THE HARP OF PROPHECY

Christianity and Judaism in Antiquity Series

Gregory E. Sterling, Series Editor

Volume 20

The University of Notre Dame Press gratefully acknowledges the generous support of Jack and Joan Conroy of Naples, Florida, in the publication of titles in this series.

THE HARP
OF PROPHECY

Early Christian Interpretation of the Psalms

EDITED BY

BRIAN E. DALEY, S.J.,

AND

PAUL R. KOLBET

University of Notre Dame Press
Notre Dame, Indiana

Manufactured in the United States of America

The Press gratefully acknowledges the support of the Institute for Scholarship in the Liberal Arts, University of Notre Dame, in the publication of this book.

Library of Congress Control Number: 2014952960

∞ *The paper in this book meets the guidelines for permanence and durability of the Committee on Production Guidelines for Book Longevity of the Council on Library Resources.*

For as the different strings of the harp or lyre, each of which gives forth a sound of its own seemingly unlike that of any other, are thought by the unmusical who do not understand the theory of harmony to be discordant because the sounds are dissimilar, so are they who have not ears to detect the harmony of God in the holy scriptures. . . . But if a reader comes who has been instructed in God's music, one who is wise in word and deed, and for this reason may be called David—which is interpreted "skillful player"—he will produce the sound of God's music. . . . For he knows that the whole scripture is the one, perfect, harmonious instrument of God, which blends the different sounds, for those who wish to learn, into one harmonious song of salvation.

—Origen of Alexandria, *Commentary on Matthew* 2 in *Philocalia* 6.2

A psalm is the blessing of the people, the praise of God, the acclaim of the masses, the applause of all, the universal speech, the voice of the church, the melodious confession of faith, devotion full of authority, the joy of liberty, the cry of delight, and resounding happiness. A psalm soothes anger, banishes anxiety, and alleviates grief. It is protection at night, instruction by day, a shield in fear, a feast in holiness, the image of tranquillity, the guarantee of peace and harmony, which produces one song from various and sundry voices in the manner of a harp.

—Ambrose of Milan, *Explanatio super Psalmos XII* 1.9

CHRISTIANITY AND JUDAISM
IN ANTIQUITY SERIES (C J A S)

The Christianity and Judaism in Antiquity Program at the University of Notre Dame came into existence during the afterglow of the Second Vatican Council. The doctoral program combines the distinct academic disciplines of the Hebrew Bible, Judaism, the New Testament, and the Early Church in an effort to explore the religion of the ancient Hebrews, the diverse forms of Second Temple Judaism, and its offspring into religions of Rabbinic Judaism and the multiple incarnations of early Christianity. While the scope of the program thus extends from the late Bronze and Early Iron Ages to the late antique world, the fulcrum lies in the Second Temple and Early Christian periods. Each religion is explored in its own right, although the program cultivates a History-of-Religions approach that examines their reciprocally illuminating interrelationships and their place in the larger context of the ancient world. During the 1970s a monograph series was launched to reflect and promote the orientation of the program. Initially known as Studies in Judaism and Christianity in Antiquity, the series was published under the auspices of the Center of the Study of Judaism and Christianity in Antiquity. Six volumes appeared from 1975 to 1986. In 1988 the series name became Christianity and Judaism in Antiquity as the editorship passed to Charles Kannengiesser, who oversaw the release of nine volumes. Professor Kannengiesser's departure from Notre Dame necessitated the appointment of a new editor. At the same time, the historic connection between the series and the CJA doctoral program was strengthened by the appointment of all CJA faculty to the editorial board. Throughout these institutional permutations, the purpose of the series has continued to be the promotion of research into the origins of Judaism and Christianity with the hope that a better grasp of the common ancestry and relationship of the two world's religions will illuminate not only the ancient world but the modern world as well.

Gregory E. Sterling, Series Editor

CONTENTS

ACKNOWLEDGMENTS

This book grew out of the spirited discussions that took place at the University of Notre Dame in October of 1998 when a number of scholars gathered to converse about early Christian interpretations of the psalms. Together we shared in the excitement that comes from discovering just how large a body of under-read early Christian sources this is and imagining the possibilities arising from the application to them of new historical tools and methods. The work continued as essays were revised and as additional scholars joined our ranks, and it finally came to fruition in this book. Even with the research presented here, early Christian psalmody promises to be a fruitful area of research for years to come, and there remains much more to learn from this central early Christian practice.

We thank the editors of *Pro Ecclesia, Harvard Theological Review*, and *Theological Studies* for permission to republish Gary A. Anderson, "King David and the Psalms of Imprecation," *Pro Ecclesia* 15 (2007): 33–55; Paul R. Kolbet, "Athanasius, the Psalms, and the Reformation of the Self," *Harvard Theological Review* 99 (2006): 85–101; Michael C. McCarthy, S.J., "An Ecclesiology of Groaning: Augustine, the Psalms, and the Making of Church," *Theological Studies* 66 (2005): 23–48; and the Society of Biblical Literature for Brian Daley, S.J., "Finding the Right Key: The Aims and Strategies of Early Christian Interpretation of the Psalms," in *Psalms in Community: Jewish and Christian Textual, Liturgical, and Artistic Traditions*, edited by Harold W. Attridge and Margot E. Fassler, 189–205 (Atlanta, GA: Society of Biblical Literature, 2003); and Cambridge University Press for David Hunter, "The Virgin, the Bride, and the Church: Reading Psalm 45 in Ambrose, Jerome, and Augustine," *Church History* 69 (2000): 281–303.

We are also deeply grateful to the University of Notre Dame for sponsoring the original conference, the University of Notre Dame Press for its commitment to this volume, and all who labored over the years to bring it to completion. Joseph Amar, Michael Compton, Hubertus Drobner, Richard Layton, Marie-Josèphe Rondeau, Stephen Ryan, and Robert Wilken also presented papers at the original conference. Peter Martens read early drafts of many of the essays. Tyler Smith assisted in the creation of the indices. Susan Ashbrook Harvey provided valuable help with the ancient Syriac sources and bibliographic materials. Sophie Lunn-Rockliffe drew our attention to the Ambrosiaster psalm materials. Special thanks are also due to Amy Egloff and Chloé Kolbet for their continued support and unwavering encouragement.

Brian E. Daley, S.J., and Paul R. Kolbet

GENERAL AND SERIES

ACW	Ancient Christian Writers (Westminster, MD: Paulist Press, 1948–)
ANF	Ante-Nicene Fathers (Edinburgh: T. and T. Clark, 1885–)
ANRW	Aufstieg und Niedergang der römischen Welt (Berlin: De Gruyter, 1972–)
AS	*Analecta sacra spicilegio solesmensi parata*, edited by J. B. Pitra (Paris: A. Jouby and Roger, 1876–91)
BA	Bibliothèque augustinienne (Turnhout: Brepols, 1933–)
CCSL	Corpus Christianorum, series latina (Turnhout: Brepols, 1953–)
CCSG	Corpus Christianorum, series graeca (Turnhout: Brepols, 1977–)
CSCO	Corpus scriptorum Christianorum orientalium (Louvain: Peeters, 1903–)
CSEL	Corpus scriptorum ecclesiasticorum latinorum (Vienna: Tempsky, 1865–)
FC	Fathers of the Church (Washington, DC: Catholic University of America Press, 1947–)
GCS	Die griechische christliche Schriftsteller der ersten Jahrhunderte (Leipzig: Hinrichs, 1901–; Berlin: De Gruyter)
GNO	*Gregorii Nysseni opera*, edited by W. Jaeger et al. (Leiden: Brill, 1952–)
LCL	Loeb Classical Library (Cambridge, MA: Harvard University Press, 1911–)
LXX	Septuagint
MA	Miscellanea Agostiniana (Rome: Tipografia Poliglotta Vaticana, 1930–31)
NPNF	Nicene and Post-Nicene Fathers, ser. 1–2 (Edinburgh: T. and T. Clark, 1886–)
OCA	Orientalia christiana analecta (Rome: Pontificio Istituto Orientale, 1935–)
PG	Patrologia graeca, edited by J.-P. Migne (Paris, 1857–66)

PL	Patrologia latina, cursus completus, edited by J.-P. Migne (Paris, 1844–1864)
PLS	Supplement to the Patrologiae cursus completus, series latina, edited by A. Hamman (Paris: Garnier Frères, 1958–63)
PTS	Patristische Texte und Studien (Berlin: De Gruyter, 1963–)
SBLTT	Society of Biblical Literature Texts and Translations (Society of Biblical Literature, 1972–99)
SC	Sources chrétiennes (Paris: Cerf, 1942–)
WSA	*The Works of St. Augustine: A Translation for the 21st Century,* ed. John E. Rotelle (Hyde Park, NY: New City Press, 1990–)

Ancient Authors

Ambrose

| Ep. | *Epistulae* |

Athanasius

Ep. Marcell.	*Epistola ad Marcellinum*
C. Ar.	*Orationes contra Arianos*
C. Gent.	*Contra Gentes*
Vit. Ant.	*Vita Antonii*

Ps-Athanasius

| *Expos. in Ps.* | *Expositio in Psalmos* |

Augustine

Cat rud.	*De catechizandis rudibus*
Conf.	*Confessiones*
Doctr. chr.	*De doctrina christiana*
En. Ps.	*Enarrationes in Psalmos*
Ep.	*Epistulae*
Exp. Gal.	*Expositio in epistulam ad Galatas*
Fund.	*Contra epistulam Manichaei quam vocant Fundamenti*
Gn. c. Man.	*De Genesi aduersus Manicheos*
Ps. c. Don.	*Psalmus contra partem Donati*
S.	*Sermones*
Simpl.	*Ad Simplicianum*
Trin.	*De Trinitate*

Basil of Caesarea
Ep.   *Epistulae*
Hom. in Ps.   *Homiliae super Psalmos*

Cassiodorus
Exp. Ps.   *Expositio Psalmorum*

Clement of Alexandria
Strom.   *Stromata*

Cyprian
Dom. or.   *De Dominica oratione*

Cyril of Alexandria
Glaph. in Gen.   *Glaphyrorum in Genesim*
In Ps.   *Explanatio in Psalmos*

Didymus the Blind
Comm. in Ps.   *Commentarii in Psalmos*

Dio Chrysostom
Or.   *Orationes*

Diodore of Tarsus
Comm. Ps.   *Commentarii in Psalmos*

Epiphanius
Pan.   *Panarion (Adversus haereses)*

Eusebius of Caesarea
Comm. in Ps.   *Commentarii in Psalmos*
Hist. eccl.   *Historia ecclesiastica*

Gregory of Nazianzus
Ep.   *Epistulae*
Or.   *Orationes*

Gregory of Nyssa
Ep.   *Epistulae*
Hom. in Ps. 6   *In sextum Psalmum*
Inscr. Ps.   *In inscriptiones Psalmorum*

Hilary
Comm. Ps.   *Tractatus super Psalmos*
Instr. Psal.   *Instructio Psalmorum*

Jerome
Ep.   *Epistulae*

John Cassian
Conlat.   *Conlationes*

Maximus the Confessor
Cap. theol.   *Capitum theologicorum et oeconomicorum*
Expos. in Ps. 59   *Expositio in Psalmum lix*
Qu. Thal.   *Quaestiones ad Thalassium de scriptura*

Origen
Comm. Cant.   *Commentarius in Canticum*
Comm. Jo.   *Commentarii in evangelium Joannis*
Comm. Rom.   *Commentarii in Romanos*
De. princ.   *De principiis (Peri Archôn)*
Fr. Jer.   *Fragmenta in Jeremiam*
Hom. Gen.   *Homiliae in Genesim*
Hom. Exod.   *Homiliae in Exodum*
Or.   *De oratione*
Phil.   *Philocalia*

Philo
Abr.   *De Abrahamo*
Conf.   *De confusione linguarum*
Congr.   *De congressu eruditionis gratia*

Ps-Dionysius the Areopagite
Cel. hier.   *De caelesti hierarchia*

Seneca
Ep.   *Epistulae morales*

Tertullian
Or.   *De oratione*

Theodore of Mopsuestia
Exp. in Ps.   *Expositionis in Psalmos*

Theodoret
Hist. eccl.   *Historia ecclesiastica*
Int. in Ps.   *Interpretatio in Psalmos*

Tyconius
Liber reg.   *Liber regularum*

Introduction

Paul R. Kolbet

The psalms antedate Christianity, became the prayer book of early Christians, and supplied the words that gave form to the earliest Christian expressions of praise and repentance. No other scriptural book is cited more frequently in the New Testament.[1] The psalms were already the language of the church well before Christians began to theorize about the identity of Jesus, compose liturgies, or engage in ascetic practices such as fasting and almsgiving. When they did so, they had the Psalter ever in mind. An unidentified fourth-century Christian observer describes the extent that the psalms pervaded all aspects of Christian life as follows:

> In the churches there are vigils, and David is first and middle and last. In the singing of early morning hymns David is first and middle and last. In the tents at funeral processions David is first and middle and last. In the houses of virgins there is weaving, and David is first and middle and last. What a thing of wonder! Many who have not even made their first attempt at reading know all of David by heart and recite him in order. Yet it is not only in the cities and the churches that he is so prominent on every occasion and with people of all ages; even in the fields and deserts and stretching into uninhabited wasteland, he rouses sacred choirs to God with great zeal. In the monasteries there is a holy chorus of angelic hosts, and David is first and middle and last. In the convents there are bands of virgins who imitate Mary, and David is first and middle and

1

last. In the deserts men crucified to this world hold converse with God, and David is first and middle and last. And at night all men are dominated by physical sleep and drawn into the depths, and David alone stands by, arousing all the servants of God to angelic vigils, turning earth into heaven and making angels of men.[2]

Carol Harrison has recently argued that much early Christian writing is inflected by practices of prayer that "might seem far removed from how we normally understand prayer."[3] Prayer, nevertheless, remains one of the most understudied subjects in early Christian studies.[4] This lacuna may well lead scholars who are searching for causal explanations for early Christian experiences—such as allegorical biblical interpretation or intra-Christian political arguments—to fail to see what was instigated by practices of deep prayer and other forms of meditation. Each of the essays in this volume uncovers in its own way something about these particularly rich early Christian practices. The essays and bibliographic materials in this book are not encyclopedic. A comprehensive account of this, the largest body of early Christian exegetical literature devoted to a single biblical book, would require at least a chapter on nearly every early Christian author.[5] This volume's limited scope is intended both to enable readers to locate and read the early Christian sources for themselves and to introduce them to the various interdisciplinary methods and perspectives that are currently being brought to bear upon the study of early Christian psalm saying.

Recovering material artifacts such as texts and buildings has been an essential task for scholars of early Christianity for as long as the discipline has existed. While great progress continues to be made in identifying the objects that garnered the attention of early Christians, it has been more difficult to determine how they experienced themselves as subjects. It is one thing to study *what* the material objects of late antique culture were, but it is another to envision *how* human subjects experienced those objects. The study of the interpretation and use of psalms is a convenient venue for seeing how early Christianity was for its adherents not only a set of objective religious beliefs but also a way of life. As it spread across the late Roman world, Christianity had a remarkable assimilative capacity that indeed made use of structures of political authority but was fueled no less by the transformative power of a personal practice that won adherents for itself on a case-by-case basis.

Although a great deal of good has been accomplished by scholars who have methodically catalogued subtle variations in belief in order to identify discrete early Christian groups, valuable work remains to be done by attending to the very disciplines and practices that have been studied relatively less because they were so widely shared.[6] For those who are accustomed to the conventional study of the history of Christian doctrine, the study of early Christian psalm practices is an invigorating descent from the heights of second-order reflection upon experience to the primary speech of prayer, struggle, and transformation. Appropriating the language of the psalms was a kind of action that engaged both the body and the mind, as bodily positions set the mind on a particular path and the mind pulled the body to transcend the limits of its own self-regard. In the early Christian psalm commentaries we see not only the emergence of the confession "Jesus is Lord" but also how that lordship was established in individual souls and made real through daily recitation. The Psalter is at the heart of the cultivation of human capacities and civic culture that early Christians referred to in shorthand fashion as "virtue." As odd as it may sound, the modern study of early Christian psalmody is still in its youth. This volume provides materials that will promote further research into the depth and range of this essential early Christian practice.

Brian Daley's opening chapter serves as a synthetic introduction to the whole collection and charts the extraordinary rise and proliferation of psalm saying and commentary during the formative centuries of Christianity, especially among urban and rural ascetics. According to Daley, early Christian exegetes brought all the tools of ancient literary criticism to bear upon the Psalter to tease out its philosophical, theological, and moral value. They interpreted the psalms within the single whole of scripture, where interpretation involved not only the intended meaning of the original authors but also the meaning as it was received in the ongoing life of Christians. They also understood that the Psalter had its own distinctive qualities and presented challenges because of its lack of a continuous narrative and its preference for a more intimate first-person point of view. This made it especially valuable as a formative instrument where doctrine, poetic phrasing, and melody combined to create a uniquely self-involving set of exercises and prayers with emotional and aesthetic power.

Contemporary scholars have applied modern critical methods to the book of Psalms but have still struggled to interpret the primal emotions and questionable ethical propositions present in it. Gary Anderson demonstrates that premodern interpreters—although their work can easily appear to be simply "precritical" by modern disciplinary standards—in fact had their own hermeneutical rules for determining correct readings. Taking perhaps the most difficult case, the hatred expressed in an imprecatory psalm such as Psalm 58 (LXX 57), Anderson shows how fruitful ancient approaches were for early rabbinic and Christian interpreters. Employing similar hermeneutical strategies, Jews and Christian both situated psalms within the unfolding circumstances of David's life and found in these emotionally charged psalms resources to overcome their own hatred inwardly before it gained outward force.

Having established in the first two chapters the general approach of early Christians to the interpretation of the psalms, the remaining essays turn to the work of representative early Christian authors. There is no better place to begin than with Origen of Alexandria. In the third century, Origen was a prolific biblical commentator and a commanding Christian intellectual who was highly learned in the ancient grammatical and philosophical disciplines and became an unparalleled source for the personally transforming reading of the psalms that is so central to this book. The problem for contemporary scholars is that enormous quantities of Origen's publications have been lost to us—including, for our purposes, every complete work on the Psalter—largely because of the controversies about him that occurred in intervening centuries.[7] Since these materials were known to other early Christian authors and influenced them greatly, it is necessary to learn as much as we can about them. Sifting through the surviving fragments preserved in the writings of other late antique authors, Ronald Heine reconstructs the main components of Origen's lost prologue to his large Caesarean commentary on the psalms based on topics customarily addressed in ancient philosophical commentaries and in Origen's preserved prologues to other biblical books. He finds in these fragments evidence of a Christian reading of the Psalter that saw it as a completely harmonious divine harp designed for the tuning of human minds.

In his study of Athanasius of Alexandria's influential letter on the psalms, Paul Kolbet follows the Origenist tradition into the next century and shows how this tradition drew upon resources available in Hellenistic philosophy to integrate the psalms into the sort of meditational practices that were the chief means of caring for oneself taught by the philosophical schools. Athanasius's letter demonstrates that the Psalter proved to be a remarkably flexible technology that could be appropriated in any number of circumstances to acquire self-knowledge and heal unhealthy emotional and intellectual responses. The self's indeterminacy was stabilized through daily exercises that employed the persuasive language of the Psalter to internalize the biblical narrative and its constitutive theological doctrines. The ultimate goal of this spiritual practice of personal prayer was to harmonize oneself with the eternal Source of the universe as one's bodily song became more and more an outward image of the internal ordering of the mind. Kolbet concludes that Athanasius's promotion of the Psalter had important political implications insofar as it was an aspect of his broader effort to unite urban and rural Christians in a shared ascetic program.

By examining neglected scholia on the psalms by the brilliant, yet controversial fourth-century Origenist Evagrius Ponticus, Luke Dysinger demonstrates how thoroughly psalmody shaped both the intellectual world and the personal practices of Christian ascetics. Evagrius applied Origen's hermeneutical system not only to the book of Psalms but also to the human psyche. He believed that the words and imagery of the psalms could be made to reflect back to the reader a carefully mapped program of personal spiritual progress, recapitulating in miniature the cosmic story of creation, fall, and reunion with God. The contemplative exegete (or *gnōstikos*) would learn to read the Psalter as a multilayered handbook of spiritual growth that could become, as Athanasius suggested, "a mirror of the soul's movements."[8] Brief texts and allegorical insights drawn from the imagery of the psalms would increase the *gnōstikos*'s own spiritual understanding and provide texts that could be recommended for meditation by those who sought advice and counsel.

The following three chapters all focus upon on Psalm 45 (LXX 44), a psalm celebrating a royal wedding that required interpreters to identify the bride and groom. Nonna Harrison examines the homilies of the prominent fourth-century bishop Basil of Caesarea. Although Basil read the psalm as a prophetic allegory about Christ and the church, the very masculine and feminine language of the Psalter invited reflection on the nature of gender, and he used it to question received values about gender roles in society, especially male roles. The practice of reading opened up space in the imagination for new expressions of masculinity because ways of speaking that were not acceptable on the literal level were broached indirectly through the force of allegorical reasoning. David Hunter uses the same psalm to show how studying the exegesis found in psalm commentaries equally discloses what broader social structures were being negotiated between leading Roman families and emerging ecclesiastical structures. He finds that Ambrose, the bishop of Milan, Jerome, the ascetic scholar and spiritual director, and Augustine, the bishop of Hippo, each enlisted the psalm in their respective arguments for their own authority amid the changing social conditions of the fourth and fifth centuries. Hunter finds that Ambrose, for example, interpreted the marital imagery of the psalm in terms favorable to consolidating his own episcopal power through the oversight of consecrated virgins, while Jerome underscored the ascetic teacher's value as an independent expert, and Augustine understood the bride to be the whole unified church (including both ascetics and all other types of Christians) rightly related to the episcopate.

Approaching Psalm 45 from yet another point of view, Ronald Cox explores the variety of exegetical approaches to the interpretation of the psalms present among early Christians. Over the past several generations it has become traditional to contrast the exegetical traditions stemming from ancient Alexandria with those of Antioch because varying educational institutions led their practitioners to bring different methodological presuppositions to their reading of scripture. By comparing Theodore of Mopsuestia's and Cyril of Alexandria's commentaries on this psalm, Cox shows how even on a psalm they agree to be about Christ their interpretations reveal strikingly different theological and exegetical approaches. John O'Keefe, nevertheless, in his own chapter examines the same traditional dichotomy by studying the psalms commentary of another, somewhat later representative of the Antiochene school, Theodoret of Cyrus. While acknowledging the very contrasts pointed to in Cox's essay, O'Keefe shows how Theodoret self-consciously departed from several interpretive rules that set his predecessors apart from the Alexandrians. For this reason,

O'Keefe counsels readers not to rely so much upon inherited overarching categories such as "Antiochene" and "Alexandrian" that they lose track of the peculiarities of individual authors.

As in other matters, the great Western bishop Augustine of Hippo left his mark upon subsequent Western interpretations of the psalms by reframing the Christian traditions he inherited in terms of his own profound intellect and spirituality. Two chapters by Michael Cameron and Michael McCarthy articulate the distinctly Augustinian viewpoint present primarily in Augustine's massive complete work on the psalms. Cameron's essay describes a shift that occurred in Augustine's thinking after his ordination to the priesthood that caused him to rethink the interpretive rules he had inherited. It was already standard practice to ask of each verse of the Psalter, "Who is the speaker?"; sometimes this could be Christ, while at other times it was the psalmist. As Cameron describes it, Augustine increasingly discerned a unity between speakers where the one Christ spoke intimately from his head and from his body, and where readers discovered their own voices in the Psalter to be the voice of the body of Christ speaking to Christ the head. In this way, for Augustine, to interpret the psalms was to experience the presence of "the whole Christ" (*totus Christus*). Michael McCarthy's essay develops this theme further by emphasizing how for Augustine an integral component of the hermeneutical act was the constitution of a community of readers who embodied the values of the scriptural text. For this reason, the "meaning" of any psalm could not easily be cut loose from the community in which that meaning was first seen. The act of reading, therefore, implies an ecclesiology, as the church comes to be what it is in time by appropriating the voicing of the Psalter. It is in the individual speaking of prayer that one discovers oneself within a larger whole. This Augustinian reading of the psalms, then, yields a view of the church that eschews the idealized spiritual perfection of an autonomous human polity to be described systematically and instead incorporates the reader into the body of the suffering, vulnerable, Christ extended in time. The travail and pain shared with others opens the interpreter of the psalms to a word that is still being spoken by God and that includes each person who identifies with it.

In the final chapter, Paul Blowers extends the scope of our volume well past Augustine into the seventh-century Greek East by supplying the first English translation and analysis of Maximus the Confessor's *Commentary on Psalm 59*. Maximus's commentary demonstrates the continued vitality in the early Byzantine period of the Origenist stress upon a personally transforming spiritual reading that led readers to ascend through the plenitude of meanings in scripture toward contemplative vision. While Blowers shows Maximus to have mastered earlier commentators and their own techniques, he also finds in the commentary evidence of Maximus's powerful synthetic mind drawing these earlier traditions into a cosmic vision centered on a highly nuanced Christology. As a consequence, the traditional quest to apprehend the various voices present in the psalm becomes in this case a dynamic exercise where insight into the incarnate Christ simultaneously illumines one's own ascetic progress, which, in turn, opens ever new avenues of perception.

Notes

1. Harold W. Attridge, "Giving Voice to Jesus: Use of the Psalms in the New Testament," in *Psalms in Community: Jewish and Christian Textual, Liturgical, and Artistic Traditions*, ed. Harold W. Attridge and Margot E. Fassler (Atlanta, GA: Society of Biblical Literature, 2003), 101. According to Attridge, "Of the 150 canonical psalms, 129 make at least a cameo appearance in the pages of the New Testament" (101). Compare William Lee Holladay, *The Psalms through Three Thousand Years: Prayerbook of a Cloud of Witnesses* (Minneapolis, MN: Fortress Press, 1993), 113–33, and Jacques Trublet, who states that appeals to the book of Psalms amount to a fourth of all citations in the New Testament and that "the fathers of the church . . . do nothing but amplify the movement started by the N. T." ("Psaumes IV: Le Psautier et le Nouveau Testament," in *Dictionnaire de spiritualité ascétique et mystique: Doctrine et histoire*, ed. M. Viller et al. [Paris: G. Beauchesne, 1980], 12.2: 2553 [translation mine]).

2. Pseudo-Chrysostom, *De poenitentia* (PG 64:12–13; trans. James McKinnon, *Music in Early Christian Literature* [Cambridge: Cambridge University Press, 1983], 90).

3. Carol Harrison, *The Art of Listening in the Early Church* (Oxford: Oxford University Press, 2013), 183–228, quote at 204.

4. As Columba Stewart observes, "Although ubiquitous in early Christian life, today the personal prayer of early Christians is one of the least-studied aspects of their experience" ("Prayer," in *The Oxford Handbook of Early Christian Studies*, ed. Susan Ashbrook Harvey and David G. Hunter, Oxford Handbooks in

Religion and Theology [New York: Oxford University Press, 2008], 744). Carol Harrison also draws attention to this weakness in the scholarly literature (*Art of Listening*, 183). See also Paul R. Kolbet, "Rethinking the Rationales for Origen's Use of Allegory," *Studia Patristica* 56 (2013): 41–50.

5. For a brief survey of the sources, see Charles Kannengiesser, *Handbook of Patristic Exegesis*, 2 vols., The Bible in Ancient Christianity 1 (Leiden: Brill, 2004), 1: 297–301, 307–9.

6. See Karen L. King, "Which Early Christianity?," in Ashbrook and Hunter, *Oxford Handbook*, 66–85.

7. It is worth noting here that a newly discovered Greek manuscript in the Bayerische Staatsbibliothek appears to contain twenty-nine previously lost homilies of Origen (some of which had been preserved in a Latin translation of Rufinus). For the first scholarly impressions of this discovery, see Lorenzo Perrone, "Rediscovering Origen Today: First Impressions of the New Collection of Homilies on the Psalms in the *Codex monacensis Graecus* 314," *Studia Patristica* 56 (2013): 103–22. Needless to say, should the manuscript be determined to be authentic Origen, the study of it in the coming years will be an important advance in our knowledge of Origen's understanding and use of the psalms.

8. Athansius, *Ep. Marcell.* 12.

ONE

Finding the Right Key

The Aims and Strategies of Early
Christian Interpretation of the Psalms

Brian E. Daley, S.J.

For the early church, the book of Psalms was "daily bread": clearly one of the most important and familiar books of the Bible. Early Christian commentary on it is more abundant than on any other book of the Hebrew and Christian canon; we still possess partial or complete sets of homilies or scholarly commentaries on the psalms—sometimes more than one set—by at least twenty Latin or Greek patristic authors before 600, and this interest did not abate in the medieval church. The main reason, undoubtedly, was the fact that the psalms were in constant use, both in public worship and in private prayer and meditation.

How the Christian liturgical use of the biblical psalms began remains a matter of scholarly debate. The earliest documentary evidence that Christians regularly sang the psalms at worship comes from the early third century of our era, in the work that is usually called Hippolytus of Rome's *Apostolic Tradition.*[1] Throughout the second century, the psalms were widely used by Christians as a prophetic text from the Hebrew scriptures and seem to have been used also for family and private prayer.[2] Because there is no clear evidence of their liturgical use, however, some scholars have suggested that the earliest Christians may have preferred to sing original compositions in praise of Christ in public worship; in fact, it may have been only the proliferation of such poetry in Gnostic circles that led orthodox leaders to decide, around the end of the second century, that biblical psalms should be used more regularly as their communities' liturgical song.[3] By the mid-fourth century, at any rate, a synod at Laodicaea in Phrygia could lay down as a canon, "It is not permitted that privately composed psalms or noncanonical books be read out in church, but only the canonical books of the New and Old Testament."[4]

With the meteoric rise of monasticism and ascetical piety during the fourth century, the recitation and chanting of psalms grew to be the mainstay of Christian daily prayer, both private and communal;[5] "meditation"— the quiet, ruminative "chewing" on the words of the psalms—was recommended by many spiritual guides as the most effective spiritual weapon against inner demons, a medicine for diseased thoughts.[6] The desert monks seem to have learned large portions of the Psalter, in some cases even the whole of it, by heart, and to have chanted the psalms constantly as they worked. Epiphanius of Salamis, the pugnacious defender of orthodoxy of the late fourth century, is said to have chided a Palestinian abbot for allowing his monks to restrict their psalmody to three canonical hours, "for the true monk should have prayer and psalmody continually in his heart."[7] The great sixth-century spiritual guide of the Gaza desert, Barsanuphius, gave familiar, well-tested advice to a young monk who asked how to be freed from the awful slavery of irreligious trains of thought (λογισμοί): resist them forthrightly, throw yourself on God's mercy, confide in your spiritual director, concentrate on your manual work. "And as far as the psalms are concerned," he adds, "do not give up studying them, for they are a source of energy; struggle to learn them by heart, for that will be completely beneficial."[8] But Barsanuphius immediately warns his correspondent against seeking too exalted a knowledge of divine mysteries, presumably through speculation on the meaning of the psalms that he mutters: "As for hearing things that are beyond your powers, don't attempt it; for you have knowledge, for the moment, fitting your own limitations, which will serve you well."[9]

Writers of a more intellectual bent, however, recognized that it was those who used the psalms every day, giving a scriptural voice to their prayer and using them as a structuring principle for their daily struggle, who most needed thoughtful and accurate Christian exegesis of the psalms if their *meditatio* was to be different from magical incantation. Diodore of Tarsus, the great Antiochene commentator of the 360s and 370s, gives this as the main reason for his own grammatical labors. He writes in the well-known prologue to his commentary that

> since this book of scripture—I mean the Psalms—is so important, I have decided to put together, just as I have myself been taught, a concise explanation of the narrative settings [ὑποθέσεις] specifically corresponding to each of the psalms, and of their word-for-word meaning, so that in the moment when they are singing them, the brethren may not simply be swept along by the sounds, or find their minds occupied by other things because they do not understand the text; but that, by recognizing the train of thought [τὴν ἀκολουθίαν] in what is said, they may "sing praise with understanding" (Ps. 46:8b: LXX), as scripture puts it—from the depths of each psalm's meaning, and not simply from the top of their heads or the tip of their lips.[10]

The driving concern of early Christian exegesis of the Psalter, in fact, seems to have been somewhat different from that which animated the interpretation of other books of the Bible: except perhaps for the psalm-homilies of Ambrose, Augustine, and Chrysostom, its audience seems to have been clergy or monks, rather than congregations of "ordinary" believers; and its point was not simply to identify the referent of a particular verse or passage, to find the "prophetic" significance of a text for the Christian reader, but to facilitate the *internalization* of these biblical prayers-in-verse, to enable the reader so to feel and grasp them, as works of divinely inspired poetry, that the reader's own thoughts and emotions, desires and passions, might be purified and transformed. Only if this could be achieved would the psalms really succeed in healing the heart of its ills and driving away its demons.

In its overall aims and methods, of course, ancient Christian exegesis of the psalms rested on the same assumptions and used the same general strategies of interpretation as all Christian biblical exegesis. It assumed, first and foremost, that God is ultimately real—transcending ordinary experience but actively present in all human history and so actively involved in both the composition and the interpretation of the scriptural text. Just as the divine artistry is constantly involved in the creation and continuance of the world, even down to the tiniest leaf and insect, Origen observes in his preliminary remarks on the first psalm, "so we must realize, with regard to everything written under the inspiration of the Holy Spirit, that the divine providence that has bestowed superhuman wisdom on the human race through the written word has sown, one might say, saving oracles [λόγια σωτήρια] in every letter—footprints of Wisdom, to the degree that that is possible."[11]

Second, ancient Christian exegesis, from Origen on, assumed that these inspired scriptures formed a single book, which told, together, a single story of creation, instruction, judgment, and salvation by a single God; thus, if one confessed Jesus to be the Messiah longed for by Israel, the promised Savior who brought to fulfillment God's historical campaign to form for himself a holy people, one was justified in seeing Jesus as the ultimate referent, the "bottom line," in every book and every verse of the whole collection.[12] Third, early Christian interpreters certainly recognized, in varying degrees, that the scriptures were written in a variety of particular times and places, by particular authors, about particular people and events; far from being unimportant, that particularity provided the "plain sense" on which all interpretation, all discovery of "deeper" or more "spiritual" references, had to be based.[13] Nonetheless, most of them also assumed that the *meaning* of any given passage in the Bible was not simply its reference to the author's own world, its "original" intentionality: it also involved *us*— the preacher, the hearer, the community that received it as part of God's Word. So the task of the interpreter was not simply to reconstruct the *Sitz im Leben* of the "original" version of the text but also to point out its *Sitz in unserem Leben*, the relevance for the community's faith and life that was seen as shaping the text's ultimate meaning within the whole Bible.

Fourth and most strikingly, early Christian exegetes tended to speak of their task—in language reminiscent of the mystery cults—as that of penetrating divine secrets: all scripture, as Origen says in the passage on Psalm 1 that we have already quoted, is a "locked door" that only "the key of David" can open, a scroll whose seal only the "Lamb who was slain" can break;[14] what some may think of as mere literary obscurities, Cassiodorus later insists, often "bear the secret sign of a great mystery."[15] Borrowing Origen's image, Jerome compared the book of Psalms to a house full of locked rooms, for which all the keys lie scattered and hopelessly confused;

the exegete's task is to enter the house by the "great door" of the Holy Spirit and then to sort through the keys to the "mysteries" of the individual psalms, matching each of them to the right door.[16] The point of such language is not simply to suggest that the central meaning of the psalms, or of any scriptural text, may be difficult to come by but also to describe the quest itself in religious, even mystagogical terms. So Hilary writes, at the beginning of his homily on Psalm 13: "We ought not to treat scripture with the vulgar familiarity of our ordinary speech; rather, when we speak of what we have learned and read, we should give honor to the author by our care for the way we express ourselves. . . . Preachers must think that they are not speaking to a human audience, and hearers must know that it is not human words that are being offered to them, but that they are God's words, God's decrees, God's laws. For both roles, the utmost reverence is fitting."[17]

These assumptions lay behind all early Christian biblical interpretation, even though they were applied by different interpreters in very different ways. The Psalter, however, presented distinctive problems for interpretation and called for distinctive strategies: above all, because it is not a book of continuous narrative or instruction but a collection of *poems.* Early Christian commentators on scripture were virtually all highly trained in the grammatical and rhetorical skills of classical *paideia* and realized that poetry is a distinctive use of language, designed to speak to the feelings as well as to the mind, to "beguile" or "divert" (ψυχαγωγεῖν) as well as to inform.[18] A common way of referring to this effect in the ancient world was to speak of the "delight" or "sweetness" that the hearer of poetry was intended to drink in—either as added motivation for taking to heart a poem's intended lesson or simply as a poem's ultimate purpose.[19] The ancient theorist of literary criticism usually known as Longinus spoke in somewhat more exalted terms of the "sublimity" or exalted character of the very best classical texts: their ability, recognized only by a person of great experience, to "lift up the soul" and fill it with "joy and exultation," giving it food for lasting thought and making "a strong and ineffaceable impression on the memory."[20] Patristic commentators, in this same tradition, tended to speak of the Psalter as characterized not primarily by its contents—which often simply mirrored or summarized what was said more at length in the Bible's narrative, prophetic, and wisdom books—but by its "sweetness," its beguiling effect. "Although every part of holy scripture breathes forth the graciousness [*gratiam*] of God," Ambrose writes (perhaps paraphrasing 2 Tim. 3:16), "the book of Psalms is especially sweet";[21] so other biblical figures—Moses, Miriam, Anna—occasionally burst into song, Ambrose observes, but David was chosen by God to do continually, in an entire biblical book, what the others do only rarely,[22] so the book of Psalms helps us fulfill our natural desire as creatures to find delight (*delectatio*) in praising God.[23] Basil of Caesarea stresses the pedagogical, medicinal effect of this aesthetic dimension of the psalms: "When the Holy Spirit saw that the human race was guided only with difficulty toward virtue, and that, because of our inclination toward pleasure, we were neglectful of an upright life, what did he do? The delight of melody he mingled with the doctrines, so that by the pleasantness and softness of the sound heard we might receive without perceiving it the benefit of the words, just as wise physicians who, when giving the fastidious rather bitter drugs to drink, frequently smear the cup with honey."[24] At the beginning of a homily, no longer completely preserved, on Psalm 41 (LXX), John Chrysostom speaks in a similar vein of the providential work of the Holy Spirit in "mixing melody with prophecy" by causing the psalms to be written, and so drawing recalcitrant human minds to the "philosophic life" by the allure of pleasure: "For nothing so arouses the soul, gives it wing, sets it free from the earth, releases it from the prison of the body, teaches it to love wisdom, and to condemn all the things of this life, as concordant melody and sacred song composed in rhythm."[25] The task of the early Christian exegete, then, was clearly not only to read the psalms for their content as moral instructions or prophecies, or as witnesses to the long divine narrative that would culminate in the story of Christ and the church, but also to read them as poems: and that meant using all the analytical tools and theoretical principles that ancient literary criticism, the art and science of γραμματική, had developed for interpreting and judging secular verse.

The study called "grammar," in the ancient Greek and Roman world, after all, was understood to be principally the art of organized literary *exegesis*: explaining the meaning of a classic literary work, usually a poetic text—epic, tragedy, or comedy; analyzing prose classics was considered the parallel work of the rhetorician. Such exegesis moved principally on a linguistic level, beginning often with an explanation of difficult words—proper names, dialect forms, unusual metaphors or allusions—but would also include a wider discussion of the passage's narrative content, its "plot" or ὑπόθεσις. The crowning moment of the grammarian's skill, however—what won his art the name "criticism"—was thought by many to be his "judgment" (κρίσις) of the poem's or the passage's value as a whole.[26] Dionysius of Halicarnassus, the antiquarian and critic active at Rome in the mid-first century BCE, wrote a whole essay "On the Examination of Speeches," in which he tried to elaborate criteria for judging the value of prose works by objective standards, rather than simply being "led along" (ψυχαγωγούμεθα) by the authors' reputations.[27] For philosophically sophisticated critics, this involved commenting not simply on the success of a work's formal composition—the "arrangement" or σύνθεσις of its images, sounds, and rhythms—but also on its ideas, its moral implications, the example and "teaching" it offered. In fact, it was in such judgment of the philosophic and ethical worth of classical epic poetry that the Stoic art of allegorical interpretation was developed.[28]

Christian interpreters of the psalms were all influenced, if in varying degrees, by the classroom practice of professional grammarians. Some, like the fourth-century Antiochene exegete Diodore of Tarsus or the sixth-century scholar-bureaucrat Cassiodorus, closely followed the formal procedures of grammatical commentary in their approach to the psalms. Diodore begins his treatment of each psalm with a brief statement of the poem's ὑπόθεσις or theme and makes a conjecture on its probable original setting within the narrative history of Israel; he then moves on to give terse explanatory paraphrases of the "plain sense" of each verse, understood within that historical setting. Cassiodorus, ever the humanist, offers a much more technical, self-consciously academic commentary on each psalm: beginning with a discussion of its number and *titulus* (if there is one); then moving on to a brief analysis of its literary structure and of the presumed speakers to whom various sections can be assigned; then on to a verse-by-verse, often word-by-word explanation of its meaning, frequently identifying the etymologies of significant words and the logical and rhetorical figures he discovers; and finishing with his own *conclusio*, in which he offers his judgment of the psalm's importance and summarizes its theological and spiritual "message" for the Christian user. All of this was, in his view, a way of demonstrating the unique *eloquentia*, the heart-transforming beauty, of these biblical poems.[29]

In the introductions—a standard feature of the grammatical genre—to their commentaries or sets of homilies on the psalms, patristic exegetes tended to concern themselves with the sort of general literary questions any grammarian might address in beginning to comment on a body of poems: the unity and arrangement of the collection, its authorship and historical origin, and the peculiar significance of the "titles" or "inscriptions" that are attached to many of them in both the Hebrew and Greek traditions. The answers they gave to these questions varied widely. Diodore, for instance—ever skeptical of attempts to find deeper significance in the apparent incoherences of the Bible—assumed that the psalms had all been written by David and that they referred prophetically to specific events—whether past, present, or future—in Israel's history;[30] but he argued that the present ordering of the psalms was haphazard and that the "titles" represented simply the pious guesswork of later editors.[31] Hilary of Poitiers, on the other hand, as well as Theodoret of Cyrus and later Cassiodorus, were convinced that the present arrangement and numbering of the psalms and the "titles" given to particular psalms, although certainly the work of later editors and of the Greek translators of the Septuagint, also were due to the inspiration of the Spirit and were an essential part of the psalms' full significance.[32] In fact, the numbering and ordering of the psalms were, in Cassiodorus's view, a constitutive element of the "particular eloquence of the Psalter," challenging the reader to divine the meaning of each psalm's number in relation to the text. For these commentators, as for Gregory of Nyssa in his elaborate treatise on the titles of the psalms, the Psalter as a whole was a kind of detailed map for growth in Christian holiness: in Hilary's phrase, an image of the *dispensatio salutis nostrae*.[33] Gregory of Nyssa, as later Jerome, took seriously the traditional Hebrew division of the Psalter into five parts or "books," perhaps in imitation of the Torah, each part ending with a solemn "Amen and Amen."[34] Hilary, on the other hand, followed by Cassiodorus, rejected this view and preferred—on the scriptural authority of Acts 1:20, which refers to "the book of Psalms"—to consider the Psalter a single whole, conceived in three units of fifty poems corresponding to the biblical years of jubilee, and hinting together at three stages of ascent in the spiritual life toward "our blessed hope," the eternal Sabbath.[35]

More important, even, than decoding the structure and order of the Psalter, for early Christian interpreters, was the task of identifying its peculiar effectiveness in guiding its users along this path of spiritual growth, as poetry written to be prayed and sung. In this regard, perhaps the fullest and most original treatment of the distinctive working of the psalms was Athanasius's *Letter to Marcellinus on the Interpretation of the Psalms*, a work so highly valued in antiquity that it was included in the early fifth-century Codex Alexandrinus of the Greek Bible, as an introduction to the book of Psalms. Athanasius presents his essay as embodying the teaching he received from "a scholarly old man"[36]—presumably an *abba* from the Egyptian desert; by this device, he situates his own explanation of the peculiar character and "grace" of the Psalter within the thought-world of monastic prayer. Athanasius begins by suggesting, as Basil of Caesarea would also do, that the actual thematic content of the psalms is not really different from that of the other books of the Hebrew Bible but rather "contains in itself what is found in all of them, like a garden, and expresses this in song."[37] What is distinctive about the Psalter in relation to other books is its more personal element, which allows the reader to identify the message with his or her inmost feelings: "It contains within itself the movements of each soul, their changes and adjustments, written out and thoroughly portrayed, so that if someone should wish to grasp himself from it, as from an image, and to understand on that basis how to shape himself, it is written there."[38]

The point of portraying the whole range of human spiritual "movements" or emotions, Athanasius goes on to explain, is not simply poetic imitation—Aristotle's μίμησις—but *therapy*: the person who recognizes his own inner state in the psalms "can possess from this, once again, the image contained in the words, so that he does not simply hear them and move on, but learns what one must say and do to heal one's disordered feelings."[39] The psalms, in other words, do not simply command us to repent of our sins, to bear suffering patiently, or to praise God for his gifts; they actually give us the words by which we can come to say and do these things for ourselves.[40]

For this, once again, is the curious thing about the psalms: that in reading the other books lectors tend to proclaim the sayings of the holy authors, whatever subjects they are talking about, as concerning those about whom the books are written, and listeners understand that they themselves are different people from those dealt with in the text. . . . But while the person who takes up this book will certainly marvel, in the same way as in other books, at the prophecies concerning the Savior, and will make an act of adoration and read on, still he will read out the rest of the psalms as if they are his own words; and the one who hears them will be deeply moved, as if he himself were speaking, and will be affected by the words of these songs as if they were his own.[41]

Athanasius's argument, in this central section of his work, is that in becoming "like a mirror to the one singing them," the psalms act as a providential corrective to the imbalance of our desires and emotions.[42] In hearing and singing them as our own prayers, in recognizing our present needs and deepest longings in them, we allow them subtly to reshape our inner life to conform with God's own Word; "for what psalm-singers express in words can become forms and models of ourselves."[43] And Athanasius recognizes in this mimetic, modeling role of the psalms an anticipation of the healing effect of the Incarnation: just as the Word, in becoming one of us, not only taught us how to live by his words but "did what he taught," providing us with a living image of "perfect virtue" in his own life, "for the same reason, even before his life among us, he made this resound from the lips of those who sing the psalms. Just as he revealed the model of the earthly and the heavenly human being in himself, so also anyone who wishes can learn in the psalms about the motions and conditions of souls and can find in them the remedy and corrective measure for each of these motions."[44]

Toward the end of the treatise, Athanasius draws on Hellenistic music theory to argue that the reason the psalms are sung and not simply read—besides the fact that this adds "breadth" and solemnity to our praise of God—is to enable them to create a harmony and order in our inner selves that parallels the harmony that the Logos, as creator and sustainer, perpetually secures in the universe.[45] "For just as we recognize the thoughts of the soul, and signify them through the words [of the psalms] we utter, so the

Lord wishes that the song that springs forth from the words should be a symbol of spiritual harmony in the soul, and has decreed that the odes be sung to melodies, and the psalms also be chanted musically."[46]

Gregory of Nyssa, in his treatise *On the Titles of the Psalms*, written a few decades after Athanasius's work, elaborates this point at much greater length, comparing the "music" produced by the order of the whole cosmos with the inner harmony of the well-ordered, virtuous human person— "the philosophy that comes through melody";[47] the psalms are given to us precisely as a way of restoring and preserving that "microcosmic" order of mind and body by the "sweetness" of poetry and music: "Since everything which is in accord with nature is pleasing to nature, and since the music which is in us has been shown to be in accord with nature, for this reason the great David combined singing with philosophical instruction concerning the virtues, thereby pouring the sweetness of honey, as it were, over these sublime teachings. In this singing, nature reflects on itself in a certain manner, and heals itself. For the proper rhythm of life, which singing seems to me to recommend symbolically, is a cure of nature."[48]

What continually amazed early Christian interpreters of the psalms, in fact, was the apparently universal ability of these poems to transform the hearts and minds of the people who regularly prayed them. Like the rest of the Bible, their eloquence and power was not quite the same as that of classical poetry: "It speaks to the heart," Cassiodorus observed (with perhaps a hint of *apologia* toward the secular connoisseurs of his time), "not to the body's ears."[49] The music of the psalms, he suggests, is in fact what "leads the words to God," giving them a "divine eloquence" that even the heart of God will presumably find persuasive.[50] The core of the Psalter's power to move and delight is its truth, its "perfect theology," its richness of moral example.[51] Yet as he and other authors insisted, it could do this in the simplest and most direct of terms, so that beginners in the spiritual life could learn from it.[52] Further, people of every rank could sing it and understand it, people of every age could find it engaging; it summoned them to silence and united them in a single song.[53] For everyone who was prepared to read or chant them in faith, the psalms worked as both a mysterious inner medicine against the passions, and a rigorous workout program, an *askesis*, for the heart. So Ambrose describes the pedagogy of the psalms, within the larger context of biblical revelation, in athletic as well as medicinal terms:

History informs, the law instructs, prophecy announces, correction chastises, moral teaching persuades; but in the book of Psalms we find the progress [*profectus*] of each person, a kind of medicine for human healing. Whoever reads it has the means of curing the wounds of passion by a special remedy. Whoever wants to see, as if in a common training ground for souls [*in communi animarum gymnasio*] and a stadium of the virtues, can choose for himself various kinds of imaginative situations, all prepared for him, which he knows will suit him well; by using them, he can more easily win the crown of victory.[54]

Yet for all their human effectiveness, this therapeutic instrument remains, at a deeper level, God's music rather than our own: a body of songs given to us by God, to enable us to speak to him in the words he is most disposed to hear. As Augustine observes at the beginning of his homily on Psalm 99: "The voice of God, whatever instrument it sounds through, is still the voice of God, and there is nothing that gives pleasure to his ears except his own voice. For even when we speak, we give him pleasure only when he speaks through us!"[55]

In the ninth book of his *Confessions*, Augustine describes the peaceful yet excited state of his own heart when he and his companions made a final decision, after years of searching for truth, to enroll themselves for baptism and to take on the yoke of being a committed disciple of Christ, a *servus Dei*. Most of his intellectual difficulties with mainstream Christian doctrine had been solved, he told us in book 7, by an immersion into Neoplatonist philosophy at Milan; his old distaste for the apparent harshness of doctrine and literary rusticity of the Bible had also found a cure there, in Ambrose's preaching. His final need was for internal transformation: a healing of the "swelling tumor" of pride that philosophy, even Neoplatonic philosophy, only seemed to aggravate, and with that healing a new freedom to move toward the goal he so desired but seemed unable to reach on his own.[56] It was only after that freedom was given him as a gift, in the garden of his house in Milan, that he came to find, in prayer and in the scriptures, the medicine for his inner ills. And he found it above all, he tells us, in the psalms:

My God, how I cried to you when I read the Psalms of David, songs of faith, utterances of devotion which allow no pride of spirit to enter in!

I was but a beginner in authentic love of you, a catechumen resting at a country villa. . . . How I cried out to you in these Psalms, and how they kindled my love for you! I was fired by an enthusiasm to recite them, were it possible, to the entire world, in protest against the pride of the human race. Yet they are being sung in all the world, and "there is none who can hide himself from your heat" (Ps. 18:7).[57]

For Augustine, as for Ambrose and so many of his contemporaries, it was essential to "sing the psalms with understanding," to seek out their meaning as texts within the context of the whole Christian narrative of salvation. But it was the emotive and aesthetic power of the psalms—their music, their "sweetness"—that enabled them to touch and transform these readers in a way no other book of scripture, no preaching or theological argument, was able to do. Augustine's own later interpretation of the psalms, delivered chiefly in the setting of public worship, would focus more often on their role as the voice of the church as the body of Christ, the *totus Christus* crying out to God in the midst of a hostile society, or as the voice of Christ, the divine Bridegroom, calling to his spouse, the church, to imitate him. But here at Cassiciacum, in the autumn of 386, Augustine had discovered the power of the psalms in a much more intimate and personal way, as Athanasius and the desert monks had done before him: their power to become part of our inner selves and to form our very thoughts and desires in the image of God.

NOTES

1. *Apostolic Tradition* 25 (Ethiopic text with translation and collation from Ethiopic and Arabic manuscripts, ed. and trans. G. Horner, *The Statutes of the Apostles, or, Canones ecclesiastici* [London: Williams and Norgate, 1904]); for singing the psalms at the third, sixth, and ninth hours, see *Apostolic Tradition* 31–38.

2. See Clement of Alexandria, *Strom.* 7.7 (psalms as table prayer and prayer before going to bed). See also, from the early third century, Origen, *Or.* 12.2; Tertullian, *Or.* 24–25; Cyprian, *Dom. or.* 34. The best general survey of early Christian practices of prayer is still Adalbert-G. Hamman, *La prière*, vol. 2, *Les trois premiers siècles* [Paris: Desclée, 1963]).

3. For a summary of this theory, and for further references to the scholarly literature supporting it, see Balthasar Fischer, "Die Psalmenfrömmigkeit der

Märtyrerkirche," in *Die Psalmen als Stimme der Kirche*, ed. A. Heinz (Trier: Paulinus-Verlag, 1982). See now also James W. McKinnon, *Music in Early Christian Literature* (Cambridge: Cambridge University Press, 1983), 10–11. For a good, brief survey of the development of the liturgical use of the Psalter in the first eight centuries, see Joseph Gélineau, "Les psaumes à l'époque patristique," *Maison-Dieu* 135 (1978): 99–116.

4. Canon 59; see E. J. Jonkers, ed., *Acta et Symbola Conciliorum quae saeculo quarto habita sunt* (Leiden: Brill, 1954), 96; Jonkers dates this synod, about which little is known, between 341 and 381. See also Basil of Caesarea, *Ep.* 207.3, for a description of his own congregation's custom of singing the psalms antiphonally during the night vigils; apparently the practice was unusual enough in 375 to elicit sharp criticism from the Church of Neocaesarea in Pontus. Augustine says he wrote a tract against a Carthaginian layman named Hilary, who had criticized the singing of psalms during the Eucharistic liturgy "before the oblation" and during the distribution of communion, a custom Augustine says was of recent origin in the Church of Carthage (*Retractationes* 2.37 [CSEL 36: 144]). See also Everett Ferguson, "Psalm-Singing at the Eucharist: A Liturgical Controversy in the Fourth Century," *Austin Seminary Bulletin* 98 (1983): 52–77.

5. The growing monastic use of the psalms seems to have had its effect, in turn, on nonmonastic liturgy: McKinnon remarks that by the mid-fourth century in the East, "the monastic office virtually inundated the cathedral office with psalmody" (*Music*, 9).

6. The fifth-century Latin writer John Cassian insists that the apex of prayer, and indeed of the human spiritual journey, is to be united to God in a total, wordless concentration of mind and heart, free from all material images and concepts (*Conlat.* 10.5–6). As the first step toward this habitual state, Cassian recommends a version of "meditation" that anticipates later practices of both Eastern and Western Christianity, as well as of some Eastern religions: constantly repeating to oneself the opening words of Psalm 70 (LXX 69), "O God, come to my assistance; O Lord, make haste to help me!" Since this verse, in Cassian's view, perfectly represents the right attitude of the creature before God, its constant use has a formative effect on the human spirit, as well as practical value for focusing the thoughts. On Cassian's approach to the psalms, see Columba Stewart, *Cassian the Monk* (Oxford: Clarendon Press, 1998), 100–105, 110–13. For general discussion of the use of the psalms in both the common and private prayer of the early monks, see García Colombás, *El monacato primitivo* (Madrid: Biblioteca de Autores Cristianos, 1975), 2: 330–35, 345–46; Lucien Régnault, *La vie quotidienne des pères du déserte en Égypte au IVe siècle* (Paris: Hachette, 1990), 118–21.

7. *Apophthegmata patrum*, Epiphanius 3 (trans. Benedicta Ward, *Sayings of the Desert Fathers: The Alphabetical Collection* [Kalamazoo, MI: Cistercian Publications, 1975], 49). Theodoret of Cyrus attests to this same practice as his reason

for undertaking his own commentary on the Psalter: "For the pupils of piety, both in the cities and in remote places, have all undertaken to focus their minds on the psalms with particular dedication; those who have embraced the ascetic life, for example, recite the Psalter orally by night and by day, as their way of singing the praises of the God of all things and of bringing under control the passions of the body" (*Int. in Ps.*, praef. [PG 80: 857d]).

8. Barsanuphius and John of Gaza, *Letter* 215 (SC 427: 666.11–13).

9. Barsanuphius and John of Gaza, *Letter* 215 (SC 427: 666.13–15).

10. Diodore of Tarsus, *Comm. Ps.*, praef. (CCSG 6: 4.33–42). Diodore's more "centrist" heir in the Antiochene tradition of exegesis, Theodoret of Cyrus, expresses a similar concern in the preface to his commentary on the psalms (*Int. in Ps.*, praef. [PG 80: 857a–860a]); see also Athanasius, *Ep. Marcell.* 1 and 33 (PG 27: 12a and 45c).

11. Origen, *Phil.*, frag. 2.4.19–24 (SC 302: 246, 11–13).

12. For a classic statement of this understanding of the scriptures, see Origen, *Comm. Jo.* 1.6–15; cf. Irenaeus, *Adversus haereses* 4.1–15, 22–26.

13. See, for example, Origen, *De princ.* 4.3.4; for a more emphatic insistence on the necessity of searching out the original situation in the narrative (ἱστορία) of Israel to which a given passage in the Bible refers, in order to avoid an arbitrary and "pagan" style of exegesis by ἀλληγορία, see again Diodore, *Comm. Ps.*, praef. (CCSG 6: 7.124–32).

14. Origen, *Phil.*, frag. 2.1.1–10 (SC 302: 240).

15. Cassiodorus, *Exp. Ps.*, praef. 9 (CCSG 97: 3.9).

16. Jerome, *Tractatus LIX in Psalmos* 1 (CCSL 78: 3.1–9), alluding to Origen, *Phil.*, frag. 2.3.1–12 (SC 302: 244), where the image of the "houseful of locked rooms" is applied to the Bible as a whole; see also Hilary of Poitiers, *Instr. Psal.* 5–6 (CCSL 61: 6–8), who takes from the same text of Origen the more general image of the risen Christ as the only "key" who can unlock the meaning of the Bible, "through the mystery of his incarnation and his divinity" (*Instr. Psal.* 8.32–33).

17. Hilary of Poitiers, *Comm. Ps.* 13.1 (CCSL 61: 76.3–6, 21–24).

18. For a discussion of the various theories held by ancient theorists on the relative importance of teaching and ψυχαγωγία in poetic diction, see Donald A. Russell, *Criticism in Antiquity* (Berkeley: University of California Press, 1981), 94–95. For the Epicurean Philodemus's discussion of this issue, see Michael Wigodsky, "The Alleged Impossibility of Philosophical Poetry," in *Philodemus and Poetry*, ed. Dirk Obbink (New York: Oxford University Press, 1995), 66–69.

19. See the famous dictum of Horace, *Ars poetica* 343–44: "Omne tulit punctum qui miscuit utile dulci, / lectorem delectando pariterque monendo." Horace here reflects more the Stoic insistence that poetry should also have a moral and didactic purpose than the usual Epicurean view that poetry is simply for amusement. Even Cicero seems to have assumed that poetry, unlike good rhetorical prose, is

simply devised to please the ears by its sounds and meter (*De or.* 162). Philodemus, however, the Epicurean thinker who exercised a great deal of influence on the Augustan literary world, seems to have shared Horace's position and may well have inspired much of his *Ars poetica*; see Wigodsky, "Alleged Impossibility," 67, and the further references there.

20. Longinus, *[Subl.]* 6, in *Classical Literary Criticism*, ed. and trans. D. Russell and M. Winterbottom, World's Classics (Oxford: Oxford University Press, 1989), 148.

21. Ambrose, *Explanatio Psalmi* 1.4 (ed. Luigi Franco Pizzolato, *Sancti Ambrosii Episcopi Mediolanensis Opera* 7 [Milan: Biblioteca Ambrosiana; Rome: Città Nuova, 1980], 40).

22. Ambrose, *Explanatio Psalmi* 6 (ed. Pizzolato, *Opera*, 7: 42).

23. Ambrose, *Explanatio Psalmi* 1–2: "Delight is something natural." On the transforming effect of the psalms' beauty and sweetness on the one who prays, see also Cassiodorus, *Exp. Ps.*, praef. (CCSL 97: 4.39–6.120). On the idea that the pleasure of singing is "natural to the soul," see also John Chrysostom, *Homily-Fragment on Psalm 41* 1 (PG 55: 157).

24. Basil of Caesarea, *Hom. in Ps.* 1.1 (PG 29: 212 b1–9; trans. FC 46: 152). A similar thought appears in the homily "On the Benefit of Singing the Psalms" (*De psalmodiae bono* 5), by Augustine's Dacian contemporary Niceta of Remesiana (ed. Andrew E. Burn, *Niceta of Remesiana: His Life and Works* [Cambridge: Cambridge University Press, 1905], 73.4–10).

25. John Chrysostom, *Homily-Fragment on Psalm 41* 1 (PG 55: 156; trans. McKinnon, *Music*, 80).

26. For references to the use of critical judgment, see, e.g., Sextus Empiricus, *Adversus mathematicos* 1.248; Quintilian, *Institutio oratoria* 10.1.40. "Longinus," in the passage referred to above (note 20), remarks that "literary judgment comes only as the final product of long experience" (Russell and Winterbottom, *Classical Literary Criticism*, 148). On the actual practice of some ancient critics in making literary judgments, see J. W. H. Atkins, *Literary Criticism in Antiquity*, 2 vols. (Cambridge: Cambridge University Press, 1934), 1: 107–16 (Aristotle); 2: 39–43 (Cicero), 2: 92–96 (Horace).

27. Dionysius of Halicarnassus, "On the Examination of Speeches" (περὶ λόγων ἐξετάσεως), *Ars Rhetorica* 11 (ed. Hermann Usener and Ludwig Rademacher, *Dionysii Halicarnassensis opera* [Leipzig: Teubner, 1904], 2: 374–87).

28. For a description of the intentions and techniques of classical grammarians, see the old but still comprehensive account of Henri-Irénée Marrou, *Histoire de l'éducation dans l'Antiquité*, 6th ed. (Paris: Seuil, 1964), 1: 250–57 (Greece); 2: 81–85 (Rome). On the allegorical interpretation of Homer and other classical texts by philosophically minded grammarians, see Robert Lamberton, *Homer the Theologian*

(Berkeley: University of California Press, 1986), esp. 1–43. On the importance of intellectual as well as aesthetic judgments of poetry, see especially Philodemus, *On Poems* 27 and 151 (ed. Richard Janko [Oxford: Oxford University Press, 2000], 215 and 361). Philodemus constantly argues against earlier the grammarians he calls "the Κριτικοί," whom he accuses of judging poetry solely by its sound; for Janko's discussion, see 120–28; cf. James Porter, "Content and Form in Philodemus: The History of an Evasion," in *Philodemus and Poetry*, ed. Dirk Obbink (New York: Oxford University Press, 1995), 139–41.

29. See Cassiodorus, *Exp. Ps.,* praef. 15 (CCSL 97: 18–21), on the distinctive "eloquence" of all scripture; *Exp. Ps.,* praef. 16 (CCSL 97: 21–22), on the particular eloquence of the Psalter.

30. The Antiochene commentators' attempts to see each psalm as referring to some concrete situation within the history of Israel in some ways resembles the practice of early rabbinic commentators, as represented in the somewhat later (ninth-tenth century) Midrash Tehillim. Braude remarks, in the introduction to his translation of this commentary, "For the authors of Midrash Tehillim, historical past, present and future are rolled up into God's single and all embracing vision of things, a glimpse of which he occasionally vouchsafes to Patriarchs, kings and prophets who move through the pages of Scripture" (William G. Braude, trans., *The Midrash on the Psalms*, 2 vols., Yale Judaica Series 13 (New Haven, CT: Yale University Press, 1959], 1.xxiv).

31. Diodore of Tarsus, *Comm. Ps.,* pracf. 107–8, 120–22 (CCSG 6: 6).

32. So Hilary, *Instr. Psal.* 8 (CCSL 61: 9). Theodoret, *Int. in Ps.,* prol. (PG 80: 864 a1–b6), does not want to discard the titles, precisely because of their presence in the Septuagint, even though he admits his uncertainty about their origin.

33. See Hilary, *Instr. Psal.* 9, 11 (CCSL 61: 9–11); Gregory of Nyssa, *Inscr. Ps.* 1.5–8 (GNO 5: 37–112); Cassiodorus, *Exp. Ps.,* praef. 16 (CCSL 97: 21–22).

34. Gregory of Nyssa, *Inscr. Ps.* 1.5 (GNO 5: 37); Jerome, *Commentarioli in Psalmos* 40; see Cassiodorus, *Exp. Ps.,* praef. 12 (CCSL 97: 15).

35. Hilary, *Instr. Psal.* 10–11 (CCSL 61: 10); Cassiodorus, *Exp. Ps.,* praef. 12 (CCSL 97: 15).

36. Athanasius, *Ep. Marcell.* 1 (PG 27: 12).

37. Athanasius, *Ep. Marcell.* 2 (PG 27: 12); see Basil of Caesarea, *Hom. in Ps.* 1.1 (PG 29: 212 a4–9).

38. Athanasius, *Ep. Marcell.* 10 (PG 27: 20), following the suggestion of the eighteenth-century editor, Johann Ernst Grabe, to read ἀπ' εἰκόνος instead of ἄπειρον. Unfortunately, there is not yet a critical edition of this important treatise; Migne's collection reprints Grabe's scholarly but obsolete edition (Venice, 1707), based on the Codex Alexandrinus of the Bible.

39. Athanasius, *Ep. Marcell.* 10 (PG 27: 20).

40. Athanasius, *Ep. Marcell.* 10 (PG 27: 21).

41. Athanasius, *Ep. Marcell.* 11 (PG 27: 21); Athanasius is thinking of the liturgical chanting of the psalms by a cantor. John Cassian also describes, albeit briefly, the same process of discovering one's own feelings mirrored in the psalms, which enables us to perceive the psalms as expressing our own experience (*Conlat.* 10.11.6).

42. Athanasius, *Ep. Marcell.* 12 (PG 27: 24).

43. Athanasius, *Ep. Marcell.* 12 (PG 27: 24).

44. Athanasius, *Ep. Marcell.* 12 (PG 27: 25).

45. Athanasius, *Ep. Marcell.* 27 (PG 27: 40).

46. Athanasius, *Ep. Marcell.* 28 (PG 27: 40). Athanasius seems here to be referring to the "odes" or canticles contained in other books of the Bible as a separate, musically more elaborate category of sung liturgical text, alongside the book of Psalms.

47. Gregory of Nyssa, *Inscr. Ps.* 1.3.18 (GNO 5: 30.23). In the parlance of the fourth-century Greek fathers, *philosophy* meant above all the practice of asceticism, grounded in Christian faith and scripture.

48. Gregory of Nyssa, *Inscr. Ps.* 1.3.23 (GNO 5: 33.7–11; trans. Ronald E. Heine, *Gregory of Nyssa's Treatise on the Inscriptions of the Psalms* [Oxford: Clarendon Press, 1995], 91 [alt.]).

49. Cassiodorus, *Exp. Ps.*, praef. 15 (CCSL 97: 18.5–6; trans. ACW 51: 36).

50. Cassiodorus, *Exp. Ps.*, praef. (CCSL 97: 4.65–5.68): "Psalmi sunt denique, qui nobis gratas faciunt esse vigilias, quando silenti nocte psallentibus choris humana vox erumpit in musicam, verbisque arte modulatis ad illum redire facit, a quo pro salute humani generis divinum venit eloquium."

51. "Perfect theology": Basil, *Hom. in Ps.* 1.2 (trans. FC 46: 153); see also Diodore of Tarsus, *Comm. Ps.*, praef. 45–67. On its richness of moral example, see Cassiodorus, *Exp. Ps.*, praef. 15; Diodore of Tarsus, *Comm. Ps.*, praef. 1–13.

52. Cassiodorus, *Exp. Ps.*, praef. 16.

53. Ambrose, *Explanatio super Psalmos XII* 1.9 (CSEL 64: 7); cf. Niceta of Remesiana, *De psalmodiae bono* 5 (ed. Burn, *Niceta of Remesiana*, 72).

54. Ambrose, *Explanatio super Psalmos XII* 1.7 (CSEL 64: 6.4–11). For a perceptive study of this same image of the psalms as an athletic training ground for the Christian affections, in patristic literature and in Luther's exegesis, see Günter Bader, *Psalterium affectuum palaestra: Prolegomena zu einer Theologie des Psalters* (Tübingen: Mohr Siebeck, 1996).

55. Augustine, *En. Ps.* 99.1 (CCSL 39: 1393.5–8).

56. See Augustine, *Conf.* 7.20.26, 7.21.27.

57. Augustine, *Conf.* 9.4.8 (CCSL 27: 137.20–28; trans. Henry Chadwick, *Confessions* [Oxford: Oxford University Press, 1992], 160).

King David and
the Psalms of Imprecation

Gary A. Anderson

For both Jews and Christians, the book of Psalms has been a staple for prayer. Countless persons recite them on a daily basis, and many have committed large portions of this book, if not its entirety, to memory. Yet for all its attractions to one inclined toward prayer, the book of Psalms is not without its difficulties. Chief among these difficulties are the so-called imprecatory psalms, those psalms that take a somewhat morbid delight in hurling verbal curses upon one's enemies. In the Catholic Church, the Liturgy of the Hours has constituted the means for daily recitation of the psalms.[1] This tradition of divine service is as old as Christian monastic devotion itself. In our own day, the imprecatory portions of the psalms are no longer required reading for priests and monastics who are obliged to pray this office daily. As concerns the practice of the religious life, they have been removed from the record.

And who could blame these reformers for editing out these trouble-some texts? Who is it, even among the most traditionally minded, who takes delight in urging divine retribution on one's enemies? "O God, smash their teeth in their mouths; shatter the fangs of the lions," our psalmist exhorts (58:6 [LXX 57:6]). If this is not sufficiently repellent, consider Psalm 137 [LXX 136], the rather well-known psalm about the destruction of Jeru-salem. Its opening lines of lamentation—"By the waters of Babylon we sat down and wept, as we gave thought to Zion"—have struck a sympathetic chord in the ears of many. But its closing lines have evoked no such sympathy: "A blessing on him who repays you in kind for what you have inflicted on us; a blessing on him who seizes your babies and dashes them against the rocks." If these wishes for destruction are not a sufficient evil, consider the fact that the psalmist will also, on occasion, implore God that he might be a witness to the desired acts of vengeance: "May the righteous rejoice when he sees revenge; may he bathe his feet in the blood of the wicked" (58:10). No shrinking violet, this fellow. Little wonder that nearly all modern commentators have found these texts a stumbling block for prayer.

Surprisingly, the barbarity of these psalms did not prove to be such a problem for premodern readers. Though one can find an occasional sign of flinching at some of the more violent images, the horror that moderns unequivocally display simply isn't there. How could this be? For children of the Enlightenment, who harbor deep suspicions about the value of religion, this can only be a confirmation of their prejudices. As these cultured despisers would have it, it is a short journey indeed from the barbarism of the biblical religion to the animosity found in a divided Ireland, the lands bounded by the former Yugoslavia, or the Middle East.[2]

Perhaps the most extreme manifestation of this reaction is that of the German psychologist Franz Buggle. In a recent book, he takes special aim at the book of Psalms. In his words, this book is "a text dominated by primitive and uncontrolled feelings of hatred, a desire for vengeance, and self-righteousness."[3] Adding insult to injury, Buggle observes that one would have no problem naming a whole crowd of people whose moral stature "would be far above that of the biblical god." Yet before we accept this characterization of the psalms as accurate, let us take into consideration a different perspective. In what may be one of the greatest short stories ever written, Shmuel Agnon's "Tehillah," we meet a woman of unparalleled kindness and moral virtue.[4] Thoroughly premodern in nearly every sense, her religious life is defined by a daily routine of reading the psalms; indeed, her name means "a psalm." In the opening lines of this story Agnon describes her thus: "She was righteous, she was wise, she was graceful, and she was unassuming. The light of her eyes was full of kindness and mercy; the lines on her face were full of blessing and peace. If it were not the case that women cannot be angels, I would have imagined her to be a veritable angel of God." If the psalms are barbaric, they have left no trace of their barbarism on this premodern woman of virtue, Tehillah.

The Psalms of Imprecation in Modern Scholarship

Not all moderns have been willing to give up on this difficult language of imprecation found in the Psalter. Erich Zenger, a Catholic biblical scholar who teaches at Münster, has made the best case for retaining the entire Psalter within the liturgy.[5] For Zenger, one must bear in mind at least two things while interpreting the imprecatory psalms. First, the very notion of God's wrath is dependent on and inextricably bound to the concept of God's personal love and involvement with his people. God's wrath should not be understood as mere irrational passion. It is rather the wrath of a loving father and judge who intervenes in human history to save. As the Egyptologist Jan Assmann has put the matter, "Wrath and mercy are mutually conditioned, and both follow, as a matter of logical necessity, from the idea of divine relationship with the world. Anyone who denies God these affects denies God's relationship to the world and makes God a *deus otiosus*, to whom no worship is due. A God who knows no wrath requires no cult: *religio esse non potest, ubi metus nullus est*."[6]

The second factor to bear in mind follows necessarily from the first. If mercy and wrath are to be understood as necessary correlates of a God who intervenes in human history to save, then both mercy and wrath must be made dependent on a higher divine attribute, that of justice. Justice, in the spiritual economy of the psalmist, is a profoundly this-worldly category. As that giant of modern biblical criticism Yehezqel Kaufman put it, there is no wider eschatological horizon to the *Lebenswelt* of the psalmist.[7] The spiritual battle in which the psalmist is engaged is a battle to affirm and confess God's just dealings with *this* world. This axiom cuts in two directions: if justice is not in evidence, then neither is God. If God is not in evidence, then there is no reason to act justly. The atheism described by the psalmist is not the aloof posture of a modern scientist who, upon gazing into the heavens above or while using an MRI to peer into our craniums below, sees no evidence of either a God directing the planetary spheres or a soul animating human life. The atheism portrayed in the psalms has a moral edge. When the psalmist observes that "the fool says in his heart 'there is no God'" (14:1) and then immediately adds, "His deeds are corrupt and loathsome," he intends that we understand these two clauses as two sides of a single coin. Because the affirmation of God's being is so closely tied to his just actions, the psalmist is continually driven to make his private moments of deliverance public knowledge:

> I have told the glad news of deliverance
> in the great congregation;
> see, I have not restrained my lips,
> as you know, O Lord.
>
> (Ps. 40:9)

On the other hand, when the psalmist suffers, his suffering is also not a private concern. His tears become his very food, and his enemies gather and taunt him with the question, "Where is your god?" (Ps. 42:4).

Seen this way, the plea for God to take vengeance on evildoers is not merely a call for *personal* and perhaps therefore petty revenge. It is rather a prayer that God underscore a principle fundamental to all human society: that good behavior will be rewarded and evil behavior punished. The imprecatory language of the psalmist is so impassioned because the very concept of justice itself is at stake. Jon Levenson has reminded us that the doctrine of Creation in the psalms is not a simple affirmation of *creatio ex nihilo*. "God's visible victory over the enemies of order is in the past," Levenson writes, "[but] the present is bereft of the signs of divine triumph."[8] The psalms give witness to the idea of *creatio continua*; the world is continually at war with the forces of chaos, and every tool and strategy is required in the ongoing battle to establish order.

PREMODERN APPROACHES TO THE PSALMS

So much for the imprecatory psalms through the eyes of modern biblical scholarship. How does the picture look in the eyes of premodern interpreters? One might expect, at least with Christian readers, an argument for a developmental perspective. On this view, the barbarism of the psalms is a stage in human history that was only slowly overcome by the monotheistic impulse. Zenger, in particular, argues with great clarity and acumen against this view, especially the tendency of Christians to ascribe the more primitive voice of these imprecations to the religion of the Jews. One might suppose that this idea, so attractive to many modern Christians, would have been of even greater appeal to premoderns. Yet here we are met with a surprising *aporia*: *I know of no early Christian writer who even entertained this argument.* How can we explain this curious fact? Certainly the reason cannot be the love of the fathers of the church for the Jews. They were never shy when it came to criticizing the Jews. For an explanation we must look to the very structure of the premodern Bible. The fathers could eschew such talk, I wish to claim, partly because of an idea they inherited from the Jews — the psalms were the prayer book of David.[9]

That the psalms were the prayer book of David is a very ancient exegetical opinion.[10] It is so ancient, in fact, that it is not really exegesis in the formal sense but a part of the biblical tradition itself. The "fact" of Davidic authorship is established in numerous psalm titles, which frequently provide historical circumstances for the composition as well. Yet strikingly, this piece of information is rarely employed by modern interpreters. This is because moderns have made the dubious assumption that what is late is secondary, and what is secondary can be ignored. David's role in authoring the psalms is alluded to, if at all, in the introductory portion of most commentaries and is then ignored for the body of the psalm itself. Indeed, some moderns, like the editors/translators of the New English Bible, do not even print the titles as part of the book of Psalms. David's role is no longer minimal; it has ceased to exist.

If we assume for a moment that the ascription of the psalms to David should be taken seriously as a hermeneutical principle, then the imprecatory psalms acquire an entirely different tenor of meaning. For now we can contextualize these psalms within the context of an individual life. As contemporary ethicists have noted, the moral life cannot be taught as a series of rules and regulations; moral learning follows best from observing how such rules and norms are embodied in practice. We become moral by imitating moral persons. And so for the religious life more generally. The formation of a godly character is a *mimetic* act; it requires a *Rav*, "teacher," and a *Talmid*, "student." In a classic essay on the demise of the rich texture of mimetic religion, Haym Soloveitchik argued that modern Jewish orthodoxy was in danger of ossifying into a wooden religion of the book alone.[11] Halakhic man, in his ideal form, is not a person bound by mere book learning but one shaped by a *culture* of religious observancy.

What is the relevance of this to our psalms? We must not isolate the text of these prayers from the person who prays them. The correlation of person to prayer is not extrinsic to interpretation but absolutely essential.

But this act of correlation is more easily suggested than done. For the harsh words of imprecation that we find in the Psalter do not easily match up with the person of David who is so severely persecuted by Saul in the books of Samuel. Instead of the angry, imprecatory voice of these prayers, we find a man ready to avoid conflict at all cost. Time and again in the stories of his rise to kingship David distances himself from any thought of vengeance upon his mortal foe, Saul. And he does so in spite of the *numerous* and *justified* opportunities that lie before him.[12]

How then do we read the imprecatory psalms in light of his character? For the rabbis and their Christian contemporary, Gregory of Nyssa, there was only one solution. *The imprecatory psalms give witness to that deep abyss of personal hatred that David, through divine grace, was able to overcome.*

Psalm 58 among Rabbinic Readers

The psalm I would like to examine as an illustration of this is Psalm 58. This psalm is the second in a string of three psalms characterized by a curious set of psalm titles. They have been clearly edited together as a group:

Psalm 57 (LXX 56): "To the leader. Do not destroy. An inscription,[13] when he fled from Saul, in the cave."
Psalm 58 (LXX 57): "To the leader. Do not destroy. Of David. An inscription."
Psalm 59 (LXX 58): "To the leader. Do not destroy. Of David. An inscription, when Saul ordered his house to be watched in order to kill him."

Like other titles in the Psalter, these three titles attribute the compositions to David and set the prayers against a particular circumstance within his life. According to Psalms 57 and 59, the context is one of dire straits—David is fleeing for his life from Saul. It would not take any great leap of imagination to put Psalm 58 in the same general context. In these three psalms we see what type of person David is under fire.

The injunction "Do not destroy" is a bit harder to place. It is both familiar and odd. It is familiar in the sense that we can find similar injunctions for royal prayers elsewhere in the ancient Near East. Here I am thinking of the dedicatory inscriptions that monarchs were wont to install in temples. These monuments, which gave public testimony to the wonderful divine acts showered on one king or another, often ended with the threat of swift and brutal punishment should that monument be effaced. Given this fact, we would assume that these prayers might have originally been executed on stone and placed in a temple or other prominent public location. Yet we possess no evidence that Israelites set up such monuments. Though modern Israel is the most intensely excavated piece of land on the face of the earth, not one such monumental inscription has been found.

But even if we conclude that this fact is merely an accident of the archaeological record—that Israelite kings set up monumental inscriptions that we simply have not been lucky enough to find—there is still something odd about our psalm title. Why would our psalmist deploy this formula, "Do not destroy," for this peculiar type of prayer? This type of formula fits better with dedicatory inscriptions that offer thanks to a god for some great and glorious deeds of deliverance. Why does the title introduce a psalm of imprecation such as Psalm 58?

A satisfactory historical explanation for this conundrum does not exist. The rabbis, however, handled this peculiar title in an ingenious way. They began by taking their cue from the title of Psalm 57, which ended, "when he fled from Saul, in the cave." It seemed altogether logical to presume that Psalm 58 was linked to the same set of events. Why else would the psalmist have been silent? Surely he was presuming that we would carry this setting forward to the next psalm. This presumption is hardly odd given that David takes shelter from Saul on two different occasions in a cave, once in 1 Samuel 24 and again in 1 Samuel 26.

But the evidence for such a narrative linkage was not to be found only in the psalm's title. The books of Samuel seemed to provide dramatic confirmation of the truth of the title. For the warning "Do not destroy" is a verbatim quotation of David during one of these dangerous encounters with Saul. As Abishai hovers precariously over Saul, wishing to thrust him through with his sharpened spear point, David recoils in horror: "*Do not destroy him*," David commands, "for who can raise his hand against the Lord's anointed and be guiltless?" (1 Sam. 26:9). The conclusion the rabbis drew was as simple as it was inevitable: David composed these two prayers while attempting to flee the hostile attacks of King Saul. He entertained thoughts of killing Saul himself—indeed, according to the words of the psalm David burned with a desire to have his vengeance—but at the fated opportunity David managed to hold these feelings in check. He spared Saul's life, even though he had every reason to take it. The key to the psalm's meaning requires that we set these words of imprecation against this particular narrative setting. We should not simply memorize the prayer of the Psalter and mindlessly rehearse it; we should learn its contents through the actions of David. The results are impressive indeed.

David in the Caves of the Judean Desert

Let me pursue this correlation of our psalm with the story of David a bit further. The biblical story of David's flight from Saul and retreat within the caves of the Judean desert is unusual in that it is told two times. As is the custom of modern scholarship, this appearance of a single event told in two similar narratives has given rise to a theory of two different literary sources. However that might be, premodern writers saw the matter very differently. They preferred to read the text as a whole and hence draw out some literary significance to this double telling. David, they surmised, must have learned something significant during the course of these two events.

In the first story, David happens upon Saul in the dark recesses of a cave *by accident* (1 Sam. 24). David's men exhort him to take advantage of this opportunity. In words that recall prayers for vengeance in the Psalter, they say: "Here is the day of which the Lord said to you, 'I will give your enemy into your hand, and you shall do to him as it seems good to you.'" At first David acquiesces to this suggestion. He stealthily draws near and cuts off a corner from Saul's garment. But David, to our surprise, does not see this as a providential occasion for meting out vengeance on one's enemy. "Afterward," our biblical writer reveals, "David reproached himself for cutting off a corner of Saul's cloak" (1 Sam. 24:6). Shamed by this action, he rebukes both himself and his men.

The story closes with David utilizing this opportunity to press his case on Saul. He presents himself before Saul after he leaves the cave in order to prove to him that he seeks him no harm. "Please, sir, take a close look at the corner of your cloak in my hand," David pleads, "for when I cut off the corner of your cloak, I did not kill you. You must see plainly that I have done nothing evil or rebellious, and I have never wronged you" (1 Sam. 24:12). Saul, struck by David's kind gesture, is dumbfounded. "You are right, not I," he declared, "for you have treated me generously, but I have treated you badly" (24:18). Acknowledging that David has every right to be king, Saul begs David not to harm his descendants.

The second story's (1 Sam. 26) relation to the first is, at first, hard to fathom. Though the first story has drawn to a close with Saul tearfully confessing David's right to kingship, the second story opens back where we began. Saul is indignantly pursuing David. The biblical writer provides no explanation for this abrupt change of spirit. The reader can conclude only one thing: Saul is not a well-balanced man. What he offers with one hand he is quick to remove with the other.

Aware of Saul's continuing malicious intentions, David takes special care to keep his eye on him. But he is not simply being watchful; he wants *to orchestrate another face-to-face confrontation*. He sends spies to check on Saul and follows closely behind them. When Saul and his men fall asleep, David alights upon them. Again David is exhorted to take vengeance: "Abishai said to David: 'God has delivered your enemy into your hands today. Let me pin him to the ground with a single thrust of the spear; I will not have to strike him twice'" (1 Sam. 26:8). Here David rebukes Abishai with words that recall the psalm title: "Do not destroy him."[14] Vengeance, David explained, is to come by divine, not human, means.[15]

As in the first story, David uses this opportunity to plead his case with Saul one more time. On this occasion he does not cut off a piece of his robe; rather, he takes his spear and water jar. He then stands at some remove from Saul's camp and cries out to Abner, the head of Saul's army. David asks Abner to account for himself. Why has he left Saul in such a vulnerable position? "As the Lord lives," David exclaimed in exquisite irony, "[all of] you deserve to die, because you did not keep watch over your lord, the Lord's anointed. Look around, where are the king's spear and water jar that were at his head?" (26:16). David, it seems, has done a better job protecting the king than the king's own militia.

Saul, stricken by his lack of faith in David, implores him to return. "I am in the wrong. Come back, my son David; for I will never harm you again, seeing how you have held my life precious this day. Yes, I have been a fool, and have erred so very much" (26:21). David, however, is not to be won over by this confession of guilt. He asks only that Saul grant him his leave and not pursue him as a common criminal: "The Lord will requite every man for his right conduct and loyalty—for this day the Lord delivered you into my hands and I would not raise a hand against the Lord's anointed. And just as I valued your life highly this day, so may the Lord value my life and may he rescue me from all trouble" (26:23–24).

The striking feature of these two stories is that David is twice enjoined to take his vengeance on his enemy. The language and logic of the occasion are strikingly similar to the implied historical background of the imprecatory psalms. Vengeance *is* called for; David *ought* to take advantage of the opportunity. Psalm 58 ends with words that should have encouraged David to take Saul's life: "The righteous man will rejoice when he sees revenge; he will bathe his feet in the blood of the wicked. Men will say, 'There is, then, a reward for the righteous; there is, indeed, divine justice on earth.'"

Yet here is our surprise: David does no such thing. David's actions cut across the diction of the psalm. And it is this tension between the words of the psalm and its deployment in the life of David that the rabbis wish to accentuate. "Do not destroy [him]" is a fitting title to a psalm in which a bloodthirsty desire for vengeance is overcome.

There is one more detail worth attending to in this midrash. As we have noted, it is not altogether clear, in the biblical narrative itself, what the purpose of this double exchange with Saul is. Why must David have two opportunities to take his life; wouldn't one have been sufficient? The rabbis provide an ingenious answer by weaving the diction of the psalm into the plot of our story in Samuel:

So David took the spear and the water jug from beside Saul's head. . . . And David cried to the people, and to Abner the son of Ner, saying: "Will you not give an answer, Abner?" by which he meant: "What hast thou to answer now? Behold the night before, you said to Saul about the events that happened in the cave: 'If David had done anything to you, we could have entered the cave and killed him at once.' But look at this spear and water jug. What will you answer now? Won't you answer me, Abner?" But Abner could give no answer. It was as though he were struck dumb and would not admit the righteousness of David. Therefore David responded: "*Will you not, O deaf one, speak [of my] righteousness?* [Psalm 58:1]. You should have spoken the truth [about me]. But instead you pretend to be dumb and do not declare my righteousness."[16]

The rabbis utilize the difficult line of the psalm "Will you not, O deaf one, speak righteously," to construct a narrative thread across the two encounters with Saul.[17] It just so happens, the rabbis surmise, that on the first occasion David's righteousness is impugned as soon as he leaves the scene. Although Saul has drawn what seems to be the clear lesson from the event—"You [David] are right, not I"—Abner thinks differently. He cut off the hem of your garment, Abner argued, only because he knew that if he killed you he would have been killed in turn.

David must orchestrate a second meeting in order to make clear that he could have slain Saul but did not. When he succeeds on this second occasion to do precisely this, he taunts Abner. "Will you continue to act as one struck dumb about my righteousness?"—that is, will you not give public testimony about my righteous demeanor toward the Lord's anointed? In one fell swoop, two problems come into focus: the necessity of the second encounter and the peculiar reference in our psalm to someone "acting as though struck dumb."

GREGORY OF NYSSA AND THE PATRISTIC TRADITION

Gregory of Nyssa was one of the most learned and formative figures in the early church. Living in Cappadocia at the end of the fourth century, he was renowned in Byzantium for his theological learning and his influential treatises *On Virginity* and the *Life of Moses*.[18] He was deeply influenced by Origen and can be placed in the same circle as Origen and Evagrius with regard to his influence on the contemplative life and his use of the psalms as a source for Christian prayer.[19] For Gregory, the psalms were the prayer book of David, but since David's life was emblematic in almost every respect to that of Christ, the psalms were always susceptible to a secondary, Christological level of meaning. Here lies the answer as to why the church fathers did not see the imprecatory psalms as evidence of a lower form of Jewish religion: they were the authentic prayers of not just any Israelite but the venerable King David.

For Gregory, the most attractive reason for comparing Christ and David was that both were established as kings over Israel and then endlessly persecuted for their roles. Their royal kingdoms were forged, established, and maintained only at great personal cost. Saul's rejection of David and his eager pursuit of him were thought to parallel the rejection of Christ by local Jewish authorities. But, in perhaps the most important parallel for the issue at hand, David, like Christ, never resorted to personal and retributory violence in order to establish his kingdom.

Gregory stood in awe of David's self-effacing virtue in the face of all Saul's onslaughts. "David was a man," Gregory wrote, "and anger was an essential part of his nature." Yet by strength that exceeded all human measurement David could contain that anger and channel it in productive ways. Two times Saul fell into David's hands, and twice David overcame his anger and was prevented from slaying Saul. "Once in the cave Saul fell into David's hands unawares, and again in the tent when he was relaxed in sleep. David stood over him when he was asleep, and when he could have satisfied all his anger by murdering the one who pursued him, he did not lay a hand on him himself, and he said to the one eager for the kill, 'Destroy not.'"[20] So struck is Gregory by David's self-control that he adds his own commentary to this sequence: "The voice which prevents destruction in the case of this man is obviously the voice of God."

How, then, should one pray this psalm? For Gregory we see none of the hand-wringing that is so common among moderns. Instead, with his eye firmly fixed on the title of this psalm, which identifies this prayer as an *inscription*, Gregory urges his audience to allow the difficult words of this psalm to be etched deeply within their memories. "For whenever the soul swells with revenge against someone who is provoking it, and the blood around the heart boils with anger against the one who has grieved the soul, then, when one has looked up at this stela which the Holy Spirit set up for David, and has read the word on it which David uttered on behalf of him who was eager for his own blood, he will not fail to calm the troubled thoughts in his soul, and appease his passion by his desire to imitate [*mimesis*] the same things."[21] For Gregory, the correlation of psalm, psalm title, and the narrative context of the books of Samuel did not just rescue or salvage an offensive biblical text. It did far more. It put this set of imprecatory psalms at the very heart of the Psalter. Indeed, Gregory devotes more space to these three psalms that treat David's flight from Saul (Pss. 57–59 in the Hebrew and English translations) than any other grouping in the Psalter.

THE PSALMS OF IMPRECATION IN THEOLOGICAL CONTEXT

It is worth pausing here to consider just what all of this has to say about the relationship between scripture and prayer. Zenger has done about as good a job as one could within the modern critical framework. He argues that before one can begin any discussion of the claims that this text makes to be revelatory we must utilize modern historical criticism "to *understand* what the texts intended to say to their hearers or readers at the time of their origins.... Only when the original and current *contexts* form part of the reflection can the *texts* themselves be understood."[22] But certainly this methodology involves a conscious choice to bracket and ignore the title of the psalm.

Unfortunately for Zenger and other moderns who follow this train of reasoning, the original biblical context of these psalms is composed of at least two layers: that stage of original composition and use about which we can only make educated guesses and that stage of canonical form about which we can know considerably more. If the life of prayer involves not merely learning words but knowing the occasions on which they are to be used, then the historical critical method will be of limited value. For the data about such mimetic activity are simply not available for historical observation.

In short, a prayer is not just a meretricious set of words; it is a script awaiting performance. There is something deeply *mimetic* about the life of prayer. It is not just a question of what is said, but *who* says it and *when*. For the rabbis and Gregory, one cannot understand Psalm 58 until one has gone over in careful, painstaking detail the events of David's life as portrayed in 1 Samuel 24 and 26. The psalm has no meaning apart from its linkage to David's life. As Brevard Childs observed in his classic essay on the psalm titles, there are some very significant hermeneutical implications here. The role these titles played in the book of Psalms "demonstrates," Childs argues, "that midrashic—or proto-midrashic—exegesis is not some postbiblical 'Jewish distortion,' but part of the biblical tradition itself, and must be taken seriously as such."[23]

This is not to say we should go forth and exegete the Bible according to the precise models staked out by the rabbis or Gregory. Gregory's penchant for connecting each and every line of the psalm to a specific moment in David's life is not likely to win many adherents. Nor is the rabbinic predilection to use Psalm 58 as the means of connecting 1 Samuel 24 to 1 Samuel 26 likely to convince. In the working out of specific details, the rabbinic and patristic voices tended toward the fanciful and clever and not the argued and true.

Yet the *overall* impetus of the rabbis and Gregory to tie the words of the psalm to the figure of David is an altogether worthy hermeneutical turn. If we think of David, or that son of David, while we pray these psalms, I do not think we will err too badly.[24] At a minimum we will have clothed the raw emotion of this imprecation with the apparel of David's character; at a maximum we may, through *mimesis*, be transformed by them, like Agnon's Tehillah.

NOTES

1. See Robert Taft, *The Liturgy of the Hours in East and West* (Collegeville, MN: Liturgical Press, 1993).

2. This is a common criticism of biblical religion. For the argument in recent dress, see Jan Assmann, *Moses the Egyptian* (Cambridge, MA: Harvard University Press, 1997).

3. Franz Buggle, *Denn sie wissen nicht, was sie glauben* (Hamburg: Reinbek, 1992), 22, quoted in Erich Zenger, *A God of Vengeance? Understanding the Psalms of Divine Wrath* (Louisville, KY: Westminster John Knox Press, 1996).

4. The story can be found in his collected works: *All the Stories of Shmuel Yosef Agnon: Ad Hennah* (Jerusalem: Shocken, 1978), 7: 178–206.

5. Zenger, *God of Vengeance?*

6. Jan Assmann, *Politische Theologie zwischen Ägypten und Israel* (Munich: Carl Friedrich von Siemens, 1992), 85–87.

7. Yehezqel Kaufman, *Toledot ha-Emunah ha-Yisraelit* [*The Religion of Israel: From Its Beginnings to the Babylonian Exile*] (Jerusalem: Mosad Bialik, 1960), 2: 705–8.

8. Jon Levenson, *Creation and the Persistence of Evil* (San Francisco: Harper and Row, 1985), 24.

9. The patristic tradition was not uniform on the matter of Davidic authorship and its significance for understanding the psalms. The interpreters from the Antiochene school were far more systematic on this matter than the Alexandrians. Yet the fact that David looms so large in the interpretations of a thinker like Gregory of Nyssa shows that the standard division of patristic writers into two schools does not fully account for the textual data in this particular matter.

10. On this, see the classic article of Brevard Childs, "Psalm Titles and Midrashic Exegesis," *Journal of Semitic Studies* 16 (1971): 137–50; A. Cooper, "The Life and Times of King David According to the Book of Psalms," in *The Poet and the Historian: Essays in Literary and Historical Biblical Criticism*, ed. R. E. Friedman, Harvard Semitic Studies 26 (Chico, CA: Scholars Press, 1983), 117–32; and James Kugel, "Topics in the History of the Spirituality of the Psalms," in *Jewish Spirituality*, ed. Arthur Green (New York: Crossroads, 1986), 113–44.

11. H. Soloveitchik, "Migration, Acculturation, and the New Role of Texts in the Haredi World," in *Accounting for Fundamentalisms*, ed. Martin Marty (Chicago: University of Chicago Press, 1994), 4: 197–235.

12. The story of David's encounter with Nabal (1 Sam. 25) contradicts a portrait of David as nonviolent through and through. In this tale, David is determined to wreak painful and bloody vengeance on his adversary (1 Sam. 25:21–22). Only the well-chosen words of Abigail bring David to his senses and prevent him from taking justice into his own hands—"the Lord who has kept you from seeking redress by blood with your own hands" (1 Sam. 25:25b–31). She effectively persuades David to allow the Lord to prosecute the matter and leave his own hands unsullied. And at the end of the tale, this is precisely what happens—Nabal is struck dead by the Lord. When David learns of the matter, he declares: "Praised be

the Lord who championed my cause against the insults of Nabal and held back his servant from wrongdoing: the Lord has brought Nabal's wrongdoing down on his own head" (v. 39).

No doubt there are at least two reasons our biblical editor has placed 1 Sam. 25 in between 1 Sam. 24 and 26—two stories of how David refrained from slaying Saul when given what seems to be a providential opportunity to do precisely that. First, it shows us that David is fully human and capable of being roused by the fiercest desire to crush his enemies. Saul falls outside the scope of David's vengeance *solely* because of his status as the Lord's anointed. Second, because of Abigail's wise counsel in chapter 25, David learns that the Lord can be trusted to execute justice. He does not require a hotheaded vigilante to assist him, even if the vigilante is in the right.

13. The underlying term in Hebrew, *Miktam* (meaning unknown), is usually emended to *Miktab* ("inscription").

14. No doubt it is significant to the rabbis that this usage of the phrase "Do not destroy" occurs in the second of the two encounters (1 Sam. 26 instead of 1 Sam. 24). They also, not by accident, understood Pss. 57 and 58 to tack a similar course. Ps. 57 concerns the first meeting, Ps. 58 the second.

15. An echo of 1 Sam. 25, where David learns precisely this lesson. See note 12.

16. Midrash Tehillim, ad Ps. 58:2.

17. It should be noted that the Hebrew construction is quite awkward and certainly textually corrupt. The English translation I have provided is what can be inferred from the way the rabbis interpret the phrase.

18. On the life and writings of Gregory of Nyssa, see Anthony Meredith, *Gregory of Nyssa* (London: Routledge, 1999).

19. On this school and its influence on Gregory, see the work of Bernard McGinn, *The Foundations of Mysticism: Origins to the Fifth Century* (New York: Crossroads, 1995).

20. The translation is from Ronald E. Heine, *Gregory of Nyssa's Treatise on the Inscriptions of the Psalms* (Oxford: Clarendon Press, 1995), 200.

21. Ibid., 201.

22. Zenger, *God of Vengeance?*, 83, italics in original.

23. B. S. Childs, "Psalm Titles and Midrashic Exegesis," *Journal of Semitic Studies* 16 (1971): 149.

24. The remarks of Robert Jenson on this score are most apt ("Hermeneutics and the Life of the Church," in *Reclaiming the Bible for the Church*, ed. C. Braaten and R. Jenson [Grand Rapids, MI: Eerdmans, 1995], 102): "The speaker of the psalms is the *totus Christus*, the community of God's people from Abraham through the last Christian saint, as this community is one with the crucified and risen One. The *totus Christus* is indeed righteous with the divine righteousness of

God the Son, and may and must indeed plead that righteousness before God the Father. The *totus Christus*, as Christ identified with us, is 'the chief of sinners,' and speaks to God also in this role. The *totus Christus* is indeed persecuted; he is Christ on the cross, and may and must indeed plead for victory over enemies. The *totus Christus* is one individual Jesus, who spoke all those psalms that are in the first person singular. And he is the whole community of Israel and the church, who spoke all those psalms that are communal liturgy. And when we pray Israel's psalms as our own, we are not imposing a 'Christian' meaning on texts that in themselves mean something else; we are praying them in the Triune space in which they were always prayed."

Restringing Origen's Broken Harp

Some Suggestions Concerning the Prologue
to the Caesarean Commentary on the Psalms

Ronald E. Heine

It is not inappropriate to refer to Origen's great work on the psalms as a harp, in line with the theme of this book, for he himself considered the whole of scripture to be "God's music" and all of the individual parts, like the strings of a lyre or harp, to combine to make that harmonious music if one knows how to interpret them. He suggested, furthermore, that the reader who knows how to bring out this harmony in the various parts would appropriately be called "David" (*Phil.* 6.2). When we look to see how Origen brought out this harmony in the psalms, however, we discover that there are only pieces of the harp remaining. This essay is an attempt to reconstruct one small piece of that broken harp.

The Extent and Nature of Origen's Work on the Psalms

What do we know about the extent and nature of Origen's work on the psalms? For this we are dependent primarily on Eusebius, Jerome, and brief remarks made by Origen concerning his expositions of the psalms in various of his works that have survived.[1]

Origen, it seems, produced four works on the psalms, if it is proper to refer to the homilies as one work. First, he wrote a commentary on the first twenty-five psalms (or perhaps the first fifteen if Jerome's *Excerpta on Psalms 1–15* refers to this work and Eusebius misread *ke* for *ie*).[2] This commentary was written during his career at Alexandria but was probably not his first published work.[3] Next, after moving to Caesarea he preached a series of sermons on the psalms. Then, in the same time frame in which he was completing the *Commentary on the Song of Songs*, he produced the large psalm commentary that is my concern in this essay, and finally, near the end of his life, in the time frame in which he produced the *Commentary on Matthew* and the *Contra Celsum*, he wrote his scholia on the entire Psalter. That, at least, is one way to reconstruct the scene. This entire corpus on the psalms has perished in its original form. And that, I think, is one of the greatest losses of Christian literature.

We are somewhat better served for the remains of the homilies than for the commentaries. We have preserved in a Latin translation of Rufinus five homilies on Psalm 36, two on Psalm 37, and one on Psalm 38. At least that is the way they have been divided up in the tradition that has come down to us. If the theory of Vittorio Peri is correct, Jerome's homilies on the psalms are little more than translations of some of Origen's psalm homilies.[4] This would add fifty-nine more homilies on the psalms. Henri Crouzel has noted, however, that Jerome specialist Pierre Jay has questioned Peri's conclusions.[5] There are also some rather extensive fragments of one or more psalm homilies covering six psalms (Pss. 125, 129, 130, 131, 132, and 133) discovered at Tura whose first editor suggested might stem from Origen.[6]

For the commentaries we have only scattered fragments preserved in the catenae. Unfortunately the catenae preserving fragments of Origen's work on the psalms have not yet been critically edited, with the exception of those on Psalm 118, which have been edited by Marguerite Harl with the collaboration of Gilles Dorival.[7] Dorival summed up the conclusions of modern research on the catenae manuscripts in an article published in 1975.[8] This research identifies the Palestinian catena as our most reliable source for fragments of Origen on the psalms, supplemented by the catena tradition represented in the manuscript Vindobonensis 8. Dorival suggests in his conclusion that neither the Palestinian catena nor that represented in Vindobonensis 8 preserves anything from the homilies, that what is preserved in Vindobonensis 8 comes from the scholia on the psalms, and that the tradition represented most fully and accurately in the Palestinian catena is drawn from the Caesarean commentary on the Psalms.[9] These suggestions, of course, may be subject to revision based on further research in the catenae.

There has been considerable work on the fragments representing the so-called Palestinian catena, though not so much on the particular fragments attributed to Origen. This catena is thought to have originated in Palestine in the sixth century. It is represented in the manuscripts classified as Type VI and Type XI in the Karo-Lietzmann list. Marcel Richard has suggested, on the basis of the manuscript tradition, that the original Palestinian catena was edited in two different forms.[10] One produced a three-volume edition in which each volume contained fifty psalms. The other was a two-volume edition with Psalms 1 through 77 in the first volume and 78 through 150 in the second volume. We know the tradition for Psalms 1 through 50 from the three-volume edition, which is preserved in Karo-Lietzmann's Type VI manuscripts, and these manuscripts, of course, contain the prologues that are the subject of my essay. We know the tradition for Psalms 78 through 150 from the two-volume edition, which is preserved in Karo-Lietzmann's Type XI manuscripts. What we know of Psalms 51 through 77 is dependent on the three-volume edition again. The primary witness, however, Turin 300, was severely damaged in a fire in 1904 and is largely useless.[11]

Robert Devreesse has produced a list of what he considers to be authentic fragments of Origen in PG 12 and 17 and in Pitra's *Origenes in Psalmos*.[12] As I noted earlier, however, we still lack a critical edition of the fragments of Origen on the psalms in the Palestinian catena, except for the fragments on Psalm 118. There is much work still to be done so far as the catena fragments of Origen's psalm commentary are concerned. For example, in reading the fragments of Origen in PG 12 and Pitra on Psalms 1 through 71 in relation to the fragments of Didymus on the same psalms in Mühlenberg's edition, which is based on the Palestinian catena, I noted sixty fragments in Mühlenberg's edition of Didymus that have partial, and sometimes extensive, parallels in the Origen material in PG 12, and four more with parallels in the Origen material in Pitra.[13] A number of these parallels are verbatim. Are these to be explained simply as incorrectly attributed to Origen in the traditions from which they are drawn in PG and Pitra? A problem with that explanation is that the parallels are rarely complete. That is, there is material interspersed either in the Origen or in the Didymus material. On the other hand, where they are alike they are too much alike for there not to be some kind of literary dependence between the texts. But from where does the dependence spring? Does it go all the way back to Didymus excerpting portions from Origen? Or does it go back to a copyist who has blended materials from different sources? Or, as I suggested at first, is it a problem of getting the name wrong in the catena tradition? I have not studied the problem, I have only noticed it as I have read, so I do not have a solution to propose.

How much have we lost in terms of the Caesarean commentary? The first problem we encounter when we try to answer this question is that we do not know the original extent of the commentary. We may rather safely assume that the list of books on the various psalms in Jerome's Epistle 33.4 "To Paula" refers to the books of the Caesarean commentary, especially if the initial reference to "Excerpta on Psalms 1–15" refers to the Alexandrian commentary.[14] The list reveals that Origen wrote one or more books on each psalm he treated. Psalms 43, 50, and 103 each received two books, and Psalm 44 was treated in three books. Jerome's list includes forty-six books on forty-one psalms. The list is not complete, however, as Marie-Josèphe Rondeau has shown that Origen himself refers to five other psalms that he had treated (Pss. 21, 31, 47, 100, 140).[15] Psalm 118 is also not among the psalms listed by Jerome, unless Pierre Nautin's guess should happen to be correct that Jerome's Psalm 103 was actually Psalm 118, but the XV has dropped out of the middle of the Roman numeral (C[XV]III).[16] I doubt that that is correct, since Jerome says there were only two books on that psalm. I cannot imagine Origen devoting only two books to the 176 verses of Psalm 118. There are, however, a number of fragments from Origen's commentary on this psalm that have been edited by Harl and Dorival, and, if Dorival is correct that the fragments in the Palestinian catena come from the Caesarean commentary, then this is another psalm treated in that commentary. We do not know how extensive the Caesarean psalm commentary was.

If, however, we may work for a moment with the forty-six books on the forty-one psalms to which Jerome refers, and if we may assume that the fragments attributed to Origen on those same psalms in volume 12 of Migne's *Patrologiae* all come from Origen, which, of course, we may not assume, we may get an idea of how little the catena fragments have preserved. An approximate average for the length of a book in the *Patrologiae* is 30 columns. Forty-six books would fill 1,380 columns, or an average-size volume of the *Patrologiae*. The fragments published in volume 12 on the forty-one psalms that Jerome mentions fill approximately 135 columns. On this way of reckoning, then, we have lost 1,245 columns of *Patrologiae* text on forty-one psalms. And, as I have noted, Jerome's list must be considered to be incomplete.

I did this little exercise in counting columns to emphasize how careful we must be in making statements about what Origen said or did not say in his *Commentary on the Psalms* based on catena fragments. A huge amount of material has been lost. This is why we must draw not only on the catena fragments but also on those later authors who knew his works and were strongly under his influence. This is especially the case where we have the writings of these later authors on the psalms in complete or more complete form.

Origen's Use of the Classical Commentary Prologue Format

In late antiquity there was a set format for prologues to commentaries on classical literary works containing topics of both a general and a particular nature. Origen knew and followed this format in his commentaries, making appropriate adaptations to the different type of material on which he was working. Jaap Mansfeld has pointed out that at the conclusion to the prologue to his *Commentary on John* Origen uses the technical expression that was used to refer to the prologues of commentaries on philosophical authors when he says, "Here, perhaps, we shall stop discussing the matters which precede the study of the things which have been written [*ta pro tēs sunanagnōseōs*]."[17]

The overall prologue format for commentaries on classical texts was very similar for all literary genres, but there were some distinctions depending on whether the work being explained was philosophical, poetical, or rhetorical. We have the prologues for four of Origen's commentaries: his commentaries on the Song of Songs, John, Romans, and Psalms. The prologue to the latter, however, exists only in catena fragments and must be hypothetically reconstructed. Ilsetraut Hadot and Bernhard Neuschäfer have each independently argued for the influence of the prologues to philosophical commentaries on Origen's prologue to his *Commentary on the Song of Songs*.[18] I have argued also for the influence of the prologues to philosophical commentaries on the prologue to his *Commentary on the Gospel of John*.[19] Caroline Bammel has suggested that the prologues to rhetorical commentaries may provide the background for the prologue to the *Commentary on Romans*,[20] and Neuschäfer has argued for the influence of the prologues to commentaries on the poets as the background for the prologue to Origen's Caesarean *Commentary on the Psalms*.[21]

The format of particular topics for the prologue to a philosophical commentary in its full form normally consisted of six points. The order of the topics was not set and varied from work to work, and various topics could be omitted or joined with another topic when appropriate. The six topics were

1. The aim (*skopos*) of the treatise, or its theme (*prothesis*)
2. Its usefulness (*to chrēsimon*)
3. Its authenticity (*to gnēsion*)
4. Its place in the order (*taxis*) of reading
5. The reason for the title (*hē aitia tēs epigraphēs*)
6. The division (*diairesis*) into heads[22]

Some additional, more general topics might also be discussed in the prologue, such as the quality of life necessary in the interpreter, the obscurity of the writing in question, and perhaps the reason for the obscurity, and it appears that some philosophical commentaries also began with a biography of the author, like the commentaries on the poets.[23]

The format for the prologue to a commentary on a poetic book, according to Donatus on Virgil, consisted of the following seven topics:

1. A life of the author (not mentioned by Donatus but he begins with a life; mentioned by Servius)
2. The title (*titulus*) of the work, including the work's authenticity
3. The occasion or reason for the work (*causa*; Servius lacks this but has *qualitas carminis*)
4. The purpose (*intentio*) of the work (Donatus later says the Greeks call this the *skopos*)
5. The number (*numerus*) of poems (if it is a collection like that of the *Eclogues*, Donatus) or of books (if it is the *Aeneid*, Servius)
6. The order (*ordo*) of poems or books
7. The interpretation (*explanatio*)[24]

The seventh point, of course, is the commentary itself, so perhaps one should speak of a six-point format here also.

I pass by the format for the rhetorical commentaries, as it is irrelevant for our purposes.[25] I must add one further prologue format, however, before turning specifically to the prologue fragments of Origen's Caesarean commentary on the psalms. This is the Christian format for prologues to commentaries on the psalms, which, I think, developed out of a combination of the two formats I have just listed with some appropriate adaptations to the peculiarities of the psalms. I have isolated this format in its fullest form in some previously published work on Gregory of Nyssa's treatise *On the Inscriptions of the Psalms*.[26] The prologue format here contains six or seven topics (Gregory joins two of the topics in his discussion).

1. The aim (*skopos*) of the Psalter
2. The division (*diairesis*) of the Psalter into sections and their order (*taxis*)
3. The meanings of the inscriptions (*epigraphai*)
4. The reason some psalms have no inscriptions
5. The meaning of *diapsalma*
6. The divergence of the order of some psalms from the historical sequence of the events to which their inscriptions allude

In my opinion it was Origen who first adapted the pagan prologue topics to Christian commentaries on the book of Psalms and who introduced the additional topics that needed to be discussed concerning the psalms before the interpretation of the individual psalms was undertaken.

The general prologue to Origen's Caesarean commentary would not have occupied a separate book but would have constituted the beginning of the book on Psalm 1. This is the normal way, at least, that the general prologues appear in the philosophical commentaries on Aristotle, in Servius's commentary on Virgil, and in Origen's *Commentary on John*. The prologue leads immediately into the first lemma in the commentary.

PREVIOUS RECONSTRUCTIONS OF PROLOGUES TO ORIGEN'S PSALM COMMENTARIES

I am certainly not the first to attempt to reconstruct a prologue to Origen's works on the psalms. Devreesse has suggested a reconstruction of the prologue to the treatment of the psalms in the Hexapla.[27] Neuschäfer has attempted a tentative reconstruction of the prologue to Origen's Caesarean *Commentary on the Psalms*.[28] Perhaps Walter Rietz's *De Origenis prologis in Psalterium: Quaestiones selectae* (1914) should also be considered an attempt at a reconstruction of the prologue to the Caesarean commentary.[29] And, of course, Nautin has attempted to reconstruct not only the prologue to the Caesarean commentary but that of the Alexandrian one as well.[30] In the provisional reconstruction of the prologue to Origen's Caesarean *Commentary on the Psalms* that follows, I differ in some respects from all of these but, as might be expected, also have certain things in common with them.

I differ from Neuschäfer in that I think the topics of prologues to philosophical commentaries have provided the basic framework for Origen's approach but that he has modified these topics in some respects that are specific to commentaries on the poets. Rietz, Devreesse, and Nautin make no mention of prologue topics. These topics can be used, it seems to me, as a kind of grid for sorting out the topics Origen most likely treated in his prologue.

My approach differs from Neuschäfer, Rietz, and Nautin also in the materials from which I attempt to build my argument. Neuschäfer built his reconstruction on the fragments in PG 12 edited by Rietz. None of the fragments edited by Rietz belong to the tradition of the more reliable Palestinian catena represented in the manuscripts Karo-Lietzmann classified as Type VI. Nautin also based his reconstruction on the texts edited by Rietz.

Nautin, Neuschäfer, and Devreesse all note that another series of prologue fragments has been attributed to Origen in an edition by J. B. Pitra, and has been attributed to Pseudo-Hippolytus in an edition by Hans Achelis.[31] Nautin considered the Ps.-Hippolytus fragments not to represent the authentic text of the prologue to the Caesarean commentary but to be a recasting of the tradition that had several agreements with Hilary and that may have preserved a few actual texts from the prologue.[32] Devreesse notes that although not all of these latter fragments are sufficiently marked in terms of their authenticity, nevertheless, a good part of them appear under Origen's name in our better catenae, namely manuscripts Vaticanus 1789 and Oxford Bodleian Baroccianus 235.[33] These two manuscripts both belong to Karo-Lietzmann's Type VI and represent the more reliable Palestinian catena. This does not guarantee, of course, that the fragments actually derive from Origen. Richard, however, was of the opinion that this catena is "the most worthy of confidence" of all the catenae on the Psalter.[34] I build my reconstruction on the material attributed to Origen in the prologue found in Baroccianus 235 (B), the major witness to the Palestinian catena.

There are, moreover, a few additional fragments from a prologue to a psalm commentary that can be attributed with certainty to Origen, preserved in the *Philocalia*, Eusebius, and Epiphanius. Nautin claimed these fragments for the prologue to Origen's Alexandrian psalm commentary. I reject Nautin's claim and argue that the fragments from the *Philocalia* and Eusebius also derive from the Caesarean psalm commentary.

I had an interesting experience during the time that I was writing this essay. I was helping my four-year-old daughter put one of her jigsaw puzzles together on a Sunday afternoon. It was a puzzle that someone had given to her in a plain box lacking the helpful picture on the lid of the box. We had, nevertheless, managed to put it all together a few months earlier, so I had a vague recollection of the picture. It seemed, however, on this Sunday afternoon, that some of the pieces were missing. We had assembled three sections of the puzzle and had them lying in what I thought had to be their appropriate locations. But there were some large holes left and the few remaining pieces of puzzle certainly were not going to fill in the holes that remained. As I looked at the puzzle I was reminded, of course, of how this fragmentary puzzle with its missing pieces was like the psalm prologue I was trying to reconstruct from a few fragments. Then my wife came into the room, and I complained that our daughter had lost several pieces of the puzzle. She looked at it and said, "You have it arranged wrong. It goes this way. It's only a small puzzle." I looked at the blocks of puzzle I had arranged and turned the one that was lying perpendicular to the base so that it was parallel to the base and all the pieces interlocked perfectly. There were no pieces missing.

What I want to suggest in regard to Nautin's proposed reconstruction of the prologue to the Alexandrian commentary is a very simple rearrangement that, I think, puts that whole prologue together with no missing pieces and leaves the fragments I mentioned above in the *Philocalia* and Eusebius for the prologue to the Caesarean commentary.

Since first reading Nautin's *Origène* several years ago I had accepted his reconstruction of the prologues to Origen's psalm commentaries, although there always seemed to me to be several rough edges and ill-fitting pieces. But if we reject that reconstruction and accept the possibility that it was only a small prologue and that Nautin used too many pieces and forced them together, we can, I think, recover the above-mentioned fragments as important pieces to the prologue to the Caesarean commentary.

If we look carefully at how Epiphanius introduces his quotation from Origen, we see that he makes three statements. First he says that he is going to quote Origen's "own words from the first psalm" (*Pan.* 64.5.9). Then he says a few lines later that because of the extensiveness of Origen's treatise he is going to select some things from his comments on the first psalm. I take this to refer to the fact that he is going to quote two passages from Origen. The first comes from the prologue and the second from his later comments on Psalm 1:5 concerning the Resurrection. Then, when he comes to actually introduce the quotation from the prologue, he says, "Let us read the psalm from the beginning [*ap' archēs*] up to the expression in question [*heōs autēs tēs lexeōs*] in Origen's own words" (*Pan.* 64.5.12). I think Epiphanius's statement means that he is quoting from the beginning of the commentary on

Psalm 1 and that he is quoting the text in its entirety up to where the words *genētou theou* occur, which is the expression he wants to discuss.

Epiphanius's quotation begins with the discussion of the sealed book and the key of David, quoting from Revelation 3:7–8, 5:1–5, Isaiah 29:11–12, and Luke 11:52. This much appears also in the Philocalian fragments (2.1–2). From this point Epiphanius's text is unique. It proceeds to quote Origen's words, "I have said this by way of preface," and addresses Origen's patron, Ambrose, who, he says, has compelled him to embark on the difficult and dangerous task of committing discussions about God to writing. Then he asks Ambrose to pray to God the Father through our Savior and High Priest, the *genētos theos,* that he may seek as he ought in his exposition. *This paragraph is clearly the end of the prologue.* Origen often requested prayer for divine guidance at the end of prologues to commentaries, prologues to individual books of commentaries, and prologues to individual homilies (cf. *Comm. Jo.* 1.89; 20.1; 28.6; *Comm. Rom.* prol.; *Hom. Gen.* 13.1; *Hom. Exod.* 1.1; 5.1; 8.1).[35]

My suggestion is that Epiphanius has quoted the entire prologue to the Alexandrian commentary on the psalms and that the fragments found in the *Philocalia* and Eusebius come from the prologue to the Caesarean commentary. When Origen later came to write the large Caesarean commentary on the psalms he did not intend that people would also read the earlier Alexandrian commentary alongside it. The Caesarean commentary was intended as a replacement for that earlier commentary. He begins this commentary with the same discussion of the closed and sealed nature of the scriptures with which he began the Alexandrian commentary. Like everyone who produces numerous published works, Origen often repeated himself when he discussed the same subject in different contexts. He set the discussion in the Caesarean commentary, however, in the context of the topics common to commentary prologues. When he came to the end of this much longer prologue he did not use the paragraph that closes the short prologue in the Alexandrian commentary, for what he said there would no longer have been appropriate at this later stage of his publishing career. He closed instead, as I will argue later, with the story, found in the Philocalian fragments, that he had learned from a Jewish teacher about the keys for unlocking the obscurities of scripture.

If my suggestion is correct, I have removed four fragments from Nautin's reconstruction of the Alexandrian prologue for use in the Caesarean prologue. I will fit them into their places at the appropriate points.

PROVISIONAL RECONSTRUCTION OF THE PROLOGUE
TO ORIGEN'S CAESAREAN PSALM COMMENTARY

In my provisional reconstruction of the Caesarean prologue, I construct the basic framework from some fragments in the manuscript group representing the Palestinian catena as they appear in manuscript B.[36] Manuscript B is a catena commentary on Psalms 1 through 50 and is the oldest and best witness to this textual tradition.[37] The prologue of B consists of excerpts drawn from Basil, Eusebius, Origen, Epiphanius, Didymus, and Theodoret. The prologue is written in two columns per page on six pages recto and verso. It occupies twenty-one and one-half columns, of which thirteen columns are derived from Origen. These thirteen columns from Origen are written as two continuous excerpts with one short (one-half-column) excerpt from Basil inserted between them. In my reconstruction I supplement these fragments in B with a few fragments drawn from other manuscript traditions, with the four fragments in the *Philocalia* and Eusebius's *Church History* that I have just discussed, and with the prologue to Hilary's later Latin *Commentary on the Psalms*, which, as is well known, was strongly influenced by Origen.[38]

I begin, as I have indicated above, with the fragment in *Philocalia* 2.1–2. The discussion found here of the sealed book and the key of David is a discussion of the hidden nature of the contents of the Bible. Origen concludes by saying, "We must consider these things to be spoken not only of the Apocalypse of John and Isaiah, but also of all divine Scripture, which is beyond question full of riddles, and parables, and dark sayings, and various other obscurities hard to be understood by men,"[39]

Mansfeld has pointed out that this discussion of obscurity (*asapheia*) is one of the themes that the later commentators on classical authors discussed in their prologues.[40] Ammonius, for example, writing in the late fifth or early sixth century, says in the prologue to his commentary on Aristotle's *Categories*, "Let us ask why on earth the philosopher is contented with obscure teaching. We reply that it is just as in the temples, where curtains are used for the purpose of preventing everyone, and especially the impure, from encountering things they are not worthy of meeting. So too Aristotle uses the obscurity of his philosophy as a veil, so that good people may for that reason stretch their minds even more, whereas empty minds that are lost through carelessness will be put to flight by the obscurity when they encounter sentences like these."[41] Origen begins his commentary on the psalms with a standard topic of commentary literature. He also begins the prologue to his *Commentary on Romans* with a similar discussion. He notes that Romans is more difficult to understand than the other Pauline letters and asks why this is so. He ends that discussion by praying that God will make him worthy, in the words of Proverbs 1:6, "to understand proverbs and figures, the words of the wise and their riddles."

In book 4 of *De principiis* Origen argues that the divine Spirit had two aims (*skopoi*) in the composition of the scriptures. The first aim was to conceal the "unspeakable mysteries connected with the affairs of men" so that those who are capable might search them out and become partakers "of all the doctrines of the Spirit's counsel."[42] The second aim was to make this previously mentioned concealment in a narrative that would be capable "of improving the multitude" of people who lacked the capability of searching for the hidden meaning.[43]

I suspect that Origen made some statement concerning the aim (*skopos*) or the theme (*prothesis*) of the book of Psalms in conjunction with his discussion of the obscurity of scripture at the beginning of his commentary, though I have not yet found anything that I think may have been that statement in the preserved fragments. Perhaps it was something like the statement with which Hilary introduces his discussion of the sealed book and the key of David in his prologue (prol. 5): "It cannot be disputed that what has been said in the psalms ought to be understood in relation to the proclamation of the gospel."

One further thing to note about Origen's discussion of the aim of the Spirit to conceal the deeper meaning of scripture is that "usefulness" (*to chrēsimon*), another topic of commentary prologues, was a subject he discussed in relation to scripture's obscurity. In *De principiis* 4.2.9 he continues, "But if the *usefulness* [*to chrēsimon*] of the law and the sequence and ease of the narrative were at first sight clearly discernible throughout, we should be unaware that there was anything beyond the obvious meaning for us to understand in the scriptures. Consequently the Word of God has arranged for certain stumbling-blocks . . . to be inserted in the midst of the law and the history . . . else by never moving away from the letter [we] fail to learn anything of the more divine element."[44] Here we learn that the "stumbling-blocks" in scripture are intended to direct us to the real "usefulness" of scripture.

In the prologue to his thirty-ninth homily on Jeremiah preserved in *Philocalia* 10, Origen again discusses the "usefulness" of scripture in relation to the subject of "stumbling-blocks" in scripture. *To chrēsimon* occurs four times in this short prologue. The saint is called a "spiritual herbalist" who discovers the meaning of the scripture and its usefulness.

All of this is to suggest that we should expect Origen to have discussed the topic of "usefulness" in the prologue to his commentary on the psalms not long after he discussed the obscurity of scripture. If we may take a hint from Hilary's prologue again, we may be able to discover at least an echo of that discussion.

After Hilary has discussed the sealed book and the key of David in a passage that parallels our fragment from the *Philocalia* discussed above, he goes on to compare the way the divine spirit has spoken through David to the form of the harp, which produces its musical sound from its upper portion. "God," he says, "is praised in song in the psalms . . . by means of this supernal spirit, in the form of the Lord's body in which the heavenly Spirit has spoken" (prol. 7).

A very similar discussion of the harp is found in B 8r at the end of the first excerpt from Origen and in B 8r-8v (= GCS 1.2, frags. 9 [p. 140.19–24] and 11) at the beginning of the second excerpt.[45] David is the only prophet, the fragment declares, to have prophesied with the instrument the Greeks call the psaltery and the Hebrews the *nabla*. This instrument, the fragment continues, is unique in that it has no curve but is straight and in that the sound comes from the upper part of the instrument. The harp is then compared to the body of Christ and his saints, which instrument alone has maintained *tēn euthutēta*, which can mean "straightness" in relation to the harp but also "righteousness" in relation to people. This harmonious, melodious, in-tune instrument, which has received no human discord, has maintained harmony with the Father in all things. This discussion, I suggest, contains an echo of Origen's discussion of the "usefulness" of the book of Psalms. The collection of psalms, prophesied with the harp that is straight and produces its music above, points us to Christ and the things that are above. The exact location of the discussion in the prologue, however, is obscure because of the different places it occupies in Hilary's prologue and in that of B.

I turn now to the most promising and problematic section of the fragments, the beginning of the excerpt from Origen at B 6r (= GCS 1.2, frag. 7). The fragment begins in Achelis's edition with the words, "And this is the *aim* and the *usefulness* of the book, but *the reason for the title* is this." This opening line indicates that a discussion of the aim and usefulness of the book of Psalms has preceded the fragment and that a discussion of the meaning of the title will follow. The discussion of the title does follow, and this part seems clearly to have come from Origen. The problem is with the words up to "the usefulness." Do they belong with this fragment and do they come from Origen?

Achelis's edition cannot be used as evidence because this entire sentence, along with most of the following sentence, is missing in Vat. 1789. Achelis supplied the sentence from Par. gr. 143, which does not belong to the Palestinian catena and which does not indicate the author of the excerpts. The sentence is present and clear in B, but the exact point at which the words of Origen begin is unclear. The scribe responsible for B writes an abbreviation of the name of the author of each excerpt to the left of the column where each excerpt begins.[46] He also, usually, writes the initial letter of the excerpt large and slightly into the left margin of the column. The abbreviation for Origen's name appears here with the top parallel to the line beginning with *chrēsimon* (usefulness). The article with *chrēsimon* is at the end of the preceding line, and *chrēsimon* does not begin with a larger letter, nor is it extended into the left margin. The bottom of the abbreviation for Origen's name parallels the line beginning with "for the title" (*tēs epigraphēs*). The article *tēs* does begin with a slightly larger letter, and the word extends slightly into the left margin. This division, however, is grammatically impossible. The article and noun "the reason" (*hē aitia*) on which the phrase "for the title" depends and to which the demonstrative pronoun *this* (*hautē*) refers are in the preceding line and, on this division, would belong to the fragment from Eusebius. Mühlenberg, who gives a list of the *incipits* and *explicits* of all the excerpts in manuscript B, ascribes the words up through "the usefulness" (*to chrēsimon*) to the preceding Eusebian fragment (= GCS 1.2, frag. 6).[47] This division has the following two points to commend it. First, it falls at a break in the sentence, giving the final clause, "but the reason for the title is this," to the Origen fragment; second, the initial words are parallel to the top of the abbreviation of Origen's name. The problem with this division is that the sentence consists of two clauses introduced respectively by "on the one hand" (*men*) and "but on the other hand" (*de*). This division would leave the *men* clause with the fragment from Eusebius and would place the *de* clause in the fragment from Origen.

It is also possible that the statement in question stems from the catenist who first compiled the catena commentary and is his way of connecting the fragments.[48] If this is the case, one should find a clear statement of the "aim" or "theme" of the commentary along with a statement of its "usefulness" in the excerpts that precede this one. The term *usefulness* appears three times in the opening fragments from Basil (B 5r-6r = PG 29: 209A–213B with omissions). The word used is not *chrēsimon* but its synonym *ōphelimos*. It appears first in a quotation of 2 Timothy 3:16 that speaks of the "usefulness" of all scripture. This appearance may be disregarded for our purposes, except that it perhaps sets the theme for the remarks that follow and supplies the particular term, *ōphelimos*, that is used. The second appearance of the term is in the statement that the book of Psalms includes what is "useful" from all the other parts of the scriptures. Finally, Basil later uses the analogy of physicians who smear the cup of medicine with honey to make the medicine easier to take in order to say that the psalms mix "the delight of singing with doctrines so that we might imperceptibly receive what is *useful* from the words." Neither of these latter two statements speaks precisely of the "usefulness" of the book of Psalms. The first refers to the materials that are useful in other parts of scripture being gathered into the psalms, and the second refers to what is useful in the doctrines one learns while singing the psalms. One might argue, nevertheless, that the catenist used the phrase "the usefulness of the book" loosely. It is more difficult, however, to discover a statement of the "aim" of the book of Psalms in the fragments that precede the fragment from Origen. There is no word in these fragments that approximates the term *skopos*, nor is there anything in the fragments from Basil that suggests a statement of the *skopos* of the book. One might argue that the opening statement in the fragment from Eusebius (B 6r = GCS 1.2 frag. 7)—"The Book of Psalms contains new teaching after the law of Moses"—could be understood as such. In contrast to these rather vague possible references to the "usefulness" and "aim" of the book of Psalms, however, the discussion of the "reason for the title" that follows in the fragment from Origen is, as we will see, quite clear and specific. Further, if the sentence in question derives from the catenist and refers to what he has already written, we must ask why he chose to reverse the order of the topics as they appear in his earlier material—first a discussion of "usefulness" and then one of "aim"—to the order first of "aim" and then of "usefulness" when he refers back to them.

The simplest and most likely answer to this problem, it seems to me, is that the entire sentence belongs to the fragment from Origen and that the scribe of B has simply written the abbreviation for Origen's name two lines further down than he should have. The original composer of the catena commentary chose to begin the prologue of his commentary with excerpts from Basil and Eusebius that praise the book of Psalms. He wanted, then, to use Origen's discussion of the title of the book and the circumstances of its composition. This discussion by Origen, however, began with a statement referring back to what he had just discussed as well as forward to the new topic he was taking up. The catenist, therefore, included Origen's statement referring to his discussion of the "aim" and "usefulness" of the book of Psalms because it formed part of the sentence introducing the discussion of "the reason for the title." It is my opinion, in other words, that Origen had discussed both the *aim* and *usefulness* of the psalms before he took up the topic of the title and that he refers to this discussion in this statement.

After the first ten words, which refer back to the aim and usefulness of the book of Psalms, the fragment beginning at B 6r takes up the reason for the title. This was another of the topics of commentary prologues. The title "Psalms of David," which the majority of Christians gave to the book, is rejected for the title "book of Psalms" on the basis of the Hebrew title and of the appearance of this title in Acts 1:20. The reason for this, the fragment goes on to explain, is that Ezra collected the psalms of many different people into one book, so that it would be inappropriate to refer the whole book to David. Nautin and Devreesse both refer to the marginal note in a tenth-century manuscript discovered by Mercati. The marginal notes do not predate the twelfth century. The author of the note claims to have found an old book containing Origen's Hexapla on the psalms. In his note he says that Origen gives the Hebrew title of the book of Psalms and then points out that all who have translated this into Greek have rendered it the "book of Psalms" and neither "of David" nor "by David."[49] This marginal note helps to confirm the authenticity of our fragment, though not, of course, that it comes from the Caesarean commentary.

The fragment then discusses the problem of determining the author of those psalms that have no inscriptions. The solution to this problem was provided by "a certain Hebrew" who held that all psalms without an inscription are to be assigned to the author named in the last inscription that precedes those psalms without inscriptions.[50] I think the catenist has summarized in general terms here a longer and more detailed discussion of this subject that can be found in manuscripts outside those representing the Palestinian catena.

The longer discussion is found in PG 12: 1056B–1057C (= Rietz III [*De Origenis prologis*, 13–14]). There the same problem is discussed, but it focuses especially on Psalms 89 through 99. Origen begins, if I may use his name at this point, by saying that he had originally thought that there was only one psalm of Moses. But after he had consulted with "Ioullus the patriarch and some of those known as wise men among the Jews" he changed his mind and accepted their suggestion about the authorship of psalms without inscriptions being written by the author named in the last preceding psalm.

Nautin has called attention to Jerome's comments about Origen's reference to the patriarch Ioullus in relation to Psalm 89.[51] "Origen certainly speaks of the patriarch Huillus who was his contemporary and confesses that he has adopted through his teaching a truer opinion than that which he previously held. He also takes as written by Moses not only the Eighty-Ninth Psalm, which is entitled 'A Prayer of Moses the Man of God,' but also, following Huillus's opinion, the eleven following psalms, which have no title."[52] Nautin also refers to the tenth-century manuscript discovered by Mercati that I noted earlier. The annotator, who claims to have found an old book containing Origen's Hexapla on the psalms, quotes the entire fragment in one of his notes and introduces it with the words, "I have found these words verbatim [*tade kata lexin*] in a book containing the Hexapla of Origen on the psalms."[53] We are, it seems, on rather secure ground when we claim this longer fragment for Origen. Whether it appeared in the Caesarean commentary is, of course, a matter of conjecture.

Neuschäfer has pointed out that Origen's discussion of the psalms without inscriptions in this fragment is a discussion of the topic of authenticity (*to gnēsion*), which appears in the ancient scholarly prologues to commentary literature. He further notes that Origen's discussion is particularly like that of the commentaries on the poets in that the discussion of authenticity is linked with the discussion of the topic of the title of the work. This, Neuschäfer notes, is like Donatus's description of the discussion of the title where Donatus says, " 'titulus,' in quo quaeritur cuius sit quid sit."[54] I think Neuschäfer is correct in relating this discussion to the tradition of commentaries on the poets.

We have thus far, then, seen two of the particular topics of ancient commentary prologues discussed in these fragments that I assign to Origen: the reason for the title and the authenticity. We have also considered at least some possibilities for the two further particular topics of the aim and the usefulness, and we have seen the general topic of "obscurity" discussed.

The next material in the Origen fragment (B 6v–8r = GCS 1.2 frag. IX) begins with the words, "Let us inquire why there are 150 psalms." This is a discussion of the topic of "number," which I think is also related to the commentaries on the poets rather than to those on philosophical treatises because the concern in this fragment is with the number of the individual psalms and not with the number of the books. About two-thirds through the fragments the further topic of the order (*taxis*) of the psalms is introduced.

The topic of the number of the psalms is discussed in relation to the mystical meaning of the numbers 50, 7, 8, and 120. The number 50 is especially important because it symbolizes remission, on the basis of Pentecost, the year of Jubilee, and the story of the debtors in Luke 7:41.[55] Origen closes this discussion in his typical fashion by stating that it would be too much to investigate each individual psalm and that he must, therefore, rest content with only the brief outline that he has provided.

Then he takes up the subject of the order of the psalms. Here he discusses the problem that psalms that refer to historical matter in their inscriptions are often not in the correct historical sequence in their appearance in the book of Psalms. He notes especially that the historical order of Psalm 50, discussing David's sin with Bathsheba and forgiveness, and Psalm 51, discussing the treachery of Doeg the Idumean, is reversed. The explanation relates back to the discussion of the number 50, whose meaning was associated with remission. The account of David's forgiveness, therefore, had to be related in Psalm 50. This use of the symbolic significance of numbers to explain the order of the psalms may sound strange to us, but it was not strange in late antiquity. Mansfeld has pointed out that what he calls "arithmology" was involved in the ordering of Plato's treatises by Thrasyllus and of Plotinus's treatises by Porphyry.[56]

Hilary has a similar discussion of the number and order of the psalms in the prologue to his *Commentary on the Psalms* (9–14, 16). Inserted into this discussion near its end (*Comm. Ps.* 15), it speaks of the number of books making up the Old Testament and lists these books. This is what Eusebius has preserved and has introduced with the words that Origen set this forth "while expounding the first psalm" (*Hist. eccl.* 6.25). Nautin wants to put this fragment in the Alexandrian commentary and thinks Hilary interrupted his use of the Caesarean commentary at the end of paragraph 14 and inserted paragraph 15 from the Alexandrian commentary.[57] I have already suggested an alternative to Nautin's reconstruction of the Alexandrian prologue that does not use this fragment from Eusebius. I suggest that the fragment in the *Philocalia* (3) that begins with "As we are dealing with numbers, and every number has a certain significance among real existences" and ends with the sentence about the twenty-two books in the Hebrew Bible corresponding to the number of letters in the Hebrew alphabet should be inserted here in close proximity to the discussion of the mystical meaning of the number of the psalms as Hilary has it in his prologue. Eusebius's list of books in the Hebrew canon begins with this same sentence about the correspondence between the number of books and the number of letters that occurs in the *Philocalia* fragment. I would insert Eusebius's list of Old Testament books immediately after the fragment from the *Philocalia*. The significance of the list for Origen consists in the fact that there are twenty-two canonical books in the Hebrew Bible, corresponding with twenty-two letters in the Hebrew alphabet. This is the same kind of discussion, in other words, that he has been engaged in when discussing the order of the psalms on the basis of the meaning of numbers. Ps. Plutarch makes a similar observation about the *Iliad* and the *Odyssey* each being divided into twenty-four books, corresponding to the number of letters in the Greek alphabet.[58]

I go now to the second long fragment from Origen in B (8v-9r = GCS 1.2 frag. 12).[59] The words "It remains to discuss," which introduce the new topic, suggest that this discussion occurred near the end of the prologue. The fragment discusses the meaning of four expressions found in the inscriptions of the psalms. Hilary has a similar discussion of the meanings of these same inscriptions immediately following his discussion of the number and order of the psalms (*Comm. Ps.* 17–21). The discussion in B is limited to those inscriptions that have one of the four titles "Psalms," "Songs," "Psalms of a Song," and "Songs of a Psalm." Each expression is defined in terms of whether it refers to the use of an instrument or the human voice, or the two in various combinations, and then the expressions are given anagogical meanings. Hilary does the same thing (*Comm. Ps.* 19–20), and Gregory of Nyssa has a very similar discussion in his treatise *On the Inscriptions of the Psalms*, part 2, chapter 3. Origen's prologue could very well have been the common source of Hilary and Gregory.

There is a long discussion of the meanings of the inscriptions of numerous psalms attributed to Origen in manuscripts outside those representing the Palestinian catena. This discussion is printed in PG 12: 1060C–1073C and edited by Rietz (1.1–15) in his edition of prologue material.[60] I do not claim this discussion for Origen because it comes from a tradition whose main manuscript witness is not very trustworthy concerning attributions to Origen.[61] Should this fragment come from Origen and belong to the Caesarean commentary, however, it would probably have been located here, after the more general discussion of the four titles involving the meaning of "Psalm" and "Song." The fact that such a discussion is absent from Hilary's prologue also suggests that it was not a part of Origen's.

The Origen fragment in B closes with a discussion of the meaning of the term *diapsalma* (B 9r–9v = GCS 1.2 frag. 13). The expression occurs, Origen says, in the LXX, Theodotion and Symmachus. He adds that he has attempted to discover whether the term was intended to mark a change in "rhythm, melody, or part." He notes that the expression does not appear in the Hebrew or in Aquila. The latter has "always" (*aei*) in place of *diapsalma*.

I suggest that the catenist responsible for this fragment has abbreviated a longer discussion, conveying the same sense but leaving out the details. A very similar discussion appears in PG 12: 1057C–1060C (= Rietz II [*De Origenis prologis*, 11–12]) and is translated by Jerome in Epistle 28.6.[62] This longer fragment goes into much more detail, of course, and includes the important details that the fifth version (used in Origen's Hexapla on the psalms) has "always" (*aei*) and that the sixth version has "to the end" (*eis telos*) where the others have *diapsalma*. Nautin and Devreesse both point out that this longer fragment is also quoted in the margins of the manuscript discovered by Mercati, to which I have already twice referred, where the author of the marginal notes claims to have found it in the "very old book of the Hexapla by Origen."[63] Nautin would put it in Origen's work that he calls "Excerpta on the Psalms,"[64] and Devreesse would put it in the preface to the psalms in the Hexapla.[65] Devreesse's suggestion has more to commend it than Nautin's, since the fragment is purportedly derived from a book containing the Hexapla on the psalms. Given Origen's tendency to repeat himself, however, when discussing the same subject, which I noted earlier, there is no reason to think that a very similar discussion should not appear in more than one prologue to the psalms. We would anticipate, at least, that, given the size of the Caesarean commentary, the discussion of *diapsalma* would be more detailed than that found in B.[66] Furthermore, we would also anticipate the inclusion of remarks concerning the fifth and sixth versions in the long Caesarean commentary. My suggestion, therefore, is that the discussion of *diapsalma* occurred in the Caesarean commentary at the place where it occurs in the fragments from the Palestinian catena but that the fragment has been abbreviated in this catena and that the discussion was actually that found in the fragment in PG 12: 1057C–1060C or something very like that.

I suggest that we take a clue from the final paragraph of Hilary's prologue and assume that Origen closed the general prologue of his Caesarean commentary and entered his discussion of the first lemma from Psalm 1:1 with that delightful story that is preserved in *Philocalia*, which I quote.

Now that we are going to begin our interpretation of the Psalms, let us preface our remarks with a very pleasing tradition respecting all Divine Scripture in general, which has been handed down to us by the Jew. That great scholar used to say that inspired Scripture taken as a whole was on account of its obscurity like many locked-up rooms in one house. Before each room he supposed a key to be placed, but not the one belonging to it; and that the keys were so dispersed all round the rooms, not fitting the locks of the several rooms before which they were placed. It would be a troublesome piece of work to discover the keys to suit the rooms they were meant for. It was, he said, just so with the understanding of the Scriptures because they are so obscure; the only way to begin to understand them was, he said, by means of other passages containing the explanation dispersed throughout them. The Apostle, I think, suggested such a way of coming to a knowledge of the Divine words when He said, "Which things also we speak, not in words which man's wisdom teaches, but which the Spirit teaches; comparing spiritual things with spiritual" [1 Cor. 2:13].[67]

My reconstruction yields the following nine-point outline of the topics of prologues found in ancient pagan commentaries on philosophical and poetical works and in Christian commentary literature on the psalms, although I bracket numbers 2 and 3 since, at this point at least, they lack what I would consider to be hard evidence.

1. The obscurity of scripture
[2. The aim of the treatise]
[3. Its usefulness]
4. The reason for the title
5. The authenticity of the treatise
6. The number of psalms
7. The order of the psalms
8. The meaning of the inscriptions of some psalms
9. The meaning of *diapsalma*

I think the prologue to Origen's Caesarean commentary on the psalms suggests that this commentary was a major work of Christian scholarship in antiquity. Origen brought to the work the rich background of his education in the Greek grammatical and philosophical schools in Alexandria;

the Hebrew learning he had acquired from Jewish teachers and conversation partners in Alexandria and Caesarea; the Christian tradition with which he had become acquainted in Alexandria, Jerusalem, Caesarea, Rome, and Athens; and his own spiritually sensitive reading of the Bible that had been developing since his childhood.

Notes

1. See P. Nautin, *Origène: Sa vie et son œuvre* (Paris: Beauchesne, 1977), 261–92; Vittorio Peri, *Omelie Origeniane sui Salmi: Contributo all'identificazione del testo latino*, Studi e testi (Rome: Biblioteca Apostolica Vaticana, 1980), 7–28; Marie-Josèphe Rondeau, *Les commentaires patristiques du Psautier (IIIe–Ve siècles)*, 2 vols., OCA 219–20 (Rome: Pontificium Institutum Studiorum Orientalium, 1982–85), 1: 44–52; Ronald Heine, *Origen: Scholarship in the Service of the Church*, Christian Theology in Context (Oxford: Oxford University Press, 2010), 115–18, 148–51, 189.

2. See Rondeau, *Commentaires patristiques*, 1: 50.

3. See Heine, *Origen*, 116–17.

4. Peri, *Omelie Origeniane*; Rondeau, *Commentaires patristiques*, 1: 158–61.

5. In Crouzel's introduction to *Origène: Homélies sur les Psaumes 36 à 38*, ed. E. Prinzivalli, SC 411 (Paris: Cerf, 1995), 13. The reference is to Pierre Jay, "Jérôme à Bethléem: Les Tractatus in Psalmos," in *Jérôme entre l'Occident et l'Orient: Actes du Colloque de Chantilly*, ed. Y.-M. Duval (Paris: Études Augustiniennes, 1988), 367–88.

6. Bärbel Kramer, "Eine Psalmenhomilie aus dem Tura-Fund," *Zeitschrift für Papyrologie und Epigraphik* 16 (1975): 164–213.

7. Marguerite Harl, ed. and trans., *La Chaîne palestinienne sur le psaume 118 (Origène, Eusèbe, Didyme, Apollinaire, Athanase, Théodoret)*, SC 189–90 (Paris: Cerf, 1972).

8. Gilles Dorival, "Origène dans les chaînes sur les psaumes: Deux séries inédites de fragments," in *Origeniana: Premier colloque international des études origéniennes (Montserrat, 18–21 septembre 1973)*, ed. H. Crouzel, G. Lomiento, and J. Rius-Camps (Bari: Istituto di Letteratura Cristiana Antica, 1975), 199–213. Dorival mentions in this article (209) his intentions to produce a critical edition of the series in Vindobonensis.

9. Ibid., 213, cf. 207–8.

10. Marcel Richard, "Les premières chaînes sur le Psautier," *Bulletin d'Information de l'Institut de Recherche et d'Histoire des Textes* 5 (1956): 88.

11. See Harl, *Chaîne palestinienne*, 1: 18–21; Ekkehard Mühlenberg, *Psalmenkommentare aus der Katenenüberlieferung*, 3 vols., PTS 15, 16, 19 (Berlin: De Gruyter, 1975, 1977, 1978), 1: xii–xiii; 3: 48–52, 131–284.

12. Robert Devreesse, *Les anciens commentateurs grecs des Psaumes* (Vatican City: Biblioteca Apostolica Vaticana, 1970).

13. Mühlenberg, *Psalmenkommentare*.

14. Jerome, *Ep.* 33.4 (CSEL 54: 256).

15. Rondeau, *Commentaires patristiques*, 1: 51.

16. Nautin, *Origène* (Paris: Beauchesne, 1977), 250.

17. Jaap Mansfeld, *Prolegomena: Questions to Be Settled before the Study of an Author, or a Text*, Philosophia Antiqua 61 (Leiden: Brill, 1994), 7; Origen, *Comm. Jo.* 1.88.

18. Ilsetraut Hadot, "Les introductions aux commentaires exégétiques chez les auteurs néoplatoniciens et les auteurs chrétiens," in *Les règles de l'interprétation*, ed. Michael Tardieu (Paris: Cerf, 1987), 99–122; Bernhard Neuschäfer, *Origenes als Philologe*, Schweizerische Beiträge zur Altertumswissenschaft 18/1–2 (Basel: Friedrich Reinhardt, 1987), 77–84.

19. Ronald E. Heine, "The Introduction to Origen's *Commentary on John* Compared with the Introductions to the Ancient Philosophical Commentaries on Aristotle," in *Origeniana Sexta: Origène et la Bible/ Origen and the Bible. Actes du Colloquium Origenianum Sextum Chantilly, 30 août–3 septembre 1993*, ed. Gilles Dorival and Alain le Boulluec (Leuven: Peeters, 1995), 3–12.

20. "Origen's Pauline Prefaces and the Chronology of His *Pauline Commentaries*," in Dorival and Boulluec, *Origeniana Sexta*, 495–513, esp. 498–507.

21. Neuschäfer, *Origenes als Philologe*, 67–77.

22. Ammonius, *In Porphyrii Isagogen sive V voces*, ed. A. Busse, Commentaria in Aristotelem Graeca 4.3 (Berlin: George Reimer, 1891), 21.

23. See Mansfeld, *Prolegomena*, 23, 30, 110, 149–61, 179, 183, passim.

24. *Vitae Vergilianae*, ed. J. Brummer, appendix in *Tiberi Claudi Donati Interpretationes Vergilianae*, ed. H. Georgii, vol. 2 (Stuttgart: Teubner, 1969), 11–19; *Servii Grammatici qui feruntur in Vergilii Carmina Commentarii*, ed. G. Thilo and H. Hagen, vol. 1 (Leipzig: Teubner, 1881), 1–5.

25. See C. Bammel, "Origen's Pauline Prefaces and the Chronology of His *Pauline Commentaries*," in Dorival and Boulluec, *Origeniana Sexta*, 499–500. She cites Manfred J. Lossau, *Untersuchungen zur antiken Demosthenesexegese*, Palingenesia 2 (Bad Homburg: H. M. Gehlen, 1964), 123–28, where Lossau identifies the following topics: date, authenticity, genre (what type of speech), historical situation, contents and aim (*hypothesis kai skopos*), and order of the speeches.

26. Ronald. E. Heine, "The Form of Gregory of Nyssa's Treatise *On the Inscriptions of the Psalms*," *Studia Patristica* 32 (1997): 130–35, and *Gregory of Nyssa's*

Treatise on the Inscriptions of the Psalms, Oxford Early Christian Studies (Oxford: Clarendon Press, 1995), 20–29.

27. Devreesse, *Anciens commentateurs grecs*, 2–3.

28. Neuschäfer, *Origenes als Philologe*, 67–77; Mansfeld's remarks on Origen's *Commentary on the Psalms* follow Neuschäfer (*Prolegomena*, 13–16).

29. Walter Rietz, *De Origenis prologis in Psalterium: Quaestiones selectae* (Jena: Pohle, 1914).

30. Nautin, *Origène*, 262–79.

31. J. B. Pitra, ed., *Origenes in Psalmos*, AS 2 (Paris: A. Jouby and Roger, 1884), 428–35; Hans Achelis, ed., *Hippolytus Werke*, GCS 1.2 (Leipzig: Hinrichs, 1897), 136–45.

32. Nautin, *Origène*, 279.

33. Devreesse, *Anciens commentateurs grecs*, 7. See also Mühlenberg, *Psalmenkommentare*, 3: 133.

34. Richard, "Premières chaînes," 89.

35. In T. Heither's edition, *Origenes commentarii in epistulam ad Romanos*, *Fontes Christiani* 2/1 (Freiburg: Herder, 1990), the lines 70.14–15 mark the end of Origen's prologue. The remainder of the prologue has been inserted by Rufinus, as Rufinus remarks at the end of the prologue.

36. The following manuscripts, according to Richard ("Premières chaînes"), represent the direct tradition of the Palestinian catena on Psalms 1–50: Oxford Bodl. Barocc. 235 (end of ninth century); Athos Iviron gr. 597 (eleventh century); Bucharest Bibl. Acad. Rom. gr. 931 + Istanbul Bibl. Patr. Panaghias Kamariotissès 9 (eleventh century); Munich Bibl. nat. Monac. gr. 359 (tenth to eleventh centuries); and Vaticanus gr. 1789 (tenth century) ("Premières chaines sur le psautier," 88). Oxford Bodl. Barocc. 235 is the prototype of this entire tradition (Richard, "Premières chaînes"); to my knowledge, it has never been used in a critical text of the prologue fragments. According to Robert Devreesse ("Chaines exégétiques grecques," in *Dictionnaire de la Bible*, ed. Louis Pirot, suppl. 1 [Paris: Letouzey et Ané, 1928], 1116), Barocc. 235 is the only complete manuscript in the group and is the only one to contain the title of the collection, since the others all lack the beginning. Devreesse, however, seems to have known only Barocc. 235, Monac. 359, and Vat. gr. 1789. It appears, from the description of Athos Iviron gr. 597 in S. P. Lambros, *Catalogue of the Greek Manuscripts on Mount Athos*, vol. 2 (Cambridge: Cambridge University Press, 1900), 181, that this manuscript also contains the beginning of the catena along with the same title that appears in Barocc. 235. I have thus far been unsuccessful in obtaining reproductions of this manuscript.

The fragments with which I am working in this reconstruction have appeared, so far as I have discovered, in three different editions. First, that of Simon de Magistris, *Acta Martyrum ad Ostia Tibernia sub Claudio Gothico* (Rome, 1795), 439–48, where they are edited in Appendix II as coming from Hippolytus. They begin with the excerpt attributed to Eusebius in Barocc. 235, which in the latter manuscript follows four columns of material excerpted from Basil. Magistris used Vat. 1789, representing the Palestinian catena, and Casanat. 1908, which does not belong to that tradition. The next edition, from 1884, is that of Pitra, *Origenes in Psalmos* (AS 2: 428–36), where the fragments are attributed to Origen and are drawn from the same two manuscripts used by Magistris. Pitra begins with the first excerpt attributed to Origen in Barocc. 235. The most recent edition, from 1897, is that of Achelis, *Hippolytus Werke* (GCS 1.2: 137–45). Achelis also used only Vat. gr. 1789 from the Palestinian catena plus two manuscripts from another tradition of Psalm catenae, Casanat. 1908 and Paris. gr. 143, and two Syriac manuscripts.

37. I thank the Oxford Bodleian Library for providing me with reproductions of the opening pages of Codex Baroccianus 235.

38. See, for example, Nautin, *Origène*, 279. I do not, however, agree with Nautin's view that Hilary was using both the Alexandrian and Caesarean commentaries when he wrote his prologue. Nautin's view depends on his earlier reconstruction of the Alexandrian prologue that I rejected above.

39. Origen, *Phil.* 2.2 (trans. George Lewis, *The Philocalia of Origen* [Edinburgh: T. and T. Clark, 1911], 31).

40. Mansfield, *Prolegomena*, 16.

41. Ammonius, *In Aristotelis Categorias Commentarium* 7 (trans. S. M. Cohen and G. B. Matthews, *On Aristotle's Categories*, [London: Duckworth, 1991], 15).

42. Origen, *De princ.* 4.2.7 (trans. G. W. Butterworth, *On First Principles* [Gloucester, MA: Peter Smith, 1973], 282).

43. Origen, *De princ.* 4.2.8 (trans. Butterworth, *On First Principles*, 285).

44. Origen, *De princ.* 4.2.9 (trans. Butterworth, *On First Principles*, 285).

45. A short excerpt from Basil (= GCS 1.2, frag. 10) on the same subject is inserted between the two parts of the excerpt. (I give the references to GCS 1.2 for convenience throughout the essay. This does not mean, however, that the text of GCS 1.2 is always exactly the same as that in B.)

46. This is true of the excerpts in the prologue. In the body of the commentary he sometimes writes the name of the author of the excerpt in the body of the text.

47. Mühlenberg, *Psalmenkommentare*, 3: 133.

48. Cf. Neuschäfer, *Origenes als Philologe*, 365 n. 104.

49. Nautin, *Origène*, 306–7; Devreesse, *Anciens commentateurs grecs*, 3 n. 14.

50. See Heine, *Origen*, 148–51.

51. Nautin, *Origène*, 278.

52. Jerome, *C. Ruf.* 1.13 (PL 23 408A; trans. NPNF, ser. 2, vol. 3, 490, modified).

53. Nautin, *Origène*, 306. See also Devreesse, *Anciens commentateurs grecs*, 3 n. 17.

54. Neuschäfer, *Origenes al Philologe*, 70–71.

55. Origen provides a similar discussion of the number 50 in *Hom. Gen.* 2.5.

56. Mansfeld, *Prolegomena*, 65.

57. Nautin, *Origène*, 262–75, 279.

58. Pseudo-Plutarch, *De Homero* 2.4 (ed. J. F. Kindstrand [Leipzig: Teubner, 1990], 9).

59. This fragment, which follows the short excerpt from Basil (= GCS 1.2 frag. 10) inserted between the two continuous fragments from Origen, begins in B with the paragraph found in GCS 1.2, frag. 11, that I have already discussed above.

60. Rietz, *De Origenis prologis* 1.16 (= PG 12: 1073D–1076B) discusses the problem of the order of the psalms.

61. Vat. 754, Ottob. 398; Devreesse, *Anciens commentateurs grecs*, 3 n. 19.

62. Jerome writes in the first person as if the comments were his own, but it is a verbatim translation of the Greek fragment.

63. Nautin, *Origène*, 306; Devreesse, *Anciens commentateurs grecs*, 3 n. 18.

64. Nautin, *Origène*, 280.

65. Devreesse, *Anciens commentateurs grecs*, 2–3.

66. The discussion in B is even shorter than that in GCS 1.2 frag. 13. The material beginning with $\bar{e}$ at the end of GCS 1.2, 142.23, and extending through *enallagma* at 143.2 is missing in B.

67. Origen, *Phil.* 2.3 (trans. Lewis, *Philocalia of Origen*, 31–32).

Athanasius, the Psalms, and the Reformation of the Self

Paul R. Kolbet

Shortly after his death, the influential fourth-century bishop Athanasius of Alexandria was recognized for introducing the contemplative traditions of the Egyptian monks to the urban Christians of Alexandria and for bringing the desert monks into communion with the Alexandrian episcopacy.[1] Athanasius accomplished this by quite intentionally bridging the distance—physical and spiritual—between desert and city. Over time, with his tireless effort, the daily spiritual practices of the monks became those of the urban Christian, and the monks came increasingly under the sway of the Alexandrian episcopacy. As a consequence of his commitment to bringing the desert closer to the city, Athanasius thoroughly integrated ascetic practice into his theology, and it proved to be a decisive component of his ecclesiastical politics.[2] A letter Athanasius wrote to a certain Marcellinus provides valuable insight into the shape of Athanasius's spiritual program, its relationship to previous Hellenistic philosophical traditions, and, especially, the crucial function of the psalms in the reformation of the self.

Although the letter provides no details concerning Marcellinus's identity, he was, in all likelihood, one of the urban Christians adopting the ascetic practices Athanasius promoted. In fact, Athanasius began his letter by congratulating Marcellinus on maintaining his spiritual practice (ἄσκησις) and then proceeded to provide a sustained reflection upon the use of the Psalter in the Christian life.[3] It is not surprising that Athanasius directed his discussion of ἄσκησις to the Psalter, since he had elsewhere already represented the psalms as a crucial component of Antony's training. In his account of the famed monk's physical and spiritual struggles, Athanasius described how Antony so perfected the use of the Psalter that the demons wailed and cried out as though severely weakened whenever he would chant psalms.[4]

The sort of letter that Athanasius wrote to Marcellinus was, in fact, quite common in late antiquity.[5] It had become fashionable for Christians and non-Christians alike voluntarily to take time to devote themselves to training that would further their spiritual progress. This training took the form of a daily struggle with their own humanity that was not unlike that undertaken by those first Christian ascetics in the desert who battled their own passions and demons. The orator Dio Chrysostom was not atypical in describing the attempt to live a truly admirable life as a more stubborn battle than that fought by famed Spartan warriors.[6] In a similar fashion, the noble senator Seneca advised the young Lucilius that he was commending to him a way of life that was itself a battle and that he should approach this struggle with his own passions as any trained soldier would a war.[7]

Representatives of the Hellenistic philosophical schools were particularly aware of the manifold resistance that human beings faced in committing to the philosophic life. Cicero lamented that "as soon as we come into the light of day . . . we at once find ourselves in a world of iniquity amid a medley of wrong beliefs, so that it seems as if we drank in deception with our nurse's milk."[8] A century later Seneca remarked, "We are not allowed to travel the straight road," for those with whom we associate "draw us into wrong" so that the "vices of the nations" are "heaped upon" the individual.[9] The manner in which false beliefs and popular customs combine to form habits deeply ingrained in both mind and body was a prevalent concern of the time.

Part of the reason that a philosophic education was valued in the Hellenistic world was that it ideally enabled one to cultivate an inner core of the self that provided one with enough stability to withstand the onslaught of temptation and tragedy.[10] This required a long process of training that amounted to far more than a mere facility in handling dialectical syllogisms or knowledge of some true axioms.[11] The person who learned doctrines without going to the trouble to live them was dismissed as a mere "sophist."[12] Seneca calls attention to the need for "something stronger than usual" to "shake off these chronic ills" and "root out our deep-seated belief in wrong ideas."[13] The self was thought to require a daily practice to facilitate the internalization of true doctrines that would overcome both one's false beliefs and the mental, physical, and emotional habits stemming from them.[14] Specific disciplines, therefore, were "designed to ensure spiritual progress toward the ideal state of wisdom," however this might be defined by a particular school of philosophy, by exercising the faculties of reason and will in a manner "analogous to the athlete's training or the application of a medical cure."[15]

Such spiritual exercises required, above all, the "memorization and assimilation of the fundamental dogmas and rules of life of the school."[16] Through the recitation of doctrines, participants in such exercises were taught, as it were, to find themselves in the words of others. When these doctrines were reiterated continually in a persuasive form, they were thought to have the potential to "form" (*formant*) the soul, so that its emotions flowed from studied convictions rather than being driven by the whims of self-interest in any particular moment.[17] The internalization of these dogmas ideally led to a transformation of those striving to make spiritual progress as the form of life implied in the school's teaching gradually took on existential reality for them.[18] With some confidence in such methods, Seneca taught that "no affections are so fierce and self-willed that they cannot be tamed by training."[19]

Philosophy was then, in this way, to be embodied in the life of the philosopher, who ideally displayed complete harmony between beliefs and deeds.[20] Paraenetic letters of instruction, like those of Seneca, describing effective spiritual exercises were greatly valued in late antiquity by Christian and non-Christian alike.[21] Christians not only shared with their philosophically inclined contemporaries the perception that the moral life was best thought of as a battle or ongoing struggle but also shared assumptions with them about what sorts of disciplines were necessary if one was going to make spiritual progress.

Athanasius's letter can best be understood within this context as commending a daily regime of psalms to be taken on voluntarily as spiritual exercises to conform the self to a certain ideal. Athanasius describes the use of psalms in language similar to that of the spiritual exercises found among the Hellenistic philosophical schools. He asserts that the recitation of psalms is a way of "attending" or "caring for oneself" (προσέχω σεαυτοῦ).[22] The psalms are a tool that one uses to "form" or "model oneself" (τυπῶ ἑαυτὸν).[23] Indeed, for Athanasius the psalms are an essential part of Christian discipline because of their unparalleled usefulness in the care of self. This is most evident in the practical advice he offers Marcellinus.

His letter sheds light on what Athanasius considered spiritual exercises to entail, what he intended them to accomplish, and why he believed the psalms particularly suitable for this task. Athanasius claims that he is not the originator of his advice and is merely relaying wisdom that he learned from an old man who was a "master of the Psalter."[24] This is likely a literary device allowing Athanasius to refrain from speaking in his own name, and, strictly speaking, this letter provides evidence only for Athanasius's teaching on the Psalter.[25] Athanasius's allusion, nonetheless, may well refer to one of the monks with whom he became acquainted during his multiple trips and exiles into the Egyptian desert or to an anonymous urban teacher. Given that other sources attest to the widespread use of the psalms among the Christians of late antiquity, and that there was clearly a "reciprocity between Athanasius and the ascetic movement of his time," it is not unlikely that Athanasius was making available to a broader constituency at least aspects of traditions that bore some resemblance to practices he had himself witnessed.[26]

Even in this letter, however, there is evidence that not all agreed with every aspect of Athanasius's program.[27] The recitation of psalms, like other instances of the spiritual exercise tradition, admitted different kinds of instruction, influenced by the diversity of piety among practitioners. Since doctrines occupied such a central place in this tradition by providing the soul with reliable guidance, it is all the more necessary first to establish what these doctrines were for Athanasius and to locate the theological framework that directed the particular pastoral instructions given to Marcellinus. When seen in terms of these doctrinal convictions, Athanasius's contention that the Psalter furnishes exercises capable of reforming the disordered movements of the soul through speaking, acting, and singing becomes more intelligible.

PSALMS AS A MEANS FOR APPROPRIATING REVELATORY KNOWLEDGE OF BOTH CHRIST AND THE SOUL

Throughout his writings, Athanasius stresses his conviction that the universe exists exclusively through God's eternal Logos and that it persists only to the extent that it conforms to the Logos. He repeatedly underscores that God the creator remains categorically distinct from all else. Creatures were made from nothing (οὐκ ὄντων) and by definition have no internal means by which to sustain their existence. All creation relies continually on the power of the eternal God for its existence and sustenance. Furthermore, all creation retains a potency for nonbeing (οὐκ ὄντων) and risks passing out of existence if separated from the source of its being. For example, Athanasius states, "The nature of created things, having come into being from nothing, is unstable, and is weak and mortal when considered by itself."[28]

Athanasius, however, often follows such statements with an equal emphasis on God's continual sustenance of creation. Indeed, he asserts that "the God of all is good" and does not "resent [φθονεῖ] the existence of any" but "desires all to exist" so that they may benefit from God's "loving kindness" (φιλανθρωεύεσθαι).[29] For Athanasius, God's goodness is manifested in the manner in which God created everything through the divine Word, who is the "orderer" (κατορθώματος) of the universe.[30] "The Word of God gives light and life, moving [κινεῖ] and ordering [διακοσμεῖ]" the universe. By the "providence" of the Logos "bodies grow, the rational soul moves and possesses life and thought."[31] Moreover, "all things subsist [συνέστηκε] through the Word of God" and have life to the degree that they maintain the original movement given them.[32] Hence, life and order imply one another, as the active ordering of the divine Logos is the source of all power and vitality.

Made in the image of God, the first man was given a certain power by the Logos that he could use to live a life in fellowship with God that was enduring and blessed.[33] His soul received from the Logos its own agency, having its own proper motion and governance of the body. The first human was intended to have always held "his mind God-ward [πρὸς τὸν θεόν] in the boldest freedom [παρρησία]" to associate "with the holy ones in that contemplation [θεωρία]" and to understand the manner in which all creation coheres in a single Logos. In this way, he was to have kept his soul in a state of such purity (τῆς ψυχῆς καθαρότης) that it would have been sufficient of itself to reflect God as in a mirror (κατοπτρίζεσθαι).[34]

Athanasius accentuates the striking disjunction between these divine intentions for humanity and their human realization. Although intended to "abide" eternally with God, human beings used the power derived from the Logos to turn away from the source of life.[35] For Athanasius, the consequence for humanity of this turning from the Logos was a marked diminishment of the human person. In so doing human beings "forgot" (ἐπιλαθομένη) that they were in the image of the good God, and no longer by the power present in their souls could they see God the Word, in whose likeness they were made. Hence, the soul lost its mirror function and "became hidden [ἐπικρύψασα]."[36] In this way, by turning from the intended order given it by God, the soul "departed from its [true] self."[37]

This human degeneration is most visible in the soul's motion, since, for Athanasius, "the movement of the soul is nothing other than its life."[38] The soul created by God to be in motion remains mobile even when misusing its powers.[39] Having discovered that it had a certain power over itself (αὐτεξούσις), that it could move the body in various ways, the soul came to believe that its "dignity" came merely from its ability to move, rather than from its ability "to move toward the term for which it was made."[40] This power of motion separated from the term of that motion subjected the soul to disordered movements, such as the passions that it suffered. Athanasius chronicles this condition by surveying humanity's progressive descent into idolatry and vice.[41]

Having turned their vision away from the living God, human beings have made the focus of their attention that which is nearer to themselves: the physical universe and its many sense impressions on the body. Yet, without knowledge of the Logos that orders the universe, people have been "carried about by everything" and "imagine what has no existence."[42] Instead of the singular vision of the life-giving God, humanity "formed a desire" for "many things" (παλλῶν) and "began to be habituated" (σχέσις) to such desires.[43] This resulted in a dispersion of the self and a dissipation of its God-given agency. In its disordered state, the soul is far from the vital order intended by the Logos, lacking both the knowledge and the power necessary to reform itself. In short, for Athanasius, sin is the habitual choice

of an order other than the one God made: an artificial order that by definition can lead to nothing other than death, since it lacks any lasting ontological ground.

The erratic movements of the soul that threaten its very existence
become ordered only through the presence of the proper term of those
motions. Each soul needs the eternal Logos to draw near to it. For this reason, although the whole cosmos still displays the design of the Creator,
God descended to humanity's diminished condition and took on a part of
it, that is, the single body of Jesus. Through his taking as his own a single
part, the truth about the whole once again became manifest: the contin-
gency of the created universe oriented toward the Logos as its source of
life and order. Athanasius asserts that the "unalterable" (ἄτρεπτος) Logos
"took alterable [τρεπτὴν] flesh, condemned sin in it," and "secured its freedom [ἐλευθέραν] and its power [δύνασθαι] henceforth to fulfill the righteousness of the law."[44] Christ took on the Passion "that he might himself
lighten these very sufferings of the flesh and free it from them."[45] Accordingly, the cross of Christ is the true "therapy of the created order."[46]

In this way, in his own transformed body, Christ revealed the truth
about human beings and showed the fullness of undiminished humanity in
complete harmony with the Source of its being. The Logos, having drawn
near in Jesus Christ, once again makes possible the task of realizing the
divine intention: that is, of conforming oneself to the vivifying Logos; the
soul renewing its agency and power, becoming truly itself for the first
time and moving toward complete stability in God. The interpreter of
Athanasius's letter should, therefore, be aware that Athanasius's Nicene
Christology informs and shapes his advice to Marcellinus. Without this
Christology, he would consider his advice to be no different from the mere
"philosophy" that Antony describes as having a degree of truth but lacking
power.[47] Likewise, according to Athanasius, an Arian Logos would share
the creaturely potency for nonbeing and thereby also lack the power to
stabilize human existence.[48]

Since the acute human disorder involves the loss of knowledge of God
and of the self, Athanasius emphasizes that the psalms are a source of revelatory knowledge of both Christ and the soul. Indeed, for this reason, he
contends that there is a plenitude to the psalms, such that the whole biblical revelation is available to the one who learns them with understanding.

He likens the Psalter to "a garden" that contains all the other canonical books.[49] In the psalms, one learns how "to remember" (ἀναμιμνήσκεσθαι) the good works of God.[50]

Athanasius maintains that the actions of the self are reformed through imitation of the divine example, or variations of that example embodied by the saints. He tells Marcellinus that "the Lord . . . performed righteous acts and not only made laws but offered himself as a model [τύπος] for those who wish to know the power [δύναμις] of acting." He asserts that a "more perfect instruction in virtue" cannot be found "than that which the Lord typified [ἐτύπωσεν] in himself."[51] Christ's example is all the more necessary on account of the "unstable character of human behavior." The Christian life requires "continual 'formation' [τυποῦν] of the self through imitation" of the "eternally consistent 'form' or 'pattern' [τύπος]" provided by the divine Word.[52]

Christ's example, however, is mediated through scripture. The psalms are a crucial vehicle through which one internalizes the victory of the Word over passions, death, and the devil.[53] Athanasius says that "it was indeed for this reason" that God made Christ's life "resound in the psalms before his sojourn in our midst," so that he could furnish "the model of the earthly and heavenly man in his own person."[54] Since Christ's life echoes throughout the psalms, the one reciting them both benefits from the power provided by his example and internalizes that example through daily vocalization.

According to Athanasius, recitation of the psalms, in addition to providing indispensable knowledge of Christ, allows one to discern the movements of one's own soul. The beginning Christian soon learns how difficult is the preliminary task of gaining an accurate image of the true contours of her or his own soul while it remains shrouded in a fog of falsehood and passion. Athanasius states, "For I believe that the whole of human existence, both the dispositions of the soul and the movements of the thoughts, have been measured out and encompassed in those very words of the Psalter."[55] He counsels Marcellinus to employ the words of the Psalter "like a mirror" permitting him to "perceive himself and the motions of his soul [ψυχῆς κινήματα]."[56] The psalms, consequently, are a secondary remedial mirror, a corrective lens, that is needed because the human soul, the primary mirror, has become occluded, weakened, and disordered, no longer functioning to reflect the divine image.[57] Therefore, Athanasius advises Marcellinus to look to the psalms, as it were, for a linguistic blueprint of the drives that inhabit his soul.

That Athanasius considered the psalms as such an effective tool for introspection is not surprising in light of the work of Walter Ong, who has written so eloquently on the particular technology of the written word. Ong asserts: "By separating the knower from the known, writing makes possible increasingly articulate introspectivity, opening the psyche as never before not only to the external objective world quite distinct from itself but also to the interior self against whom the objective world is set. Writing makes possible the great introspective religious traditions."[58] Therefore, the fixed otherness of the psalms exposes the fluidity of the human soul and allows the Christian to perceive the rhythms of his or her own life.

In the same way that representatives of the Hellenistic philosophical schools drew attention to the therapeutic potential of the speech of the philosopher, Athanasius points to the words of the Psalter as not only providing knowledge of every stirring of the human soul but furnishing as well "the therapy [θεραπεία] and correction [διόρθωσις] suited for each motion [κινήματος]."[59] This therapy consists in subjecting uncontrolled passions to the form imposed upon them by scripture. In this way, the irrational motions of the soul become ordered by scriptural reason, which is none other than the presence of the eternal Word in the words of scripture.[60] A brief anecdote from the *Apophthegmata patrum* illumines how Athanasius envisions the stabilizing effects of the Psalter. We are told, "It was said of the same Abba John that when he returned from the harvest or when he had been with some of the old men, he gave himself to prayer, meditation and psalmody until his thoughts were re-established in their previous order [τάξιν]."[61]

Athanasius does not link the healing capacity of self-knowledge to discerning how one's emotional life connects with past experiences or one's formative history.[62] Instead, he understands it to have more to do with the knowledge of one's place in the universe and the adjustment of one's emotions to suit that context. Athanasius focuses on how the recitation of certain psalms influences the way individuals perceive the particular situations in which they find themselves. In much of his letter, Athanasius commends specific psalms as means to realize the human ideal as determined by his theological outlook in various situations. For example, he says that the one who is afraid should recite Psalm 118:6 (LXX 117:6): "The Lord is my helper, I will not fear what a human being can do to me."[63] Evidently Athanasius understands fear to be the result of a faulty belief, such as the following proposition: "Since I am vulnerable to being harmed by human beings, I will fear any that desire me harm." Although this proposition may appear reasonable, Athanasius would not consider it so, especially when the fear inhibits virtuous action. Through the exercise of saying the psalm, the one who fears can seek to replace the proposition driving the fear with the verse from the Psalter, which then becomes the dominant conviction of the moment.[64]

Although each passion presents the illusion of being unique to a particular situation, the one saying psalms discovers that no such affliction is his or hers alone. Through speech, passion is brought into the open and made a part of a more universal human struggle. Athanasius, for example, suggests that when someone has been "taken captive" by "foreign thoughts" (ἀλλοτρίων λογισμῶν) repents but even after repenting must continue to live in the situation in which one was overcome, he should say Psalm 137 (LXX 136).[65] This psalm begins with Israel lamenting by the waters of Babylon that it has been taken captive and carried away, and proceeds with a spirited exhortation not to forget Jerusalem. Athanasius then suggests that since such trials test the soul, one can give thanks for them with Psalm 139 (LXX 138). This would entail declaring God's thorough knowledge of one's soul and exclaiming how it is not possible to flee from God's presence, whether one seeks to hide in the heavens, in Hades, or in darkness or night. Thus the saying of the psalm initially provides access to the feeling that might otherwise lie fallow or erupt in an undirected manner. Once the emotion is expressed through the psalm, it is immediately reframed and integrated into the larger scriptural narrative. It becomes, as it were, another plant growing in the biblical garden and is thereby perceived differently by the one saying the psalm. The emotion of any given moment, in this way, is situated within the broad horizon of creation and redemption. The chaos of passion finds its form in the Logos in the same way that the primeval universe once did. The psalm functions here and elsewhere as a means of remembering and participating in God's intended order for creation, where the Logos pervades and gives life to the whole universe—or, in the figurative language of the Psalter, of not forgetting Jerusalem.

The Exercises of Speech, Actions, and Song

Cleaning the mirror of the soul and regaining its functionality requires the development of new habits of thought and of relating to the world. These habits are developed through exercises (ἄσκησις) that attempt to internalize the knowledge of Christ and self and to recover for the soul its proper order and agency. This is why Athanasius gives specific directions on *how* psalms should be sung or said in order to be most effective. Thus he says that in addition to teaching that passion is to be disregarded the psalms teach more importantly "also *how* one must heal [θεραπεύω] passion through speaking [λέγω] and acting [ποιῶ]."[66]

Utilization of the Psalter first of all involves speaking its language. Athanasius says that readers of the other books of scripture "consider themselves to be other [ἄλλοι] than those about whom the passage speaks." The reader can only marvel (θαυμάζω) and aspire to imitate from afar such biblical figures as the Patriarchs, Moses, and Elijah.[67] Each reader of the psalms, however, "utters them as his own words [ὡς ἴδια ῥήματα], and each sings them as if they were written concerning him"; he "accepts them and recites them not as if another [ὡς ἑτέρου] were speaking, nor as if speaking about someone else," but as one "affected by the words of the songs."[68] Thus saying the psalms is something like learning a second language. As one becomes a fluent speaker of the language of the psalms, one is able to linguistically transcribe the *world* into biblical *words*.

The biblical words have such influence on the life of the Christian because the psalms are a kind of technology. As Walter Ong reminds us, "Technologies are not mere exterior aids but also interior transformations of consciousness, and never more than when they affect the word."[69] Furthermore, he observes "that intelligence is relentlessly reflexive, so that even the external tools that it uses to implement its workings become 'internalized,' that is, part of its own reflexive process."[70] Ong notes that internalizing a technology takes "years" of constant "practice," such as that of an organist or violinist. Through this practice, the tool can become "a second nature" that "can enrich the human psyche, enlarge the human spirit, intensify its interior life."[71]

This interiorization of technology can be seen in Athanasius's assertion that the Psalter should be rewritten by the Christian in her or his own being. Thus Athanasius counsels Marcellinus to "inscribe" (γράφω) the Psalter "on your soul as on a monument" (στήλη). The soul of the Christian then can be described as "inscribed with words" (στηλογραφίας).[72] In this case, the tool has shaped its user and has become a "second nature."

Precisely because he sees the very language of the psalms as such a formative influence in the Christian life, Athanasius proscribes any alteration in the words themselves. He admonishes Marcellinus not to "let anyone amplify these words of the Psalter with the persuasive phrases of the profane," nor to let anyone "attempt to recast or completely change the words." Instead one must "recite and chant, without artifice [ἀτεχνῶς], the things written."[73] In this way, Athanasius insists that the psalms, even when they are memorized and transmitted orally, retain a textual fixity. The psalms, therefore, are neither merely the avenue the Christian uses to express prior religious feelings nor a pliable neutral medium that conforms itself to the reader. Appropriating the very words of the Psalter as one's own is an ascetic act in which one temporarily suspends one's accustomed form of expression in order to adopt as normative the logic and values inherent in the language of scripture.[74]

Given his understanding of sin as weakening human agency and eroding the proper power given to creatures by the Logos, Athanasius suggests that the Psalter is an effective tool in the Christian life because its words are not only truer than other ones but "more powerful" (ἰσχυρότερα) as well.[75] He appeals to a tradition asserting that "long ago in Israel they drove demons away and turned aside the treacheries directed against them by merely [μόνος] reading the Scriptures."[76] Athanasius, therefore, likens the recitation of scripture to the ark that contained the tablets of the law that went before the Israelites into battle and "provided sufficient help to them in the face of every army."[77] In the same way as the ark manifested the Lord's presence, so "the Lord himself is in the phrases [τὰ ῥήματα] of the Scriptures [τῶν γραφῶν]."[78] The one who recites these same words can be "confident" (θάρρος) like Antony, whose psalmody weakened the demons.[79]

In addition to supplying models for moral imitation, scriptural language, and its accompanying power, the psalms furnish melodies for singing. Athanasius is quick to declare that the "sweetness of sound" in the psalms should lead no one to believe that "the psalms are rendered musically for the sake of the ear's delight."[80] The musical aspect of the psalms, instead, according to Athanasius, is yet another means of attending to the soul. The task of singing them according to their melodies is commended to Marcellinus as an important exercise as well. Athanasius maintains that the one singing the psalms should sing "with the mind" as well as "with the tongue."[81] The melody of the phrases "is a symbol of the mind's well-ordered and undisturbed condition." He asserts that the musical instruments mentioned in the psalms are "a figure and sign of the parts of the body coming into natural concord like harp strings, and of the thoughts of the soul becoming like cymbals."[82]

The outer musical harmony not only expresses the inner concord of the soul but also contributes to it. Athanasius says that the one "beautifully singing praises brings rhythm" to the "soul and leads it . . . from disproportion to proportion." The soul gains "its composure by singing the phrases" of the Psalter, "rejoices" as it "becomes forgetful of the passions," and conceives the "most excellent thoughts" while it "sees in accordance with the mind of Christ."[83] The mathematical precision of the melody acts on the self to order it according to God's intention. Thus the harmony of the sung psalms signifies a well-ordered human being, and the harmonious person who practices psalmody manifests the message of the Psalter.

———

As he sought to unify the Egyptian Church through an ascetic program shared by Christians in the desert and the city, Athanasius promoted the use of the Psalter in the Christian life. He did so employing language and concepts that had been used previously by Hellenistic philosophers to describe their methods of shaping the soul and disciplining its passions. The daily recitation of psalms, for Athanasius, is an essential part of Christian spiritual practice because it is particularly useful in the care of self. It provides resources that are necessary to reform the self: knowledge of Christ and the soul, powerful models for imitation, a language that reveals the true state of the world, and daily exercises that bring the discordant motions of the soul into proper harmony.

Knowing well the resistance that human life gives to its own perfection, Athanasius understood the Psalter to be all the more necessary in appropriating the Christian faith. Not unlike contemporary Hellenistic philosophers, Athanasius believed that personal practice convinced the mind as much as any proof.[84] He therefore advised Marcellinus to adopt a regime of physical actions that would occupy the mind and train the body. Athanasius was acutely aware of the manner in which the malleability of the human person is a source of greatness and wretchedness. For the same instability of form that brings with it the possibility of falling into nothingness simultaneously presents the capacity for training and amendment of life. The daily chanting of psalms then is a therapy that gradually heals the human person. The language of the Psalter progressively "counters the instability of selfhood" with the stability of a written text that becomes a second nature when it is written in the soul.[85]

NOTES

1. Gregory Nazianzen, *Or.* 21.19–20 (SC 270: 148–53).

2. See David Brakke's *Athanasius and Asceticism* (Baltimore: Johns Hopkins University Press, 1998). Susanna Elm concludes, "Athanasius used his interpretation of 'rural' Egyptian asceticism to control and organize inner-urban asceticism, and it was his modified from of pseudo-'rural' ascetic life, created in response to urban requirements, that was then exported to the West; but it was also reintroduced into the rural environment to control and organize the original, 'rural', ascetic movement according to its ideals" (*Virgins of God: The Making of Asceticism in Late Antiquity* [Oxford: Clarendon Press, 1994], 371).

3. Athanasius, *Ep. Marcell.* 1 (PG 27: 12a). All citations, except where noted otherwise, are from the translation of Robert C. Gregg, in *Athanasius: The Life of Antony and the Letter to Marcellinus*, Classics of Western Spirituality (New York: Paulist Press, 1980). Two other English translations that include prefatory comments are available: one by Pamela Bright in *Early Christian Spirituality*, ed. Charles Kannengiesser (Philadelphia: Fortress Press, 1986), 56–77, and the other by Everett Ferguson, "Athanasius, Epistle to Marcellinus," *Ekklesiastikos Pharos* 60 (1978): 378–403.

4. Athanasius, *Vit. Ant.* 39.6 (SC 400: 242). On *Ep. Marcell.* as a work of the mature Athanasius, see Herman-Joseph Sieben, "Athanasius über den Psalter:

Analyse seines Briefes an Marcellinus," *Theologie und Philosophie* 48 (1973): 157. Athanasius describes Antony as devoting himself to "exercise [ἄσκησις] rather than the household, attending [προσέχω] to himself and patiently training [ἄγων] himself" (*Vit. Ant.* 3.1 [SC 400: 136.7–9]). Antony later encourages others to do the same (*Vit. Ant.* 19).

5. Athanasius wrote a number of other letters, including his annual "festal" letter to the Egyptian Christians, advocating, among other things, various spiritual practices.

6. Dio Chrysostom, *Or.* 77/78.40 (LCL 385: 296).

7. Seneca, *Ep.* 37.1 (LCL 75: 252–54), 96.5 (LCL 77: 106).

8. Cicero, *Tusculanae disputationes* 3.1.2 (trans. LCL 141: 226); see also 5.27.78 (LCL 141: 504–6).

9. Seneca, *Ep.* 94.54–55 (trans. LCL 77: 44–46).

10. See Gretchen Reydams-Schils, "Roman and Stoic: The Self as a Mediator," *Dionysius* 16 (1998): 35–62, and *The Roman Stoics: Self, Responsibility, and Affection* (Chicago: University of Chicago Press, 2005).

11. Seneca, *Ep.* 94.69 (LCL 77: 54). Musonius Rufus speaks of the "longer and more thorough training" that philosophy requires, since its students have been "born and reared in an environment filled with corruption and evil" (Cora E. Lutz, trans., *Musonius Rufus: "The Roman Socrates,"* Yale Classical Studies 10 [New Haven, CT: Yale University Press, 1947], 52–54).

12. Maximus of Tyre, *Dissertationes* 27.8 (ed. Michael B. Trapp, Bibliotheca Scriptorum Graecorum et Romanorum Teubneriana [Stuttgart: B. G. Teubner, 1994], 159–68).

13. Seneca, *Ep.* 95.34 (trans. LCL 77: 78).

14. Seneca, *Ep.* 95.34–35 (LCL 77: 78).

15. Pierre Hadot, "Forms of Life and Forms of Discourse," in *Philosophy as a Way of Life: Spiritual Exercises from Socrates to Foucault,* ed. Arnold Davidson, trans. Michael Chase (Cambridge: Blackwell, 1995), 59. *Ascesis,* nonetheless, is a term that had a long history even by the time of Athanasius. On such philosophical exercises, see also Hadot's *The Inner Citadel: The Meditations of Marcus Aurelius,* trans. Michael Chase (Cambridge, MA: Harvard University Press, 1998), esp. 35–53, as well as his *What Is Ancient Philosophy?,* trans. Michael Chase (Cambridge, MA: Harvard University Press, 2002); Paul Rabbow, *Seelenführung: Methodik der Exerzitien in der Antike* (Munich: Kösel-Verlag, 1954); Robert J. Newman, "*Cotidie Meditare:* Theory and Practice of the *Meditatio* in Imperial Stoicism," in *Philosophie, Wissenschaften, Technik: Philosophie (Stoizismus),* edited by Wolfgang Haase, ANRW 2.36.3 (Berlin: De Gruyter, 1989), 1473–1517; Martha C. Nussbaum, *The Therapy of Desire: Theory and Practice in Hellenistic Ethics,* Martin Classical Lectures, n.s. 2 (Princeton, NJ: Princeton University Press, 1994); B. L. Hijmans, *Askesis: Notes on Epictetus' Educational System,* Wijsgerige teksten en studies 2 (Assen: Van Gorcum,

1959). Michel Foucault has commented notably on this tradition. He describes "technologies of the self" by which people intentionally "not only set themselves rules of conduct, but also seek to transform themselves, to change themselves in their singular being, and to make their life into an *œuvre* that carries certain aesthetic values and meets certain stylistic criteria" (*The History of Sexuality*, trans. Robert Hurley, 3 vols. [New York: Random House, 1985], 2: 10–11). Elsewhere he refers to "technologies of the self, which permit individuals to effect by their own means or with the help of others a certain number of operations on their own bodies and souls, thoughts, conduct, and way of being, so as to transform themselves in order to attain a certain state of happiness, purity, wisdom, perfection, or immortality" ("Technologies of the Self," in *Technologies of the Self: A Seminar with Michel Foucault*, ed. Luther H. Martin, Huck Gutman, and Patrick H. Hutton [Amherst: University of Massachusetts Press, 1988], 18). Pierre Hadot has criticized the historical accuracy of Foucault's work as overemphasizing "self" at the expense of the importance this tradition has historically ascribed to conforming the self to universal principles of nature ("Reflections on the Idea of 'Cultivation of the Self,'" in *Philosophy as a Way of Life*, 206–13). Charles Taylor is similarly critical of Foucault's proposals and insightfully examines the positive and negative implications of the more classical view represented by Athanasius, among others, which understands selfhood as achieved by conforming oneself to a preexistent ideal (*Sources of the Self: The Making of the Modern Identity* [Cambridge, MA: Harvard University Press, 1989], 488–90, 518–21).

16. P. Hadot, "Forms of Life," 59; see also his *Inner Citadel*, 51. The *Kuriai Doxai* of Epicurus are the most conspicuous example from antiquity; see Diogenes Laertius, *Lives of Eminent Philosophers* 10.139–54 (LCL 185: 662–76). In his *Letter to Herodotus*, Epicurus says that "mental tranquility means being released from all these troubles and retaining constantly in memory the general and most important principles [κυριωτάτων]" (Diogenes Laertius, *Lives* 10.82 [trans. LCL 185: 610]). Musonius Rufus refers to "habituating" (ἐθίζεσθαι) oneself to act according to the principles of a particular teaching (λόγου) (Fr. 5 [trans. Lutz, *Musonius Rufus*, 50]). Epictetus observes, "It is not easy for a person to acquire a proper judgment [δόγμα], unless each day the same principles are said and heard, and at the same time applied to life" (Fr. 16 [trans. LCL 218: 460]). Marcus Aurelius exhorts himself to always have his "doctrines" (δόγματα) ready, just as physicians have their instruments always "in hand" (πρόχειρα) (*De rebus suis* 3.13 [trans. LCL 58: 60]).

17. Seneca, *Ep.* 94.47 (LCL 77: 40); See Dio Chrysostom's description of how "doctrines abide in the soul" (δόγματα ἐν τῇ ψυχῇ) of one who has received "a good education" (ἀγαθῆς παιδείας) (*Or.* 4.31–2 [trans. LCL 257: 182]).

18. See Seneca: "One who has learned and understood what he should do and avoid, is not a wise man until his mind is metamorphosed [*transfiguratus*] into the shape of that which he has learned" (Ep. 94.48 [trans. LCL 77: 42]).

19. Seneca, *De ira* 2.12.3 (trans. LCL 214: 192).

20. Seneca is typical: "Let speech harmonize with life. That man has fulfilled his promise who is the same person both when you see him and when you hear him" (*Ep.* 75.4 [trans. LCL 76: 138]). Philo describes how Moses "demonstrated his philosophical doctrines [δόγματα] by his daily actions, saying what he thought and acting according to his words, so that speech and life were in harmony, and thus life [βίος] was found to be like the speech [λόγος] and the speech like the life, just like those who play together [in tune] on a musical instrument" (*De vita Moysis* 1.29 [trans. LCL 289: 290]).

21. For example, see Seneca, *Epistulae morales ad Lucilium*; Porphyry, *Ad Marcellam*; and the texts made available by Abraham J. Malherbe, *Ancient Epistolary Theorists* (Atlanta, GA: Scholars Press, 1988).

22. Athanasius, *Ep. Marcell.* 19 (PG 27: 32b; trans. Gregg, *Athanasius*, 117). Athanasius also uses this phrase in *Vit. Ant.* 3.1; 27.4; 91.3. Porphyry extols Plotinus's continual "attention to himself" (πρὸς ἑαυτὸν προσοχήν) (*Vita Plotini* 8.20–21 [trans. LCL 440: 30–31]). Finding the phrase in Deut. 15:9 (LXX), Basil devoted a homily to the subject (PG 31: 197c–217b). See P. Hadot's comments on what he describes as "a technical term of ancient philosophy" in "Ancient Spiritual Exercises and 'Christian Philosophy,'" in *Philosophy*, 130–40.

23. Athanasius, *Ep. Marcell.* 10 (PG 27: 20c; trans. [altered] Gregg, *Athanasius*, 108).

24. Athanasius, *Ep. Marcell.* 1 (PG 27: 12a; trans. Gregg, *Athanasius*, 101).

25. Sieben, "Athanasius über den Psalter," 157.

26. Charles Kannengiesser, "Athanasius of Alexandria and the Ascetic Movement of His Time," in *Asceticism*, ed. Vincent L. Wimbush and Richard Valantasis (Oxford: Oxford University Press, 1995), 479. See also Elm, *Virgins of God*, 331–72. The daily recitation of the psalms is widely attested in the writings of early Christians. It is commonly referred to in the *Apophthegmata patrum*. One saying of Abba Epiphanius asserts that "the true monk should have prayer and psalmody continually in his heart" (Epiphanius 3 [PG 65: 164c; trans. Benedicta Ward, *The Sayings of the Desert Fathers: The Alphabetical Collection* [Kalamazoo, MI: Cistercian Publications, 1975], 57). Douglas Burton-Christie describes the consensus that "the most frequently cited Old Testament texts [in the *Apophthegmata patrum*] are the Psalms" (*The Word in the Desert: Scripture and the Quest for Holiness in Early Christian Monasticism* [Oxford: Oxford University Press, 1993], 97). Theodoret of Cyrus describes Syrian monks vocalizing psalms from early morning to late afternoon during daily walks into the desert (*Historia religiosa* 2.5 [SC 234: 204–6]). Cyril of Scythopolis indicates that the learning of the psalms was an essential skill that Sabbas required novices in Palestine to master before they could move from the *cenobium* to the *laura* (*Lives of the Monks of Palestine*, trans. R. M. Price [Kalamazoo, MI: Cistercian Publications, 1991], 113.1–20). The practice

was also integral to Cappadocian asceticism. See Basil, *Hom. in Ps.* (PG 29: 209–493) and *Reg. fus. tr.* 37 (PG 31: 1009c–1016c), and Gregory of Nyssa's *Inscr. Ps.* (SC 466).

27. Athanasius refers to "some of the simple among us" who mistakenly consider music of the psalms to be "for the sake of the ear's delight" (*Ep. Marcell.* 27 [PG 27: 37d]) and implies that there are others who "embellish the words of the Psalter with the persuasive phrases of the profane" (*Ep. Marcell.* 31 [PG 27: 41d]).

28. Athanasius, *C. Gent.* 41 (SC 18bis: 188.18–20). See also *De Incarnatione* 11 (SC 199bis: 302). For earlier attestations to *creatio ex nihilo*, see Philo, *Legum allegoriae* 3.10 (LCL 226: 306); Irenaeus, *Adversus haereses* 2.10.4 (SC 294: 90); Origen, *De princ.* praef. 4 (SC 252: 80).

29. Athanasius, *C. Gent.* 41 (SC 18bis: 188.20–24); see Plato, *Timaeus* 29e (LCL 234: 54).

30. Athanasius, *C. Gent.* 1 (SC 18bis: 50.6).

31. Athanasius, *C. Gent.* 44 (SC 18bis: 198.7–16). See also *C. Gent.* 40–45 (SC 18bis: 184–202).

32. Athanasius, *C. Gent.* 40 (SC 18bis: 184.25–26). For further elaboration, see Khaled Anatolios, *Athanasius: The Coherence of His Thought* (New York: Routledge, 1998).

33. Athanasius, *C. Gent.* 2 (SC 18bis: 54.8–11).

34. Athanasius, *C. Gent.* 2 (SC 18bis: 56.1–6). On the soul as a "mirror," see Andrew Hamilton, "Athanasius and the Simile of the Mirror," *Vigiliae Christianae* 34 (1980): 14–18. His analysis, however, does not address Athanasius's extension of this simile from the soul to the scripture as discussed below.

35. μενῶ (Athanasius, *C. Gent.* 3 [SC 18bis: 56.10]). A key term for Athanasius, which he repeats often; see its use in *C. Ar.* 2.74 (PG 26: 305a).

36. Athanasius, *C. Gent.* 8 (SC 18bis: 72.6–10).

37. ἔξω δὲ ἑαυτῆς γενομένη (Athanasius, *C. Gent.* 8 [SC 18bis: 72.8–9]).

38. ἡ γὰρ κίνησις τῆς ψυχῆς οὐδὲν ἕτερόν ἐστιν ἢ ζωὴ αὐτῆς (Athanasius, *C. Gent.* 33 [SC 18bis: 160.12–13]).

39. Athanasius, *C. Gent.* 4 (SC 18bis: 60.3–5).

40. Athanasius, *C. Gent.* 4 (SC 18bis: 60.8); οὐκ εἰδυῖα ὅτι ἁπλῶς κινεῖσθαι, ἀλλ᾿ εἰς ἃ δεῖ κινεῖσθαι γέγονε (Athanasius, *C. Gent.* 4 [SC 18bis: 62.8–11]).

41. Athanasius, *C. Gent.* 8–29.

42. Athanasius, *C. Gent.* 8 (SC 18bis: 72.9–13).

43. Athanasius, *C. Gent.* 3 (SC 18bis: 58.14–16).

44. Athanasius, *C. Ar.* 1.51 (PG 26: 120a).

45. Athanasius, *C. Ar.* 3.56 (PG 26: 440c–441a). He can even speak of the flesh being "made Word" (λογωθείσης) (*C. Ar.* 3.33 [PG 26: 396a]).

46. τὸν σταυρὸν μὴ βλάβην ἀλλὰ θεραπείαν τῆς κτίσεως γεγονέναι (Athanasius, *C. Gent.* 1 [SC 18bis: 48.11–12]).

47. Athanasius, *Vit. Ant.* 78. For the extensive influence that Athanasius's Nicene commitments had upon his depiction of Antony's asceticism, see Robert C. Gregg and Dennis E. Groh, *Early Arianism: A View of Salvation* (Philadelphia: Fortress Press, 1981), 131–59.

48. "If the Son be a creature . . . no help [βοήθεια] will come to creatures from a creature, since all need grace from God" (Athanasius, *C. Ar.* 2.41 [PG 26: 233b]; see also 2.67).

49. Athanasius, *Ep. Marcell.* 2 and 9. Note Basil's similar comments in *Hom. in Ps. 1* (PG 29: 209a–212a).

50. Athanasius, *Ep. Marcell.* 19 (PG 27: 32c; trans. [altered] Gregg, *Athanasius*, 117–18).

51. Athanasius, *Ep. Marcell.* 13 (PG 27: 25a–b; trans. Gregg, *Athanasius*, 112).

52. Brakke, *Athanasius and Asceticism*, 167. Athanasius describes this himself: "Imitation [μίμησις] of these natural [κατὰ φύσιν] qualities [in God] is particularly protective in the case of human beings, as has been said; for inasmuch as they [God's qualities] endure and never change while the conduct of human beings is easily changed, it is possible, by looking to what is unchangeable by nature, to flee evil deeds and to re-form [ἑαυτὸν ἀνατυποῦν] oneself to better things" (Athanasius, *C. Ar.* 3.20 [PG 26: 365]; trans. Brakke, *Athanasius*, 167). Burton-Christie observes, "Perhaps the primary means through which the Bible entered and affected the imaginations of those who took up life in the desert was the vivid images of holy exemplars from Scripture—that is, through exemplary interpretation. The biblical saints to whom the monks looked for guidance included figures from both the Old and the New Testament, though of course distinct from them in important ways was the person of Christ" (*Word in the Desert*, 167).

53. Brakke comments that although "all human beings receive the incorruption of the Word's assumed body, they must individually appropriate it through lives of ascetic discipline within the Church" (*Athanasius*, 151–52).

54. Athanasius, *Ep. Marcell.* 13 (PG 27: 25b; trans. Gregg, *Athanasius*, 112). Athanasius's insistence here on the Christological focus of the Psalter accords with his more general hermeneutic. See James D. Ernest, "Athanasius of Alexandria: The Scope of Scripture in Polemical and Pastoral Context," *Vigiliae Christianae* 47 (1993): 341–62, and *The Bible in Athanasius of Alexandria* (Boston: Brill Academic Publishers, 2004).

55. Athanasius, *Ep. Marcell.* 30 (PG 27: 41c; trans. Gregg, *Athanasius*, 126).

56. Athanasius, *Ep. Marcell.* 12 (PG 27: 24c; trans. Gregg, *Athanasius*, 111). I have altered Gregg's translation wherever he has translated κινήματα as "emotions." Athanasius's use of this term has a broader semantic range than "emotion," since it includes among other things, the reasoning faculty (cf. *Ep. Marcell.* 27 [PG 27: 40a]). John Cassian also likens the psalms to a mirror. He says that "all these feelings that we find expressed in the psalms" allow us to understand "whatever

happens as in a very clear mirror [*speculo purissimo*]"; *Conlat.* 10.11 (CSEL 13: 305.15–17). The comparison between the soul and Homer's *Odyssey* was also known in antiquity; see Aristotle's reference to Alcidamas's description of the *Odyssey* as "a beautiful mirror [κάτοπτρον] of human life" (*Rhetorica* 1406b [trans. LCL 193: 366]).

57. Athanasius appears to have seen not just the Psalter but the whole of scripture as effective in acquiring true knowledge of the self. Elsewhere he describes how Antony used to tell himself that the ascetic ought to employ the scriptural example of Elijah as a "mirror" to "acquire knowledge of his own life" (*Vit. Ant.* 7.13 [SC 400: 154–56]). Hence, this quality of scripture emerges most directly in the Psalter but is not limited to it.

58. Walter J. Ong, *Orality and Literacy: The Technologizing of the Word*, New Accents (London: Methuen, 1982), 105. Elsewhere he contrasts the written word with the oral: "Oral communication unites people in groups. Writing and reading are solitary activities that throw the psyche back on itself" (69; see also 54–55).

59. Regarding the Hellenistic philosophical schools on the therapeutic potential of the speech of the philosopher, see, for instance, Plutarch's instruction that one should listen for "the purpose of amending his life by means of what is there said" (τῷ λόγῳ τὸν βίον ἐπανορθωσόμενος) (*Moralia* 42a [trans. LCL 197: 226]). The Athanasius quote is from *Ep. Marcell.* 13 (PG 27: 25b). See also similar expressions in *Ep. Marcell.* 12 (PG 27: 24d) and 15 (PG 27: 28c). Elsewhere Athanasius says, "See: these are all the medicines of God's house, existing for the soul's healing. Often you hear the holy words and psalms: through them you will make your vows spiritually to the one who called you to eternal life" (frag., CSCO 150: 124; trans. Brakke, *Athanasius*, 316).

60. "The Lord himself is in the phrases [τὰ ῥήματα] of the Scriptures [τῶν γραφῶν]" (Athanasius, *Ep. Marcell.* 33 [PG 27: 45a]).

61. John Colobos 35 (PG 65: 216c [trans. Ward, *Sayings*, 92]). Note also Athanasius's remark that "from the movements" of Antony's body "it was possible to sense and perceive the stable condition of the soul" (*Vit. Ant.* 67.6 [SC 400: 312]; trans. Gregg, *Athanasius*, 81).

62. A view famously explicated by Sigmund Freud, *Five Lectures on Psycho-Analysis*, ed. and trans. James Strachey (New York: Norton, 1977).

63. Athanasius, *Ep. Marcell.* 28 (PG 27: 40d).

64. A strategy characteristic of the Hellenistic schools. See, for example, Marcus Aurelius, *De rebus suis* 4.7 (LCL 58: 72), and Nussbaum, *Therapy of Desire*, 37–40, 104–36, 366–72.

65. Athanasius, *Ep. Marcell.* 25 (PG 27: 37a; trans. [altered] Gregg, *Athanasius*, 122).

66. Emphasis mine; Athanasius, *Ep. Marcell.* 10 (PG 27: 20d; trans. Gregg, *Athanasius*, 108).

67. Athanasius, *Ep. Marcell.* 11 (PG 27: 21c; trans. Gregg, *Athanasius,* 109).

68. Athanasius, *Ep. Marcell.* 11 (PG 27: 24a–b; trans. [altered] Gregg, *Athanasius,* 110). John Cassian offers a similar description of those who sing psalms: "Vivified by this nourishment continually, he will take in to himself all the affections of the psalms and will begin to sing them in such a way that he will utter them with the deepest compunction of heart, not as if they were the compositions of the psalmist, but rather as if they were his own utterances and his very own prayer; and will certainly take them as directed at himself, and will recognize that their words . . . are fulfilled and accomplished daily in his own case" (*Conlat.* 10.11 [CSEL 13: 304.16–23]).

69. Ong, *Orality and Literacy,* 82.

70. Ibid., 81.

71. Ibid., 83. See also where Ong describes how "the deadness of the text, its removal from the living human lifeworld, its rigid visual fixity," are the features that assure "its endurance and its potential for being resurrected into limitless living contexts by a potentially infinite number of living readers" (81).

72. Athanasius, *Ep. Marcell.* 20 (PG 27: 33a; trans. [altered] Gregg, *Athanasius,* 118). Describing Antony's "reading" of scripture "that is enacted in life," Geoffrey Harpham refers to "the readers' recreation or rewriting of the text not on paper but in his own being. . . . The reception of the Biblical text becomes a form of ascesis, of self-overcoming in which the reader or hearer aspires to an identification with the text that is simultaneously original and derivative" (*The Ascetic Imperative in Culture and Criticism* [Chicago: University of Chicago Press, 1987], 42). Athanasius is preceded by Origen, who wrote that the treasure of divine wisdom "is written more clearly and perfectly in our hearts" (*De princ.* 4.1.7 [SC 268: 290]), as well as by Philo of Alexandria, who uses a similar expression regarding the realities referred to in scripture being "graven as though on stone [ἐστηλιτευμένα] on the heart of the wise" (*De confusione linguarum* 74 [trans. LCL 261: 50]). Athanasius appears to employ this principle when he states that Antony "paid such close attention to what was read that nothing from Scripture did he fail to take in—rather he grasped everything, and in him the memory took the place of books" (*Vit. Ant.* 3.7 [SC 400: 138]; trans. Gregg, *Athanasius,* 32). Douglas Burton-Christie observes that several of the stories in the *Apophthegmata patrum* speak of "the need to *attain* a saying from Scripture, an indication that the practice of Scripture should lead one to become or appropriate completely its message. This appropriation was seen as a difficult but necessary part of the process of coming truly to understand and realize the meaning of the Scripture. . . . Attaining a saying from Scripture, realizing its truth within oneself, implied a deep moral and spiritual transformation" (*Word in the Desert,* 153).

73. Athanasius, *Ep. Marcell.* 31 (PG 27: 41d; trans. Gregg, *Athanasius,* 127).

74. See Harpham's discussion of the ascetic quality of reading, since "the very condition of intelligibility" in reading is the submission of the reader to the "extrasubjective" text (*Ascetic Imperative*, 134).

75. Athanasius, *Ep. Marcell.* 31 (PG 27: 44a; trans. Gregg, *Athanasius*, 127).

76. Athanasius, *Ep. Marcell.* 33 (PG 27: 44d–45a; trans. Gregg, *Athanasius*, 128).

77. Athanasius, *Ep. Marcell.* 32 (PG 27: 44d; trans. Gregg, *Athanasius*, 128).

78. Athanasius, *Ep. Marcell.* 33 (PG 27: 45a; trans. [altered] Gregg, *Athanasius*, 129).

79. Athanasius, *Ep. Marcell.* 32 (PG 27: 44b; trans. Gregg, *Athanasius*, 127). For Antony, see note 4. Conversely, those who change the words do not benefit from the divine presence in them and "expose themselves to being mocked by demons" (*Ep. Marcell.* 33 [PG 27: 45a; trans. Gregg, *Athanasius*, 129]).

80. Athanasius, *Ep. Marcell.* 27 (PG 27: 37d; trans. Gregg, *Athanasius*, 123).

81. Athanasius, *Ep. Marcell.* 29 (PG 27: 41a; trans. Gregg, *Athanasius*, 125).

82. Athanasius, *Ep. Marcell.* 29 (PG 27: 41b; trans. Gregg, *Athanasius*, 126).

83. Athanasius, *Ep. Marcell.* 29 (PG 27: 41b; trans. [altered] Gregg, *Athanasius*, 126); See Basil's similar comments on the beneficial qualities of the Psalter's melodies (*Hom. in Ps.* 1.1–2 [PG 29: 212b–213c]; trans. FC 46: 152–53). In a speech addressing the citizens of Alexandria, three centuries prior to Athanasius, Dio Chrysostom stated, "Music is believed to have been invented by human beings for the healing [θεραπείας] of their passions, and especially for transforming souls which are in harsh and savage state. That is why even some philosophers attune themselves to the lyre at dawn, thereby striving to quell the confusion caused by their dreams. And it is with song that we sacrifice to the gods, for the purpose of insuring order and stability in ourselves" (*Or.* 32.57 [trans. LCL 358: 226–28]). The use of music for philosophical ends was often associated with the Pythagoreans. For example in his *De vita Pythagorica*, Iamblichus describes how Pythagoras employed music in spiritual exercises to "correct human characters and ways of life by means of music": "The entire Pythagorean school created what is called 'musical arrangement' and 'musical combination' and (musical) treatment, skillfully reversing dispositions of the soul to opposite emotions with certain suitable tunes.... There are cases in which they healed emotions [πάθη] and certain sicknesses, as they say, truly by means of singing as an incantation" (ἐπᾴδοντες) (25.114, also discussed in 25.110–13, and 32.224; trans. John Dillon and Jackson Hershbell, *On the Pythagorean Way of Life: Texts, Translation, and Notes* [Atlanta, GA: Scholars Press, 1991]). See also Maximus of Tyre, *Dissertationes* 37.5, and the useful collection by Andrew Barker, ed., *Greek Musical Writings*, 2 vols., Cambridge Readings in the Literature of Music (Cambridge: Cambridge University Press, 1984).

84. See Seneca, *De ira* 2.12.3–6 (LCL 214: 192–94).

85. The quoted phrase is from Harpham, *Ascetic Imperative*, 41.

Evagrius Ponticus

The Psalter as a Handbook for
the Christian Contemplative

Luke Dysinger, O.S.B.

Until recently the name of Evagrius Ponticus (345–99) would seldom have arisen in discussions of patristic exegesis. While his influence on the theory and practice of Christian asceticism was consistently acknowledged (often pejoratively) in the centuries following his death in 399, neither Evagrius's critics nor those sympathetic to his cause ever attributed to him commentaries on the scriptures. This is surprising, since it has become clear that biblical scholia constitute a very large part, perhaps the majority, of Evagrius's literary output.[1] It was only in the twentieth century that fragments from his biblical commentaries were reliably identified in catenae and ascetical anthologies. Publication of these recovered fragments facilitated critical editions of his commentary on Proverbs in 1989 and in 1993 of his commentary on Ecclesiastes.[2] Evagrius describes his commentaries as belonging to the established genre of *scholia*, literally "marginal annotations," on successive, selected verses.[3] His biblical scholia vary in form from paragraph-length, narrative expositions of particularly rich texts to the much more common brief definitions and summaries that, stripped of the biblical verses they explicate, often reappear as *kephalaia* or *gnomai* ("chapters" or "sentences") in his ascetical texts. Evagrius's *Scholia on Psalms* is his longest extant work, containing more than 1,350 scholia explicating texts from all the psalms except Psalm 117 (LXX 116).[4]

That Evagrius would devote so much energy to interpreting the psalms is hardly surprising, given the increasingly important role of the Psalter in the Egyptian monastic culture where he flourished. During the latter half of the fourth century the Psalter came to occupy an increasingly prominent place in Christian worship, both in liturgical gatherings and in private devotion. In the fourth century the book of Psalms gradually displaced other biblical texts used at the so-called "canonical prayers" of both the urban cathedral liturgies and the rapidly expanding Christian monastic movement.[5] One historian of music has described this "psalmodic movement" as "an unprecedented wave of enthusiasm for the singing of psalms that swept from east to west through the Christian population in the closing decades of the fourth century."[6] Different reasons have been adduced for the increasing popularity of the Psalter; but whatever the cause, by the 380s, when Evagrius became a monk, the central place of the Psalter in monastic ascetical practice was well established, and the need for a spiritual rationale for reciting the Psalter was widely felt. Athanasius's *Letter to Marcellinus*, discussed in the preceding chapter of this book, represents one response to this growing need, as do the commentaries of Hilary of Poitiers, Gregory of Nyssa, and Augustine. Unlike these more popular introductions and commentaries, however, Evagrius's *Scholia on Psalms* was directed toward a specific and small "target audience": namely the Christian contemplative whom he called *gnōstikos*.

The *Gnōstikos* and the Psalter

The term *gnōstikos*, used as an honorific to describe the mature Christian spiritual guide and contemplative exegete, was rendered acceptable by Clement of Alexandria, whose writings along with those of Origen were part of Evagrius's early pastoral and later monastic training. Born in Pontus (modern-day northern Turkey) around 345, Evagrius was in his mid- to late twenties when Basil of Caesarea ordained him lector. He served in the famous bishop's clergy until Basil's death in 379. Devastated by the sudden death of his patron and mentor, he fled to Basil's friend Gregory Nazianzen in Constantinople, where Gregory ordained him deacon. Evagrius appears to have inherited from these two Cappadocians an appreciation for Alexandrian exegesis, typified by their compilation in the *Philocalia* of an array of passages drawn from an extensive range of Origen's works.[7] Evagrius remained in the imperial capital after Gregory's departure and played an active role during the First Council of Constantinople in 381. He then traveled to Jerusalem, where he encountered two more enthusiastic proponents of Alexandrian spirituality, Rufinus and Melania the Elder, who convinced him to become a monk. After they had provided initial monastic training in their monastery on the Mount of Olives, Melania urged Evagrius to continue his studies in Egypt with renowned desert *abbas* and *ammas* with whom she and Rufinus were in close contact.

Evagrius lived for two years in the monastic settlement of Nitria, thirty miles southeast of Alexandria, then withdrew to the nearby hermit colony of Kellia, where he spent the remaining fifteen years of his life. He became a disciple of the desert fathers Macarius of Alexandria and Macarius the Egyptian and in time came to be regarded as a gifted *abba* in his own right. As such he played a leading role in the intellectual "Origenist circle" in Kellia, whose members included the so-called "tall brothers," Ammonius, Euthymius, Dioscorus, and Eusebius, who had all been disciples of the famous Abba Pambo. Evagrius's own disciples included John Cassian and the later bishops Palladius of Helenopolis and Heraclides of Cyprus. He died in 399, thus escaping by only a few weeks the expulsion from Egypt and exile that befell many monastic intellectuals during the first Origenist crisis. His reputation, however, did not escape, and his name was eventually linked with Origen and Didymus in anti-Origenist anathemas of later ecumenical councils.[8]

Evagrius's condemnation divided and scattered his literary legacy, dismembering his sophisticated program of monastic pedagogy.[9] He had intended his texts to both analyze and assist in the project of monastic spiritual progress. He composed elementary ascetical treatises for *praktikoi*, monks who struggled against the eight principal *logismoi* or tempting thoughts of gluttony, lust, avarice, sadness, anger, *acedia*, vainglory, and pride.[10] Their labors in the realm of *praktikē* (asceticism) would be rewarded by God with acquisition of the virtues, especially love, and with the gift of *apatheia*, dispassion or freedom from compulsion.[11] *Apatheia* would, in turn, facilitate progress from asceticism to contemplation, enabling the *gnōstikos* to undertake the more intricate labors of contemplative biblical exegesis, spiritual guidance, and teaching. Evagrius composed progressively more sophisticated and compact treatises for *gnōstikoi,* contemplatives searching for the divine *logoi,* inner meanings and purposes of God hidden beneath the surface appearances of nature, history, and the texts of sacred scripture. These treatises include collections of *gnomai* (sentences) and *kephalaia* (chapters) as well as biblical scholia. They take the form of brief expositions, usually no more than a few sentences in length, syllogisms, parables, and definitions that often become progressively more compact and cryptic as the work progresses. This progression is deliberate, requiring careful meditation and familiarity with Evagrius's model of spiritual progress in order to decode meanings and subtle interconnections.[12] In the wake of his condemnation the ordering and interrelationship of these works and the significance of their intrinsic pedagogy were lost. His straightforward ascetical treatises survive in the original Greek, often under pseudonyms of more reputable authors. The more advanced and speculative collections such as the *Gnōstikos* and *Kephalaia Gnostica* were retained, although often expurgated, in the Syriac and Armenian Christian patrimony, whose monks and bishops were undeterred by Chalcedonian anathemas. The fate of his exegetical treatises was mixed: some survived as dislocated fragments; others were incorporated wholly or in part into the Greek biblical *catanae,* often attributed to Origen or Athanasius.

The modern recovery of Evagrius's exegetical scholia on Psalms, Proverbs, and Ecclesiastes has facilitated a reappreciation of the monastic pedagogy underlying all his works. Hardly recognizable as "commentaries" in the modern sense, often having the appearance of allegorical glossaries, his collections of scholia were intended for use by *gnōstikoi,* contemplative *abbas* and *ammas* who were expected to offer biblical texts to their disciples in response to their regular plea, "Give me a word!" For Evagrius, biblical exegesis entailed the search for scriptural texts that would benefit both the *gnōstikos* and those who sought spiritual counsel. He wrote that the *gnōstikos* must be able to "give a word to each, according to his [level of spiritual] attainment."[13] This presupposes the ability to discern the disciple's level of spiritual maturity and draw from the large store of biblical wisdom provided in the scholia. Evagrius also expected the *gnōstikos* to be familiar with the different levels of meaning contained in sacred scripture. These included spiritual (often allegorical) definitions of biblical terms and familiarity with both the "customary expressions of scripture" and the rules for allegorical exegesis.[14] Evagrius succinctly presents his exegetical program in *Gnōstikos* 18. It clearly derives from Clement of Alexandria and Origen,[15] but Evagrius has superimposed his own schema of spiritual progress on the Alexandrian exegetical models he inherited.

> *Gnōstikos* 18. It is necessary to search for allegorical and literal passages pertaining to the *praktikē, physikē*, and *theologikē*.
>
> > [1] If the passage concerns the *praktikē* it is necessary to determine whether it concerns *thumos* and its effects, or *epithumia* and its consequences, or whether it concerns the movements of the *nous*.
> >
> > [2] If the passage pertains to the *physikē*, it is necessary to note whether it reveals a doctrine concerning nature, and which one.
> >
> > [3] Or if it is an allegorical passage concerning *theologikē* it should be determined as far as possible whether it reveals the doctrine of the Trinity.[16]

Evagrius thus expected the *gnōstikos* to explicate biblical texts according to three principal criteria. First was their usefulness in the battle against temptation and the acquisition of virtue (*praktikē*), divided according to the three subdivisions of the Platonic tripartite soul. Second was what they revealed of the inner purposes of God in history and creation (*physikē*). Third was whether they hinted at the ineffable mysteries of the divine nature or the transcendent experience of pure prayer (*theologikē*). In what follows, Evagrius's exegetical program will serve as a framework for studying examples from the *Scholia on Psalms*.

THE LITERAL SENSE OF THE PSALMS

The exegetical schema of *Gnōstikos* 18 clarifies Evagrius's focus on the utility of biblical texts in Christian ascetical and contemplative practice. There are only a very few scholia on psalms in which he attempts to explain words in their historical context, most often with regard to points of geography or natural history. Thus in Psalm 47:8, mention of "the ships of Tarsis" evokes the explanation, "'Tharsis' refers to a region of Ethiopia, while 'Tarsus' is the city that is called 'Tharsis' in the Book of Jonah."[17] And in Psalm 88 Evagrius responds to the verse, "Tabor and Hermon will rejoice in your name," with the observation: "Tabor, the chosen! Tabor is the mountain of Galilee on which Christ was transfigured. Hermon is the mountain on which lies the city of Naim, where Christ raised the widow's son."[18]

Such comments on the historical context of scripture are uncommon in the *Scholia on Psalms*,[19] but Evagrius regarded the literal sense as very useful in the practice of *antirrhesis*, the "contradiction" of harmful thoughts by meditation on or verbal recitation of a biblical passage. He wrote an extensive treatise, *Antirrhetikos*, on this practice and recommended it as an essential ascetical technique in *Praktikos* and *On Prayer*.[20] In the *Scholia on Psalms* Evagrius recommends antirrhetic verses for use not only against the demons and their *logismoi* but also against sinful tendencies within the self, and even more broadly as "refutations" of particular groups of people and forms of behavior. He also provides antirrhetic texts from the psalms intended to console the tempted soul and to remind it of virtues opposed to the *logismoi*. Finally, *antirrhesis* includes the offering to God of succinct biblical prayers. Part of the reason Evagrius found the book of Psalms such a rich source of antirrhetic verses, both in the scholia and in the *Antirrhetikos*, may be that he regarded the Psalter as a kind of handbook that had served King David in his own journey of spiritual progress: "I expound openly the entire contest of the monastic way of life, [that contest] which the Holy Spirit taught David by means of the psalms, and which was also handed on to us by the blessed fathers."[21]

What may be called "direct *antirrhesis*"—that is, verses intended solely to contradict a particular species of demon or its attendant *logismos*—is uncommon in the *Scholia on Psalms*. Examples include Evagrius's recommendation that those afflicted by "demons who become visible to us and thus tempt us to be terrified" should recite Psalm 91:12 (LXX): "My eye has seen my enemies and my ear will hear the wicked who rise against me."[22] Those troubled by the *logismos* of pride should remind themselves of their need for God's help in the words of Psalm 126:1 (LXX): "Unless the Lord build the house, in vain do they labor who build it; unless the Lord keeps watch over the city, in vain does the watcher keep vigil."[23] More typical of the *Scholia on Psalms* are thirteen antirrhetic scholia intended to induce compunction and repentance. Four of these concern the misuse of wealth, such as Psalm 61:11 (LXX), recommended to reprove the greedy: "If wealth should flow in, do not set your heart upon it."[24] Five scholia are directed toward those who scorn virtue or engage in worldly pursuits.[25] Four are intended to exhort or rebuke erring monks and aspiring *gnōstikoi*, such as those who are "neglectful of nocturnal prayers" or who lack discretion in their exegesis of scripture.[26]

In contrast to these thirteen texts intended to induce compunction are eight antirrhetic scholia intended to encourage persons in distress, such as scholion 6 on Psalm 41:12, where the soul "given over to grief" is encouraged to recite the verse, "Why, then, are you sad, my soul? And why do you trouble me?"[27] Four of these consoling scholia are antirrhetic prayers, such as scholion 1 on Psalm 24:1–3, where those required to bear witness to their faith are encouraged to pray, "To you, O Lord, have I lifted up my soul."[28]

Antirrhetic verses in the *Scholia on Psalms* thus serve a wide variety of spiritual purposes. Texts are recited in order to confound the demons and neutralize their effects in the soul, as well as to encourage repentance and spiritual improvement. In such *antirrhesis* the relationship between prayer and recitation of psalm verses sometimes becomes one of identity: texts that have been memorized through the practice of psalmody may serve as the soul's own words to God in times of temptation and affliction.

The antirrhetic passages in Evagrius's works reveal a progression from preoccupation with one's own spiritual improvement in the ascetical texts and the *Antirrhetikos* to a broader concern for others in the exegetical scholia such as the *Scholia on Psalms*. Whereas most of the biblical verses in the *Antirrhetikos* are intended for a single demon, habit of thought, or afflicted soul, the antirrhetic scholia are generally intended for groups of people who share a common affliction. To some extent this corresponds to Evagrius's model of spiritual progress. Whereas Christian ascetics or *praktikoi* employ the weapons of the *Antirrhetikos* in the battlefield of their own souls, contemplative *gnōstikoi* discover in the *Scholia on Psalms* healing texts that not only are therapeutic for themselves but also may be offered as remedies to the diverse groups of people who seek their advice.

ASCETICAL WISDOM IN THE PSALTER

A significant number of Evagrius's scholia interpret the Psalter at the level of *praktikē*, the ascetical project of developing virtue and avoiding vice. The *Scholia on Psalms* differ from his ascetical treatises in that he assumes the reader of the scholia to be spiritually mature, practicing asceticism *gnōstikoteros*, that is, with increasing contemplative wisdom and understanding.[29] The scholia thus contain little of the detailed advice on overcoming temptation characteristic of his ascetical writings. Instead, Evagrius presumes the *gnōstikos*'s desire to uncover symbolic significance in the imagery and events of the psalms, to recognize allegorical allusions to virtues, vices, and certain hidden *logoi* (inner purposes of God). Evagrius alludes to the relationship between the scholia and the ascetical treatises in his first scholion on Psalm 143.

> Ps.143:1. *Blessed be the Lord my God, who teaches my hands to fight, and my fingers to do battle.*
> Scholion 1. Taught by the Lord is one who battles against the opposing powers, who is well versed in the *logoi* of virtues and vices and of various [tempting] thoughts, and of the signs and stages of *apatheia*. And he also knows the *logoi* of nocturnal phantasms that arise during sleep: namely, which of these originate in the reasoning part of the soul [*logistikon*], thus activating the memory; which come from the irascible part [*thumikon*]; and which come from the desiring part [*epithumetikon*]. But I have written more extensively and in more detail concerning these in *The Monk*. As regards investigating the *logoi* of ethical matters, we have set forth there what we were taught by the Lord: namely, how those who wish may withstand the battle.

Here Evagrius employs the traditional image of the *praktikē* as spiritual warfare and refers the reader to his text *Praktikos*, subtitled "The Monk," for detailed information on the subject.[30] He explains that perception of the *logoi* or inner dynamics of this spiritual struggle requires knowledge of the inner structure of the soul. Following Plato and the later Aristotelian tradition, Evagrius considered the soul tripartite, ruled (when all goes well) by the *logistikon* or reasoning faculty, chiefly responsible for developing the virtues of prudence, understanding, and wisdom.[31] It rules over the *pathetikon*, the portion of the soul subject to passion and the source of the powers of *epithumia* (desire) and *thumos* (indignation).[32] These powers or energies, "yoked to [the soul] as helpmates," are intended by God to be used "according to nature" (*kata phusin*);[33] but they will over-whelm the soul as passions if misused or present in excess. When exercised according to nature, the *epithumetikon* contributes the virtues of temper-ance, love, and continence, while the *thumikon* provides courage and pa-tient endurance.[34] Through the practice of discernment (*diakrisis*), the as-cetic or *praktikos* learns to employ these "helpmates" as they are experienced in interpersonal relationships, in dreams, and in thoughts, es-pecially thoughts that occur during prayer.[35]

Evagrius expected the *gnōstikos* to detect in the Psalter symbolic refer-ences to virtues and spiritual warfare. Defensive imagery, such as "walls" or "gates," could stand for "gates of justice . . . , prudence, fortitude, love, and patient endurance, through which the knowledge of God enters."[36] Simi-larly, weapons such as "arrows" could evoke the whole panoply of the virtues:

> Ps. 44:6. *Your arrows are sharp, O mighty one.*
>> Scholion 6. Arrows of Christ are the *praktikē* virtues. And he shoots with justice at the unjust, with prudence at the imprudent, and with temperance at the sexually immoral; and again he shoots with courage at the coward, with self-control at the undisciplined, with patient endurance at the irascible, and with faith at the unbeliever. And it seems as if the arrow of faith appears before the other arrows are sent, since, according to Paul, "Whoever would draw near to God must first believe that he exists" (Heb. 11:6).[37]

Agricultural imagery such as "fruit" reminds the reader that "the fruit of the Spirit is love, joy, peace" (Gal. 5:22), while "leaves" are a symbol of "patient endurance, courage, . . . blessing, silence, and praise."[38] Mention of anger (*thumos*) in Psalm 6 invites deeper reflection on the proper use of righteous indignation, adapting a saying from Clement of Alexandria:

"Indignation is an impulse of desire in the civilized soul rising up for defense."[39]

The virtue of gentleness (*praotes*) is emphasized in Psalm 24. "The gentle are those who put an end to the faithless warfare of anger and desire in their souls, and to all that is subject to the passions."[40] The same virtue is associated with the "path" of freedom from wrath (*aorgesia*) in Psalm 131. "For *gentleness* is [the state] of being undisturbed by wrath when confronted by the loss of perishable pleasures."[41] Both of these hint at the spiritual goal of *apatheia*, symbolized by the "peaceful borders" of Psalm 147. "*The borders of peace* are said to be *apatheia* of the soul."[42] Unlike the ascetical treatises, where *apatheia* is a principal goal of the *praktikē*, in the *Scholia on Psalms apatheia* is less a goal than a starting point from which the *gnōstikos* begins the ascent to spiritual vision and knowledge. Thus the invitation in Psalm 4 to "sacrifice the sacrifice of justice and hope in the Lord" invites the observation: "The *sacrifice of justice* is the reasoning soul's *apatheia*, offered up to God; while *hope* is eager expectation of true knowledge."[43]

One of the *logoi* of the *praktikē* that frequently recurs in the *Scholia on Psalms* is the "*logos* of abandonment." Cries of anguish and pleas for divine assistance in the Psalter permit Evagrius to explain that God sometimes abandons the soul, not in condemnation but rather out of mercy.[44] Sometimes abandonment feels like the withdrawal of divine providence;[45] however, this seeming abandonment is not withdrawal of divine or angelic assistance but a providential act of God that serves to test or prove the tempted soul. Thus the lament in Psalm 37:12, "My nearest [relatives] stood afar off," evokes the observation: "Certain holy powers withdraw in the time of temptation so that the one tempted may be proven or punished."[46] Another providential effect of abandonment is its power to humble the soul and turn it back to God: "Sometimes *a man is turned back to humility* [Ps. 89:3] when [God] abandons him on account of his sin."[47] Finally, the claim in Psalm 36:25, "I have not seen the just one forsaken" invites Evagrius to explain that abandonment may reveal hidden virtue, as in the case of Job: "Because the just are indeed abandoned for a [brief] time for the sake of testing, the Lord says to Job: 'Do not think I have dealt with you for any other [reason], than that you might appear just'" (cf. Job 40:3).[48]

The Cosmos in the Psalter

Evagrius expected the *gnōstikos* to read and pray the Psalter *sub specie aeternitatis*, in the light of a divine origin and eternal destiny. His scholia interpret the words and events of the psalms as symbols and allegories of the great cosmic drama of the Fall, the Incarnation, and the ultimate eschatological reunion of all reasoning beings with God. This is the subject of *theōria physikē*, contemplation of the inner workings of God's creation; and it embraces the whole natural order, including the nature of demons, angels, judgment, providence, successive cosmic ages, and the saving work of Jesus Christ.

Scholia concerned with such lofty matters do not necessarily arise from correspondingly exalted texts. The origins of sin and the demonic powers were discernible to Evagrius in images as mundane as the "curdled milk" of Psalm 118:70. He explains: "Just as there was [a time] when the curd was not a curd, so there was [a time] when the demons were not evil. For if the milk is older than the curd, this indicates that virtue is older than vice."[49] The existence of different species of demons is perceptible in the nations that "encircled" ancient Israel in Psalm 117:11. "Concerning the demons, one kind *encircles* the *praktikos*, the others *encircle* the contemplative: the first are repelled by justice; the second by wisdom."[50] Further details concerning the different types of demons are evoked by the images of "sea" and "the depths":

> Ps.134:6. *All that the Lord willed he did in heaven, and on earth, and in the sea, and in the depths.*
>> Scholion 2. Just as heaven is a dwelling for the holy powers, so is the earth for human beings. For [scripture] says, "The heaven of heavens belong to the Lord, but the earth he has given to human beings" (Ps. 113:24). And just as in the figuratively interpreted "seas" dwell the demons that oppose us, within them as well is "the dragon you made to play in them" (Ps. 103:26). So also in the allegorically interpreted depths there are the subterranean demons, to which the terrestrial demons pleaded in the Gospels that Christ would not send them (cf. Matt. 8:31). The more accurate knowledge of their worlds and their various bodies is stored up in the *logoi* concerning judgment.[51]

The "*logos* of judgment [*krisis*]" that Evagrius mentions in this scholion does not refer to punishment or condemnation: it describes, rather, God's gift to all reasoning beings of the bodies and environments ("worlds") they require in order to make spiritual progress.[52] "Judgment" describes a series of progressive transformations. The "first judgment" was God's original providential creation of the material universe in response to the *kinesis*, the "movement" or fall of the reasoning beings he had brought into being. Subsequent to this first judgment, all reasoning beings undergo a series of transformations through which each receives a new body and environment suited to its changed spiritual state. The final judgment designates the complete transformation that will restore all things to union with God. Evagrius explains this almost at the beginning of the *Scholia on Psalms* in his comments on the first psalm:

> Ps.1:5. *Therefore the ungodly shall not rise in judgment, nor sinners in the counsel of the just.*
>> Scholion 8. Judgment for the just is the passage from a body for asceticism to an angelic one: but for the ungodly it is the change from a body for asceticism to a darkened and gloomy one. For the ungodly will not be raised in the first judgment, but rather in the second.[53]

Evagrius hoped that meditation on the *logos* of judgment would enable the *gnōstikos* to interpret the rich diversity of the cosmos, including the unique qualities and circumstances of each person, as God's gracious gift of a specific environment and body that would facilitate the return of each reasoning being to the divine unity from which all had fallen. The complexity and variety of creation and of human experience reflected in the varied imagery of the Psalter would thus serve as a constant reminder to the *gnōstikos* of the diverse paths and circumstances that lead to God.

Closely related to the *logos of* judgment is what Evagrius called the *logos* of providence. As has already been noted, even the experience of seeming abandonment by God may be understood by the contemplative as a divine act of providential care. The mediators of God's providence are human beings and angels, who are metaphorically described in the psalms as God's "hand": "Now, *hands* means the providence of God,"[54] and "The holy angels are the beneficent *hand* of God, through which God providentially cares for the sensible world, which [angels] are opposed by the demons who do not wish *all men to be saved and come to knowledge of the truth* (1 Tim. 2:4)."[55] The angels are also exemplars and mediators of that higher knowledge of God that in the Psalter is called God's "face":

> Ps. 4:7. *The light of your face has been manifested to us.*
>   Scholion 6. Now, the angels continually see the face of God, while human beings [see] the light of his face. For the face of the Lord is spiritual contemplation of everything that has come to be on the earth, while the light of his face is partial knowledge of these things, since, according to the wise woman Tekowitha, David was "like an angel of God," seeing everything upon the earth (cf. 2 Sam. 14:20).[56]

CHRIST IN THE PSALTER

The theme encountered most frequently in the *Scholia on Psalms* is Jesus Christ, whom Evagrius explicitly mentions at least once in 107 of the 149 psalms on which he comments, referring to Christ by name, by title, or by citation of Christ's words from the Gospels.[57] Of the numerous instances where Evagrius refers to Christ by quoting Christ's words in the Gospels, most frequent are citations employing the phrase "I am" (*egō eimi*), all but two of which are taken from Christ's "I am" statements in the Gospel of John.[58]

An association between Christ and the Psalter is common in patristic authors; however, Evagrius's approach differs significantly from that of his predecessors and contemporaries. Evagrius's constantly recurring references to Jesus Christ in the *Scholia on Psalms* only rarely represent what Marie-Josèphe Rondeau termed "prosopological" attribution to Christ of the sentiments expressed in the psalm.[59] Instead, Evagrius invokes the person or sayings of Christ in order to explicate the inner meaning of the psalm, that *dunamis* which he considered the goal of undistracted psalmody and which reveals the *logoi*, the divine purposes, concealed beneath the images and words of the psalms.

In the *Scholia on Psalms*, Evagrius particularly identifies Christ with the wisdom of God, especially the "richly diverse wisdom" of Ephesians 3:10.[60] He thus offers Christ as the exegetical key to the Psalter in a wide variety of ways. Sometimes his only explication of a verse consists of a brief citation of Christ's words from the Gospels, such as the "I am" sayings described above. More often he presents Christ as the underlying meaning of images that recur throughout the Psalter, such as "king," "shepherd," "judge," "wisdom," and "sun." In his exegesis of Psalm 126:1, Evagrius offers a rationale for this approach, explaining that Christ will be perceived and comprehended in various ways according to one's level of spiritual maturity:

> Ps. 126:1. *Unless the Lord builds the house, in vain do they labor who build it; unless the Lord keeps watch over the city, in vain does the watcher keep vigil.*
>
>> Scholion 2. Insofar as the soul may be compared to a house, it possesses within itself the Christ as master of the house; if it then becomes a city it possesses within itself the Christ enthroned as king. And if it then becomes a temple, it possesses the Christ within itself as the existing God. For it is through the *praktikē* that it acquires him as master of the house, through natural contemplation as king; and finally through *theologia* as God.[61]

Thus at the level of *praktikē* Christ is "master of the house": he provides a model of correct behavior as well as ethical instruction in the struggle to avoid sin and attain virtue. To this level correspond many of the scholia that describe the struggles of the *praktikē* in general terms,[62] as well as scholia that mention particular virtues and vices. At the level of *physikē* Christ is "enthroned as king" of his "city": that is, the universe which he created. The majority of Evagrius's *Scholia on Psalms* are concerned with this level. As has been described, they encourage the reader to interpret the words and images of the Psalter as symbols of the great cosmic drama of creation, fall, and redemption. Evagrius's frequent evocation of the person and sayings of Christ enables the language and imagery of the Psalter to reflect Christ's work as creator, redeemer, and cause of our sanctification.

A few scholia reach beyond *physikē*, the saving action of Christ in creation, and hint at *theologia*, contemplation of the divine nature and acknowledgment of Christ as "our God."[63] In addition to these are five scholia in which Evagrius employs a unique definition of Christ as "the Lord who with God the Word has come to dwell among us."[64] In his explanation of Psalm 104 Evagrius uses this definition to highlight both Christ's relationship with creation and his unique status:

> Ps. 104:15. *Do not touch my anointed ones.*
>> Scholion 10. Because those who are kind partake of Christ they are called "kind" [χρηστοί]; whereas the Christ who partakes of the Father is called "Christ" [Χριστός = anointed]. By "Christ" I mean the Lord who, with God the Word, has come to dwell among us.[65]

In this scholion Evagrius distinguishes Christ from created beings. He does this by contrasting two similar words: the title *ho Christos*, "the anointed one," and the appellation *hoi chrēstoi*, "the kind ones" or "the honest folk." This contrast between *christos/annointed* and *chrēstos/kindly* is traditional patristic wordplay that Evagrius may have encountered in Clement of Alexandria or Didymus the Blind, and that he evidently enjoyed, since he makes use of it both here and in scholion 7 on Psalm 33:9.[66] To engage in this wordplay Evagrius paraphrases the text of Psalm 104:15, changing the object of the sentence from "my anointed ones" (*christoi*) to "those who are kind" (*chrēstoi*).[67] He explains that the title *Christos* signifies that Christ "partakes of the Father" (*tou patros metechōn*). He employs the verb *metechō*, "to partake in, share" or even "to have communion" in something, to define Christ's anointing: the title *Christos* signifies Christ's relationship of communion with the Father. In an analogous way, but at a significantly lower spiritual level, "those who partake of Christ" (*Christou metechontes*) are "kindly folk" (*chrēstoi*). Evagrius establishes a link between these two analogous but distinct forms of communion through his concluding definition of Christ as "the Lord who, with God the Word, has come to dwell among us." By employing this definition Evagrius draws attention to both Christ's mediation of communion with the Father (his coming among us) and his role as the unique manifestation of God the Word.

The Blessed Trinity in the Psalter

For Evagrius the highest *gnōsis*, and thus the most exalted form of biblical exegesis, concerns *theologia*, doctrine and experience of the Blessed Trinity. Shortly after the Second Ecumenical Council in 381 he wrote a treatise on the Trinity, *The Letter of Faith*, that until recently was attributed to Basil and considered an orthodox précis of Cappadocian theology.[68] In later years he became more cautious, preferring to hint at aspects of the divine nature and eschatological reunion with God in obscure passages of the *Kephalaia Gnostica* and the *Great Letter*. However, these doctrines together with their subjective counterparts in what Evagrius called "pure prayer" are readily discernible in the *Scholia on Psalms*.

Although he uses the term *doctrine* (*dogma*) in his definition of *theologia*, "knowledge of the Blessed Trinity" in Evagrius's sense is not primarily doctrinal:[69] it is, rather, an ever-deepening relationship. Eschatological union with the Blessed Trinity is the goal and limit, the fulfillment and proper end of all human and angelic *gnōsis*. Evagrius responds to the plea of Psalm 38:5, "Lord, make me know my limit [*peras*]" with the assertion "The *limit* of reasoning nature is the knowledge of the Holy Trinity."[70] This limit or end, however, is not static. In words that may reflect Gregory of Nyssa's doctrine of eternal progress in heaven, Evagrius responds to a reference to God's unlimited greatness in Psalm 144 with a succinct meditation on the limitless, infinite nature of *theologia*:[71] "The contemplation of all [created] beings is *limited* [*peperatōtai*]: only knowledge of the Blessed Trinity is *unlimited* [*aperantos*]; for it is essential wisdom."[72] The dynamic image of spiritual progress in heaven recurs in his explication of Psalm 144, where Evagrius evokes Origen's notion of heaven as a classroom where all will learn (or teach) whatever is necessary for a deepening union with God that both reflects the dynamic unity of persons in the Blessed Trinity and fulfills the high priestly prayer of Jesus in John 17.[73]

> Psalm 144:13. *Your kingdom is a kingdom of all the ages: and your dominion through all the generations of generations.*
>
>> Scholion 5. If the kingdom of God is the contemplation of beings and of ages to come, then it is rightly said, "Your kingdom is a kingdom of all the ages." And even more does "generation to generation

unto the ages" signify that some will be teachers and others students. But in the Blessed Trinity "generation to generation" is a way of saying that all will become one in God, according to the prayer of Christ when he says, "Grant to them that they may be one in us, just as you and I, Father, are one" (John 17:21).[74]

A foretaste of this eschatological union is perceptible in the present life, first in the ascent from *praktikē* to *gnōstikḗ*, and then in the progressive movement from contemplation of corporeal and incorporeal beings to contemplation of the mystery of the Blessed Trinity. In his comments on Psalm 54 Evagrius portrays this as ascent on "the wings of a dove": "*Wings* are the holy wings of the contemplation of corporeal and incorporeal [beings] by which the *nous* is raised up to be at rest in the knowledge of the Holy Trinity."[75] Evagrius uses the terms *knowledge* (*gnōsis*) and *contemplation* (*theōria*) of the Blessed Trinity interchangeably; however, both terms become increasingly metaphorical the nearer one draws to God. True knowledge of God reaches beyond words and conceptual understanding.[76] True vision of God is possible only when sense images and even the representations (*noēmata*) and *logoi* of angelic "incorporeal natures" are transcended. Nevertheless, Evagrius insists that this highest *gnōsis* can indeed be described as a kind of vision, an experience of "seeing" the Blessed Trinity:

> Ps. 138:7. *Where shall I go from your Spirit? And where shall I flee from your countenance?*
>> Scholion 3. There is no place that is without the knowledge of God and the *logoi* of beings: for the *nous* fleeing from corporeal beings then experiences their *logoi*; . . . And if the *nous* breaks beyond the *logoi* of incorporeal natures, it then sees the Holy Trinity, which is limitless [*aperantos*] knowledge and essential wisdom.[77]

For Evagrius this possibility of "seeing" the Trinity is associated with his conviction that the *gnōstikos* is capable of apprehending God in a spiritually perceptible light within the *nous*, at the deepest level of the self where the person is most fully the image of God.[78] This experience of mystical, inner light is not as prominent a theme in the *Scholia on Psalms* as is in more advanced texts; however, Evagrius hints at it in his description of a "sun of justice" that all reasoning beings bear within their *nous*. In Psalm 148, mention of the "heaven of heavens" evokes Evagrius's comment that "the noetic *heaven* is reasoning nature that carries within itself the 'sun of justice.'"[79] More prominent in the *Scholia on Psalms* are descriptions of the precondition for this spiritual vision: namely, "angelic" undistracted psalmody and "pure" imageless prayer:

> Ps. 137:1. *and before the angels I will chant psalms to you.*
>   Scholion 1. To chant psalms before the angels is to sing psalms without distraction: either our mind is imprinted [τυπουμένου] solely by the realities symbolized by the psalm, or else it is not imprinted. Or perhaps he who chants psalms before the angels is apprehending the meaning [δύναμιν] of the psalms.[80]

Here Evagrius offers three definitions of chanting psalms "before the angels," which he equates with undistracted psalmody. In the first phrase he states that undistracted psalmody refers to two seemingly opposite experiences. Either the mind is passive with regard to the psalm's inner meanings and receives only their impressions, or it receives no impression at all, presumably because it is solely attentive to the God to whom the psalm bears witness. In the first definition Evagrius recommends that during psalmody the mind, which is particularly subject to being formed and impressed by external matters, should be receptive during psalmody, capable, like wax, of being imprinted (*tupomenos*) by the matters "signified" or "symbolized" by the psalm. By attending exclusively to the realities signified by the psalm, the mind will be formed and shaped only by them. The second definition, according to which the mind is not imprinted at all, alludes to the final goal of psalmody and indeed of every spiritual practice: namely, that the mind be occupied solely with God, who, being incorporeal, leaves no imprint on the *nous*.[81]

In the second phrase Evagrius provides a third definition of undistracted psalmody that complements the first but is less passive. Undistracted psalmody is not merely a willingness to be "stamped" by the matters symbolized by the psalm; it is also an active search for the *dunamis*, the "meaning," the "potentiality," or even the "power" of the psalm. In other words, undistracted psalmody is exclusive attentiveness to the inner meanings of the psalm, those meanings that his scholia on the psalms are intended to reveal.

There thus emerges something of Evagrius's purpose in composing the *Scholia on Psalms*. Undistracted psalmody attentive solely to the inner *dunamis* of the psalm is no easy task. The rich variety of images and events found in each psalm, as well as the poetic beauty of the Psalter, can captivate the mind and distract it from the real end of psalmody: namely, God himself, the only legitimate "distraction" of the soul.[82] Undistracted psalmody requires the ability to move backwards and forwards through the history of salvation amid the rich diversity of creation while perceiving this complexity and variety as a reflection of God's "manifold wisdom." Evagrius's exegetical methods become comprehensible when the *Scholia on Psalms* is viewed as a guide to the practice of undistracted psalmody and an encouragement to that higher state he calls "pure" or imageless prayer:

> Ps. 140:2 *Let my prayer be set forth as incense before you.*
>> Scholion 1. His prayer is set forth like incense who is able to say: we are the fragrance of Christ to God among those who are being saved and among those who are perishing (2 Cor. 2:15). And one form of prayer is "a conversation of the *nous* with God"[83] with the *nous* remaining unstamped. And by *unstamped* I mean that at the time of prayer the *nous* is completely without corporeal fantasies. For only words and names [of corporeal things] stamp an imprint on our *nous* and shape the meanings of what is sensed, while the *nous* at prayer ought to be completely free of what is sensed. And the concept [νόημα] of God necessarily leaves the *nous* unstamped, for he is not corporeal.[84]

The image of incense, floating and seemingly incorporeal, enables Evagrius to reflect on the nature of pure, wordless prayer in which the innermost self, the *nous,* is attentive only to God, free from distractions, "unstamped" by external concerns or temptations. In the liturgical practice of the late fourth century, and especially in monastic communities, opportunities for such prayer recurred regularly frequently throughout the day and night. The term *psalmodia* referred to corporate or private chanting of psalms, interrupted at regular intervals by pauses for prayer. These pauses occurred at the end of psalms or between divisions in longer psalms and generally entailed a change or a series of changes in ritual posture. The prayer offered during these pauses could be vocal or silent and of variable duration (although generally not protracted), depending on circumstances, local practice, and whether the monk lived alone as a hermit or with others in a community (*coenobium*).[85] The intimate relationship between chanted psalmody and the pauses for prayer that punctuated it was such that late fourth-century sources often refer to the practice of psalmody as "the psalms and prayers" or simply as "the prayers." Evagrius's emphasis on undistracted psalmody and imageless prayer are an invitation to the *gnōstikos* to use the *Scholia on Psalms* as a guidebook for entry into either the contemplation of God's diverse glory in creation or the transcendent experience of God that silences all speech and unites into simplicity all thoughts and images.

Conclusion: Reading the Book of God

Evagrius wrote the *Scholia on Psalms* as a handbook for the Christian *gnōstikos.* Chanting the psalms with the aid of the scholia would evoke within the *gnōstikos* reflection on an intertwining spiritual dynamic: *praktikē*, the ongoing struggle for virtue, *apatheia*, and *agape*; and *theōretikē*, contemplation of the origin, nature, and final goal of the universe, and rest in the experience of pure prayer. But the scholia were intended to be more than an aid to the *gnōstikos*'s personal spiritual progress. Such an experience of the Psalter would enable the *gnōstikos* to apply newfound exegetical skills to the "book" that consists of each individual's personal salvation history:

> Ps.138.16 [2] *And in your book all shall be written.*
>> Scholion 8. The book of God is the contemplation of corporeal and incorporeal beings, in which the pur[ified] *nous* comes to be written through knowledge. For in this book are written the *logoi* of providence and judgment, through which book God is known as creator, wise, provident, and judging: creator through the things that have come from nonbeing into being; wise through his *logoi*,

concealed within them; provident, through what is accomplished for our virtue and knowledge; and furthermore judge, through the variety of bodies of the reasoning beings, and through the multiform worlds and the ages they contain.[86]

In this scholion Evagrius describes a "Book of God" in which the *nous,* the deepest level of each person, is somehow inscribed with the mysteries of angels and divine *logoi.* This notion of the individual *nous* and the whole of creation together constituting a "divine book" did not originate with Evagrius, and it would enjoy a long and fruitful history in the later history of Christian spirituality, becoming a commonplace among medieval authors and their later admirers. However, for Evagrius, unlike many later authors, the concept of a book of God that contains both the external creation and the interior cosmos of ideas (*noēmata*) is not simply an attractive metaphor: rather, it reflects both Evagrius's pastoral methodology and his conviction that the arts of biblical exegesis and spiritual guidance are profoundly interrelated. Evagrius's approach to both biblical exegesis and spiritual guidance may be summarized as an attempt to perceive and describe everything in the light of a divine origin and an eternal destiny, or as Columba Stewart has described it, within a "unified vision of everything."[87] As a biblical exegete, Evagrius's *gnōstikos* would discover in the book of Psalms symbols and allegories of the great cosmic drama of the Fall, the Incarnation, and the eschatological reunion of all reasoning beings with God. As spiritual guide the *gnōstikos* could then, as it were, look up from the Bible to perceive the movements and experiences of each disciple and pilgrim as part of the "Book of God," a miniature iteration and reflection of the universal cosmic journey toward reunion. Thus the drama of each soul's inner struggle would be illuminated by the sweeping movements and symbolic imagery of biblical salvation history.

Notes

1. Extant are Evagrius's scholia on the books of Psalms, Proverbs, Ecclesiastes, and Job. He probably also wrote a commentary on the Song of Songs and perhaps on other biblical books as well, but of these no certain traces remain. Hans Urs von Balthasar discusses fragments suggestive of commentaries, now

lost, on books of the Pentateuch and the Song of Songs: "Die *Hiera* des Evagrius," *Zeitschrift für katholische Theologie* 63 (1939): 87–89. Also suggestive of a lost commentary on the Song of Songs are recently discovered *kephalaia* in which Evagrius deliberately imitates both the style and the themes of the Song of Songs: Paul Géhin, "Evagriana d'un Manuscrit Basilien (*Vaticanus Gr. 2028; olim Basilianus 67*)," *Muséon* 109 (1996): 71–73.

2. *Scholia on Ecclesiastes* (ed. and trans. Paul Géhin, *Évagre le Pontique Scholies a L'Ecclésiaste*, SC 397 [Paris: Cerf, 1993]); *Scholia on Proverbs* (ed. and trans. Paul Géhin, *Évagre le Pontique Scholies aux Proverbes*, SC 340 [Paris: Cerf, 1987]).

3. Evagrius, scholion 5 *on Psalm* 88.9 (AS 3, 88.9[2]: 160).

4. Although still awaiting a critical edition, the majority (over 95 percent) of the scholia in Evagrius's *Scholia on Psalms* may be assembled from printed sources, according to a key published by Marie-Josèphe Rondeau, "Le commentaire sur les Psaumes d'Évagre le Pontique," *Orientalia Christiana Periodica* 26 (1960): 307–48. Rondeau's reconstruction is based on MS Vaticanus Graecus 754 (tenth century, 395 ff., *Psalmi et cantica cum catena*, Karo-Lietzman Cat.: 39–41). For a working edition of Evagrius's *Scholia on Psalms*, based on Rondeau's key and my own reworking of Rondeau's trancription of MS VG 754, see Evagrius, "Scholia on Psalms," trans. Luke Dysinger, http://ldysinger.stjohnsem.edu/Evagrius/08_Psalms/00a_start.htm. This is the text upon which I have based my translations of Evagrius's *Scholia on Psalms*. I refer to the PG text only for the convenience of readers who lack access to the Vatican MS, but readers should keep in mind that the text I employ frequently departs from PG.

5. A. Veilleux argues that in the primitive Pachomian office of the early fourth century there was no particular preference for psalmody and that the office consisted largely of consecutive scripture readings, each followed by the prayers Cassian describes in book 2 of the *Institutes* (*La liturgie dans le cénobitisme pachômien au quatrième siècle*, Studia anselmiana 57 [Rome: IBC Libreria Herder, 1968]: 276–323).

6. J. McKinnon, "Desert Monasticism and the Later Fourth-Century Psalmodic Movement," *Music and Letters* 75 (1994): 506. With regard to this widespread, accelerating enthusiasm for psalms in the fourth century, the same author asserts, "Nothing quite like it has been observed either before or after in the history of Christianity or Judaism" ("The Fourth Century Origin of the Gradual," *Early Music History* 7 [1987]: 98).

7. For Greek text and a French translation, see Marguerite Harl, *Sur les écritures: Philocalie, 1–20*, SC 226 (Paris: Cerf, 1983), and Éric Junod, *Sur le libre arbitre: Philocalie 21–27*, SC 302 (Paris: Cerf, 1976). There is an English translation by George Lewis, *The Philocalia of Origen* (Edinburgh: T. and T. Clark, 1911).

8. Precisely when Evagrius was first condemned remains something of a mystery. The Lateran Synod of 649 is the first council to explicitly name Evagrius in a list of twenty-one condemned authors. However, it is widely believed that his

name may have appeared in anathemas of the sixth century. In the surviving texts of the fourteen anathemas of the Second Council of Constantinople (the Fifth Ecumenical Council) in 553 there is no mention of Evagrius; however, accounts by two contemporaries of the council who had access to the conciliar decrees suggest that the surviving texts may be incomplete and that the names of both Evagrius and Didymus may originally have appeared together with that of Origen in the list of condemned heretics.

9. See Columba Stewart, "Evagrius Ponticus on Monastic Pedagogy," in *Abba, the Tradition of Orthodoxy in the West: Festschrift for Bishop Kallistos (Ware) of Diokleia,* ed. John Behr, Andrew Louth, and Dimitri Conomos (Crestwood, NY: St. Vladimir's Seminary Press, 2003), 241–71.

10. These roughly correspond to the divisions of the Platonic tripartite soul, beginning with the *epithumetikon* (concupiscible faculty), moving through the *thumikon* (irascible faculty), and concluding with intellectual temptations. See "Ascetical Wisdom in the Psalter" below on Evagrius's assignment of different virtues to each of these parts of the soul.

11. *Apatheia* does not mean freedom from temptation, since Evagrius emphasizes that certain temptations will continue until death (*Praktikos* 36); rather, it refers to freedom from the inner storm of passions' irrational drives, which in their extreme forms would today be called obsessions, compulsions, or addictions (*Praktikos* prol. 8, ch. 81).

12. Stewart, *Evagrius Ponticus,* 254–68. Jeremy Driscoll also discusses the complex interrelationships and progressive nature of Evagrius's sentences in *The Ad Monachos of Evagrius Ponticus: Its Structure and a Select Commentary,* Studia anselmiana 104 (Rome: Pontificio Ateneo S. Anselmo, 1991).

13. Evagrius, *Gnōstikos* 44 (SC 356 [1989]: 174).

14. On spiritual definitions of biblical terms, see Evagrius, *Gnōstikos* 17 (SC 356 [1989]: 114–16); on the customary expressions of scripture, see Evagrius, *Gnōstikos* 19 (SC 356 [1989]: 118 f); on allegorical exegesis, see Evagrius, *Gnōstikos* 20–1 (SC 356 [1989]: 118–21).

15. Clement, *Strom.* 1.28.179, 3–4; Origen, *Comm. Cant.* prol. 3.6.

16. Evagrius, *Gnōstikos* 18 (SC 356 [1989]: 116–18).

17. Evagrius, scholion 4 *on Psalm* 47:8 (PG 12: 1440).

18. Evagrius, scholion 8 *on Psalm* 88:13 (PG 12: 1548).

19. In addition to the two examples given, Evagrius cites Josephus on the fate of Jerusalem in scholia 1 and 2 *on Psalm* 73.

20. The *Antirrhetikos* consists of 494 brief texts from the scriptures, each preceded by a description of the *logismos* the text is intended to counteract. It is divided into eight chapters, each devoted to one of the eight principal *logismoi* of gluttony, lust, avarice, sadness, anger, *acedia*, vainglory, and pride. Of the 494 verses in this work, 91 are taken from the book of Psalms. For a modern translation with

introduction and commentary, see David Brakke, *Evagrius of Pontus: Talking Back, Antirrhetikos, A Monastic Handbook for Combating Demons* (Collegeville, MN: Cistercian Publications, 2009). The recommendations of a practice of *antirrhesis* in Evagrius's other works are in *Praktikos* 42 and *De oratione* 94–99, 134–35. Bunge speculates that Evagrius may at one time have intended the *Antirrhetikos* to be published as part of the *Praktikos*, or at least to be read in conjunction with it; G. Bunge, "Evagrios Pontikos: Der Prolog des *Antirrhetikos*," *Studia Monastica* 39 (1997): 83.

21. Evagrius, *Antirrhetikos*, prol. (ed. Wilhelm Frankenberg, *Euagrius Pontikos*, Abhandlungen der Königlichen Gesellschaft der Wissenschaften zu Göttingen, Philologisch-historische Klasse, Neue Folge, 13.2 (Berlin: Weidmannsche Buchhandlung, 1912), 474–75.

22. Evagrius, scholion 7 *on Psalm* 91:12 (AS 3, 91.12: 172).

23. Evagrius, scholion 1 *on Psalm* 126:1 (PG 24: 20).

24. Evagrius, scholion 6 *on Psalm* 61:11 (AS 3, 61.11[3]: 70). The other three verses intended for the wealthy are: are scholion 14 *on Psalm* 10:30; scholion 8 *on Psalm* 38:7; and scholion 4 *on Psalm* 14:5 (particularly directed against usurers).

25. Scholion 16 *on Psalm* 108:24; scholion 4 *on Psalm* 100:5; scholion 4 *on Psalm* 25:5; scholion 5 *on Psalm* 37:8; scholion 5 *on Psalm* 101:10.

26. On neglect of prayers, see Evagrius, scholion 27 *on Psalm* 118:62 (PG 12: 1600). On lack of discretion in exegesis of scripture, see Evagrius, scholion 4 *on Psalm* 111:5 (AS 3, 111.5[2]: 231; PG 12: 1572). The other two are scholion 44 *on Psalm* 118:100 and scholion 37 *on Psalm* 118:85.

27. Evagrius, scholion 6 *on Psalm* 41:12 (AS 3, 41.8: 37). Additional encouraging antirrhetic scholia include scholia 6 and 8 *on Psalm* 89:12; scholia 10 *on Psalm* 43:17 and 6 *on Psalm* 100:6.

28. Evagrius, scholion 1 *on Psalm* 24:1–3 (PG 27: 144). The other three antirrhetic prayers are scholia 31 *on Psalm* 118:71; 7 *on Psalm* 25:9; and 8 *on Psalm* 26:12.

29. Evagrius, *Praktikos* 50.

30. The concept of spiritual warfare was popular with both biblical and Alexandrian writers. St. Paul describes both a "warfare against the law of the mind" (Rom. 7:23); and "passions of the flesh that wage war on the soul" (2 Cor. 10:3–4). Similar imagery is also employed by the authors of 1 Tim. 1:18 and 1 Peter 2:11. Origen invokes the notion of spiritual warfare in *Phil.* 15, *Or.* 3, *Contra Celsum* 8.44, *Homiliae in Lucam* 3 (Homily 10 on Luke 1:67–76), and *Peri Pascha* 48.

31. Evagrius, *Praktikos* 89 (SC 171: 680–84). Plato's description of the tripartite soul is found in *Phaedrus* 246a and *Republic* 4.440–42. As for the later Aristotelian tradition: the beginning of chapter 89 of Evagrius's *Praktikos*, where the virtues are divided among the soul's three divisions, is modeled closely on an anonymous first-century peripatetic treatise, *On Virtues and Vices*, in *Aristotelis opera*, ed. Immanuel Bekker, vol. 2 (Berlin: Reimer, 1831): 1249a 26–1251b 37.

32. Evagrius, scholion 2 *On Psalm* 107:3 (AS 3, 107.3: 220).

33. Evagrius, *Peri Logismon* 17 (SC 438: 210).

34. Evagrius, *Praktikos* 89 (SC 171: 680, 682).

35. Evagrius, *Praktikos* 25; *De oratione* 12, 13, 24, 25.

36. Evagrius, scholion 4 *on Psalm* 23:7 (PG 12: 1268).

37. Evagrius, scholion 6 *on Psalm* 44:6 (PG 12: 1429).

38. Evagrius, scholion 5 *on Psalm* 22:1.

39. Evagrius, scholion 1 *on Psalm* 6:2 (AS 2, 6.2–3: 456). Adapted from Clement of Alexandria: "Wrath is the impulse of concupiscence in a mild soul, prominently seeking irrational revenge," *Strom.* 5.5.27–28.

40. Evagrius, scholion 3 *on Psalm* 24:4 (PG 12: 1269).

41. Evagrius, scholion 1 *on Psalm* 131:1 (PG 12: 1649; AS 3, 131.1, 1: 329).

42. Evagrius, scholion 2 *on Psalm* 147:3 (PG 12: 1677).

43. Evagrius, scholion 5 *on Psalm* 4:6 (AS 2, 4.6.1: 453). In scholion 2 *on Psalm* 1.1, Evagrius writes similarly, "Blessedness is *apatheia* of the soul together with true knowledge of things that exist" (PG 12: 1085).

44. In *Gnōstikos* 28 Evagrius recommends study of "the five reasons for abandonment," a doctrine that was taken up and adapted by later monastic authors, including Maximus the Confessor (*Centuries on Charity* 4.96) and the Pseudo-Damascene (cited by Nicetas, PG 96: 1412). This doctrine ultimately derives from Origen, who discussed it in the context of the hardening of Pharaoh's heart (*De princ.* 3.1, *Or.* 29.17). Jeremy Driscoll discusses Evagrius's teaching on providential abandonment in "Evagrius and Paphnutius on the Causes for Abandonment by God," *Studia Monastica* 39 (1997): 259–86.

45. Evagrius, scholion 8 *on Psalm* 93:18 (PG 12: 1553).

46. Evagrius, scholion 8 *on Psalm* 37:12 (PG 12: 1368). Evagrius cites and interprets Psalm 37:12 in the same way in *Antirrhetikos* 6.17.

47. Evagrius, scholion 1 *on Psalm* 89:3 (AS 3, 89.3[1]: 167).

48. Evagrius, scholion 20 *on Psalm* 36:25 (AS 3, 36.25[1]: 11–12).

49. Evagrius, scholion 30 *on Psalm* 118:70 (PG 12: 1600–1601).

50. Evagrius, scholion 2 *on Psalm* 117:10 (PG 12: 1580).

51. Evagrius, scholion 2 *on Psalm* 134:6 (PG 12: 1653; AS 3, 134.5–6.3: 333–34).

52. Evagrius, scholion 275 *on Proverbs* 24:22 (SC 340: 370).

53. Evagrius, scholion 8 *on Psalm* 1:5 (PG 12: 1097–1100).

54. Evagrius, scholion 1 *on Psalm* 94:4 (PG 12: 1555).

55. Evagrius, scholion 7 *on Psalm* 16:13 (cf. PG 12: 1221).

56. Evagrius, scholion 6 *on Psalm* 4:7 (AS 2, 4.7[1]: 453–54). The same interpretation and citation from 2 Sam. is found in scholion 7 *on Psalm* 29:8 (PG 12: 1296).

57. The title *christos* is explained or employed in 159 scholia, and of 130 scholia in which Evagrius comments on the title *kurios*, he applies this title to Christ in the majority of instances. Christ is invoked as "Savior" in twenty-four scholia, and the name "Jesus" appears in eight.

58. These citations are distributed fairly evenly throughout the *Scholia on Psalms*, appearing thirty-one times in twenty-nine different scholia: "I am the life" (John 11:25, 14:6) is used in nine scholia; "I am the way" (John 14:6) in eight; "I am the truth" (John 14:6) in five; "I am the bread which came down from heaven" (John 6:41) in four; "I am the good shepherd" (John 10:11, 14) in two; "I am the light of the world" (John 8:12, 9:5) once; "I am (lit. 'it is I')—do not fear" (Mark 6:50) once; and "I am your salvation" (Ps. 34:3) once.

59. In her study of patristic commentaries on the Psalter, Rondeau coined the term *l'exégèse prosopologique* to describe the widespread interest of early commentators in the question, "Whose face [*prosōpon*] lies behind the psalm?" Or put more simply, "Who is praying the psalm?" She points out that patristic exegesis of the Psalter often begins with the determination whether a text should be regarded as David's prayer, as the prayer of Jesus Christ, or as our own prayer (Marie-Josèphe Rondeau, *Les commentaires patristiques du Psautier (IIIe–Ve siècles)*, 2 vols., OCA 219–20 [Rome: Pontificium Institutum Studiorum Orientalium, 1982–85], 2: 21–89).

60. On the identification of Christ with the wisdom of God, see Evagrius, scholia 3 *on Psalm* 21:7(1); 6 *on Psalm* 21:15(2); 8 *on Psalm* 21:19(1); 1 *on Psalm* 30:2(2); 1 *on Psalm* 32:1(1); 2 *on Psalm* 33:3(1); 15 *on Psalm* 34:26(1); 10 *on Psalm* 76:15(1); 2 *on Psalm* 79:5(1); 3 *on Psalm* 84:10(1); 9 *on Psalm* 93:15(1); 2 *on Psalm* 118:3; 4 *on Psalm* 131:6(2); 4 *on Psalm* 135:23; 3 *on Psalm* 141:6(3). This identification of Christ with the wisdom of God is also found in *Kephalaia Gnostica* 2.2; 2.21; 3.3; 3.11; 3.81; 4.4; 4.7; 5.5; and 5.84. On the identification of Christ with the wisdom of Eph. 3:10, see Evagrius, scholia 8 *on Psalm* 44:10, and 1 *on Psalm* 122:1.

61. Evagrius, scholion 2 *on Psalm* 126:1 (PG 12: 1641–44).

62. Christ is example or teacher of the *praktikē* in scholia 4 *on Psalm* 18:9; 1 *on Psalm* 26:2; 2 *on Psalm* 27:2; 1 *on Psalm* 30:2; 8 *on Psalm* 32; 9 *on Psalm* 32; 15 *on Psalm* 42:23; 3 *on Psalm* 44:4; 4 *on Psalm* 44:5; 6 *on Psalm* 44:6(1); 13 *on Psalm* 67:19; 7 *on Psalm* 85:11; *on Psalm* 100:8; 13 *on Psalm* 108:19; 25 *on Psalm* 118: 61; 2 *on Psalm* 119:4; 4 *on Psalm* 119:7; 1 *on Psalm* 126:1; 4 *on Psalm* 136:7; 5 *on Psalm* 136:9; 1 *on Psalm* 143:1; 5 *on Psalm* 143:7–8.

63. Evagrius, scholion 7 *on Psalm* 47:15(1.3): "The Christ is our God who shepherds us" (PG 12: 1441); scholion 1 *on Psalm* 49:2(2): "For our God is the Christ" (PG 12: 1449 and PG 27: 229–32); scholion 4(b) *on Psalm* 49:6(2): "The divine judge is the Christ" (PG 12: 1452, PG 27: 232); scholion 10 *on Psalm* 76:15: "*You are the God who works wonders. . . .* This is the Christ; for Christ is *the power and the wisdom of God* (1 Cor 1:24)" (PG 12: 1540).

64. Evagrius employs this definition five times with minor variations in the *Scholia on Psalms*: scholia 7 *on Psalm* 44:3; 10 *on Psalm* 104:15; 2 *on Psalm* 118:3; 5 *on Psalm* 131:7; and 4 *on Psalm* 88:7(2). Antoine Guillaumont maintained that this formula and the scholia containing it attest to a "christologie très particulière" that contributed to Evagrius's eventual condemnation for heresy (*Les "Kephalaia Gnostica," d'Evagre le Pontique et l'histoire de l'Origénisme chez les Grecs et chez les Syriens*, Patristica Sorbonensia 5 [Paris: Editions du Seuil, 1962], 147). F. Refoulé has undertaken a detailed study of Evagrius's Christology, generally agreeing with Guillaumont's findings, in "La christologie d'Évagre et l'Origénisme," *Orientalia Christiana Periodica* 27 (1961): 251–66. Their findings and conclusions are accepted by A. Grillmeier in his influential study (*Christ in Christian Tradition: From the Apostolic Age to Chalcedon (451)*, rev. ed., trans. John Bowden [Atlanta, GA: John Knox Press, 1975], 377–84). Recent Evagrian scholarship (Gabriel Bunge, "Origenismus-Gnostizismus: Zum geistesgeschichtliche Standort des Evagrios Pontikos," *Vigiliae Christianae* 40 (1986): 25–27; Luke Dysinger, *Psalmody and Prayer in the Writings of Evagrius Ponticus*, Oxford Theological Monographs [Oxford: Oxford University Press, 2005], App. 1: "The *Nous* of Christ in the *Kephalaia Gnostica*," 199–211; Augustine Casiday, *Reconstructing the Theology of Evagrius Ponticus: Beyond Heresy* [Cambridge: Cambridge University Press, 2013]) has generally emphasized that Evagrius's definition would have been considered at least marginally orthodox from the perspective of late fourth-century Christology, if not by the standards of later councils, although some scholars (such as Julia Konstantinovsky, *Evagrius Ponticus: The Making of a Gnostic* [Farnham: Ashgate, 2009]) continue to favor Guillaumont's conclusions.

65. Evagrius, scholion 10 *on Psalm* 104:15 (PG 12: 1564). Evagrius's wordplay and distinctions (*christoi/chrēstoi*) are not apparent in the version of this text in the PG; they become clear only when corrected by the version in MS Vat. Gr. 754, fol. 258v.

66. Clement, *Strom.* 2.4.18.3.1; 6.17.149.5; Didymus, *De Trinitate* 39.712.6. In commenting on the verse "Taste, and see that the Lord is kind [*chrēstos*]," Evagrius explains, "If the Lord is tasted, it is through faith that he is tasted; and if he is kind [*chrēstos*], it is through knowledge that he is [known as] Christ [*christos*, 'anointed']" (PG 12: 1308).

67. His decision to paraphrase the biblical text in this way is noteworthy, since he was unquestionably familiar with another time-honored wordplay that would have permitted him to leave the text intact. The comparison between Christ's title and the baptismal chrismation that allows the newly baptized to be called *hoi christoi*, "the christs," is extremely common in patristic sources: indeed, Evagrius was present in Constantinople when Gregory Nazianzen preached his Fifth Theological Oration, which makes this very point.

68. Joel Kalvesmaki, "The *Epistula fidei* of Evagrius of Pontus: An Answer to Constantinople," *Journal of Early Christian Studies* 20 (2012): 113–39.

69. For his definition of *theologia*, see Evagrius, *Gnōstikos* 18, cited above. See Gehín's defense of *dogma* as the most probable rendering of the Syriac and Armenian versions of the text (SC 344: 114).

70. Evagrius, scholion 3 *on Psalm* 38:5 (PG 12: 1388–89).

71. Gregory writes of eternal *epektasis*, "straining forward" toward God: Gregory of Nyssa, "Homily 12 on the Song of Songs," *Canticum canticorum (homiliae 15)* (GNO 6: 291, 352).

72. Evagrius, scholion 2 *on Psalm* 144:3 (AS 3, 144.3[2]: 354).

73. Origen, *De princ.* 2.6.

74. Evagrius, scholion 5 *on Psalm* 144.13 (AS 3, 114:13[1–2]: 355–6; PG 12: 1673).

75. Evagrius, scholion 2 *on Psalm* 54:75 (PG 12: 1466).

76. Evagrius positively describes "one ignorance which has an end [*peras*] and another without end" (*Praktikos* 87 [SC 171: 678]). However, such explicitly apophatic language is rare in the *Scholia on Psalms*, where the term *ignorance* (*agnosia*) is generally understood negatively, paired with *vices* (*kakia*) to describe the manifestation of evil in the reasoning intellect.

77. Evagrius, scholion 3 *on Psalm* 138:7 (AS 3, 138.7: 342).

78. Evagrius mentions the "light of the *nous*" in *Praktikos* 64, *Gnōstikos* 45, *De oratione* 74, *Skemmata* 25, *Kephalaia Gnostica* 5.42, *Antirrhetikos* 2.36, and *Peri Logismon* 30, 37, 40, 43. Columba Stewart discusses this theme in "Imageless Prayer and the Theological Vision of Evagrius Ponticus," *Journal of Early Christian Studies* 9 (2001): 173–204.

79. Evagrius, scholion 3 *on Psalm* 148:4 (PG 12: 1680).

80. Evagrius, scholion 1 *on Psalm* 137:1 (AS 3, 137.1: 340).

81. See scholion 1 *on Psalm* 140:2(1), cited below, on the susceptibility of the *nous* to being imprinted or molded (*tupoō*) by the external world through the senses.

82. In *On Prayer* 34 Evagrius uses the term *distracted* in a positive sense: "For what is higher than conversing with God and being occupied in [lit: 'being distracted by' (*perispasthai*)] communion with him?" (PG 79:1173; trans. Simon Tugwell, *Evagrius Ponticus: Praktikos and On Prayer* [Oxford: Oxford University, Faculty of Theology, 1987], 8).

83. Evagrius employs this same definition of prayer in *On Prayer* 3: it is taken from Clement of Alexandria, *Strom.* 7.7.38.6.

84. Evagrius, scholion 1 *on Psalm* 140:2 (PG 12: 1665; AS 3, 140.2[1]:148).

85. Cassian describes the monastic practice of psalmody interspersed with intervals for prayer in *Institutes* 2.5–8. Bunge discusses the implications of this practice for Evagrius's texts on psalmody in *Das Geistgebet, Studien zum Traktat "De oratione" des Evagrios Pontikos* (Cologne: Luthe, 1987), 13–14. Elsewhere Bunge

speculates concerning the *Sitz im Leben* of the *Scholia on Psalms*: he concludes that these texts and Evagrius's recommendations of undistracted psalmody are less applicable to the common recitation of the monastic office in communities than to the more leisurely, solitary meditation on the Psalter practiced by hermits like Evagrius in the privacy of their cell. "'Der Mystische Sinn der Schrift' Anlässlich der Veröffentlichung der Scholien zum Ecclesiasten des Evagrios Pontikos," *Studia Monastica* 36 (Rome: Collegio Sant' Anselmo, 1994), 142.

    86. Evagrius, scholion 8 *on Psalm* 138:16 (PG 12: 1662).

    87. Stewart, "Imageless Prayer," 174.

Gender Allegories in Basil of Caesarea's Homily on Psalm 45

Nonna Verna Harrison

Psalm 45, or 44 in the Septuagint numeration Basil used, is unusual in that it celebrates a royal wedding. It appears to have originated in the northern kingdom of Israel, and scholars of Hebrew scripture have suggested that it may actually have been written to honor the marriage of Ahab and Jezebel.[1] If this is true, its subsequent interpretations manifest the irony of historical process and perhaps disclose the sublime humor of divine providence. Early Christian exegetes understood this psalm to be prophesying and praising the marriage between Christ and the church, a reading that has deep roots in the biblical story of love between God and Israel. To borrow a phrase from Gregory Nazianzen, the Ahab and Jezebel of canonical scripture are not types but antitypes of this divine love relationship.[2] Yet in the mind of the Christian community through the centuries, their presence in Psalm 44 has been forgotten and displaced by a greater presence.

In Christian theology, this psalm's interpretation became a privileged locus of Christological reflection. This began already in the New Testament. In Hebrews 1:8–9, Psalm 44:5–6 is quoted and read as referring to Christ. In an excellent monograph, Elisabeth Grünbeck traces the variations in the psalm's exegesis among early Christian writers and shows how they express the Christological concerns and controversies in each period from the second to the fifth centuries.[3] By Basil's time, its reading as a prophetic allegory of Christ and the church is a universal and long-standing tradition. The psalm is read together with the Song of Songs in a common context. Basil elsewhere explicitly disapproves the use of allegory and often focuses on the literal meaning of scripture, looking for what God directs people to do.[4] Yet in this homily we see his work as an allegorical exegete. Pio Tamburrino has shown how he borrows from Origen in this text.[5]

Like all of the material to which we have alluded, this homily is also interesting because the imagery of bride and groom is replete with masculine and feminine symbolism. This chapter will examine these themes as part of my investigation of gender language in the Cappadocian fathers. This task involves a number of complexities whose character I will now elucidate.

THE COMPLEXITIES OF GENDER LANGUAGE

The concepts and imagery of male and female that occur in patristic writings belong largely to three categories that correspond to the three levels of biblical meaning that Origen identifies in *De principiis* 4.2.4 and links to body, soul, and spirit. First is the "literal" level, referring to the biology of the human body or the ontology of the human person, as when men and women are said to be created in the image of God. The ontology of the divine nature, in which the Cappadocians believe the created property of gender is absent, also belongs to this category. Second is the moral or psychological level, which in the Middle Ages would be called "tropology." On this level, human faculties, virtues, and vices that occur in both men and women are symbolized through the gender categories of late antique culture as masculine and feminine. Much of the descriptive and prescriptive language about the "masculine woman" as soldier and athlete and the implicitly "feminine" man as virgin and mother belongs in this category. A third level of allegory refers to mystical, anagogical, and eschatological relationships between divine and human persons, above all between Christ and the church. Although these three levels of meaning are clearly interrelated, gender concepts function differently in the context of each.[6]

In Basil's view, the divine image and likeness are central and definitive in human ontology. It follows that the most important aspects of what men and women are, and what they are called to do and become, are common to all human beings. He summarizes his position in his *Homily on Psalm 1*: "For the virtue of man and woman is one, since also the creation is of equal honor for both, and so the reward for both is the same. Listen to Genesis. 'God,' It says, 'created the human; in the image of God he created him; male and female he created them.' And as the nature is one, their activities also are the same; and as the work is equal, their reward also is the same."[7] Moreover, as he says in his treatise *On Baptism*, in the life to come likeness to Christ and unity in him will displace characteristics such as class, ethnicity, and gender that in this life divide and limit the full actualization of human perfection.[8] Thus, as he says in his *Homily on Psalm 114*, "There is no male or female in the Resurrection, but there is one certain life and it is of one kind, since those dwellings in the land of the living are well pleasing to their Master."[9] Accordingly, as I have shown elsewhere, for Basil as for Gregory Nazianzen and Gregory of Nyssa, the gender distinction is a secondary and temporary feature of the human condition.[10]

Because concepts and symbols of male and female do not denote ultimate realities on a literal or ontological level, Basil is free in his *Homily on Psalm 44* to transfer them to allegorical usages that serve as verbal icons through which he can perceive or depict the realities of God's kingdom that transcend actual maleness and femaleness. Gregory of Nyssa will carry this mode of reflection further, especially in his *Commentary on the Songs of Songs*. The first sentence of the homily identifies its primary concern; he says that Psalm 44 "seems to be one that is adapted to perfecting human nature and that provides assistance for attaining the prescribed end for those who have elected to live in virtue."[11] Thus the themes will be ascetic spirituality and the theology of the human person, topics that Philip Rousseau has identified as among Basil's major interests.[12] These themes point to contexts in which moral and psychological allegories naturally arise, so the homily emphasizes this level of meaning. However, the imagery of bride and groom and the tradition of Christian interpretation he has inherited lead Basil first of all to develop Christological and ecclesiological allegories. As Grünbeck has shown, in opposition to Eunomius and the Neo-Arians, he stresses the full divinity of Christ.[13] The homily will therefore enable us to explore examples of moral and psychological uses of gender language as naming human faculties and virtues perceived as masculine and feminine, language depicting Christ and the church as "spiritually" masculine and feminine, and ways in which these two levels of figurative meaning connect with each other.

CHRIST AS MORAL EXAMPLE

Once concepts of masculine and feminine are used figuratively as referring to aspects of spiritual life, many conjunctions, crossovers, and paradoxes that would not have been acceptable in speaking of "literal" late antique social roles become not only possible but necessary.[14] On the moral and psychological level, this happens in a relatively straightforward way. The human faculties, virtues and vices perceived as masculine and feminine in late antiquity, are actually characteristics belonging to men and women alike. Allegory enables Basil and his contemporaries to bypass culturally prescribed stereotypes and speak of these aspects of universally human moral and ascetical experience. Their aim is simply to encourage people to grow toward a wholeness that includes the virtues associated with both genders. In our homily, we can expect to find that Basil recommends to his audience, which probably includes both women and men, both the "masculine" virtues he perceives in Christ the Bridegroom and the "feminine" virtues he perceives in the church as bride.[15]

However, because of other theological concerns, what emerges is somewhat different from this simple balanced picture. Much of what he says about the groom is Christological, analyzing who our Lord is rather than prescribing his example for others. This is especially true of passages that emphasize his divine nature and mighty works, some of which we will analyze below. Yet in two places Christ is proposed as an example. When commenting on the text "You have loved justice and hated iniquity" (Ps. 44:8), Basil begins by contrasting Jesus and fallen humans. While our Lord naturally is drawn to good and turns away from evil, others achieve an inclination toward virtue and a disinclination toward vice only through labor and ascetic practice. Still, Basil declares that people can follow Christ's example: "Yet it is not hard for us, if we wish it, to take up a love for justice and a hatred for iniquity. God has advantageously given all power to the rational soul, as that of loving, so also that of hating, in order that, guided by reason, we may love virtue but hate vice. It is possible at times to use even hatred in a praiseworthy manner."[16]

This is a perceptive psychological point about how human reason can use strong emotions for good purposes, even in the case of hatred. Here one discerns the late antique masculine ideal of rational control over emotion, but it is transformed to reflect the more positive stance toward emotions found in the psalm. The capacity to experience them is a gift of God, and they provide the energy needed to strive zealously for virtue and turn resolutely away from evil. However, this is more of an issue of human psychology as such than a matter of gender.

Jesus is also offered as an example in Basil's discussion of Psalm 44:5, "Because of truth and meekness and justice." In this paragraph, our Lord's truth is said to point to his rule among humans held captive by sin and deceit so as to "sow the truth again," since he is the truth.[17] The language of sowing alludes to the Parable of the Sower and may hint in passing at figuratively masculine spiritual generativity, but the reference is to his divine truth and sovereignty. Christ's justice in not discussed in this paragraph, though it is discussed elsewhere in the homily. His meekness is what Basil proposes as a moral example, addressing the Lord directly: "'Because of meekness,' in order that by your example all may be led forth to clemency and goodness. Wherefore, the Lord also said: 'Learn from me, for I am meek and humble in heart' (Matt. 11:29). And he showed this meekness in his works themselves; 'when he was reviled, he was silent' (1 Pet. 2:23); when he was scourged, he endured."[18]

If this is a portrayal of masculine virtue, as it surely is, the content of the manly ideal has been radically transformed from the usual late antique depiction of the victorious soldier or the powerful civic leader. Endurance of hardship can indeed be a military virtue and clemency an aspect of good civic leadership, but Jesus's humility, gentleness, and patient acceptance of suffering are more like the virtues associated with women in late antique culture. This is a masculinity radically transformed by the values of the gospel, and above all by the example of Jesus himself.

The cultural revision Basil suggests here echoes his own choice to renounce the traditional career of a civic notable and teacher of rhetoric for the sake of monastic life. Feminist scholars have devoted much attention to the ways in which Christianity challenged, transformed, and/or reaffirmed late antique ideals of feminine behavior.[19] More recently, a similar attentiveness to the new religion's impact on masculine ideals has also emerged.

Basil and his patristic colleagues devote much attention to critiquing received manly values. Such critiques often take the form of attacks on worldly desires for wealth, power, and status, the standard goals of the aristocratic male. The gendered character of much of this rhetoric is genuine and important, though the texts seldom refer to it explicitly. It is often masked by the unreflective androcentrism presupposed by late antique Christian writers and echoed by many of their modern commentators, so that it appears simply as moral instruction for all human beings. It is worth considering whether Christian values challenged late antique norms of masculine conduct far more than the corresponding norms of feminine conduct. Women, after all, were trained by the culture to be meek and chaste, while men were not.[20]

Most of the moral instruction in the homily is associated with the figure of the bride, who is both the queen standing at the right hand of Christ and his beloved daughter (cf. Ps. 44:10–11). Basil identifies her both with the church and with the "soul which is joined to the Word, its bridegroom, not subjected by sin but sharing the kingdom of Christ"[21]— that is, the human person living a truly Christian life. We will now consider the bride in further detail.

THE FIGURE OF THE BRIDE

The place of gender in Christological and ecclesiological allegories is difficult to assess because of the complexities involved in who and what Christ and the church are in patristic theology. Following biblical usage, the fathers often speak figuratively of the church as a kind of corporate entity represented as vine, flock, temple, et cetera, as well as body and bride of Christ. This way of thinking is rooted in the Hebrew notion of God's people Israel as a "corporate personality," and it expresses the early Christians' experience of profound spiritual and ontological unity in the church. Yet the church is not itself a person, a divine or human hypostasis; rather, it is a communion of persons united by love and mutual indwelling. In the broadest sense, this communion includes the Holy Trinity together with the angels, the saints, and all the faithful of every time and place.

Thus, in texts such as patristic homilies on Psalm 44 or the Song of Songs, the figure of the bride could have a number of different referents and often slips quickly from one to another. She could be the company of all the faithful acting as one in their common love of Christ. She could be a part of that company who love and serve God in an exemplary way, such as apostles, saints, virgins, bishops, Mary, or individual Christians striving for spiritual perfection. The church may mean the heavenly community of saints to which the preacher's audience hopes one day to be joined, but in another sense the listeners already are the earthly church. The bride could be the Mother of God or the daughter of the King. On the one hand, she bears the apostles and bishops as her children, and on the other hand, they give birth to her in the baptismal font.[22] In these variegated images, the bride in her familial relationships with her husband, parents, and children depicts many of the rich and diverse ways in which God's people interact in love with each other and with Christ and God. In this kaleidoscope of figurative language it is sometimes difficult to pin down which human persons are at issue, how they are being labeled as figuratively feminine or masculine, and to what exactly this gender language refers. Clearly, great variety is possible in the details of each allegorical interpretation.

Although Basil's homily speaks specifically of two groups within the church, apostles and virgins, for the most part he identifies the bride as the ideal Christian and focuses on her duties and virtues, which are symbolized by her raiment as depicted in the psalm. His description of this figure is a summary of this teaching about the spiritual life. Thus the emphasis is on moral and psychological allegory.

The bride as ideal Christian is well educated in scripture and theology, that is, adorned with varied teachings, moral, natural, and contemplative.[23] This list parallels the three stages of spiritual life later identified by Evagrius Ponticus as practice, contemplation of nature, and contemplation of God.[24] Here Basil appears to refer approvingly to the allegorical interpretation of the Bible and the multiple levels of meaning discovered through this method. This is significant given his negative remarks about allegory, cited above.

He then says that the bride is a daughter adopted and taught by Christ. This imagery would not have appeared strange in late antique culture, since mature men often married teenage girls half their age, assumed the role in loco parentis from their fathers, and educated their wives.[25] Basil says that the bride of Christ is to be trained in the contemplation of the natural world and through it the contemplation of God. She is to listen humbly to the words and stories of the Gospels. Through conversion she is to renounce inherited pagan religious practices and instead submissively adore her Spouse and King, Jesus Christ. Basil adds that this submission and adoration pertain to "all creation."[26] Thus in some sense all created beings function as bride in their encounter with Christ. In a certain sense creaturehood as such is symbolically feminine, since it involves the reception of life from God.

The bride's glory is "within," that is, she prays and does good works in secret (cf. Ps. 44:14, Matt. 6:1–6), not for public display. Such inwardness and hiddenness contrast sharply with the ostentation and competition for status characteristic of late antique aristocratic culture. They correspond to the private roles expected of women, whose primary tasks were associated with the indoors, with private as opposed to public space.[27] Moreover, the bride is to be clothed with the virtues linked to the image of God in the human being. Interestingly, the virtues Basil lists here are "the heart of mercy, kindness, humility, patience, and meekness" (Col. 3:12), quite a "feminine" catalogue. This demonstrates that Basil does not identify the *imago Dei* with masculinity, as "the fathers" are sometimes alleged to do. In a striking reversal of the metaphor of clothing oneself outwardly, he adds that the bride must "put on the Lord Jesus" (Rom. 13:14) inwardly, so that the remembrance of God may cover her whole mind. Her interior garments are to be made of words interwoven with deeds,[28] that is, in a commonplace of Greek patristic ascetic theology, action combined with contemplation.

This passage summarizes major themes in Basil's ascetical and mystical theology. As is characteristic of him, he relies heavily on scripture. The points he stresses here are commonplace, not original, or speculative, and this is why the uses of gender imagery in this text are particularly significant. They reflect standard early Christian modes of thought. Basil emphasizes virtues and modes of activity that his culture would regard as feminine and prescribes them for every member of the church, perhaps even for every creature standing in the presence of the Creator. This mode of activity involves the receptivity of eyes open to contemplate God's beauty and of ears open to hear his teachings. Such spiritual perceptiveness is more like sense perception, which is symbolically feminine in late antiquity, than it is like the symbolically masculine controlling reason. Humility, submissiveness, obedience, and above all adoring love are needed to accept the revealed truth and self-manifestation of a transcendent God. Mindfulness of the overawing presence of such a God decenters the self within one's inward awareness, and acceptance of this decentering presupposes humility and produces greater humility.[29] Such remembrance of God requires a habitual inwardness and hiddenness in one's attitude, whatever the outward circumstances. The natural fruits of this stance in life are gentleness, compassion, meekness, and patience, received in the heart from the Holy Spirit. All these qualities are genuine virtues, without which a deep authentic Christian spiritual life is impossible. They are a natural expression of creaturehood as such and are elicited by the presence of the Creator. They are above all the virtues of the contemplative. It is not too surprising that women brought up in late antiquity could practice these virtues, in which they had been trained from childhood. The radical message of the gospel embodied in Basil's homily is that they can and must belong to men also, indeed to all created beings, including the hosts of angels.

Because in this imperfect world self-serving men have often demanded that women yield absolute submission to themselves (which is ultimately idolatrous, since absolute worship belongs to God alone), today there is an understandable propensity to reject the idea of submission altogether, even that offered to God, along with the cluster of "feminine" receptive virtues that accompany it.[30] Among scholars this tendency is often coupled with a reductive methodology that seeks to explain all human interactions and all historical occurrences in terms of competition for status and power. It is tragic and at the same time implausible to imagine that human motivation and culture could be reducible to this. If this were so, Basil's teaching in the passage we are discussing would be a mere instrument of social control. If this were his real purpose, it would indeed be irremediably unjust and oppressive. Yet such an interpretation misses the central focus and aim of the text, namely to lead people toward human perfection understood as communion with God. In this context the "feminine" virtues he names are entirely appropriate. The early Christians would surely have experienced them as liberating and life-giving for both women and men when used appropriately in ascetical and mystical practice. The language identifying the church and all its members as symbolically and allegorically feminine could have emerged in late antique culture as a "natural" expression of this experience.

The homily comments specifically on two exemplary groups within the church, virgins and apostles. Basil depicts the virgins through strongly "feminine" imagery as sacred vessels dwelling in the temple of God.[31] This suggests the idea of the holy woman as a receptacle indwelt by the divine presence. The apostles, bearers of Christ's message, are represented as extensions of his being and depicted through "masculine" imagery. They are the lips of Christ speaking his words and the arrows of Christ piercing the hearts of those who believe.[32] Finally, they, and all the saints whose way of life is comparable to theirs, are the sons of the church who will be established through their virtue as princes ruling the earth (cf. Ps. 44:17).[33] Here, at the end of the homily, Basil redirects the aristocratic male quest for mastery toward the spiritual realm and teaches that it can be more truly achieved by virtue than by worldly power. Once again, the masculine ideal of the culture is reconfigured. Ambition is transformed into the driving force that enables spiritual striving. This illustrates how for Basil "masculine" as well as "feminine" virtues are essential to spiritual life.

CHRISTOLOGY AND GENDER

When interpreting the bridegroom in Psalm 44 and the Song of Songs, Basil and other early Christian exegetes bring all the concepts, questions, and controversies of their Christological discussions to their reading of the text. In his preface to what would become the great medieval textbook on the psalms, Cassiodorus identifies three aspects of Christ as depicted in the biblical text. He provides an apt summary of much patristic interpretive practice, as follows: "For the instruction of the faithful, the psalms speak of the person of the Lord Jesus Christ in three ways; first, in a manner recognizably referring to his humanity. . . . Secondly, he is shown to be equal to and coeternal with the father. . . . Thirdly, in connection with the limbs of the church, whose Leader and Head is Christ himself."[34] That is, the psalmist may be understood as referring to Christ's humanity, his divinity, or the people he saves who become members of the *totus Christus*. Cassiodorus adds that often there are quite sudden shifts among these three aspects of Christological meaning.[35] In Psalm 44, for example, for Basil and many of the other fathers the eternal throne in verse 5 pertains to Christ's divinity, the anointing in verse 6 to his humanity and to his anointed people, and the myrrh in verse 7 to his death and burial.

In "literal" discussions of the ontology of Christ among the fathers, his human maleness is accepted without question as historical fact, but it is rarely mentioned as having Christological significance. The primary concern is with his humanity as such, since he shares this with all human beings, and it thus becomes the medium through which he acts to save them and unite them with God. As Gregory Nazianzen says, "What is not assumed is not healed, but what is united to God" in the Incarnation, "that also is saved."[36] Since our Lord does not share maleness with all other humans, its significance is secondary within his human ontology. Patristic writings, for this reason, do not focus on Jesus's human maleness in a biological or ontological sense. Nor do they find maleness in his divine ontology, where the creaturely attribute of gender is strictly absent. Rather, they find it most centrally in allegories of the Bridegroom based on such biblical texts as John 3:29, Psalm 44, and the Song of Songs. Therefore, to arrive at an adequate understanding of the place of gender in patristic Christology and anthropology it is essential to examine how this allegorical maleness functions in the fathers' thought, as it interacts with the corresponding allegorical femaleness of the church. In reading Basil's homily, we will consider which of Cassiodorus's three kinds of Christological reference this maleness refers to, and in what sense—to our Lord's divinity, his humanity, or the members of his body.

It is important in this context to distinguish Christology from anthropology and to analyze the complex relationship between them. In the allegorical sense, Christ is predominantly masculine not because of his human maleness but because of his divinity.[37] The allegorical predominance of the masculine over the feminine reflects the ontological asymmetry within his own person described by John Meyendorff.[38] In the Cyrilline

Chalcedonian terminology that states more precisely the understanding already implicitly present in Basil's homily, Christ is a divine hypostasis who has both divine and human natures. The subject present and active in him is divine, and he exists and acts fully in both divine and human ways. Thus the divine takes the lead and the human cooperates. We will see that in Basil's homily the imagery of masculine excellence is ascribed to Christ's divinity, while his humanity is implicitly feminized in relation to it.

Three sections of the homily employ figurative language that highlights the Bridegroom's masculinity. They concern his beauty as object of the bride's desire (Ps. 44:3), the sword girded to his thigh (v. 4), and his sharp arrows (v. 6). Basil locates Christ's beauty in his divinity, not his humanity, which he declares in the words of Isaiah 53:2–3 to be lacking in beauty. He speaks in Platonic fashion of the soul's ascent to the truly beautiful through love. He says that the psalmist

> calls the Lord ripe in beauty when he fixes his gaze on his divinity. He does not celebrate the beauty of the flesh. "And we have seen him, and he had no sightliness, nor beauty, but his appearance was without honor and lacking above the sons of men" (Is. 53:2–3). It is evident, then, that the prophet [David], looking upon his brilliancy and being filled with the splendor there, his soul smitten with this beauty, was moved to a divine love of the spiritual beauty, and when this appeared in the human soul all things hitherto loved seemed shameful and abominable.[39]

The homily goes on to identify this beauty with the glorious radiance that Peter, James, and John saw on the mount of transfiguration.[40] Subsequently, Basil speaks of the bridegroom's arrows in erotic terms and cites the Song of Songs, again in the context of Platonic love for divine beauty. "'Your arrows are sharp.' The souls which have received the faith are wounded by these arrows, and those inflamed with the highest love of God say with the spouse, 'I languish with love' (Cant. 2:5). Indescribable and inexpressible are the beauty of the Word and the ripeness of the wisdom and of the comeliness of God in his own image. Blessed, therefore, are those who are fond of contemplating true beauty."[41] Basil thus locates the beauty of Christ not in his human form but in his divine nature, which is manifested in the transfiguration and identified as the sublime goal of the quest for union with God.

The link between this passage and erotic masculinity is clear from the way Basil's discussion of the sharp arrows echoes the interpretation of the sword on the thigh that precedes it in the homily. Basil begins by citing Psalm 44:4. "'Gird your sword upon your thigh, O most mighty. With your ripeness and your beauty.' We believe that this refers figuratively to the living Word of God, so that he is joined with the flesh, who is 'efficient and keener than any two edged sword'" (Heb. 4:12).[42] In the Hebrew Bible, *thigh* is a common euphemism for the male genitalia. Basil is well aware of this fact and interprets the psalm verse accordingly.

> For, the thigh is a symbol of efficiency in generation. "For these," [scripture] says, "are the souls that came out of Jacob's thigh" (cf. Exod. 1:5). As, then, our Lord Jesus Christ is a life and a way, and bread, and a grapevine, and a true light, and is also called numberless other names, so, too, he is a sword that cuts through the sensual part of the soul and mortifies the motions of concupiscence. Then, since God the Word was about to unite himself to the weakness of flesh, there is added beautifully the expression, "O most mighty," because the fact that God was able to exist in the nature of man bears proof of the greatest power.[43]

Basil adds that the creation of the universe does not show the power of the Logos as much as his incarnation and "condescension to the lowliness and weakness of humanity."[44]

Like the arrow, the sword initially appears as an obvious phallic symbol, a representation of male sexual prowess. In Basil's interpretation, its meaning and the ideal of masculinity it symbolizes have undergone a twofold transformation. Masculine identity is first transferred from sexual prowess to the control of one's sexuality. This idea is standard in late antiquity among philosophers and ascetically minded Christians, who connect a man's dignity with moderation and self-restraint.[45] Thus the sword "cuts through the sensual part of the soul and mortifies the motions of concupiscence." In this context, a man's own sensuality and desire are correspondingly feminized in a negatively charged way, though Basil does not state this explicitly. Unfortunately, this kind of rhetoric easily tempts early Christian writers to project men's fleshly weaknesses onto women.

Basil's reading of Psalm 44:4 includes the standard ascetic transformation of the masculine ideal but also transforms it a second time by placing it in a Christological context. The sword is the divine Logos. It is he who enables the ascetic to master his sensual desires. The sword thus denotes one aspect of Christ's salvific activity, just as the names *life, way, bread, vine,* and *light* denote other aspects. His grace is what rightly orders the irrational part of the soul and overcomes the weakness of the flesh. To Basil this human fleshliness is a formidable obstacle to sanctification. He portrays Christ's ability to master it through the Incarnation as a greater manifestation of divine power than the creation of the universe.

Notice how the role of the ascetic is thus subtly transformed. Besides exercising his own self-restraint, he has to be receptive to grace. The idealized masculinity is transferred to the divine Logos, and the human ascetic, beset by weaknesses of the irrational soul and the flesh, is implicitly feminized in relation to him. This means that the implicit femininity of human weakness also undergoes a transformation as it is redirected from sensual instability to receptivity toward the Logos. It no longer is only negatively charged and instead comes to have a positive function in spiritual life.

This text contains a further extraordinary ambiguity. Basil has equated the girding of the sword to the thigh with the joining of the Logos to the flesh. This clearly points to the imparting of grace to the ascetic Christian, but it refers more directly to the Incarnation itself. Thus the Logos is first said to master the irrational soul and flesh within the humanity he has assumed in the Incarnation, and this is represented as a mighty work of divine power. Grünbeck suspects the influence of Apollinaris here,[46] as if the Logos displaced Jesus's human mind in governing his irrational soul and flesh. This is not necessarily the case. Basil's ideas are equally compatible with the Christology contained in Gregory Nazianzen's classic refutation of Apollinarianism. Perhaps Jesus's human mind, like "a little torch brought close to a great blaze[,] is neither destroyed, nor is it seen, nor is it extinguished; but it is all one blaze, the greater prevailing over the other."[47]

The subtext of this passage in Basil's homily is that Jesus's humanity is implicitly feminized in relation to his divinity, though unfortunately in quite a negative way. This feminization becomes explicit, and its more positive dimensions are suggested in Augustine's commentary on the same psalm. "The nuptial union is effected between the Word and human flesh, and the place where the union is consummated is the Virgin's womb. It is flesh, very flesh, that is united to the Word; as scripture says, 'They are two no longer, but one flesh' (Matt. 19:6; see Eph. 5:31). The Church was drawn from the human race, so that flesh united to the Word might be the Head of the Church, and all the rest of us believers might be the limbs that belong to that Head."[48] Augustine makes the same point succinctly in Exposition 1 of Psalm 18:6: "He proceeded from a virgin's womb where God was joined with human nature as a bridegroom is united with his bride."[49] It is also presupposed in Byzantine hymnody, where the Mother of God is often called a bridal chamber in which the incarnate Lord's divine and human natures are mysteriously united to each other.[50] Moreover, Christ's humanity is the bridge linking his divinity to the church's members. In Augustine's commentary on Psalm 44:4, although his humanity is called the head, that is, symbolically the husband, this status depends on the prior bridal union with divinity in the Virgin's womb. Here headship means inclusion in the body of which the head is the leading member. In his responsiveness to the divine in himself and his obedience to his Father, Jesus as human leads and models the church's bridal response to God's love. It is perhaps ironic that Christ's humanity, the only place in him where maleness is literally present, thus becomes the locus of an allegorical femininity. However, caution is needed in using this imagery to avoid a Nestorian splitting of Christ into two persons, a variant of the classic "two sons" error in which they have become a son and a daughter.

THE RELATIONSHIP BETWEEN CHRIST AND THE CHURCH

Thus the gender concepts that express the relationship between Christ and the church are also complex. The church functions as both body and bride of Christ. As body it is an extension and manifestation of his own presence and activity, as the hand manifests the person to whom it belongs. In this sense Basil portrays the apostles as our Lord's arrows. Yet the church is also the other, the opposite juxtaposed and conjoined to him, the personality who faces him and encounters him in love. Christians are called to play both roles as they interact with their Lord and with each other; they manifest him to others and encounter him in others in diverse ways. For example, in Basil's homily the apostles are both the lips of the Bridegroom and the sons of the bride. They embody in themselves both Christ and the church, both his body and his bride. This makes them symbolically both masculine and feminine. The language of church as body and bride involves a profound reciprocity or indeed a superimposition of the two images, and frequently each passes into the other.

There is a striking expression of this reciprocity and superimposition in the first of Tyconius's rules of biblical interpretation as explained by Augustine in *De doctrina christiana*. This passage describes a phenomenon that occurs often in patristic exegesis:

> The first rule is "On the Lord and his body." Sometimes we know that a single being, consisting of a head and a body, that is, Christ and his church, is being presented to us; for it was said to the faithful, not without reason, "So you are the seed of Abraham" (Gal. 3:29), although there is but a single seed of Abraham, namely Christ. In such cases we should not be puzzled when scripture moves from head to body or vice versa, while still dealing with one and the same person. For it is a single person that says, "He has placed a garland on me as on a husband and has arrayed me with ornament like a wife" (Is. 61:10).[51]

Thus the union between Christ and the church is so close that they can be represented as a single figurative person, who is symbolically both male and female.

In Basil's homily, the images of the church as body included within Christ and Christ as head included within the church both find vivid expression. The first, the concept of the *totus Christus*, is developed in Basil's interpretation of Psalm 44:3b, "God has blessed you forever." These words are addressed to the bridegroom, and for the Cappadocian opponent of Arianism they immediately involve a Christological problem. If Christ is himself God, how can he be the recipient of a blessing? Basil answers this question by proposing two interpretations. First he suggests that the verse refers to Christ's humanity, since as man he "grew in wisdom and age and grace" (cf. Luke 2:52). In the same way he is said to be the recipient of anointing and exaltation (Ps. 44:8, Phil. 2:8).[52] The second interpretation of Psalm 44:3b is that the blessing is given to Christ's body.

> Since the church is the body of the Lord, and he himself is the head of the church, just as we have explained that those ministering to the heavenly Word are the lips of Christ (even as Paul, or anyone else much like to him in virtue, had Christ speaking in himself), so also we, as many of us as are believers, are the other members of the body of Christ. Now, if anyone refers to the Lord the praise given to the church, he will not sin. Therefore, the saying: "God has blessed you"; that is to say, he has filled your members and your body with blessings from himself for eternity, that is to say, for time without end.[53]

This passage expresses the profound continuity between Christ and those united to him in faith. Basil extends to all members of the church the affirmation that the Lord dwells in Paul and speaks through him. The underlying idea is that God's blessing, which fills his only begotten Son's human nature, spreads from there to permeate all other humans who are united to him as members of the church. Gregory Nazianzen expresses this important soteriological concept through the image of yeast that spreads to permeate a whole lump of dough and make it rise.[54] According to the Cappadocians, this is how divine life is able to reach humankind through the Incarnation.

The imagery of Christ included within the church appears in Basil's interpretation of Psalm 44:13b, "The rich among the people will entreat your face." He understands this entreaty as worship, which it is inappropriate to offer to the church. "For the church will not be worshipped," he says, "but Christ, the head of the church, whom scripture calls the 'face.'"[55] Augustine's commentary on the same verse develops the idea further: "Both those who seek that face, and the queen whose face is entreated, are all the one bride, all one queen, for mother and children together all belong to Christ, belong to the Head."[56] Here Christ is worshipped by the bride but is also part of the bride.

In early Christian theology, this mutual indwelling and reciprocity are also said to be present in a human marriage, where, in the language of the Letter to the Ephesians, the husband is the wife's head and the wife is the husband's body. It shows that "he who loves his wife loves himself" (Eph. 5:28). Likewise, Gregory Nazianzen writes of his mother Nonna that she could not bear the unbelief of her husband, since it meant that she was "but half-united to God, because of the estrangement of him who was part of her."[57] This parallels Basil's and Augustine's language about Christ as face of the church. Perhaps it follows that through their union in marriage a wife can share in her husband's masculine mode of existence and a husband can share in his wife's feminine mode of existence, insofar as they are distinctive. This mutual indwelling would then enable the couple to grow toward moral and psychological wholeness together by learning from, imitating, and participating in each other's virtues, including those linked to gender.

An analogous mutual indwelling occurs in the relationship between Christ and the church. In Basil's imagery, the faithful are members of the Bridegroom who share his blessing, and he is the face of the bride. This means that because of the union and continuity between them, the church shares Christ's symbolic masculinity and Christ shares the church's symbolic femininity.

The church and the human persons gathered in it are allegorically both masculine and feminine. As we have seen, gender conjunction, crossover, and paradox are inherent in the structure of the allegorical discourse that describes them. Thus the divine Logos as Head and Bridegroom through the mediation of his own humanity becomes the source of life, activity, and virtue both for the figuratively masculine body that manifests him and for the figuratively feminine bride that receives and responds to his love. Human wholeness includes both of these dimensions. The recitation of psalms, in this way, became for Basil and other early Christians a deeply formative practice challenging cultural constructions of gender and influencing the concrete experience of individuals.

Notes

1. William L. Holladay, *The Psalms through Three Thousand Years: Prayerbook of a Cloud of Witnesses* (Minneapolis, MN: Fortress Press, 1993), 28.

2. Cf. Gregory Nazianzen, *Or.* 45.22 (PG 36: 653b–c), where he says that Moses's bronze serpent is not a type but an antitype of Christ on the cross, that is, a contrast rather than a likeness, since it is dead instead of being the source of life.

3. Elisabeth Grünbeck, *Christologische Schriftargumentation und Bildersprache: Zum Konflikt zwischen Metapherninterpretation und dogmatischen Schriftbeweistraditionen in der patristischen Auslegung des 44. (45.) Psalms* (Leiden: Brill, 1994). For Christological but especially ecclesiological interpretations, see also Lucien Robitaille, "L'église, épouse du Christ, dans l'interprétation patristique du Psaume 44 (45)," *Laval Théologique et Philosophique* 26 (1970): 167–79, 279–306, and 27 (1971): 41–65.

4. Basil, *Homilia de fide* (PG 31: 464b–465c). See also his remarks in *Hexaemeron* 9.1 (PG 29: 188b–189a; trans. NPNF, ser. 2, 8: 101–2): "There are those truly, who do not admit the common sense of the scriptures, for whom water is not water, but some other nature. . . . who, giving themselves up to the distorted meanings of allegory, have undertaken to give a majesty of their own invention to scripture."

5. Pio Tamburrino, "Osservazioni sulla sezione cristologica dell' *Hom. In Ps. XLIV* di San Basilio," *Revista di Cultura Classica e Medioevale* 8 (1966): 229–39.

6. I have described these categories of gender language briefly in "The Feminine Man in Late Antique Ascetic Piety," *Union Seminary Quarterly Review* 48 (1994): 49–71, and have discussed them further in "The Maleness of Christ," *St. Vladimir's Theological Quarterly* 42 (1998): 111–51.

7. Basil, *Hom. in Ps.* 1 (PG 29: 216d–217a). Translations not otherwise attributed are my own.

8. Basil, *De baptismo* (ed. Umberto Neri, *Basilio de Cesarea. Il Battesimo. Testo, traduzione, introduzione e commento* [Brescia: Paideia, 1976], 604–6).

9. Basil, *Hom. in Ps.* 114 (PG 29: 492c).

10. Verna E. F. Harrison, "Male and Female in Cappadocian Theology," *Journal of Theological Studies*, n.s., 41 (1990): 441–71.

11. Basil, *Hom. in Ps.* 44 (PG 29: 388a; trans. FC 46: 275).

12. Philip Rousseau, *Basil of Caesarea* (Berkeley: University of California Press, 1994).

13. Grünbeck, *Christologische Schriftargumentation*, 294.

14. See David Dawson, *Allegorical Readers and Cultural Revision in Ancient Alexandria* (Berkeley: University of California Press, 1992).

15. Jean Bernardi, *La prédication des pères cappadociens: Le prédicateur et son auditoire* (Paris: Presses Universitaires de France, 1968); and Daniel F. Stramara Jr., "Double Monasticism in the Greek East, Fourth through Eighth Centuries," *Journal of Early Christian Studies* 6 (1998): 269–312.

16. Basil, *Hom. in Ps.* 44 (PG 29: 405b; trans. [modified] FC 46: 289).

17. Basil, *Hom. in Ps.* 44 (PG 29: 401a; trans. FC 46: 286).

18. Basil, *Hom. in Ps.* 44 (PG 29: 401b; trans. FC 46: 286).

19. For a useful analysis and extensive bibliography of the burgeoning literature addressing women, gender, and religion in late antiquity, see Ross S. Kraemer, "Women and Gender," in *The Oxford Handbook of Early Christian Studies,*

edited by Susan Ashbrook Harvey and David G. Hunter, Oxford Handbooks in Religion and Theology (New York: Oxford University Press, 2008), 465–92. See particularly the many contributions of Elizabeth A. Clark, such as *Ascetic Piety and Women's Faith: Essays on Late Antique Christianity* (Lewiston, NY: Edwin Mellen Press, 1986), "Ideology, History, and the Construction of 'Woman' in Late Ancient Christianity," *Journal of Early Christian Studies* 2 (1994): 155–84, and "The Lady Vanishes: Dilemmas of a Feminist Historian after the 'Linguistic Turn,'" *Church History* 67 (1998): 1–31.

20. On the other hand, aristocratic women often shared the same desires for wealth, ostentation, power, and status as their male relatives. These appear to be universally human temptations, after all, though class is obviously a factor, and though, in a culture with many social roles determined by gender men and women frequently pursued these goals in different ways. When encountering the masculine "default mode" in late antique reflections on the human condition, one needs to carefully distinguish between genuine discussions of masculinity and consideration of what is universally human. This can prove difficult because ancient authors seldom articulated this question explicitly. Matthew Kuffler, *The Manly Eunuch: Masculinity, Gender Ambiguity and Christian Ideology in Late Antiquity* (Chicago: University of Chicago Press, 2001), argues that in general classical and late antique reflections about human identity and ethics are actually a discourse about masculinity. In other words, ἄνθρωπος means the same as ἄνηρ, and *homo* the same as *vir*. His study is thoroughly documented and makes a good case that concern about manly ideals is a major theme. However, in my view ancient authors also show great concern for what is universally human, and evidence of misogyny is far from monolithic. More attention to nuance and multiple levels of meaning is needed, as is care to avoid reductionism.

21. Basil, *Hom. in Ps.* 44 (PG 29: 408c; trans. FC 46: 291).

22. See Robitaille, "Église, épouse du Christ."

23. Basil, *Hom. in Ps.* 44 (PG 29: 408c).

24. Antoine Guillaumont and Claire Guillaumont, eds., *Évagre le Pontique. Traité pratique, ou Le moine,* 2 vols., SC 170–71 (Paris: Cerf, 1971), 2: 498. Evagrius was a student and coworker of Basil as a young man, and his theology and spirituality surely manifest the influence of his teacher and mentor. The character of this influence merits further study, as Augustine Casiday notes in his masterful survey of the current renaissance in Evagrian studies, "Gabriel Bunge and the Study of Evagrius Ponticus," *St. Vladimir's Theological Quarterly* 48 (2004): 249–97.

25. See Paul Veyne, *A History of Private Life,* vol. 1, *From Pagan Rome to Byzantium,* trans. Arthur Goldhammer (Cambridge, MA: Harvard University Press, 1987), 33–49.

26. Basil, *Hom. in Ps.* 44 (PG 29: 409b–c).

27. See Karen Torjesen, *When Women Were Priests: Women's Leadership in the Early Church and the Scandal of Their Subordination in the Rise of Christianity* (San Francisco: HarperSanFrancisco, 1993), 111–32.

28. Basil, *Hom. in Ps.* 44 (PG 29: 409d–412d).

29. This dimension of ascetic practice is described perceptively in Carol A. Newsom, "The Case of the Blinking I: Discourse of the Self at Qumran," *Semeia* 57 (1992): 13–23.

30. Kerstin Aspegren, *The Male Woman: A Feminine Ideal in the Early Church*, ed. René Kieffer (Uppsala: Uppsala Universitet, 1990); and Kari Elisabeth Børresen, ed., *Image of God and Gender Models in Judaeo-Christian Tradition* (Oslo: Solum, 1991). For a broad historical and systematic exploration of these issues, see Sarah Coakley, *Powers and Submissions: Spirituality, Philosophy, and Gender* (Oxford: Blackwell, 2002).

31. Basil, *Hom. in Ps.* 44 (PG 29: 413a).

32. Basil, *Hom. in Ps.* 44 (PG 29: 397a, 404a–b).

33. Basil, *Hom. in Ps.* 44 (PG 29: 413b).

34. Cassiodorus, *Exp. Ps.*, praef. 13 (CCSL 97: 16; trans. ACW 51: 34).

35. Cassiodorus, *Exp. Ps.*, praef. 13 (CCSL 97: 16; ACW 51: 35).

36. Gregory Nazianzen, *Ep.* 101 (SC 208: 50).

37. See V. Harrison, "Maleness of Christ."

38. John Meyendorff, *Byzantine Theology: Historical Trends and Doctrinal Themes* (New York: Fordham University Press, 1974), 154. See also Meyendorff's *Christ in Eastern Christian Thought* (Crestwood, NY: St. Vladimir's Seminary Press, 1987).

39. Basil, *Hom. in Ps.* 44 (PG 29: 396c; trans. FC 46: 282).

40. Basil, *Hom. in Ps.* 44 (PG 29: 400c–d).

41. Basil, *Hom. in Ps.* 44 (PG 29: 401c–d; trans. FC 46: 287).

42. Basil, *Hom. in Ps.* 44 (PG 29: 400a; trans. [modified] FC 46: 284).

43. Basil, *Hom. in Ps.* 44 (PG 29: 400a–b; trans. [modified] FC 46: 284–85).

44. Basil, *Hom. in Ps.* 44 (PG 29: 400b; trans. FC 46: 285).

45. Michel Foucault, *The History of Sexuality*, vol. 3, *The Care of the Self*, trans. Robert Hurley (New York: Pantheon Books, 1986); Peter Brown, *The Body and Society: Men, Women, and Sexual Renunciation in Early Christianity*, 2nd ed. (New York: Columbia University Press, 2008), 5–32.

46. Grünbeck, *Christologische Schriftargumentation*, 305–6.

47. Gregory Nazianzen, *Ep.* 101 (SC 208: 54; trans. John A. McGuckin, *St. Cyril of Alexandria: The Christological Controversy* [Leiden: Brill, 1994], 395).

48. Augustine, *En. Ps.* 44.3 (CCSL 38: 495; trans. WSA III.16: 282).

49. Augustine, *En. Ps.* 18(1).6 (CCSL 38: 102–3; trans. WSA III.15: 200).

50. See, for example, the *Akathistos Hymn*, Ikos 10.

51. Augustine, *Doctr. chr.* 3.31.44 (CCSL 32: 104; trans. [slightly modified] R. P. H. Green, *Saint Augustine: On Christian Teaching* [Oxford: Oxford University Press, 1999], 90). For Tyconius, see *Liber reg.* (trans. William S. Babcock, *Tyconius: The Book of Rules* [Atlanta, GA: Scholars Press, 1989]).

52. Basil, *Hom. in Ps.* 44 (PG 29: 397b–c).

53. Basil, *Hom. in Ps.* 44 (PG 29: 397c–400a; trans. FC: 284).

54. Gregory Nazianzen, *Or.* 30.21 (SC 250: 272). See Matt. 13:33 and 1 Cor. 5:6–8.

55. Basil, *Hom. in Ps.* 44 (PG 29: 409c; trans. [modified] FC 46: 292).

56. Augustine, *En. Ps.* 44.28 (CCSL 38: 514–15; trans. [slightly modified] WSA III.16: 305–6).

57. Gregory Nazianzen, *Or.* 18.11 (PG 35: 997c; trans. FC 22: 127).

The Virgin, the Bride, and the Church

Reading Psalm 45 in Ambrose, Jerome, and Augustine

David G. Hunter

Within the past decade or so, historical studies of early Christianity have been affected by what has been called the "linguistic turn."[1] This development has entailed a new appreciation of the varied forms of Christian "discourse" and their importance in shaping the cultural, political, and social worlds of late antiquity.[2] For example, historians of religion and culture, such as Judith Perkins and Kate Cooper, have drawn attention to the way in which narrative representation in early Christian literature functioned to construct Christian identities and to negotiate power relations both within the church and in society at large.[3] It has become increasingly difficult for historians to ignore the power of rhetoric in shaping the imaginative (and, therefore, real) worlds of late ancient Christians.

These new perspectives have created some dilemmas for church historians. For example, feminist scholars have become sensitized to the way in which male writers used women to "think with."[4] Literary representations of women by men are increasingly recognized as problematic, and feminist historians are less optimistic than they once were about the possibility of recovering the histories of "real women" from the stories about them in early Christian literature.[5]

Although it has created these difficulties for historians, attention to the figural character of Christian discourse has also opened up new avenues of historical investigation and rendered a greater variety of "texts" more susceptible to historical inquiry. As Judith Perkins has noted: "The recognition that literary, religious, and technical discourses all contribute to generating a cultural world has revealed that the traditional distinctions made between historical documents and other texts was [*sic*] essentially arbitrary. If historians wish to approach an understanding of the dynamics of a past period, they must incorporate the testimony of many different kinds of discourses."[6] Christian biblical interpretation, for example, is now mined for evidence of the way in which texts were deployed as rhetorical strategies for creating and maintaining symbolic worlds, which in turn sustained actual social and religious communities.[7]

Sensitivity to the rhetorical character of male representations of women may contribute similarly to the study of Christian history. If male descriptions of women can no longer be taken at face value as reflecting the actual experience of "real" women, it has become plausible to read such stories for evidence of how the rhetoric of female virtue could serve in an economy of power relations among men. As Kate Cooper recently has argued regarding the representation of women in the early Christian apocryphal acts: "The challenge by the apostle to the householder is the urgent message of these narratives, and it is essentially a conflict *between men* [her emphasis]. The challenge posed here by Christianity is not really about women, or even about sexual continence, but about authority and the social order."[8] In other words, Christian discourse about the virtue and purity of women may tell us more about the thinking of the men who wrote the texts (and about their own struggles for status and authority) than about the women who are represented there.

The aim of this essay is to suggest that these new historical perspectives are useful in reading certain aspects of Christian biblical exegesis. The biblical image of the virgin bride of Christ is a literary trope that especially lends itself to analysis in terms of its social and political function, and not merely as an episode in the history of biblical interpretation. In the later years of the fourth century the ascetic and monastic movements led male Christian writers to devote an extraordinary degree of attention to the bodies of women, especially celibate women. In the hands of ascetic authors the traditional biblical image of the virgin bride acquired new life. The "bride of Christ" became the celibate Christian woman.

The most notable example of this development can be found in interpretations of the Song of Songs. As Elizabeth Clark has demonstrated, Western writers, such as Ambrose and Jerome, taking their cue from aspects of Origen's spiritual exegesis, applied the bridal imagery of the Song to the life of the ascetic Christian. The "virgin bride," traditionally used as a figure of the church, became the celibate Christian, particularly the female virgin, and ultimately the preeminent virgin, Mary.[9] By contrast, Augustine of Hippo stood aloof from the ascetic interpretations of his contemporaries. As Clark has noted, Augustine discussed the Song only to counter the attempts of the Donatists to enlist the text on behalf of their own elitist ecclesiology.[10]

The contrast between Augustine and the more ascetic interpreters suggests that readings of the virgin bride were by no means univocal in the late fourth century, even among authors with ascetic interests. Moreover, if we include the opponents of asceticism, we find even greater diversity. For example, Jovinian, one of the central figures in the Western resistance to the ascetic ideal, cited both 2 Corinthians 11:2 and the Song of Songs to argue that virginity is a distinguishing mark of the church as a whole. All baptized Christians, Jovinian reasoned, share equally in the holiness of the church. Therefore, distinctions based on the ascetic merit of individuals can have no ultimate relevance in the kingdom of God. In response to Jovinian, Jerome argued that the church is honored with the title of "virgin" precisely because virginity is superior to marriage.[11] In the ascetic controversies of the late fourth century, the identity of the virgin bride—and specifically the question of the relationship between the individual Christian as virgin and the church as virgin—was clearly a point of contention.

In this essay I will examine the different uses of the image of the virgin bride in the three Western writers most closely engaged in the ascetic controversies: Ambrose, Jerome, and Augustine. Each of these authors had his own particular interest in asceticism and his own perspective on the place of ascetics in the church. These distinct perspectives, I will argue, can be seen reflected in each author's distinctive interpretations of the virgin bride. Furthermore, the question of asceticism is not the only issue being negotiated in the early Christian texts. In each of these commentators, I will suggest, the figure of the virgin bride is also related to a particular self-representation, that is, to a construction of the author's own authority, specifically in relation to ascetic women. The increasing prominence of ascetic women in late fourth-century Christianity created a crisis of authority for the male leaders of the church. In different ways, Ambrose, Jerome, and Augustine each responded to this development by employing the discourse of the virgin bride to render a particular image of male authority, one that pertained directly to his own status and authority in the church.

Rather than use the better-known text of the Song of Songs, I will focus on interpretations of Psalm 45 (Psalm 44 in the Vulgate enumeration).[12] The primary reason for this choice is the wording of the psalm itself. The first ten verses of the psalm speak of an anointed king and thus lend themselves naturally to a Christological interpretation. The remaining eight verses are addressed to the prospective bride of the king, who is described both as a queen clad in gold (v. 10) and as the daughter of a king (v. 14). But Psalm 45 speaks not only of the bride but also of the "virgins" who accompany the bride into the palace or temple of the king (v. 15). This wording naturally led the different interpreters to reflect on who the "bride" is, who the "virgins" are, and what it means to accompany the bride to the king. In other words, the phrasing of the text itself tended to force commentators to address the question of the relationship between celibate Christians (the "virgins") and the church (the "bride"). Analysis of the diverse interpretations of Psalm 45, therefore, will enable us to discern different approaches to the issues of asceticism, gender, and authority in the church among our three authors.

AMBROSE: THE CONSECRATED VIRGIN AS BRIDE OF CHRIST

In his various treatises on virginity, composed between the years 377 and 395, Ambrose cited the Song of Songs more than fifty times.[13] Citations of Psalm 45 are much less frequent, but they do occur, and in significant places. Most references to the psalm are found in *De virginibus*, Ambrose's earliest extant literary work. *De virginibus* was compiled from a collection of sermons and later reworked into a single treatise dedicated to Ambrose's sister, the virgin Marcellina. Originally, however, the sermons were addressed not just to celibate women but to the entire church community, and the concerns of a wider audience are reflected in the work.[14] For example, throughout *De virginibus* Ambrose appears somewhat defensive about encouraging young women to embrace the life of perpetual virginity, and he constantly reports the complaints of parents who object to their nubile daughters' adopting the ascetic life. Ambrose's *De virginibus* and his later treatise, *De virginitate,* both indicate that at Milan there was considerable resistance to Ambrose's efforts to foster the practice of ascetic renunciation.

The context of Ambrose's remarks in *De virginibus,* therefore, is one of controversy over the ascetic life, and the use of marital imagery is central to Ambrose's apologetic argument on behalf of asceticism. Early in the work he first appeals to the virginity of the church, which, as the bride of Christ, embodies the paradoxical quality of spiritual fertility: "Notice another merit of virginity: Christ is the spouse of a virgin, and Christ is, one might say, the spouse of virginal chastity. For virginity belongs to Christ, not Christ to virginity. Thus it was a virgin who married, a virgin who carried us in her womb, a virgin who gave birth, a virgin who nursed with her own milk."[15] A few paragraphs later Ambrose again argues for the superiority of heavenly brides over earthly ones by invoking the figure of the church as the virgin bride of Christ:

> And so holy church, who is free from the stain of intercourse and fruitful in childbirth, is a virgin by her chastity, a mother by her offspring. As a virgin she conceived us, full of the Spirit, not of a man; as a virgin she gave birth to us, not with bodily pain, but with the joys of angels. She nourished us, not with bodily milk, but with the milk of the apostle, who nursed the tender infancy of a people that was still growing [cf. 1 Cor. 3:2]. What married woman has as many children as does the church, who is a virgin in her sacraments and a mother in her peoples? Her fecundity is given testimony in the words of scripture: "For the children of the deserted woman will be greater in number than the children of her who has a husband" [Isa. 54:1].[16]

While our mother the church does not have a human husband (*virum*), Ambrose maintains, she does have an eternal spouse (*sponsum*); she is wedded to the eternal Word of God without loss of purity, both as the whole church and as the individual human soul.[17]

After thus establishing the "virginity" of the whole church as a foundation for the value of ascetic renunciation, Ambrose proceeds to apply this argument to the life of the individual Christian virgin. At this point Psalm 45 becomes central to his discussion. Like the church itself, the consecrated virgin has Christ as a spouse. Girls who are about to marry, Ambrose notes, often boast about the beauty of their future husbands. But they cannot compare to Christian virgins who can say in the words of Psalm 45:3, "Your beauty is greater than that of men; grace is poured out upon your lips."[18] The virgin's spouse is not one who pursues trivial activities or who takes pride in transient riches; rather, her partner is the one who, in the words of Psalm 45:7, possesses a "throne that endures forever." By characterizing the consecrated virgin as the "bride of Christ," Ambrose is able to ascribe to the individual Christian virgin all of the purity and spiritual stature that he previously attributed to the church.

This dimension of Ambrose's rhetorical strategy becomes especially clear as he proceeds to discuss the later verses of Psalm 45, in which he assimilates the Christian virgin to the prospective bride of the text. For example, he quotes the following verses from Psalm 45: "The daughters of kings are there in his honor; at his right hand stands the queen in gold garments, surrounded by a variety of virtues. Hear, O daughter and see, incline your ear, and forget your people and your father's house, for the king has desired your beauty, for he is your God" (Ps. 45:10–12).[19]

Although the text of the psalm clearly distinguishes the "daughters of the king" (*filiae regum*) from the "queen" (*regina*) clad in gold, Ambrose proceeds to blur the distinction between the two. He notes that the Holy Spirit, speaking through the divine scriptures, has assigned to the virgin three special gifts: royalty, gold, and beauty. Royalty refers to her status as the bride of the king, as well as to the fact that the virgin's soul does not fall captive to the enticements of pleasure.[20] Gold, a metal that becomes more precious when refined by fire, refers to the virgin's body; its appearance becomes more splendid when consecrated by the divine Spirit. And of beauty, Ambrose writes: "Who can imagine greater beauty than that of her who is loved by the king, approved by the judge, dedicated to the Lord, consecrated to God? She is ever the spouse, ever unwedded, so that she can have love without end and chastity without corruption."[21] Ambrose then invokes several verses from the Song of Songs (4:7–8) and concludes that these phrases show the perfect and faultless beauty of the virginal soul. When consecrated at God's altars and intent on the mysteries of God, she wins for herself a lover whose heart is filled with joy.[22] Clearly, one feature of Ambrose's defense of ascetic renunciation involves characterizing the Christian virgin as the bride of Christ and ascribing to her the spiritual "beauty," "purity," and "royalty" that earlier Christian commentators (and he himself earlier in the sermon) tended to reserve for the church.

Another aspect of Ambrose's argument in *De virginibus* is equally noteworthy, though perhaps less obvious. In *De virginibus* Ambrose is concerned exclusively with young women who have embraced perpetual virginity and who have undergone the formal rite of virginal consecration, that is, the *velatio* or veiling of virgins. Ambrose speaks explicitly of the virgin's body as "consecrated by the divine spirit," "dedicated to the Lord," "consecrated to God," and "consecrated at God's altars," all of which suggest a formal ritual of consecration.[23] When Ambrose speaks of the individual Christian as the "virgin bride" in *De virginibus*, he is referring specifically to the consecrated virgin and not to others who may have embraced the celibate life. In this regard, it is significant that in his treatise "On Widows" (*De viduis*), composed shortly after *De virginibus*, Ambrose never once cites Psalm 45 or the Song of Songs and never once refers to the consecrated widow as the "bride of Christ." This suggests that for Ambrose the consecrated virgin functioned as a bride of Christ in a manner that was simply not open to other Christians, not even to other celibate Christians.

Why was Ambrose so interested in the consecrated virgin? The answer may lie in the ritual of veiling itself and in the role that the bishop played in the life of the consecrated virgin. The ritual of consecration of virgins had become a formal practice in the Western church only at the end of the fourth century.[24] Ambrose, in fact, is one of the primary sources of evidence for it, and he seems to have been one of the primary movers behind this distinctively Western development. The taking of the veil (*flammeum*) in a ceremony modeled after a Roman wedding established a new formal relationship of the virgin to Christ and to the Christian community, a relationship mediated by the Christian bishop. The bishop customarily presided at the ceremony, bestowed the veil, offered the liturgical benediction, and delivered a sermon of exhortation. The relationship of the consecrated virgin to the bishop continued after the ceremony as well, since the bishop now exercised ecclesial supervision over the virgin who had taken the veil.[25]

The role of the bishop in the life of the *virgo velata*, I would suggest, is relevant to an interpretation of Ambrose's rhetoric of the virgin bride. By participating in the ritual of virginal consecration the bishop took on a public, quasi-parental role in relation to the consecrated virgin. He became, in effect, a new *paterfamilias*. Ambrose himself alludes to the "fatherly" status of the bishop at several places in his ascetic writings. For example, in *De institutione virginis*, a sermon delivered circa 391 on the occasion of the veiling of the virgin Ambrosia, Ambrose referred to Ambrosia as "she whom I offer in my role as priest, whom I commend [to Christ] with fatherly affection."[26] Bishops would address the virgin to be veiled as "my daughter," which helped to confirm the quasi-paternal relationship.[27] In some cases bishops were required to supervise the physical care of virgins as well as their spiritual needs. For example, the Council of Hippo in 397 entrusted bishops with the task of placing consecrated virgins in the care of proper Christian women upon the death of their biological parents.[28]

The prominent role of the bishop in the veiling and supervision of consecrated virgins suggests, therefore, another way to read Ambrose's rhetoric of the virgin bride. Ambrose's defense of consecrated virginity in *De virginibus* may reflect not only the bishop's concern with the issue of asceticism but also an effort to defend or enhance his own authority as bishop. In his biography of Ambrose, Neil McLynn has noted that *De virginibus* was composed at a time when Ambrose was still relatively new to his see and still consolidating his position vis-à-vis the majority of his clergy who were sympathetic to the former bishop, the Homoian Auxentius. According to McLynn, Ambrose used the dramatic ritual of virginal consecration for the purposes of establishing himself in the see of Milan and advertising his ascetic program.[29] McLynn's argument helps to explain why Ambrose appeared so defensive in his early treatises on virginity and why it was so essential that he assimilate the consecrated virgin to the church as the virgin bride of Christ. As Peter Brown has demonstrated in a number of contexts, it was increasingly important in late antiquity for the Christian clergy to harness the power of holiness, and the rhetoric of the virgin bride was central to Ambrose's efforts in this regard.[30] Ambrose's rhetoric of the "virgin bride" thus would have functioned not only to enhance the status of consecrated virgins in the church but also to construct an authoritative persona for the Christian bishop, that of the surrogate *pater*.

JEROME: THE CELIBATE WOMAN AS BRIDE OF CHRIST

When we turn to Jerome's reading of the bridal imagery of Psalm 45, we find significant differences in interpretation, differences that suggest a rather different ascetic outlook from that of Ambrose. Jerome was not a bishop but an ascetic teacher and scholar. His treatment of Psalm 45 reveals someone more interested in the work of ascetic formation than in the event of virginal consecration.[31] The opening lines of Jerome's famous Letter 22 to Eustochium are fairly typical of his approach. He quotes Psalm 45:11–12 ("Hear, O daughter, and see, and incline your ear and forget your people and your father's house; and the king will desire your beauty"). Jerome notes that in the psalm God is telling the human soul that it should follow the example of Abraham and forsake the Chaldeans, that is, the demons.

Then, applying the text to the life of the young virgin, Jerome writes: "But it is not enough for you to go out from your native country, unless you forget your people and your father's house and, despising the flesh, are united in your bridegroom's embraces."[32] Jerome follows this up with a number of quotations or allusions to scripture, stressing the theme of ascetic renunciation: Genesis 19:17 ("Do not look back or stay anywhere on the plain; flee to the mountains or else you will be taken captive"); Luke 9:62 ("No one who puts a hand to the plow and looks back is fit for the kingdom of God"); and Matthew 24:17–18 ("The one on the housetop must not go down to take what is in the house; the one in the field must not turn back to get a coat"). Returning to Psalm 45, Jerome notes that to "forget your father's house" must be read in the light of John 8:44 ("You are of your father the devil, and the desires of your father you will do"). Unlike Ambrose, Jerome invokes the psalm not to glorify the consecrated virgin but to urge her to engage in the lifelong struggle for ascetic virtue.

Another difference between Jerome and Ambrose is found in Jerome's willingness to apply the bridal imagery of Psalm 45 not only to the consecrated virgin but to other celibate women as well. In his Letter 54 to the widow Furia, composed about the year 394, Jerome urges Furia to be faithful to her ascetic resolve with a string of verses from Psalm 45 and the Song of Songs: "'Honor your father,' the commandment says; but only if he does not separate you from your true father. Recognize the tie of blood, but only as long as your parent recognizes his creator. Should he fail to do so, David will sing to you: 'Hear, O daughter, and see, and incline your ear. Forget your people and your father's house, and the king will desire your beauty, for he is the Lord your God' (Ps. 45:11–12)."[33] Jerome leaves no doubt that he intends to apply the text of the psalm to the ascetic resolve of the widow Furia, for he goes on to address her directly: "*You* have heard, *you* have seen, *you* have inclined your ear, *you* have forgotten your father's house; therefore the king will desire your beauty and shall say to you, 'You are fair my love; there is no spot in you' (Song of Songs 4:7)." What can be fairer, Jerome notes alluding to Psalm 45:10, than a soul that is called the "daughter of God"? "She believes in Christ and enriched with this ambition, she makes her way to her spouse, who is both her Lord and her husband."[34]

Jerome's use of the language of Psalm 45 and the Song of Songs clearly reflects his preoccupations as an ascetic teacher and a mentor to ascetic women. Many of his closest associates were widows, Marcella and Paula being only the most prominent examples. Unlike Ambrose, who as a bishop was intimately involved in the consecration and ecclesial supervision of women who were veiled as virgins, Jerome was less formally involved and more oriented to the role of spiritual director and biblical teacher. Furthermore, unlike Ambrose, Jerome lacked the status of a bishop. His authority as a teacher and spiritual guide, therefore, was more fluid than that of Ambrose and depended on the success of his clientele in establishing themselves as learned and virtuous ascetics.

It is well known, however, that precisely Jerome's involvements with ascetic women, particularly Paula, were regarded with great suspicion and hostility, especially among the Roman clergy.[35] Jerome's status as an authoritative teacher of ascetic women was something that needed to be defended and could not simply be taken for granted. In one letter of Jerome we find this concern with women's education and ascetic training expressed clearly in the context of a commentary on Psalm 45. Jerome's Letter 65 was addressed in 397 to the virgin Principia, a lifelong companion of the widow Marcella. This letter is Jerome's only extant attempt to write a full-scale commentary on Psalm 45. Not only does he present a scholarly, philological examination of the psalm, but he provides Principia with an interpretation that applies the psalm to her life as a consecrated virgin. Letter 65, therefore, provides an unusually clear view of Jerome's approach to the bridal imagery of the psalm and its varied applications, both ascetic and ecclesial.

Jerome begins the letter with an extensive apology for directing his biblical commentary to a woman. He notes that he has often been criticized for writing to women and for preferring the "weaker sex" to males. Jerome then provides a long list of biblical examples of women who have distinguished themselves for virtue or learning. Commenting, for example, on the fact that Priscilla and Aquila gave instruction in the faith to Apollos, Jerome notes wryly: "If it was not shameful for an apostle to be instructed by a woman, why should it be shameful for me to teach women?"[36] Jerome then assures Principia that he has provided this litany of female saints so that she will not be ashamed of her female sex. He even presents Principia's companions, Marcella and Asella, as "instructors both in the study of scripture and in chastity of mind and body." The widow Marcella, Jerome notes, will lead Principia through the verdant fields and dappled flowers of the sacred scriptures until she comes to the one who says in the Song of Songs: "I am the flower of the field and the lily of the valley" (Song 2:1). Likewise, the virgin Asella, "who is herself a flower of the Lord," will hear together with Principia the words of the Bridegroom: "As a lily among the brambles, so is my love among the maidens" (Song 2:2).[37]

Like Ambrose, Jerome here uses the bridal imagery of the Song of Songs and Psalm 45 to exalt the ascetic Christian. Unlike Ambrose, Jerome stresses not the ritual of virginal consecration but the tasks of biblical study and ascetic formation, embodied, respectively, by Marcella and Asella. These, of course, were the very tasks in which Jerome took a central role as mentor and for which he had received so much criticism. Jerome's apology for the capacity of women to study scripture and to practice asceticism, therefore, also appears to be an apology for his own authority as a spiritual guide and mentor to ascetic women.

When Jerome moves into the commentary on Psalm 45 itself, he, like Ambrose, works on the assumption that the bridal language of Psalm 45 can be read on several levels at once. Although he occasionally points to

certain phrases that apply in a special way to Principia as a virgin, Jerome's more usual approach is first to identify the bride of the psalm as
the church.[38] For example, commenting on Psalm 45:10 ("The queen sits
at your right hand clothed in gold"), Jerome notes that the queen is "the
Catholic Church founded on the rock of Christ, as on a stable root; she is
the one dove, the perfect one, the beloved."[39] Turning to the daughters of
the king who stand in attendance, Jerome observes that these can be understood "both as the souls of believers and, in a special way [*proprie*] as
the choir of virgins."

Continuing through the psalm, Jerome comes to verses 11–12 ("Hear,
O daughter, and see, and incline your ear. Forget your people and your father's house, and the king will desire your beauty, for he is the Lord your
God"). Again Jerome prefers a multileveled reading of the text, but one that
starts with the church as the bride of the king. She is the church gathered
from the nations, like Abraham who left Chaldea; she has forgotten her former father (again, the devil, borrowing from John 8:44) and has been
adopted by God. Although Jerome acknowledges that "each person should
also apply the text to himself and to the soul of the believer," his dominant
line of interpretation points first to the church as the virgin bride of Christ
and only then to the individual Christian or ascetic as the bride.[40]

Toward the end of Letter 65, however, Jerome does move overtly toward a more ascetic interpretation of Psalm 45. In the course of doing so
he also reveals most clearly his sense of the role of asceticism within the
church. When he reaches verses 15 and 16 of the psalm ("Behind her the
virgins shall be brought to the king, her companions shall follow her; with
joy and gladness they are led into the temple of the king"), Jerome notes
that here Psalm 45 must be read in the light of the Song of Songs, which
teaches that "there is a great difference among the souls who believe in
Christ."[41] The Song of Songs states that "there are sixty queens, eighty concubines, and maidens without number. One is my dove, my perfect one,
my beloved" (6:8–9). About this perfect one, Jerome points out, the Song
of Songs says: "The daughters saw and blessed her; the queens and the
concubines praised her" (6:9). Reading the psalm in the light of the Song
of Songs, Jerome discerns a hierarchy based on ascetic merit. The ones in
the first rank, that is, the "sixty queens" who follow the church most
closely, must be those "who have persevered in virginity of body and soul,"

such as Principia herself. Next come the widows and married people who live in continence; they are the "eighty concubines," all of whom are led into the temple of the king with gladness and joy.

As for the average, noncelibate Christians, they are the "maidens without number," or, as Jerome describes them, "the diverse multitude of believers, who are not yet able to be joined to the embraces of the spouse or to produce children by him."[42] They follow the bride at a distance but do not (at least not in this life) attend her at the wedding. Jerome's ascetic reading of Psalm 45 has now merged with his ecclesial reading, and the result is a strongly "asceticized" portrait of the church. Those who follow the church most closely, who are led by the king into the temple, are celibate Christians: that is, the consecrated virgins, widows, and continent married persons who serve the king as "queens" and "concubines." For Jerome Psalm 45, like the Song of Songs, portrays the church as an ascetic hierarchy, ranked according to degrees of sexual renunciation. His reading of the bridal imagery creates a symbolic world in which celibate Christians, especially women, have priority of place by virtue of their ascetic resolve.

One further aspect of Jerome's letter should be noted. Letter 65 to Principia was written in 397, near the end of the decade that witnessed the Jovinianist controversy in the West. Jovinian's efforts to resist the formation of an ascetic elite in the church and his views on the essential equality of married and celibate Christians had met with ecclesiastical censure at Rome under Pope Siricius and at Milan under Ambrose in the early 390s. Nevertheless, Jovinian's ideas had continued to spread and to influence Western Christians. In 396, for example, Ambrose had to write a lengthy letter to the church at Vercelli, urging them to resist the efforts of some followers of Jovinian, the monks Sarmatio and Barbatianus, to influence the episcopal election at Vercelli.[43] Augustine also, about the year 400, wrote two treatises on marriage and virginity, *De bono coniugali* and *De sancta virginitate*, which he says were necessary because of the continued spread of Jovinian's ideas.[44]

It is well known that Jerome's own treatise *Against Jovinian* had been roundly criticized at Rome for its excesses and even taken out of circulation by his friends.[45] Moreover, during the years 393–97 Jerome had already become embroiled in the Origenist controversy, a bitter debate that was eventually to alienate Jerome from lifelong friends, such as Rufinus of Aquileia.

Jerome had even briefly suffered excommunication at the hands of Bishop John of Jerusalem.[46] Jerome's stature as an ascetic teacher and biblical scholar, therefore, was very much under attack in these years. His interpretation of the virgin bride, particularly as it emerged in his commentary on Psalm 45, was perhaps something more than simply a rhetorical argument on behalf of the ascetic movement. Letter 65 to Principia, with its vigorous defense of the education of women and its zealous apology for ascetic hierarchy, can also be read as an apology for Jerome's own authority as a teacher in the domains of biblical study and ascetic practice.

AUGUSTINE: THE CHURCH AS THE BRIDE OF CHRIST

This brings me to my final commentator, Augustine of Hippo. As noted above, Augustine showed little interest in the Song of Songs and its bridal language. His use of the Song, as Elizabeth Clark has noted, is restricted almost entirely to refutations of the attempts of the Donatists to claim the text as a descriptor of their own ecclesial body.[47] The case of Psalm 45, I would argue, is somewhat different. Here Augustine shows a greater appreciation of the bridal imagery of the psalm, especially when it is applied to the church. Furthermore, when Augustine is compared to Ambrose and Jerome, the contrast is striking. Rather than use the bridal imagery of Psalm 45 or the Song of Songs to refer to Christian ascetics, Augustine uses it to refute any form of ecclesial elitism, whether Manichean or Donatist. And when Augustine was faced with the verses of the psalm that speak of the bride and her virginal companions, he used the text to stress the priority of the church and to remind celibate Christians that their celibacy would not save them apart from the church. An examination of a representative sample of Augustine's citations of Psalm 45 will demonstrate the difference between Augustine and his ascetic contemporaries Ambrose and Jerome.

Augustine treats Psalm 45 in a variety of works: letters, sermons, and polemical treatises. In all of them his interpretation is consistently ecclesial. His use of the text appears as early as the treatise *Contra Faustum Manichaeum*, composed circa 398 just after the *Confessions*. Here Augustine cites several verses of the psalm to argue against the Manichean claim to be the pure bride of Christ. The appearance of the true church, the bride of Christ, was prophesied, Augustine argues, in Psalm 45. The psalmist uttered numerous prophecies about the coming of the chaste virgin. The fact that these prophecies have now been fulfilled is evidence that the Old Testament prophets spoke truly.[48] In this passage of *Contra Faustum* Augustine's argument against the Manichees is essentially about the validity of the Hebrew scriptures and not about the church per se. Nevertheless, Augustine's early use of Psalm 45 against the Manichees may have helped confirm in his mind the idea that the virgin bride of Psalm 45 is first and foremost the Catholic Church.

Augustine's argument about the existence and spread of the church as the fulfillment of prophecy was to become increasingly prominent in his writings during the next two decades, particularly in apologetic argument against pagans and in debate with the Donatists. In the *City of God*, for example, Psalm 45 is the very first text Augustine cites as clear evidence of the psalmist's prophetic testimony about Christ and the church. The first ten verses of the psalm, which describe an anointed king, Augustine argues, clearly refer to Christ; the remainder of the psalm, which describes the queen, refers to Christ's church "wedded to so great a husband by a spiritual marriage and a divine love." After quoting the entire text of Psalm 45, Augustine goes on to state: "I do not imagine that anyone is such a fool as to think that some mere woman is here praised and described, as the wife, that is, of one who is thus addressed. . . . Obviously, this is Christ, anointed above his Christian followers. For they are his followers, from whose unity and concord in all nations that queen comes into being, who in another psalm is described as 'the city of the great king.'"[49] Augustine's point is that the text of Psalm 45 describes both a transcendent king (Christ) and a transcendent bride (the church), which is the spiritual Zion or Jerusalem. This queen, he goes on to note, has been set free from Babylon, the city of the devil, by baptismal rebirth: "That is why she is told to 'forget your people and your father's house.'"[50] This city contains both the prophets and patriarchs of old, as well as the Gentiles who enter by faith. Commenting on the final verses of Psalm 45, Augustine notes: "Thus what we now see fulfilled was said in prophecy so long before to this queen, 'In place of your fathers there are sons born to you; you will make them princes over all the earth' (Ps. 45:17); for it is true that from her sons throughout all the earth come her leaders and fathers, since the people acknowledge her pre-eminence, as they flock together to confess her everlasting praise for all time to come."[51] Augustine's treatment of Psalm 45 in the *City of God* shows that a high ecclesiology dominates his discussion of the virgin bride. No mere human being can be the object of the text's reference. For Augustine the virgin bride of Psalm 45 can be no one other than the church, the "city of God." Only such a queen can truly embody the virgin who is the bride of so great a king.

Augustine's stress on the church as the prophetic fulfillment of Psalm 45 is also developed in an anti-Donatist direction in several sermons preached during the first decade of the fifth century. In Sermon 138, for example, Augustine cites Psalm 45:14 ("The beauty of the king's daughter is all within") in the midst of discussing Song of Songs 1:6 ("Tell me, O you whom my soul has loved, where do you graze your flock, where do you make it lie down *in meridie*?"). As Maureen Tilley has demonstrated, this text from the Song was used by Donatists to express their view that the true church of Christ was present "in the south" (*in meridie*), that is, in North Africa.[52] For Augustine the text of the Song of Songs must be read in the light of Psalm 45. The bride, whose "beauty is all within," signifies the church. She must be beautiful not only in her external gifts (which are possessed by heretical communities, as well as orthodox ones) but internally as well. For Augustine, this internal beauty signifies her unity and universality: "that she is one, that she is found among all nations, that she is chaste, that she ought not to be corrupted by perverse conversation with evil companions."[53]

In another sermon, 360A, recently discovered and edited by François Dolbeau, Augustine also uses Psalm 45 against the Donatists to portray a church whose universal spread is the prophetic fulfillment of scripture. Citing Psalm 45:11 ("Hear, O daughter, and see, and forget your people and your father's house"), Augustine says that the words of the psalm were addressed both to our ancestors in faith and to us: "They *heard* the promises, we *see* the fulfillment."[54] The promise was made in Genesis 22:18 ("In your seed all the nations shall be blessed"). Augustine argues that "this is *seen* by us because it is *fulfilled* in us."[55]

Moving on to verses 14–15, the passage about the queen dressed in gold and robed in many colors, Augustine develops the theme of the universalism of the Catholic Church in contrast to what he regards as Donatist provincialism. The "many colors" of the queen's robes are the many languages in which Christianity has spread: Latin, Greek, Punic, Hebrew, Syriac, Indian, Cappadocian, and Egyptian. In the church, he writes, there is "variety of color, but unity in weave." For Augustine the text of Psalm 45 is used to create the image of a church whose universal spread guarantees the authenticity of her existence as the fulfillment of prophecy. His interpretation (like the rival interpretations of his Donatist contemporaries) was intended to construct an ecclesial world that would fortify his congregation against alternative readings of the virgin bride of scripture.

But what about the ascetic use of the virgin bride? Surely Augustine was aware of the exegetical tendencies of Ambrose and Jerome regarding the bride of Psalm 45 or the Song of Songs. As noted above, he too was engaged in the ascetic debates of the late fourth century. His own treatises, *De bono coniugali* and *De sancta virginitate*, were written as an attempt to find a middle ground between Jovinian's equation of marriage and celibacy and Jerome's excessive depreciation of marriage. What is Augustine's view of the ascetic readings of the virgin bride, such as those we have seen in Ambrose and Jerome? In his commentary on Psalm 45, which is found among his *Enarrationes in Psalmos* and was preached probably in 404, there is perhaps an answer.

In his *enarratio* on Psalm 45, whenever Augustine discusses any verses of the psalm that pertain to the virgin bride or to her attendants (the "daughters of kings" of Psalm 45:10), his interpretations are resolutely ecclesial. The "daughters of kings" are "all the souls that have been born through the activity of preaching and evangelization, and the churches, who are the daughters of the apostles, are the daughters of kings."[56] The multicolored robe of the queen is, once again, the spread of Christian doctrine in a multitude of languages.[57] When the prophet addresses the queen, as in verse 11 ("Hear, O daughter, and see, incline your ear, and forget your people and your father's house"), Augustine says that he is addressing each one of us as well, "provided that we know where we are, and endeavor to belong to that body, and do belong to it in faith and hope, being united in the members of Christ."[58]

Throughout his discussion of Psalm 45 Augustine continues to stress the ecclesial interpretation until he comes to verse 15 ("After her the virgins shall be brought to the king, her companions shall follow her"). Only here does Augustine raise the question of celibate Christians, and he does so in a decidedly unsympathetic way: "Truly this has happened. The church has believed; the church has been formed throughout all nations. To what extent do virgins now seek to find favor with that King? How are they moved to do so? Because the church has preceded them. 'Behind her the virgins shall be brought to the king, her companions shall follow her' (Ps. 45:15). For those who follow her are not estranged from her but are her companions who belong to her."[59] Augustine notes that the text speaks of the virgins as "companions" or "loved ones" (*proximae*) of the queen, not strangers (*alienae*). They must belong to the church, *ad eam pertinentes*, in order to enter into the king's presence.

As Augustine proceeds to discuss verse 16 ("With joy and gladness they are led into the temple of the king"), he makes an even more surprising suggestion—the temple of the king, into which the bride and her companions enter, is the church itself. To enter into the temple is to enter into the church. Such an interpretation is possible, Augustine says, because the temple of the king is constructed out of God's faithful spread throughout the world, that is, the "living stones" of 1 Peter 2:4, "whose mortar is charity." The temple of the king consists in unity; it is not divided by schism. "Therefore," Augustine writes, "those virgins who stand outside of the church are heretical virgins. Yes, they are virgins, but what profit does it bring them if they do not enter the temple of the king? . . . Even those who have chosen to be virgins cannot find favor with the king, unless they are led into the temple of the king."[60] Unlike Ambrose and Jerome, who assimilated the Christian virgin to the church as bride of Christ as she entered the temple of the king, Augustine assimilates the church as bride of Christ to the temple of the king itself. Such an exegetical maneuver underscored Augustine's point that it was only as a member of the church that one entered the temple of the king.

Compared to the readings of Psalm 45 by Ambrose and Jerome, Augustine's interpretation of the bridal imagery is remarkable for its inclusion of all Christians in the one body of Christ. In other contexts, to be sure, most notably in his writings on marriage and celibacy, Augustine could argue for the superiority of celibacy over marriage. Nevertheless, even in these works, he was reluctant to invoke the bridal imagery of Psalm 45 or of the Song of Songs to support this view.[61] On the rare occasions when Augustine does make use of bridal imagery, he does so only to remind celibate Christians that they and their married sisters are members of the same church. As he wrote concerning celibate women in his treatise *On the Good of Widowhood*: "The church itself, of which they are members, is the bride of Christ, and the church itself is ever a virgin by the integrity of faith, hope, and charity, not only in holy virgins, but also in widows and the wedded faithful. Indeed, it is to that universal church, of which all these are members, that the apostle says: 'I promised you in marriage to one husband, to present you as a chaste virgin to Christ' (2 Cor. 11:2)."[62] After decades of polemic against Manichean asceticism and Donatist exclusivism, it seems that Augustine was skeptical of any type of elitism that threatened to compromise the unity of the church. Therefore, he was willing to apply these texts of marital intimacy and sublime purity only to the whole church, celibate and married.

But Augustine's commentary on Psalm 45 did not end with the entry of the virgins into the temple of the king. Verse 17 of Psalm 45 speaks one final exhortation to the virgin bride: "In place of fathers, sons will be born to you. You will establish them as princes over all the earth." Who are these "fathers" and "sons"? According to Augustine, the "fathers" must refer to the apostles, whose preaching gave birth to the church. It was not possible, however, for the "fathers" to stay forever with the church. Since God would not leave the church bereft at the death of the apostles, he has appointed "sons" to rule in their place, that is, the bishops: "The apostles were sent as 'fathers.' In place of the apostles, 'sons' are born to you, that is, bishops are appointed. From what source have they been born, the bishops who are spread throughout the world today? The church itself calls them 'fathers'; she herself has given birth to them and has established them on the seats of the 'fathers.'"[63] The bishops who have been appointed to take the place of the apostles have, in the words of Psalm 45, been established "as princes over all the earth." For Augustine, the universal character of the episcopate grounds the universal character of the true church. *Haec est catholica ecclesia*, he writes: "Her sons have been established as princes over all the earth; her sons have been established in place of the fathers. Let those who are cut off acknowledge this, let them come into unity, let them enter the temple of the king. God has established his temple in every place [*ubique*]; God has made firm the foundations of the prophets and apostles in every place [*ubique*]. The church has given birth to sons; she has established them in place of the fathers as princes over all the earth."[64] In the closing words of his discourse on Psalm 45, Augustine stresses a dimension of the "virgin bride" that is largely absent from the ascetic discourses of Ambrose and Jerome.[65]

By focusing on the language of "fathers" and "sons," Augustine has introduced a decidedly paternal and patriarchal dimension into his interpretation of the psalm. In contrast to Ambrose and Jerome, whose reflections on the virginal church as bride of Christ led them naturally to speak of the celibate Christian or consecrated virgin as bride of Christ, Augustine resisted this ascetic reading. For Augustine, episcopal authority, rather than ascetic effort, defined the contours of the true church. Profoundly influenced by his struggle against Donatism, Augustine's reading of Psalm 45 emphasized the authority of the (male) bishop in establishing the universal character of the (female) church. Rather than serving as a warrant for sexual asceticism, Augustine's discussion of the bridal imagery of Psalm 45 created an image of the church whose universal character, embodied in the universal episcopate, vastly overshadowed any individual's ascetic effort.

———

In this essay we have seen that the biblical image of the virgin bride was put to a variety of uses by Western ecclesiastical writers in the late fourth and early fifth centuries. Analysis of the treatment of Psalm 45 in Ambrose, Jerome, and Augustine has suggested that each of the various (male) authors used the (female) image to construct his own particular vision of the church, asceticism, and ecclesiastical authority. It was, perhaps, not accidental that each of these different church "fathers" chose the image of a virgin bride (and "mother") to express his own deepest convictions regarding the church, the body, and society. As Averil Cameron has argued in *Christianity and the Rhetoric of Empire*, it was precisely such a "discourse of paradox," expressed in antinomies such as "virgin mother" and "spiritual marriage," that was adopted by leaders of the church to articulate their own sense of the boundaries between church and world. "It was a discourse that worked by metaphor and paradox, and that boldly exploited the very imagery it was ostensibly denying. . . . As virginity is the perfect state, so virginity is a figure for Christianity itself."[66]

In the fourth and fifth centuries the question of the place of Christianity in the late Roman world, as well as the correlative question of the nature of the true Christian life, was particularly pressing to thoughtful Christians.[67] All of the authors we have considered used the figure of the virgin bride to express both their ideal Christian community and their own authoritative role within that community. Their intensive resort to the language of paradox indicates, perhaps, the risks and ambiguities inherent in negotiating a course for the church in the post-Constantinian establishment. The rhetoric of virginal purity became all the more prevalent at a time when the actual identity of the church was most susceptible to compromise.[68] Not surprisingly, it was Augustine, with his thoroughgoing sense of human sinfulness, who most strongly resisted the tendency to assimilate the Christian ascetic to the virgin bride. Believing that the purity of the church was only an eschatological prospect, Augustine insisted on maintaining a distinction between the ideal of a virginal church and the present ecclesial reality.[69]

Notes

An earlier version of this chapter was delivered at the University of Notre Dame as part of the symposium "The Harp of Prophecy: The Psalms in Early Christian Exegesis," October 16–18, 1998. I am grateful to Brian E. Daley, S.J., for his kind invitation to the symposium and his generous support of it. A somewhat different version was delivered at the annual meeting of the American Society of Church History, January 7–10, 1999, as part of the session "The Bible in North Africa and Maureen Tilley's *The Bible in Christian North Africa.*" I have also benefited very much from the comments of the anonymous reviewers for *Church History.*

1. For an explication of the theoretical influences on this development and a helpful exploration of its practical implications for church historians, see Elizabeth A. Clark, "The Lady Vanishes: Dilemmas of a Feminist Historian after the 'Linguistic Turn,'" *Church History* 67 (1998): 1–31.

2. Averil Cameron has been a notable proponent of this perspective. See *Christianity and the Rhetoric of Empire: The Development of Christian Discourse,*

Sather Classical Lectures 55 (Berkeley: University of California Press, 1991), and her essay, "Virginity as Metaphor: Women and the Rhetoric of Early Christianity," in *History as Text: The Writing of Ancient History*, ed. Averil Cameron (Chapel Hill: University of North Carolina Press, 1989), 181–205. Behind many of the current developments stands the work of Michel Foucault. See Averil Cameron, "Redrawing the Map: Early Christian Territory after Foucault," *Journal of Roman Studies* 76 (1986): 266–71.

3. Judith Perkins, *The Suffering Self: Pain and Narrative Representation in the Early Christian Era* (London: Routledge, 1995); Kate Cooper, *The Virgin and the Bride: Idealized Womanhood in Late Antiquity* (Cambridge, MA: Harvard University Press, 1996). For a somewhat different application of the same approach, see Virginia Burrus, "Reading Agnes: The Rhetoric of Gender in Ambrose and Prudentius," *Journal of Early Christian Studies* 3 (1995): 25–46, and " 'Equipped for Victory': Ambrose and the Gendering of Orthodoxy," *Journal of Early Christian Studies* 4 (1996): 461–75.

4. Clark, "Lady Vanishes," 27, with reference to Peter Brown, *The Body and Society: Men, Women, and Sexual Renunciation in Early Christianity* (New York: Columbia University Press, 1988), 153.

5. See, for example, the important cautions expressed by Clark, "Lady Vanishes," 24–30.

6. Perkins, *Suffering Self*, 5.

7. A notable example in early Christian studies is Maureen Tilley, *The Bible in Christian North Africa: The Donatist World* (Minneapolis, MN: Fortress Press, 1997). Adopting insights from the sociology of religion, Tilley charts changes in the Donatist use of the Bible over several generations and correlates these changes with alterations in the social and political environment of the Donatist community.

8. K. Cooper, *Virgin and the Bride*, 55. Cf. Kate Cooper, "Insinuations of Womanly Influence: An Aspect of the Christianization of the Roman Aristocracy," *Journal of Roman Studies* 82 (1992): 150–64.

9. Elizabeth A. Clark, "The Uses of the Song of Songs: Origen and the Later Latin Fathers," in *Ascetic Piety and Women's Faith: Essays on Late Ancient Christianity* (Lewiston, NY: Edwin Mellen, 1986), 386–427, esp. 401–6.

10. Ibid., 407–10.

11. See Jerome, *Adversus Jovinianum* 1.37, 2.19, 2.30 (PL 23: 275–76, 328, 341). A fuller discussion of Jovinian's arguments can be found in David G. Hunter, "Resistance to the Virginal Ideal in Late-Fourth-Century Rome: The Case of Jovinian," *Theological Studies* 48 (1987): 45–64, and "Helvidius, Jovinian, and the Virginity of Mary in Late Fourth-Century Rome," *Journal of Early Christian Studies* 1 (1993): 47–71.

12. I will cite the verses of Psalm 45 according to the enumeration in the Vulgate edition, which differs slightly from that found in contemporary English

versions. See R. Weber, ed., *Biblia Sacra iusta vulgatam versionem* (Stuttgart: Württembergische Bibelanstalt, 1975), 824.

13. Clark, "Uses of the Song," 404. The treatises in question are *De virginibus* (ca. 377), *De virginitate* (possibly ca. 378), *De institutione virginis* (ca. 391–92), and *Exhortatio virginitatis* (ca. 393–95). I have followed the dating of these treatises proposed by Maria Grazia Mara, the editor of Part III, "Ambrose of Milan, Ambrosiaster and Nicetas," in *The Golden Age of Latin Patristic Literature*, vol. 4 of *Patrology*, ed. Angelo di Berardino, trans. P. Solari (Westminster, MD: Christian Classics, 1986), 167–69, substantially confirmed by Boniface Ramsey, *Ambrose, The Early Church Fathers* (London: Routledge, 1997), 60–61, 71.

14. For a discussion of the dating and composition, see Y.-M. Duval, "L'originalité du *De virginibus* dans le mouvement ascétique occidental," in *Ambroise de Milan: XVIe centenaire de son élection episcopale*, ed. Y.-M. Duval (Paris: Études Augustiniennes, 1974), 11–12.

15. Ambrose, *De virginibus* 1.22 (ed. Franco Gori, *Verginità e vedovanza*, 2 vols., Opera omnia di sant'Ambrogio 14.1–2 [Rome: Città Nuova Editrice, 1989], 1: 28).

16. Ambrose, *De virginibus* 1.31 (ed. Gori, *Verginità e vedovanza*, 1: 132).

17. Ambrose, *De virginibus* 1.31 (ed. Gori, *Verginità e vedovanza*, 1: 132): "Nostra virum non habet, sed habet sponsum, eo quod siue ecclesia in populis siue anima in singulis dei uerbo sine ullo flexu pudoris quasi sponso innubit aeterno effeta iniuriae, feta rationis."

18. Ambrose, *De virginibus* 1.36 (ed. Gori, *Verginità e vedovanza*, 1: 136).

19. Ambrose, *De virginibus* 1.36 (ed. Gori, *Verginità e vedovanza*, 1: 136).

20. Ambrose, *De virginibus* 1.37 (ed. Gori, *Verginità e vedovanza*, 1: 138).

21. Ambrose, *De virginibus* 1.37 (ed. Gori, *Verginità e vedovanza*, 1: 138).

22. Ambrose, *De virginibus* 1.38 (ed. Gori, *Verginità e vedovanza*, 1: 138–40): "Quibus indiciis ostenditur perfecta et inreprehensibilis virginalis animae pulchritudo altaribus consecrata diuinis inter occursus et latibula spiritalium bestiarum non inflexa mortalibus et intenta mysteriis dei meruisse dilectum, cuius ubera plena laetitiae."

23. Ambrose, *De virginibus* 1.37–38 (ed. Gori, *Verginità e vedovanza*, 1: 138–40): "spiritu consecrata divino . . . dicatur domino, consecratur deo . . . altaribus consecrata divinis." In another work, *De institutione virginis*, composed as a homily for the consecration of the virgin Ambrosia, Ambrose again invoked Psalm 45 and the Song of Songs to speak of virginal consecration. See *De institutione virginis* 1.2–5 (ed. Gori, *Verginità e vedovanza*, 2: 110–12).

24. For the ceremony of virginal consecration, see René Metz, *La consécration des vierges dans l'église romaine* (Paris: Presses Universitaires de France, 1954); and R. D'Izarny, "Mariage et consécration virginale au IVe siècle," *Vie Spirituelle*, suppl., 6 (1953): 92–107. It has recently been argued that the liturgy of virginal

consecration in Ambrose's day actually included the formal recitation of the Song of Songs. See Nathalie Henry, "The Song of Songs and the Liturgy of the *Velatio* in the Fourth Century: From Literary Metaphor to Liturgical Reality," in *Continuity and Change in Christian Worship: Papers Read at the 1997 Summer Meeting and the 1998 Winter Meeting of the Ecclesiastical History Society,* ed. R. N. Swanson (Woodbridge: Boydell, 1999), 18–28.

25. Canonical literature from the later fourth century frequently contains instructions for bishops on how to handle cases of consecrated virgins who have lapsed from their profession. In a decree of Pope Siricius, for example, the consecrated virgin who subsequently married was considered excommunicated until the death of her (human) spouse. See Siricius, *Ep.* 10.1.3 *Ad Gallos episcopos* (PL 13: 1182).

26. Ambrose, *De institutione virginis* 107 (ed. Gori, *Verginità e vedovanza,* 2: 186): "Quam sacerdotali munere offero, affectu patrio commendo."

27. See, for example, *De virginibus* 3.1 (ed. Gori, *Verginità e vedovanza,* 1: 206), where Ambrose cites the words of Pope Liberius in his sermon on the veiling of Marcellina.

28. Canon 31, in *Concilia Africae, a. 345–a. 525,* ed. Charles Munier, CCSL 149 (Turnholt: Brepols, 1974), 42. According to Ambrose it was also the bishop's responsibility to decide whether a virgin was mature enough to receive the veil and whether the circumstances of her home were conducive to the success of her vow. See *De virginitate* 7.39 (ed. Gori, *Verginità e vedovanza,* 2: 38).

29. Neil McLynn, *Ambrose of Milan: Church and Court in a Christian Capital* (Berkeley: University of California Press, 1994), 60–68. The actual candidates for consecration, McLynn suggests, were imported from outside Milan by episcopal allies of Ambrose, since he himself had failed to elicit much interest in the virginal life at Milan. Cf. Daniel H. Williams, *Ambrose of Milan and the End of the Nicene-Arian Conflicts* (Oxford: Clarendon Press, 1995), 128: "Ambrose was acutely aware of his own deficiencies upon assuming the reins of ministry at Milan, referring to himself as 'indoctus' (unlearned) and an 'initiate in religious matters.'"

30. See, for example, Brown's discussion of the importance of clerical celibacy in generating the power of the clergy in *Body and Society,* 357–58, and David G. Hunter's "Clerical Celibacy and the Veiling of Virgins: New Boundaries in Late Ancient Christianity," in *The Limits of Ancient Christianity: Essays on Late Antique Thought and Culture in Honor of R.A. Markus,* ed. W. Klingshirn and M. Vessey (Ann Arbor: University of Michigan Press, 1999), 139–52.

31. This is not to say that Jerome was completely uninterested in the ritual of virginal consecration. For example, in *Ep.* 130, written in 414 on the occasion of the veiling of the virgin Demetrias, Jerome could describe her consecration at the hands of the bishop with a string of verses from Psalm 45 and the Song of

Songs. See *Ep.* 130.2 (CSEL 55: 176–77). Nevertheless, the ritual does not seem to have had the same significance for Jerome as it did for Ambrose.

32. Jerome, *Ep.* 22.1.1 (CSEL 54: 143–44).

33. Jerome, *Ep.* 54.3 (CSEL 54: 468).

34. Jerome, *Ep.* 54.3 (CSEL 54: 468).

35. It is virtually certain, for example, that a charge of immorality was made against Jerome and that this was the primary reason for his departure from Rome after the death of Pope Damasus. See the discussion in J. N. D. Kelly, *Jerome: His Life, Writings, and Controversies* (New York: Harper and Row, 1975), 111–14. The primary source of evidence is Jerome's *Ep.* 45.

36. Jerome, *Ep.* 65.1 (CSEL 54: 618).

37. Jerome, *Ep.* 65.2 (CSEL 54: 619).

38. For examples of phrases applying to Principia as a virgin, see Jerome, *Ep.* 65.12, 14.

39. Jerome, *Ep.* 65.15 (CSEL 54: 637).

40. Quote from Jerome, *Ep.* 65.16 (CSEL 54: 639). Here Jerome interprets Psalm 45:11–12 as the soul abandoning its vices and putting away its past way of life.

41. Jerome, *Ep.* 65.20 (CSEL 54: 642).

42. Jerome, *Ep.* 65.20 (CSEL 54: 643).

43. Ambrose, *Ep.* 14 extra collectionem (CSEL 82/3). In this letter Ambrose makes extensive use of the image of the church as a virgin bride in order to argue for the superiority of virginity over marriage.

44. See Augustine's comments on *De bono coniugali* in his *Retractationes* 2.22 (CCSL 57: 107–8). It is significant in this context that Augustine's arguments in *De bono coniugali* were directed as much against the excesses of Jerome's *Adversus Jovinianum* as they were against Jovinian's positions.

45. See Jerome, *Ep.* 48, 49, 50.

46. J. Kelly, *Jerome*, 195–209; cf. Elizabeth A. Clark, *The Origenist Controversy: The Cultural Construction of an Early Christian Debate* (Princeton, NJ: Princeton University Press, 1992), 121–32, who stresses the connection between the Jovinianist and Origenist controversies.

47. Clark, "Uses of the Song," 407–10.

48. Augustine, *Contra Faustum Manichaeum* 15.11 (CSEL 25/1:438–39).

49. Augustine, *De civitate Dei* 17.16 (CSEL 40/2: 249.5–250.3; trans. Henry Bettenson, *Augustine: Concerning the City of God against the Pagans* [New York: Penguin, 1972], 747).

50. Augustine, *De civitate Dei* 17.16 (CSEL 40/2: 250.11–12; trans. Bettenson, *City of God*, 748).

51. Augustine, *De civitate Dei* 17.16 (CSEL 40/2: 251.5–11; trans. Bettenson, *City of God*, 748).

52. Tilley, *Bible*, 148–49.

53. Augustine, *S.* 138.8 (PL 38: 767).

54. Augustine, *S.* 360A.1 (ed. François Dolbeau, *Augustin d'Hippone: Vingt-six sermons au people d'Afrique* [Paris: Études Augustiennes, 1996], 42).

55. Augustine, *S.* 360A.2 (ed. Dolbeau, *Augustin d'Hippone*, 43).

56. Augustine, *En. Ps.* 44.23 (CCSL 38: 510).

57. Augustine, *En. Ps.* 44.24 (CCSL 38: 512).

58. Augustine, *En. Ps.* 44.25 (CCSL 38: 512).

59. Augustine, *En. Ps.* 44.30 (CCSL 38: 515).

60. Augustine, *En. Ps.* 44.31–32 (CCSL 38: 515–16).

61. In *De bono coniugali* and *De sancta virginitate*, for example, there are no references to the Song of Songs. In *De sancta virginitate* Augustine alludes to Psalm 45:3 on three occasions but does not develop the theme of the consecrated virgin as bride of Christ at any length. See *De sancta virginitate* 11.11, 37.38, 44.55.

62. Augustine, *De bono viduitatis* 10.13 (CSEL 41: 319). Cf. 3.4 and 6.8.

63. Augustine, *En. Ps.* 44.32 (CCSL 38: 516).

64. Augustine, *En. Ps.* 44.32 (CCSL 38: 516).

65. At the end of *Ep.* 65 (CSEL 54: 644), Jerome presents several different interpretations of the "fathers" and "sons" of Psalm 45:17. One possible reading he offers is that the "sons" begotten by the church are those who have become teachers (*magistros*): "O, church, your sons, to whom you have given birth, are turned into your fathers, when you make into teachers those who were formerly disciples and when you establish them in the priestly order [*in sacerdotali gradu*] by the testimony of all." Jerome, however, develops this interpretation no further.

66. A. Cameron, *Rhetoric of Empire*, 175.

67. See the stimulating discussion of this problem in R. A. Markus, *The End of Ancient Christianity* (Cambridge: Cambridge University Press, 1990), especially 19–83.

68. Cf. Brown, *Body and Society*, 353, who thus characterizes Ambrose's concern with perpetual virginity: "What was at stake was the absolute nature of the boundaries that separated the Catholic Church from the world, as well as those which rendered individual virgins irrevocably 'sacred' by reason of their vocation, and separate from their families."

69. See, for example, the conclusion of *En. Ps.* 44 (CCSL 38: 517), where Augustine contrasts the final destiny of the church with its current state, in which her full identity is unknown even to herself.

A Sharp Pen versus Fragrant Myrrh

Comparing the Commentaries of Cyril of Alexandria and Theodore of Mopsuestia on Psalm 45

Ronald R. Cox

The context of Psalm 45 (LXX 44) is a wedding between a king and his bride.[1] Much like the Song of Songs, this was suggestive material for early Christian exegesis. Still, even were one not predisposed to understand the king to be representative of Christ, and the king's bride representative of the church, the psalm's citation in the New Testament (Heb. 1:8–9) practically provides a mandate for such an understanding. Hence, if we wish to gain a window into the world of early patristic exegesis, Psalm 44 is an ideal test case. This is especially so if we are interested in comparing and contrasting the exegetical tendencies of the Alexandrian and Antiochene "schools," since the mandate just mentioned constrains *both* schools to deal with the Christological significance of the psalm.

While in many ways Cyril of Alexandria's exegesis can be distinguished from that of earlier commentators usually designated as belonging to the Alexandrian "school," he is in his Christological exegesis most definitely indebted to the Origenist approach to scripture.[2] Indeed, as John O'Keefe has said, Cyril, "more than any other patristic author, focuses his exegesis on the reality of Christ as present, in shadow and type, in the Old Testament. It was part of his method to focus on how the text testified to the reality of Christ. . . . According to Cyril, Christ was always there [in Scripture], always just below the surface of the letter of the text waiting for an occasion . . . to burst forth for all but the most blind and foolish people to see."[3] With regard to the psalms in particular, Cyril—writing probably between 400 and 420—believed David had prophesied in them everything about Christ, his life and teaching, and even the experiences of the first Christians.[4]

Theodore of Mopsuestia is usually placed at the opposite end of the spectrum from the Alexandrians in terms of the theological interests that drive his exegesis and in terms of the resulting emphases in his interpretations. Theodore, a student of Diodore of Tarsus, seems to have composed his *Commentary on the Psalms* in the early 370s, when he was himself in his early twenties; his work embodies the Antiochene emphasis on *historia* (questions of philological and historical scholarship) in his interpretation of the Old Testament, and his treatment of the psalms is no exception.[5] Like Diodore, his primary concern in interpreting any given psalm is usually to determine its place within the longer narrative of Israel's history. Yet, while he is generally hesitant to accept a Christological interpretation of the psalms, Theodore does interpret Psalms 44, 2, 8, and 109 (LXX) as Davidic prophecies about Christ. All four of these psalms are viewed as prophecies of Christ in the New Testament. Beyond its New Testament use, Theodore justifies his departure from his usual approach by observing that the language used of the king in Psalm 44 (the king is called "God" and is told that his throne is "forever") has no proper referent among the kings of Israel. Such language is appropriate only for Christ.[6]

What makes these two writers' comments on Psalm 44 such a valuable case study in varieties of ancient approaches to Old Testament exegesis is that both Cyril and Theodore are in agreement that this psalm is a prophecy about Christ and his church. In what follows, I compare the comments of Theodore and Cyril on Psalm 44 as they pertain to three areas that I think best illuminate the differences and similarities between their exegesis of the psalm: (1) their method of reading the psalm and especially how they identify the speaker of the psalm; (2) the use of the Jews as a foil for sketching out what these commentators regard as the true— that is, Christian—interpretation; and (3) their Christology, or what this psalm in fact says to each of them about the person and work of Christ. For the sake of brevity and focus, I will limit my analysis to the verses that speak specifically about Christ—for both authors, this is the first eight (Cyril) or nine (Theodore) verses of the psalm. For both, the remainder of the psalm is a prophecy about the king's bride, the church.

Before I begin the study proper, I must point out that while Robert Devreesse has given us a reliable edition of Theodore's *Commentary on the Psalms* (up to Psalm 80), the reliability of Cardinal Mai's edition of Cyril's "commentary" on the psalms as preserved in Patrologia Graeca 69 has been questioned.[7] However, while much can be considered spurious in the comments that Mai edited for us, Marie-Josèphe Rondeau suggests that significant portions are probably Cyrillian.[8] With respect to Psalm 44, Devreesse has identified sections of the Mai edition that are probably authentic, and it is those sections that I use for this study.[9]

PART ONE:
WHO IS SPEAKING ABOUT WHAT IN PSALM 44?

Probably no other part of their commentaries on Psalm 44 sets off the methodological differences between Theodore and Cyril more than how they interpret verse 2.[10] Here the psalm reads, "My heart has uttered a good word; I declare my works to the king: my tongue is the pen of a quick writer." Theodore understands this verse to serve as David's prologue to the prophecy contained in the remainder of the psalm. As such, this prologue communicates the importance of the prophecy, that it is a "good" word. Theodore concludes from this that the prophecy is "surer than all the words of address found in the other psalms."[11] The reason for this astounding claim is that unlike the other psalms, which deal with earthly rulers and events, this psalm has "good" subject matter—"and what could be greater than what concerns the Christ."[12] According to Theodore's logic, the prophet would not call an "encomium of Solomon and his bride" or even a prophecy about Hezekiah "good."[13]

In addition, the prologue validates the prophet as messenger. The message is from the prophet's heart, denoting his deep assent to what is prophesied.[14] Theodore interprets "I will speak my works to the king" (Ps. 44:2b) to mean that the psalmist is engaged in a work of prophecy about the king for the benefit of others.[15] But it is beyond the prophet's abilities to speak a "good" word about the king. Hence he says, "My tongue is the pen of a quick writing secretary" (v. 2c). That secretary is "the first-rate scribe" whom we know as the Spirit, who "fills the heart with an understanding of revelation as if it were ink, and from there enables the tongue to utter it and to form words as if they were letters, and to articulate a message for those who wish to receive its benefit."[16] Thus the prologue (i.e., Ps. 44:2) affirms the credibility of the messenger: since he is not speaking of the king from his own thoughts but drawing on the revelation of the Spirit and expressing it like the pen in a writer's hand, his prophecy is worthy of belief.

It is true that the object of Psalm 44:2—the king—is the same for both Theodore and Cyril, namely, Christ. Cyril's reading of verse 2 is, however, markedly different. While Theodore thinks the psalmist is the one who speaks this verse, Cyril maintains that the speaker is actually God the Father. So when the psalm reads, "My heart pours forth a good word," we are to understand here that God the Father is talking about the eternal generation of the Logos. "For it is not permitted for mind, or heart, to ever be without expression; nor indeed for a word to be something that is not from the mind and directed toward the mind, or toward the heart and in the heart. By way of analogy, then, admitting God has a heart and mind, let us turn the eyes of our mind toward what is beyond the senses, and let us think of generation as something fitting for the Logos of God, which in the form of a word the Father 'poured forth from his heart.'"[17] And the Word is called "good" since "on account of the salvation of the world and of life he chose to suffer the voluntary emptying, out of the natural gentleness and calmness proper to God."[18] In other words, the praise of this word as good is rooted in the psalmist's sense of the economy of salvation.

Cyril's commentary continues this line of prosopological interpretation by asserting that it is God the Father who says, "I speak my deeds to the king."[19] Here it is not the value of the psalmist's prophecy but Christ's teaching that is affirmed as coming from God. As Jesus himself said: "The words which I speak are not mine, but are from the one who sent me" (John 12:16).[20] We discuss the significance of this further in the next section when we speak of Cyril's polemic against the Jews, but suffice it to say that in this verse God names Jesus as his instrument of revelation. This is supported in the last line of verse 2: "My tongue is the pen of a swift scribe." Here Cyril reads that Christ is both God's tongue and the pen of a swift writer. Like the tongue, Christ transmits "the things of [God's] heart and mind to those in the outside world."[21] And notice that where Theodore had the psalmist claim for himself the role of a pen in the hand of the Spirit, Cyril holds that Christ is the pen and that the scribe is not God's Spirit but God the Father himself. As this pen, "the unique Word of God fulfills just this [purpose], spiritually inscribing on the hearts of believers the great and wise and true will of the Father."[22]

So while Theodore claims that Psalm 44:2 prepares the reader for what is to come in the psalm, expressing both the importance of the message (it is the good word about Christ) and the reliability of the messenger (David is a compliant instrument of the skilled Holy Spirit), Cyril holds that God speaks directly here of Christ. Christ comes from God, like a word from the mind or the tongue expressing the things of the heart, and relays reliably all that his Father has entrusted to him.

Clearly, Cyril and Theodore are reading the psalm differently from the outset. But the contrast, in terms of their sense of the psalm's context and divinely intended significance, is even greater than what my observations suggest. It is no small thing to say that Theodore and Cyril perceive different subjects speaking this verse. And in fact, the speaker changes often in Cyril's comments on this psalm. He interprets Psalm 44:3bc as a word about Christ spoken by "the chorus of holy prophets."[23] Just before (v. 3a), it is God the Father who speaks. A little later, a line of the psalm will express the sentiment of the saints in general. Theodore, on the other hand, considers such assumed prosopological changes as demonstrating exegesis done "without sophistication, by the chance process of mental guesswork."[24]

Theodore's comments on Psalm 44 are of value for understanding how he believes the psalms in general must be read. In addition to establishing that David is a reliable prophet, Theodore spends a considerable amount of time discussing the fact that David is the sole voice we hear in the whole psalm as well. Indeed, nearly a quarter of his commentary on this psalm concerns the second verse ("I speak my works to the king"), and most of that on the issue of whether there can be a change of speakers in a psalm.[25] He wants it clearly understood that "in truth, there is never a change of speakers in the psalms."[26]

Theodore ridicules other interpreters who claimed (as Cyril would do forty years later) that this second verse was spoken not by David to God but by God to David.[27] Then David, according to these simple, unsophisticated readers, would be the one speaking in the following verses. This change of speakers "corrupts the sense of the whole psalm," with the result that "if David is referring to himself as 'king' in this verse, according to their interpretation, then in the whole psalm he is speaking of himself as king and no longer of the Lord Christ, to whom alone all that follows can apply. There is one speaker [*prosōpon*], then, throughout."[28] As we will discuss further when considering Theodore's Christology, he holds that Psalm 44 makes claims about a king that apply to no earthly king but only to Christ. By assuming that the whole psalm should be attributed to one speaker, Theodore understands himself to be not only reading it properly (i.e., with sophistication) but also preserving the quality of the prophecy about Christ.

Part Two:
The Jews as Foil in the Exegesis of Psalm 44

The persons Theodore blames for promoting this "corrupt" manner of reading the psalms as spoken by changing voices are the Jews. As he says, "It is not a good idea to omit saying [there is no change of speakers], especially because of the Jews, who use this notion to attack the true understanding [*dianoia*]" of the psalm.[29] Further, Christians who introduce this confusion of speakers are guilty of "cooperating with the Jews in their abuse of the text."[30] As we have said, a change of speakers allows the term *king* in Psalm 44:2b, in Theodore's view, to signify someone other than Christ, namely David. In light of this, Theodore exhorts, "We must therefore devote ourselves to making [the proper] interpretation, especially since the Jews have the audacity to turn this psalm in their own direction."[31]

According to Theodore, the Jews, by reading the psalm as about another king beside Christ, explain the psalm according to "their own principles of interpretation" and so turn the psalm into "more of a joke than a prophecy." Verses 7 and 8 (which we discuss further below) then read as if an earthly king is said to have an everlasting throne or that he is called "God." Even worse, the Jews actually claim this Davidic prophecy to have been addressed to Solomon and his bride. Such an encomium of Solomon and his bride by God would result in the "worst route of ignorance" imaginable, for the Jews would be "turning the sayings of the inspired prophet to naught, and making them into women's hymns and chants of praise."[32]

I cannot help but think that Theodore has in mind the Song of Solomon as he writes these comments, though he makes no explicit reference to that work. For it is important to note that Theodore, almost alone of early Christian exegetes, not only denies the allegorical reading of the Song as pertaining to Christ and his bride but even denies the book's inspiration entirely.[33] The Song of Solomon has no utility for the church, Theodore apparently argued, and should have no place in the canon, precisely because it was, in his opinion, a "woman's hymn," a poem about romantic love.[34] Such a strong stance makes one wonder how Theodore would have interpreted Psalm 44 if it had not been cited in the New Testament, or if he would have even bothered to attempt an interpretation. But for the New Testament, this psalm—which clearly had to do originally with the wedding of an Israelite king—probably would have suffered the same fate at Theodore's hand as Solomon's song.

We do not need to speculate about whether Cyril had the Song of Solomon in mind as he interpreted Psalm 44; in fact, he both refers to the book by name and quotes from it. In his interpretation of the verse "You are more beautiful than the sons of men" (Ps. 44:3a), he writes, "For who will compete with Christ? No one whatsoever! For indeed on account of this, the bride who is introduced in the Song of Songs—playing the part of the church—though the opportunity is given her to peruse the writings of the all-wise Moses, as well as those of the prophets, thirsts for the word about Christ; as she in fact says, 'Show me the sight of you, and let me hear your voice, because sweet is your voice and fair is the sight of you' (Song 2:14)."[35]

This passage not only reveals Cyril's favorable view of the Song but also shows that he, like Theodore, is mindful of the Jews as he interprets scripture. Cyril implies here that he understands Christ's word as superior to that of Moses and the prophets—a comparison we find frequently in his comments on Psalm 44. When speaking of Christ as the pen of the swift scribe, for instance, he writes: "The pen of God is very sharp indeed! For on the one hand the law through Moses foreshadows with great circularity and through much difficulty, faintly and scarcely—I speak of the literal sense—what is necessary; on the other hand, the Savior and Lord of the Universe, apart from every distraction, concisely reveals to us . . . the will of the Father."[36] And when the psalmist says, "God speaks his works to the king" (cf. Ps. 44:2b), this means—as we noted already—that Christ's teachings are directly from God. "For since, having rejected the shadow of the law, he says he himself is the truth; he teaches worship and service in spirit and truth."[37]

Whereas Theodore was concerned with how the Jews improperly interpreted scripture, Cyril is concerned with how Christianity has come to supersede Judaism *in toto*. As Robert Wilken states, when Cyril deals with Judaism in his exegesis, his central notion is "that Christianity is the result of a transformation of Judaism into a more God-pleasing way of life marked by worship in spirit and in truth."[38] The key to this transformation is Christ, the object of our psalm's prophecy. In this way, the prophecy of Psalm 44 appears to function in the same manner as Deuteronomy 18:18, a passage Cyril refers to in his commentary: "But we remember that God gave the promise concerning Christ to Israel gathered together on Mt. Horeb, saying to the hierophant Moses, 'I will raise up a prophet for them from among their brothers, like you; I will give my words in his mouth and he will speak to them according to all which I shall command him.'"[39] It is interesting to consider that Hebrews, the very New Testament book that quotes Psalm 44, addresses this same issue about the relationship between Judaism and Christianity. And its conclusion is the same as Cyril's: "Long ago God spoke to our ancestors in many and various ways by the prophets, but in these last days he has spoken to us by a Son" (Heb. 1:1–2).

Although Theodore and Cyril use the Jews as a negative contrast in divergent ways (for one to exemplify those who use improper exegesis, for the other to exemplify those involved in an outmoded means of worship), their purpose for doing so is the same: to acknowledge Christ as the real object of our psalm's prophecy.

PART THREE:
THE CHRISTOLOGY OF PSALM 44

That the psalm is, for both interpreters, about Christ results in a polemical bent in their interpretation, a polemic directed not just against the

Jews but against any who would diminish the ontological identity and work of Christ. But, as we shall observe momentarily, the identity and work of Christ according to our psalm are interpreted differently by Theodore and Cyril. Indeed, it is here where the most significant differences arise between Cyril and Theodore, differences not of exegetical presuppositions or method but of theology.

As we have already pointed out, Theodore thinks it foolish for the Jews to claim that the object of the psalm is an earthly king. After all, Psalm 44:5 ascribes to the king truth, justice, and gentleness; as the gospels show, Christ's ministry revealed in him all of these characteristics. Furthermore, "It is clear from . . . all of this that he is not speaking about a human king. For no human being, who is full of eagerness to establish kingly rule for himself, takes up arms and all that goes with them in order to teach his followers gentleness; on the contrary, in order to gain power and eradicate his enemies he exerts himself in every way to make his followers terrible to their enemies."[40] The subsequent line "Your throne, O God, is for ages and ages" (Ps. 44:7a) underscores that such characteristics cannot be ascribed to an earthly king.

According to Theodore, the prophet's saying to Christ "Your throne, O God, is forever" is meant to prevent anyone from thinking that Christ's kingship has come to him only recently or that he can lose it again. Christ "does not possess kingly power as something alien" to himself.[41] And that the psalmist calls the king "God" in one verse (Ps. 44:7a) but then says to the king, "God, your God, has anointed you" in the following verse (v. 8b) is not a problem for Theodore. This shows that what is said in both verses is said about Christ, "in whose case he [David] has here divided the natures in a marvelous way for our benefit, and has shown the unity of his person [prosōpou]. He divides the natures by using words expressive of different ideas—for there is a great difference between 'Your throne, O God, is for ever and ever' and 'Therefore God, your God has anointed you'—but he shows the unity by saying these things about one person."[42]

Christ's two natures lie also behind Theodore's reading of the verse "Myrrh and aloes and cassia radiate from your garments" (Ps. 44:9a). With the term garments Theodore understands the psalmist to refer to Christ's body, "since it is something wrapped around him from without, while his godhead is within, according to the principle of indwelling."[43] Myrrh, used in the anointing of the dead, signifies Christ's "passion and the glory of his passion."[44] "And having mentioned 'myrrh,' the prophet connects it well to the phrase 'from your garments,' so that we might realize that the godhead is free from passion."[45]

This understanding of the two natures of Christ, one divine and one human, may lie behind Theodore's rather concise interpretation of the verse "Therefore God has blessed you forever" (Ps. 44:3c). "That is," Theodore explains, "he made you blessed and so caused you to be praised by all people."[46] And here Cyril's comment on the same verse is of interest to us. The Alexandrian writes, "It says 'he has blessed you' and not 'he has made you blessed'"—refuting exactly Theodore's phrase.[47] While we cannot prove that Cyril is responding directly to Theodore, we do know he read his works; it is at least possible that Cyril here shows knowledge of Theodore's views on this psalm.[48] What is clear is that Cyril does not view such a rephrasing of the psalm positively. He is concerned "lest anyone say it is granted to the Son by the Father to be blessed along with us."[49] Rather, the proper reading of this verse sees it denoting the *kenōsis* of Christ, "that the things he has as God naturally, these he is said to receive humanly."[50]

This last line efficiently sums up the two aspects of Cyril's Christological agenda in his interpretation of Psalm 44: first, that "all the things of the Father are Christ's naturally." Thus Cyril interprets "Gird your sword on your thigh" (Ps. 44:4a) as speaking about what is Christ's naturally. The psalmist says "your sword," and not that of some other, so that we will understand that "nothing, whether from without or by introduction, can be added to Christ, but what is his own is reasonably conceived to be that which is fitting to God."[51] And with respect to the verse "Your throne, O God, is forever: a rod of justice is the rod of your reign" (v. 7) we are to notice that the psalmist calls the incarnated one "God." "For God was in the form of one of us, but he was not existing apart from what he was because of this; rather, he remained in his own preeminence and continued holding the rod of righteousness."[52] And on the verse "I speak my works to the king" (v. 2), Cyril writes "it is exceedingly good that the Father calls the Son 'king,' so that the mystery might not somehow seem to remove him— by the limits of the Incarnation—from the rank and preeminence over all things that inhere naturally in him."[53]

The second item on Cyril's agenda is to clarify what the Word received humanly in becoming flesh, and why. The *kenōsis* of the Divine Word is not about what he gave up naturally but rather about what he underwent—"the most human of limitations"—on our behalf.[54] Hence, when the psalmist says of Christ that "God has blessed you," we are to understand not something done for Christ's benefit but something done for ours. Cyril explains:

> it was necessary for the Son—having become human, and having been styled the second Adam, and having been established as a second root for those upon the earth—it was necessary for him to be blessed by God as a human, so that the power of the curse might then be ended, which was inflicted on the one who was both from the earth and out of clay: namely, the first root of humanity, Adam. For if in that one we came to be accursed, so also we have been blessed in Christ, who has conveyed to the whole race the grace given him as a human.[55]

Similarly, when the psalmist says, "God, your God, has anointed you" (Ps. 44:8b), this anointing is again not for Christ's benefit but for ours. Understanding the anointing to be of the Spirit, Cyril says, "On the one hand the Son is the bestower of the Holy Spirit—since all things of the Father are present to him naturally; on the other hand, he himself humanly receives the Sprit with us, when he becomes one of us, he did not add anything to himself, by which he is understood to be God and Logos; but by himself, the first of human kind, he secures on our behalf the Spirit of exultation."[56]

Both Theodore and Cyril want to interpret Psalm 44 as containing prophecies that instruct us about Christ. They agree that this psalm speaks to the superiority of Christ's teaching and the majesty of his reign, the humility of his passion and the glory of his exultation. But they differ, as we might expect from their other writings, in how they understand the person and natures of Christ. For Theodore, who seeks to safeguard God's deity, the psalm shows clearly that Christ, though one person (*prosōpon*), has two natures, one divine and impassible, the other human and capable of suffering. Cyril seeks to safeguard the mystery of the union brought about through the *oikonomia*: namely, the *kenōsis* of Christ in which Christ's one, divine nature undergoes and transcends human limitations so that we might experience divine exultation.

The Purpose of Psalm 44 and of Its Interpretation

Contrasting Theodore's and Cyril's comments on Psalm 44 in these three areas—the voice(s) of the psalmist, the use of the Jews as a foil, and Christology—helps to bring into fresh light how Antiochenes and Alexandrians typically compared in their reading of scripture. We have found basic similarities between these leading representatives of their respective exegetical schools, but connected to these similarities are substantial differences. Theodore and Cyril agree that none other than Christ is the object of this psalm's praise, but Cyril violates the rules against confusion of speakers that Theodore considers so important. This is telling about both interpreters. Theodore spends a great deal more time discussing how to read the psalm properly than explaining the psalm's content—so much so that we might suspect that for Theodore the claim that the psalm is about Christ actually dictates the proper method of reading the psalm, rather than vice versa. That Cyril changes speakers is evidence of his desire to do whatever it takes to "unpack" the Christology of the psalm; unlike Theodore, he seems to consider the psalm's literary integrity to be less important than its subject matter.

Again, both Theodore and Cyril use the Jews as a foil for their Christological exegesis. But we should notice that Theodore is, once again, more concerned about the improper exegetical method he identifies with the Jews, while Cyril is more concerned that Christ, and the worship he inaugurated, be seen to be superior to Judaism and its worship.

With respect to Christology, the differences are also pronounced, but of another kind. Here Theodore is not trying to protect the literary character of the psalm, as in the first two cases; rather, by means of asserting the two natures of Christ's one person, Theodore is attempting to protect God from being too closely tied to passible humanity. Cyril also is striving to protect God from being improperly understood, but in his case that means any understanding that diminishes what God, *qua* God, does in the economy of the Incarnation.

In evaluating the results of Theodore's and Cyril's interpretation of Psalm 44, it would be possible to conclude that, in terms of Christology, the psalm in itself is of little importance for either writer—it is merely a cipher for either one's theology. I would disagree. Even if, as most modern exegetes would assume, the psalm was originally composed as an encomium of a king at his wedding, it was also, at least in a secondary way, a song of praise addressed to that king's God. As such an instrument of double praise the psalm is significant to both of our writers, and to the church, which continues to use it in its worship. Theodore would have us focus our reading of the psalm on what is praiseworthy about God in his transcendent, divine nature, with Christ's human nature held safely at a distance. Cyril would have us focus on what is praiseworthy about the mystery of God's Son, who humbled his divine self to our lowly state for our sake. It is left to subsequent readers to learn from Theodore's and Cyril's varying theological emphases and exegetical strategies and to make their own judgments about how best to interpret a psalm that both early Christian writers believed forced readers to make decisions about their fundamental intellectual commitments.

NOTES

1. I use LXX versification rather than that of the Masoretic text throughout.

2. For theological interpretation of this psalm prior to Cyril and Theodore, see Rowan Williams, "Christological Exegesis of Psalm 45," in *Meditations of the Heart: The Psalms in Early Christian Thought and Practice*, ed. Andreas Andreopoulos, Augustine Casiday, and Carol Harrison, Studia traditionis theologiae 8 (Turnhout: Brepols, 2011), 17–32. For discussion of Cyril's exegetical influences, see John O'Keefe, "Interpreting the Angel. Cyril of Alexandria and Theodoret of Cyrus: Commentators on the Book of Malachi" (PhD diss., Catholic University of America, 1993), 33–44. The most comprehensive treatment of Cyril's Old Testament exegesis remains Alexander Kerrigan, *St. Cyril of Alexandria: Interpreter of the Old Testament*, Analecta biblica 2 (Rome: Pontifical Biblical Institute, 1952). Cyril explicitly references one of his Origenist forebears in his comment on Ps 44:3a: "The same ideas . . . Eusebius of Caesarea says in his second exegesis, even if

not with such an abundance of witnesses from scripture" (*In Ps.* 44 [PG 69: 1032 B3–4]). The English translation of Cyril's *Explanatio in Psalmos* as found in PG 69 is my own. See the discussion below about the reliability of this edition.

3. O'Keefe, "Interpreting the Angel," 39–40. Cf. Robert Wilken, "St. Cyril of Alexandria: The Mystery of Christ in the Bible," *Pro Ecclesia* 4 (1999): 478.

4. Cf. Cyril, *In Ps.*, praef. (ed. G. Mercati, *Osservazioni a Proemi del Salterio, di Origene, Ippolito, Eusebio, Cirillo Alessandrino e altri,* Studi e testi 142 (Vatican City: Biblioteca Apostolica Vaticana, 1948), 140–44. On this preface, see Marie-Josèphe Rondeau, *Les commentaires patristiques du Psautier (IIIe–Ve siècles),* 2 vols. (Rome: Pont. Institutum Studiorum Orientualium, 1982–85), 1: 132: "Cette préface se caractérise par un désintérêt total à l'égard des questions d'érudition philologique et historique et met tout l'accent sur la signification théologique, c'est-à-dire christique, du recueil." Compare Kerrigan, *St. Cyril of Alexandria,* 230.

5. Studies on Theodore's exegesis include Robert Devreesse, *Essai sur Théodore de Mopsueste,* Studi e testi 141 (Vatican City: Biblioteca Apostolica Vaticana, 1948); M. F. Wiles, "Theodore of Mopsuestia as Representative of the Antiochene School," in *The Cambridge History of the Bible,* vol. 1 (Cambridge: Cambridge University Press, 1970), 489–509; and D. Zaharopoulos, *Theodore of Mopsuestia on the Bible: A Study of His Old Testament Exegesis* (New York: Paulist Press, 1989).

6. For further discussion of why Ps. 44 can refer only to Christ, see below and Harry Spero Pappas, "Theodore of Mopsuestia's Commentary on Psalm 44 (LXX): A Study of Exegesis and Christology," *Greek Orthodox Theological Review* 47 (2002): 55–79.

7. Robert Devreesse, *Le commentaire de Théodore de Mopsueste sur les Psaumes (I–LXXX),* Studi e testi 93 (Vatican City: Biblioteca Apostolica Vaticana, 1939). English translations of Devreesse's edition in this chapter are from Brian Daley, "Theodore of Mopsuestia: Commentary on Psalm 44 (45)," unpublished paper, 1993. On the reliability of Mai's edition, see Kerrigan, *St. Cyril of Alexandria,* 230: "The fact that many of the fragments on the Psalms, that have been published under Cyril's name, are of dubious authenticity prevents our using them in this study." Cf. Wilken, "Mystery of Christ," 456–57.

8. See Rondeau's discussion about the state of Cyril's psalm commentary in *Commentaires patristiques,* 1: 131–34. See also M. Assunta Rossi, "Ancora sul Commento ai Salmi di Cirillo: A proposito di un recente lavoro sui commentari patristici al Salterio," *Annali di Storia dell'Esegesi* 1 (1984): 45–52.

9. Robert Devreesse, *Les anciens commentateurs grecs des Psaumes,* Studi e testi 264 (Vatican City: Biblioteca Apostolica Vaticana, 1970), 229.

10. This is actually the first verse in the psalm where we can compare the two writers. Verse 1 in the LXX is the superscription. Theodore does not view superscriptions as authentic and so does not comment on them. Devreesse (*Anciens*

commentateurs, 229) does not include the comments on Psalm 44:1 (LXX) as reliably Cyril's.

11. Theodore of Mopsuestia, *Exp. in Ps.* 44 (ed. Devreesse, *Commentaire,* 278, lines 6–7).

12. Theodore, *Exp. in Ps.* 44 (ed. Devreesse, *Commentaire,* 278, lines 14–15).

13. Theodore, *Exp. in Ps.* 44 (ed. Devreesse, *Commentaire,* 278, lines 9–12).

14. See Theodore, *Exp. in Ps.* 44 (ed. Devreesse, *Commentaire,* 279, lines 2–3): "He takes such joy in the importance of what is being said."

15. See Theodore, *Exp. in Ps.* 44 (ed. Devreesse, *Commentaire,* 279, lines 16–18).

16. Theodore, *Exp. in Ps.* 44 (ed. Devreesse, *Commentaire,* 282, lines 16–20).

17. Cyril, *In Ps.* 44 (PG 69: 1028 A11–B3).

18. Cyril, *In Ps.* 44 (PG 69: B5–8).

19. Prosopological exegesis is exegesis "in which one tries to determine exactly who is speaking, who is spoken to, who is being referred to" (Michael Slusser, "The Exegetical Roots of Trinitarian Theology," *Theological Studies* 49 [1988]: 468).

20. See Cyril, *In Ps.* 44 (PG 69: 1028 D7–8).

21. Cyril, *In Ps.* 44 (PG 69: 1029 C2–4).

22. Cyril, *In Ps.* 44 (PG 69: C7–10).

23. Cyril, *In Ps.* 44 (PG 69: 1032 B11).

24. Theodore, *Exp. in Ps.* 44 (ed. Devreesse, *Commentaire,* 280, lines 13–14).

25. Theodore's discussion on whether there can be a change of speakers extends from page 280, line 1, to page 282, line 11, of Devreesse's *Commentaire.*

26. Theodore, *Exp. in Ps.* 44 (ed. Devreesse, *Commentaire,* 280, lines 9–10).

27. "For the words, 'I speak my works to the king' do not belong to another speaker, as some think, as if God were saying about David that he was going to speak his works to him!" (Theodore, *Exp. in Ps.* 44 [ed. Devreesse, *Commentaire,* 279, lines 24–26]).

28. Theodore, *Exp. in Ps.* 44 (ed. Devreesse, *Commentaire,* 282, lines 6–8).

29. Theodore, *Exp. in Ps.* 44 (ed. Devreesse, *Commentaire,* 280, lines 10–13).

30. Theodore, *Exp. in Ps.* 44 (ed. Devreesse, *Commentaire,* 280, line 2).

31. Theodore, *Exp. in Ps.* 44 (ed. Devreesse, *Commentaire,* 277, lines 18–19).

32. Theodore, *Exp. in Ps.* 44 (ed. Devreesse, *Commentaire,* 277, lines 21–22).

33. This is an assertion, at least, of Leontius of Byzantium in his polemical work against the Antiochene school, *Deprehensio et triumphus super Nestorianos* 15 (PG 86:1365D).

34. See Wiles, "Theodore of Mopsuestia," 495.

35. Cyril, *In Ps.* 44 (PG 69: 1032 A9–B3).

36. Cyril, *In Ps.* 44 (PG 69: 1029 D1–6).

37. Cyril, *In Ps.* 44 (PG 69: 1028 D6–1029 A2).

38. Robert L. Wilken, *Judaism and the Early Christian Mind* (New Haven, CT: Yale University Press, 1971), 74.

39. Cyril, *In Ps.* 44 (PG 69: 1029 A6–12).

40. Theodore, *Exp. in Ps.* 44 (ed. Devreesse, *Commentaire*, 285, lines 4–8).

41. Theodore, *Exp. in Ps.* 44 (ed. Devreesse, *Commentaire*, 286, line 29, through 287, line 1).

42. Theodore, *Exp. in Ps.* 44 (ed. Devreesse, *Commentaire*, 289, line 25, through 290, line 3).

43. Theodore, *Exp. in Ps.* 44 (ed. Devreesse, *Commentaire*, 290, lines 14–15).

44. Theodore, *Exp. in Ps.* 44 (ed. Devreesse, *Commentaire*, 290, lines 19–20).

45. Theodore, *Exp. in Ps.* 44 (ed. Devreesse, *Commentaire*, 291, lines 1–3).

46. Theodore, *Exp. in Ps.* 44 (ed. Devreesse, *Commentaire*, 284, lines 1–2).

47. Cyril, *In Ps.* 44 (PG 69: 1032 C1–2).

48. For Cyril's reading of Theodore's biblical commentaries, see O'Keefe, "Interpreting the Angel," 145–47.

49. Cyril, *In Ps.* 44 (PG 69: 1032 C6–7).

50. Cyril, *In Ps.* 44 (PG 69: C15–D1).

51. Cyril, *In Ps.* 44 (PG 69: 1033 A14–B1).

52. Cyril, *In Ps.* 44 (PG 69: 1037 B3–6).

53. Cyril, *In Ps.* 44 (PG 69: 1029 B3–7).

54. Cyril, *In Ps.* 44 (PG 69: 1028 C15).

55. Cyril, *In Ps.* 44 (PG 69: 1032 D2–1033 A5).

56. Cyril, *In Ps.* 44 (PG 69: 1040 A6–12).

NINE

Theodoret's Unique Contribution to the Antiochene Exegetical Tradition

Questioning Traditional Scholarly Categories

John J. O'Keefe

In studies narrating the history of patristic exegesis, few distinctions have been more sharply drawn than that between the exegetical schools of Antioch and Alexandria.[1] The Alexandrians, we are told, embraced Origen's spiritual exegesis and were resisted by the Antiochenes, who both rejected figural reading and embraced a method more rooted in history and fact. This alleged historical bias has led to considerable scholarly interest in Antiochene theology and to high hopes that some of their methods could be retrieved for modern use as a form of exegesis that is historically sensitive without being historically reductionist.[2] However, more recent scholarly studies of the difference between Alexandria and Antioch point to conclusions that differ somewhat from the consensus built up over the course of the last several generations of scholarship. Alexandrian and Antiochene exegetical practices differed from each other, but those differences do not, it turns out, fit easily in the space provided by neat distinctions between "allegorical and typological" or "ahistorical and historical."[3]

Rather than focus on this debate as such, in this essay I will consider one representative of the Antiochene style, Theodoret of Cyrus, who was the school's last great exegete.[4] By looking closely at Theodoret's interpretation of the psalms, I hope to underscore the veracity of those studies

that suggest the distinction between Alexandria and Antioch is more refined than neat antitheses allow. In the history of exegesis Theodoret is
usually treated as "the third of three." That is, Theodoret is usually mentioned along with Diodore of Tarsus and Theodore of Mopsuestia. The
tendency to lump Theodoret together with his predecessors has obscured
the many and significant ways that his work differs from theirs. A careful
consideration of Theodoret reveals that he moved creatively within the
intellectual environment that formed him. He was no mere copy of his
teachers. Indeed, we might say that at a critical juncture he recognized the
limitations inherent in the work of his masters and attempted to move
beyond them. Theodoret's independence asserts itself throughout his exegetical works, including his *Commentary on the Psalms*. Recognizing this
independence gives weight to the scholarly arguments favoring a revised
understanding of the relationship between Antiochene and Alexandrian
approaches.

This distinctive aspect of Theodoret can be difficult to locate because,
despite his uniqueness, he was still an Antiochene author. For example, in
his Christology, he was vehemently anti-Alexandrian; he especially opposed the Christology of Cyril of Alexandria.[5] Likewise, his exegetical practices resemble in significant ways the methods of his predecessors Diodore
and Theodore. In the *Commentary on the Psalms*, the psalms are subjected
to a careful grammatical analysis.[6] For each psalm, Theodoret seeks to uncover the basic *skopos*, or subject of the text, he comments on obscure
vocabulary, and he engages in text-critical analysis of his edition of the
Septuagint. He makes corrections based upon comparisons with other
translations, including those of Aquila, Theodotion, Symmachus, and a
text that he calls simply "the Syrian."

Throughout the commentary, Theodoret reveres the *historia* of the
text, a commitment that he shares with his predecessors Diodore and
Theodore. Although *historia* could be translated as "history," that would
be misleading. All three of these authors were interested in *historia* as a
way to honor the literal narrative. They were not attempting to reconstruct the past from diverse source material in the manner of modern historical criticism. Antiochenes, including Theodoret, were historical, but
they were not historical-critical. They wanted to know about the past.
They were concerned about the accuracy of their texts and their contexts.

However, they made no effort to get "behind" the text to the real story that the text itself obscured. Their historical explorations were distinctly premodern.

The psalm commentaries of Diodore, Theodore, and Theodoret all exhibited this premodern approach to *historia*. Grasping this fact is critical to understanding how they interpreted the psalms. For example, they all were interested in identifying the proper context of psalms, but that context was not articulated with appeals to an extrabiblical historical narrative. Rather, they simply accepted the context that the Bible provided in its more historical books. Antiochene exegetes assumed that the Old Testament historical books provided the chronological framework within which to fit the books that were not historical. That is, these exegetes used the sequence of events narrated in the historical books, like Kings and Chronicles, to control and influence their reading of nonhistorical books, like the prophetic books and the book of Psalms. Thus, uncovering the *historia* of the psalms was, for them, not, as it is for many modern critics, an attempt to separate actual history from mythic history. Rather, it was to figure out how the psalms fit on the time line of Chronicles and Kings. Theodoret's *Commentary on the Psalms* is, at this level, deeply Antiochene and quite consistent with Diodore and Theodore. For these authors, especially Diodore and Theodore, the tendency was to see the project of interpreting the psalms as restricted to the identification of each psalm's particular *historia*. The idea that a psalm could also have a *theōria*, a theological or figural meaning, was generally avoided, as will be discussed below. So in this sense at least Theodoret seems indistinctive because he shares these basic sensibilities with other Antiochene interpreters.

Theodoret's distinctiveness is obscured in another way. In the scholarly discussion of the school of Antioch, Theodoret has often been dismissed as an exegete riding on the shoulders of giants but making no real contribution himself. Theodoret's knowledge of the works of Diodore and Theodore is beyond dispute, but the originality of his own voice has often been questioned and has needed to be recovered. Earlier in the twentieth century, G. Bardy recognized the influence Theodore had upon Theodoret. Bardy characterized Theodoret as a compiler of the work of others and declared him "un commentateur sans originalité."[7] As a compiler, Bardy added, Theodoret shared company with Jerome, except that Jerome, because of his superior intelligence and knowledge of the Bible, avoided slipping into "banalité."[8] H. B. Swete was more lenient: "[Theodoret's] imitation of Theodore seldom, if ever amounts to a verbal reproduction. Theodoret recasts Theodore's matter in his own words. . . . It is not indiscriminate. Theodoret . . . holds aloof from the speculations of Theodore when they would have led him away from the Catholic faith."[9]

Jean-Noël Guinot, an important interpreter of Theodoret, agrees with Swete. According to Guinot, Theodoret steadfastly defended Theodore as a "master" (διδάσκαλος) of the Antiochene tradition. For Guinot, Theodoret's loyalty did not include slavish adherence to Theodore's exegetical method. On the one hand, again according to Guinot, Theodoret clearly revered his masters. For example, in Letter 16, Theodoret responded to complaints from a certain Irenaeus, which seem to have been addressed to him because, in an earlier work, he had neglected to include the names of Diodore and Theodore in the catalogue of church teachers (διδάσκαλοι).[10] Theodoret responded that he had no intention of omitting these saints and that if he had done so he would have been guilty of ingratitude toward these teachers. Likewise, in his *Ecclesiastical History,* Theodoret again described the two as διδάσκαλοι and noted with approval their contribution to the fight against heresy.[11] Similarly, in *Eranistes* Theodoret explained that Eranistes himself, the person for whom the treatise was named, because of his Apollinarian biases would never appreciate the "interpretations of Diodore and Theodore, the victorious combatants of piety."[12]

Yet the prefaces to his biblical commentaries also offer hints that Theodoret's attitude toward his teachers was complex and nuanced. In some of these prefaces, Theodoret acknowledges a debt to his predecessors in a way that seems to affirm the charges that his work is merely derivative. For example, in the preface to the *Commentary on the Minor Prophets,* he compares his works to the widow's contribution of two coins, which is described in Luke 21:1–4. Later in the same preface, drawing upon the image of the construction of the temple, he likens himself to women who are too poor to offer gold, precious stones, and other materials on their own but who possess the skill to "spin and weave" wool offered by others: "Just like women who spun and wove wool that had been offered by others and who prepared the leather covering of the tabernacle, we, by gathering from various places what has been well said, will weave, with God's help, a single work from all of these."[13] While Theodoret's expressions of humility are best understood as a standard rhetorical device, statements like these have helped to reinforce the idea that he was a compiler.

In other prefaces, however, it is clear that Theodoret signaled a willingness to go beyond the work of his predecessors and even to correct them. For example, in the preface to his *Commentary on the Song of Songs*, he lists the names of great exegetes who have preceded him. On the list are Eusebius, Origen, Cyprian, Basil, Gregory of Nyssa, Gregory of Nazianzus, Diodore of Tarsus, and John Chrysostom. Theodore of Mopsuestia is conspicuously absent.[14] In the same preface Theodoret criticizes those who interpret the Song of Songs too literally. The likely target of this charge of excessive literalism is Theodore of Mopsuestia, who seems to have been unwilling to see the text as anything but love poetry "written by Solomon concerning his marriage to an Egyptian princess."[15] On this occasion Theodoret is deliberately distancing himself from the interpretations of his "master."

A similar indication of Theodoret's willingness to depart from the insights of his predecessors is found in the preface of his *Commentary on the Psalms*. Here he urges his readers not to think of his work as a waste of time simply because so many others have commented upon it. He says that he will offer something different: his work will avoid both the "excesses of allegorical interpretation" and "an overemphasis on *historia*" that helps the Jews but offers nothing nourishing to those who have faith.[16]

This statement is especially instructive. In a previous article, I argued that Diodore's and Theodore's insistence on a rigid attention to *historia* in their interpretations was motivated by resistance to Origenist readings of scripture.[17] Here Theodoret signals that while he wants to avoid the excessive allegory associated with Origen, he does not think that a draconian exclusion of *theōria* is the way to do it. Theodoret has in mind a middle path between the spiritual exegesis of Origen and the more literal practices of Diodore and Theodore. When Theodoret claims that others have overemphasized *historia* he can be referring only to his masters in the exegetical enterprise, Diodore and Theodore.

Surprisingly, however, modern students of Theodoret often miss these differences and continue to lump him together with "the Antiochenes," ignoring the extent to which *theōria*, or spiritual exegesis, informed his actual exegetical judgments. However, it is clear that when he composed his *Commentary on the Psalms* in the 440s, Theodoret was discontented with the limits of *historia* as a method of interpretation and probably had been for some time already.[18]

The discontent, however, was not simply methodological. When Theodoret says that interpretations of the psalms that overemphasize *historia* help the Jews but offer nothing nourishing to those who have faith, he means these interpretations are insufficiently Christian. A close examination of the psalm commentaries of Diodore and Theodore helps to explain Theodoret's concern. Diodore's commentary begins with a general introduction to the psalms as a whole in which he reflects upon his methodology. His opening remarks illuminate not only his strategy but also that of his disciple Theodore, whose own commentary follows a similar pattern. Diodore expresses his desire to enhance the understanding of those who are "singing the psalms in worship." He explains that while the psalms offer spiritual consolation, they also provide interesting religious teaching and insight into the history of Israel. Some psalms offer moral correction, some express joy in the Lord, others defend the existence of God, and still others warn against Greek notions of fate, or chance. According to Diodore, the psalms narrate the story of David, and they foretell the captivity in Babylon and the return from exile. Some even look ahead to the time of the Maccabees. Theodore's commentary exhibits the same basic judgments.

Both Diodore and Theodore control the interpretation of the psalms through the implementation of a strict hermeneutic that Diodore details in his prologue.[19] Unlike some exegetes who lapse into allegorical reading, Diodore writes, he will present an interpretation "on the basis of the narrative and the text" (κατὰ τὴν ἱστορίαν καὶ τὴν λέξιν).[20] This will not, he insists, prevent him from offering typological readings (τὴν ἀνογωγὴν).[21] It is simply that this higher meaning will derive from the natural flow of the narrative. In this way the interpreter can both avoid introducing foreign ideas into the text and escape "the stranglehold" of Judaism.[22]

Both Diodore and Theodore may claim that their interpretations allow for Christian readings, but such readings are rare.[23] Throughout most of the commentaries they content themselves with a simple paraphrase of the text to which they often add a brief moral reflection. By far their most pressing concern is to establish a sense of the sequence of events and the place of the psalms in an overall narrative framework encompassing the historical books of the Old Testament. For them, the main question is, Where on the time line of Kings does a particular psalm fit? Despite what they say in their prologues, the actual scope of their interpretive project is quite narrow. They are, for example, far more interested in fitting the psalms into a chronological sequences derived from other parts of the Bible than in connecting the psalms to the mystery of Christ and to the Christian life. This, Theodoret implies, is a high price to pay in resisting Origen and his allegories, and it is precisely here that Theodoret's difference emerges most clearly.

Unlike Diodore and Theodore, Theodoret tends to interpret the psalms in the light of his experience as a bishop and monk. In key places throughout his commentary, the events recorded in the psalms are reoriented and understood as a prophetic witness to the ascetical life. Monks reading such passages would recognize themselves in the text and be able to say: "That psalm is about me." Hence, while interpreting verse 83 of Psalm 118 (LXX)—"I have become as a wine skin in the frost, but have not forgotten your ordinances"—Theodoret turns to Paul in 1 Corinthians 9:27—"I punish my body and enslave it so that after proclaiming to others, I myself should not be disqualified." He explains that the text is about the way David surmounted his passions through his struggle with Saul. But by connecting David to Paul through 1 Corinthians Theodoret also shows a deeper ascetical meaning relevant to the Christian life.[24]

Figurative readings like this set Theodoret apart from his predecessors. The interpretation of Psalm 22 (LXX 21) reinforces this impression. The second verse of Psalm 22 has a famous pedigree. According to the Gospel of Matthew, while hanging on the cross, Jesus cries out, "My God, my God, why have you forsaken me," quoting this psalm (Matt. 27:46). The psalm also contains other references traditionally associated with Jesus. Verse 16 reads, "They pierced my hands and my feet," and verse 17 declares, "They parted my garments among themselves and cast lots upon my raiment." Both Diodore and Theodore certainly knew that these texts had been used to refer to Jesus, but they insist that, according to the *historia* of the text, the proper context for interpreting the entire psalm, including these verses, is David and his problems with Absalom.[25] Both Diodore and Theodore seem embarrassed by their conclusions. Aware he is on dangerous ground, Theodore says that Jesus used the psalm in the way that anyone suffering anguish might use it. However, the psalm is not about Jesus. Similarly, Diodore says sheepishly that, if we are careful, we can see a likeness here to Jesus as long as we do not get carried away and forget that the true reference of the text is David and David's life. Both Diodore and Theodore allow this provision only because the New Testament makes the link between Jesus and Psalm 22, but they do not take this as a license to pursue an expanded program in figural reading. For them, the psalm must fit in the historical chronology offered by Kings; that is the primary meaning. To read it in any other way would represent a breach of methodological purity and risk the possibility of reckless allegorical indulgence.

Theodoret, on the other hand, declares at the beginning of his commentary on Psalm 22 that it "predicts the suffering and resurrection of the Lord Christ as well as the call of the Gentiles and the salvation of the world." He ascribes great significance to the psalm's inscription: *For the end, concerning the morning aid, a psalm of David.* Theodoret takes *morning* to mean "the suffering and resurrection of the Lord" and contrasts that with *the end* (τέλος) or the day of resurrection. He declares as well that we should rely on the testimony of the holy apostles for the interpretation of this psalm. He then allows himself a moment for Christological reflection—a relatively rare occurrence in his exegesis. The phrase "My God, my God, why have you forsaken me?" indicates that the Godhead was present to the one suffering in the "form of a slave." Yet, he is careful to point out, "the godhead itself did not receive the suffering."[26] Hence, the term *forsaken* does not mean that the Word had left his godliness behind.

The Christological references continue when he explains that when the psalmist laments being "far from salvation," he is describing our nature without Christ. Verse 3 refers to Jesus's desire to let the cup pass, and verse 4 alludes to the saving body of the Lord. There are allusions to the Virgin Birth, to the betrayal by the disciples, and to wicked scribes and Pharisees. When the psalmist mentions "bones" in verse 14, Theodoret hears "apostles," because the strength of a body is its bones. When the psalmist mentions "dogs" in verse 16, Theodoret hears "Gentiles," because of Matthew 15:26–27, where Jesus declares to the Gentile woman, "It is not right to take the food of the children and throw it to the dogs." And she says in reply, "Please Lord, even the dogs eat the scraps that fall from the table of their masters."

In his exegesis of this psalm, Theodoret engages in other flights of intertextual indulgence. Here is a final sample. In verse 27 the psalmist writes, "The poor shall eat and be satisfied." Theodoret understands this to mean that the Gentiles will be called. In verse 30 the psalmist writes, "All that go down to the earth shall fall down before him." Theodoret understands this to mean that in the resurrection all will bend the knee. The "seed" that will serve him, mentioned in verse 31, is the people that has been washed clean in holy baptism.

A second major example is Psalm 72 (LXX 71). Theodore argued that this psalm referred only to Solomon, to whom the psalm is dedicated. In contrast, Theodoret opens his interpretation by declaring that "the present psalm in no way applies to Solomon."[27] "On the contrary," he says, it "shows the person spoken of by the inspired author to be more ancient than the sun and moon": that is, "Christ the Lord." The psalm foretells that Christ will bring peace to all the nations. As Thedoret's interpretation unfolds, explicit references to the Christian economy continue. In verse 3, when the psalmist proclaims, "May the mountains restore peace to the people, and the hills righteousness," Theodoret believes it to be a promise that has been fulfilled by the rise of "those who have embraced the angelic life," a clear reference to Christian monasticism.

Theodoret is especially intrigued by the Christological implications of verse 5 ("He will endure as long as the sun, and generations of generations before the moon") and verse 17 ("His name will be blessed forever, his name will abide beyond the sun"). Theodoret interprets both of these texts in the light of the association in Hebrews between Christ and Melchizedek. According to Hebrews, Christ is "without father, without mother, without genealogy, having neither beginning of days nor end of life, but resembling the Son of God, he remains a priest forever" (7:3). For Theodoret the psalmist's reference to the king's enduring as long as and beyond the sun clearly prefigures the revelation of the cosmic Christ and his role in the divine economy. Similarly, when the psalmist declares in verse 6 that "he will come down like a shower on a fleece, and like a drop falling on the ground," Theodoret sees a hint of the Incarnation: "Through this he gave us a clear glimpse of the human birth happening silently, very tranquilly, and secretly."

Finally, when verse 17 goes on to proclaim, "All the nations will declare him blessed," Theodoret discerns a reference to the universal mission of the church. This is a reality that the psalmist longed for under the inspiration of the Holy Spirit: "The inspired author knew this through the grace of the Spirit, and inflamed with desire he prays for it to happen and for the prophecy to take effect."

These examples illustrate clearly that Theodoret's interpretations are often at odds with the interpretations offered by his masters. They are consistently more likely to include figural connections to Christ and the church that are excluded by Diodore and Theodore. Still, it is also clear in his *Commentary on the Psalms* that Theodoret was deeply indebted to his predecessors in all kinds of ways. He employed the same methodology that they had employed. For the most part he agreed with them that David's life was the primary reference point for all the psalms and that the text could be illuminated through correlation with the book of Kings. Indeed, the modern reader can study page after page of Theodoret's exegesis of the psalms and find scarcely a mention of Christ and the church. Yet the evidence suggests that he also recognized the limitations of the methods he had inherited. The commentaries of Diodore and Theodore did not go far enough. In the end, Theodoret said "no" to his masters in some key areas.

We cannot know exactly why Theodoret departed from his master in this way. Certainly it was in part the company he kept: we know he read Origen, he may have read Cyril, he says he knew Gregory of Nyssa.[28] He was also a monk who wanted to apply the text of the Bible to his life. These forces clearly moved Theodoret beyond the strict school exegesis of Diodore and Theodore.

Theodoret's "no" offers us yet another reason to reconsider the categories "Alexandrian" and "Antiochene" in our effort to understand early Christian exegetical practices. On the one hand these categories are helpful, but on the other they flatten out the individuality of the authors concerned. Clearly Theodoret's exegesis is more interesting, more complex, and more nuanced than the label "Antiochene" implies.

Notes

1. Although this chapter contains pieces of the original conference paper delivered in 1998, it has been significantly revised for this volume. It should also be noted that the original conference paper led to other publications, which contain parts of the original paper: "A Letter That Killeth: Toward a Reassessment of Antiochene Exegesis, or Diodore, Theodore, and Theodoret on the Psalms," *Journal of Early Christian Studies* 8 (2000): 83–104; "Rejecting One's Masters: Theodoret of Cyrus, Antiochene Exegesis, and the Patristic Mainstream," in *Syriac and Antiochian Exegesis and Biblical Theology for the 3rd Millennium,* ed. Robert D. Miller (Piscataway, NJ: Gorgias Press, 2008). Research on this topic has been greatly assisted by the publication of translations of Theodore's and Theodoret's psalm commentaries. See *Theodore of Mopsuestia: Commentary on the Psalms,* trans. Robert C. Hill (Atlanta, GA: Society of Biblical Literature, 2006) and *Theodoret of Cyrus: Commentary on the Psalms,* 2 vols., trans. Robert C. Hill, FC 101–2 (Washington, DC: Catholic University of America Press, 2000–2001).

2. The following studies are illustrative: Rowan Greer, *Theodore of Mopsuestia, Exegete and Theologian* (Westminster: Faith Press, 1961); R. P. C. Hanson, *Allegory and Event* (Richmond, VA: John Knox Press, 1959); G. W. H. Lampe and K. J. Woollcombe, *Essays on Typology* (Naperville, IL: Alec R. Allenson, 1956); Paul Ternant, "La θεωρία d'Antioche dans le cadre des sens de l'écriture," *Biblica* 34 (1953): 135–58, 354–83, 456–86; Alberto Vaccari, "La θεωρία nella scuola esegetica di Antiochia," *Biblica* 1 (1920): 3–36.

3. Frances Young, in her book *Biblical Exegesis and the Formation of Christian Culture* (Cambridge: Cambridge University Press, 1997), makes this point forcefully. See also Peter Martens, "Revisiting the Allegory/Typology Distinction: The Case of Origen," *Journal of Early Christian Studies* 16 (2008): 283–317; John J. O'Keefe and R. R. Reno, *Sanctified Vision* (Baltimore: Johns Hopkins University Press, 2005); O'Keefe, "Letter That Killeth." For a study of the Christological issues, see Paul Clayton, *The Christology of Theodoret of Cyrus: Antiochene Christology from the Council of Ephesus (431) to the Council of Chalcedon (451),* (Oxford: Oxford University Press, 2007).

4. For recent discussions of his legacy, see István Pásztori-Kupán, *Theodoret of Cyrus* (New York: Routledge, 2006), and Theresa Urbainczyk, *Theodoret of Cyrrhus: The Bishop and the Holy Man* (Ann Arbor: University of Michigan Press, 2002).

5. I have argued elsewhere that it is a mistake to interpret Antiochene resistance to Alexandrian Christology as rooted in a defense of the human nature of Jesus. The primary Antiochene motive in their Christological reasoning was to defend the impassibility of God; John O'Keefe, "Impassible Suffering? Divine Passion and Fifth-Century Christology," *Theological Studies* 58 (1997): 39–60.

6. I accept Frances Young's argument that Antiochene exegesis was not proto-historical-critical in a modern sense. Rather, it was deeply influenced by the ancient rules of grammatical analysis; see "The Rhetorical Schools and Their Influence on Patristic Exegesis," in *The Making of Orthodoxy: Essays in Honour of Henry Chadwick*, ed. Rowan Williams (Cambridge: Cambridge University Press, 1989), 182–99.

7. G. Bardy, "Commentaires patristiques de la Bible," in *Dictionnaire de la Bible Supplément*, vol. 2, ed. I. Pirot et al. (Paris: Letouzey et Ané, 1934), 102.

8. Ibid.

9. H. B. Swete, ed., *Theodori Episcopi Mopsuesteni in Epistolas B. Pauli Commentarii. The Latin Version with the Greek Fragments*, 2 vols. (Cambridge: Cambridge University Press, 1880–82), quoted in Paul Parvis, "Theodoret's Commentary on the Epistles of St. Paul: Historical Setting and Exegetical Practice" (PhD diss., Oxford University, 1975), 109.

10. Jean-Noël Guinot, "L'importance de la dette de Théodoret de Cyr à l'égard de l'exégèse de Théodore de Mopsueste," *Orpheus* 5 (1984): 68–109.

11. Theodoret, *Hist. eccl.* 27, 39 (PG 82: 1256D, 1277A–B).

12. G. H. Ettlinger, ed., *Eranistes* 1 (Oxford: Clarendon Press, 1975): 95.5–12; translation mine. For an alternate English translation of the whole work, see Gerard H. Ettlinger, *Theodoret of Cyrus: Eranistes* (Washington, DC: Catholic University of America Press, 2003), 66.

13. Theodoret, *Interpretatio in duodecim Prophetas Minores* praef. (PG 81: 1548B). The translation is my own.

14. Theodoret, *Interpretatio in Canticum Canticorum* praef. (PG 81: 32B). Cf. Guinot, "Importance," 76.

15. Dimitri Zaharopoulos, *Theodore of Mopsuestia on the Bible: A Study of His Old Testament Exegesis* (New York: Paulist Press, 1989), 33–34.

16. Theodoret, *Int. in Ps.* praef. (PG 80: 860C–D); translation mine.

17. O'Keefe, "Letter That Killeth," 90–92.

18. For this date, see Jean-Noël Guinot, *L'exégèse de Théodoret de Cyr* (Paris: Beauchesne, 1995), 48.

19. This hermeneutic probably was adapted from the tradition of ancient rhetorical schools. See note 6 above.

20. Diodore, *Comm. Ps.* 7.125 (CCSG 6: 7.125–26).

21. Diodore, *Comm. Ps.* 7.125 (CCSG 6: 7.126).

22. It is somewhat ironic that Diodore says he is trying to avoid Jewish interpretation when that is the very charge that Theodoret implicitly levels against him. Exegetes in the fourth and fifth centuries often criticized the interpretations of their Christian opponents as being too Jewish. While these exegetes may have had contact with Jewish exegetical traditions, these accusations could also be simply a stylized way of saying that the interpretation is not very good. For a discussion of

Jewish and Christian exegesis in antiquity, see Marc Hirshman, *A Rivalry of Genius: Jewish and Christian Biblical Interpretation in Late Antiquity* (Albany: St. University of New York Press, 1996).

23. Theodore of Mopsuestia, for example, believed that Old Testament prophecy was fulfilled within the confines of the Old Testament. Hence, in his *Commentary on the Minor Prophets* he identifies only five messianic prophecies: Amos 9:11, Micah 5:1–2, Joel 2:28–29, Zechariah 9:9–10, and Malachi 3:1. In his commentary on the psalms, only Psalms 2, 8, 44, and 109 refer to Christ. Cf. Guinot, "Importance," 109.

24. Theodoret, *Int. in Ps.* 118 (PG 80: 1848C).

25. Diodore of Tarsus, *Comm. Ps.* 21 (CCSG 6: 126.5–10); Theodore, *Exp. in Ps.* 21 (CCSL 88A: 107.1–5).

26. Theodoret, *Int. in Ps.* 21 (PG 80: 1009); translation mine.

27. Theodoret, *Int. in Ps.* 71 (PG 80: 1428–41; trans. Hill, *Theodoret of Cyrus,* 1: 413–20.

28. See the preface to his *Commentary on the Song of Songs* (PG 81: 32B). See also Jean-Noël Guinot, "Théodoret à-t-il lu les homélies d'Origène sur l'ancien Testament?" *Vetera Christianorum* 21 (1984): 285–312.

The Emergence of *Totus Christus* as Hermeneutical Center in Augustine's *Enarrationes in Psalmos*

Michael Cameron

Augustine made an ambitious and famously programmatic statement about the scope of his spiritual pursuits within weeks of his conversion: "I desire to know God and the soul. Nothing more? Nothing at all" (*Soliloquies* 1.2.7).[1] But then he spent decades winding round and round up the spiritual mountainside trying to reach the peak of that lofty sentence. Along the way he found that the best way to learn about God and the soul was to attend to the God who took up a human soul, that is, the divine Word who became a crucified Man. As Augustine studied the truth about Christ more closely, he became absorbed with Christ the Man and his unbreakable bond with the chosen ones he came to save. Christ the head and the church his body appeared more clearly as the only proper context for searching out God and the soul; indeed, they became the primary means to "know" them.

Nowhere is this clearer than in the striking exegesis of Augustine's massive *Enarrationes in Psalmos*, where the work of reading scripture is dominated by the theme of the "whole Christ," or *totus Christus,* the one body of Christ composed of head and members.

The expression *totus Christus* occasionally refers in Augustine to the person of Christ as considered in the fullness of his divine and human natures.[2] But most of the more than two hundred passages where it appears or is discussed refer to Christ and the church as head and body of a single great spiritual entity that Augustine does not hesitate to describe as a single "person."[3] Though scholarship has paid relatively little attention to the theme (see the bibliographical note below), not only have many analysts seen *totus Christus* as the heart of Augustine's psalms interpretation, but it has also been called the center of Augustine's mature theology.[4] More than a simple object of analysis within the text, for Augustine *totus Christus* was woven deeply into the fabric of the Psalter. The whole Christ was part of the psalms' content as fulfilled prophecy and so acted as a tight-binding filament of scriptural unity. The whole Christ was the very means of salvation for readers, for the church saw itself and heard its own voice in the praises and prayers of the ancient text. Reading oneself in the whole Christ therefore was also a way of participating in God's saving action. The self-discovery brought about by this reading *of* the text invited readers to project themselves *into* the text as the present subject of the past (or future) saving action of God portrayed there. Thus was *totus Christus* the hermeneutical center of the psalms, irradiating God's saving plan in every direction. Though this chapter can do so only briefly, it will take up some prominent threads of this important and richly textured theme in order to get a view of its origin and direction in Augustine's work on the psalms. These threads converged when Augustine hit upon the theme of *totus Christus* early in his ministry at Hippo and allowed it to interweave lines that were pastoral, polemical, exegetical, and grammatical-rhetorical. It begins to appear about 394–395, in expositions that immediately predate his ordination as bishop. The resulting exegetical knot held together Augustine's thinking on Christ's divine and human natures, Christ's saving work before and after his death and resurrection, Christ's relationship to the church, and Christ's unifying presence in the Old and New Testaments.

Pastoral Thread:
"How Shall I Minister to These Little Ones?"

Augustine needed to reexamine his approach to scripture after being ordained unexpectedly at Hippo in 391. It threw him into a crisis of action to which he was not accustomed. As he wrote plaintively to his new bishop Valerius, "How [*quomodo*] do I minister this very thing for the salvation of others, 'not seeking what is advantageous to me, but what is advantageous to the many, that they may be saved'?" (1 Cor. 10:33).[5] "*How* do I minister?"—*Quomodo?* Clearly it was the *quomodo* question that drove Augustine's anxiety: not about *what* he knew but about *how* he knew what he knew; not about knowing more for himself but about bringing knowledge to "the many"—beginners in faith (*rudes*), catechumens and *competentes* on the brink of baptism, and the horde of baptized but unreflective faithful who all looked up dizzily "from below" at the daunting spiritual climb that lay before them. Augustine had suddenly thrust upon him the responsibility for their salvation, and so also the need to reorient his prodigious intellectual skills upon faith's basic "advantage." One of his assignments was instructing candidates for baptism; it helped to hone his skills in studying and preaching scripture for the simple.[6]

Exegetical Thread: Reading the Psalms through the Gospel and the Apostle

The psalms had been interpreted Christologically from the earliest days of the church.[7] Images of the righteous sufferer that undergird the Passion narratives of the Gospels give evidence of early layers of Christological psalm interpretation. Throughout the New Testament the psalms remained crucial instruments for unfolding the meaning of Christ (cf. Luke 24:44), particularly his crucifixion (Pss. 21 and 68), resurrection (Pss. 15 and 117), and session at God's right hand (Ps. 109). New Testament interpretations of Jesus's mission grew to include a dimension of joint participation of humanity in his death and resurrection. This was especially evident in the apostle Paul, who reasoned out the comprehensive effect of Jesus's death (2 Cor. 5:14; Gal. 2:20, 3:13; Rom. 6:3). The apostle's related vision of the body of Christ (1 Cor. 12:12–27; Rom. 12:4–5) originally served as a metaphor for spiritual interdependence within the local Christian community. Later writings of the Pauline tradition interpreted and extended the metaphor to include the glorified Jesus Christ as head for the body of the universal church (Eph. 1:22–23; Col. 1:18) and led to beginning speculation on the dynamic relationship that this union entailed (Eph. 5:21–33; Col. 1:24). After the New Testament the postapostolic and early patristic periods continued to develop the identification of the speaking *ego* in the psalms as the voice of the Lord, from Irenaeus's concept of recapitulation through the teaching on divinization in Athanasius and Hilary.[8] Augustine digested it by reading Ambrose and Hilary, whose interpretations he refers to on occasion.[9]

First Grammatical-Rhetorical Thread: The Work of Prosopological Exegesis

One of the more remarkable interpretive tools Augustine used identified *Christ as the speaking voice of the psalms*. Not only do various voices in the Psalter describe or speak about Christ: Christ himself speaks. Even if only a few in ancient Israel faintly heard his voice, Christ nevertheless really spoke. Then after amplifying his voice in the Incarnation, he was clearly audible to Christians who chanted the psalms. Augustine's tool for distinguishing Christ's voice behind the other voices in the text came from adapting a standard practice of his grammatical and rhetorical training called "prosopological exegesis." A number of fine studies of this practice have appeared.[10] Briefly, *prosopological exegesis* refers to the work of literary analysis that identifies the various speaking voices in a poetic text. The speaking person, *prosopon* in Greek (literally, "face," which Latin writers often translated as *persona*, "person"), had to be identified in texts without cues, line breaks, punctuation, or even spaces between letters. Grammatical exercises taught the young how to distinguish and identify voices in passages of Homer or Virgil. Grammarians also trained readers to attend to the form of a verb that indicates its "person," that is, the first-person *I*, the second-person *you*, or the third-person *he, she,* or *it*. Framing the text as a dialogue between interlocutors required a disciplined analysis that rigorously discriminated between each speaking voice. The distinctive features emerging from each *prosopon* built up a distinct profile for each character in the story and shaped the reader's overall comprehension of the text. Prosopological exegesis was therefore an important tool for literary understanding.

Early Christian writers adapted prosopological analysis to identify the speaking voices of biblical texts, especially poetic texts like the book of Psalms and the Song of Songs. They routinely identified the speaking "I" (*ego*) of the psalms as Christ. Augustine's early expositions also often answer the question "Who is speaking here?" Augustine resorted often to prosopological analysis in the earliest psalm expositions; he identified the voices of Christ the Son, God the Father, and the church (*En. Ps.* 5.1) along with a number of individuals like the "perfected soul" of Psalm 7 (*anima perfecta*; 7.1) and the "Catholic soul" of Psalm 10 (*anima catholica*; 10.6). Augustine at times discriminated between alternating voices within a single psalm (2.6–7; 9.4, 7), differentiated between voices within a portion of a psalm (9.6), or even recast and reinterpreted an entire psalm in a different voice (3.9–10; 7.20). Prosopological analysis was especially important for explaining Psalm 3. He established the interpretive base line in verse 6's death and resurrection imagery: "I rested and fell asleep, and I arose" compels us, he contends, to read the psalm as though spoken "in the person of Christ" (*ex persona Christi*).[11] This Christological reading proceeded through the whole psalm in *Enarrationes in Psalmos* 3.1–8 as the prayer of the head of Christ's body. But then in 3.9 he backtracked to reread the entire psalm from the beginning as the words of a different *persona*, that is, Christ's body the church journeying through the time of temporal affliction. Then in 3.10 he returned to the start once more to reread the psalm as the prayer of an individual member of the body. Augustine thus sharply distinguished at least three speaking voices and their different perspectives. This self-conscious and fastidious approach shows Augustine still experimenting with his style of exegesis.[12] But it also points to his concern not to confuse the divinely transcendent and humanly immanent perspectives.

The Donatist interpreter Tyconius advanced the tradition when his *Liber regularum* (ca. 380) became the first to articulate the body of Christ as an *exegetical* principle. He developed the Pauline idea of head and the body as a critical principle for distinguishing the alternating voices of Christ and church throughout the scriptures.[13] Augustine shared some basic categories with Tyconius, but his thought on the theme of the body of Christ predates his exposure to Tyconius, and he developed the Donatist's thought in fundamental ways.

Second Grammatical-Rhetorical Thread:
The Impersonating Voice-within-Voice
(*Prosopopoeia*)

A striking figure of speech appears in these first expositions that transcends the distinctions made by prosopological exegesis. The psalmist-prophet in Psalm 7 at first seems to relay the words of the "perfected soul" who sings God's mysteries; but close reading shows that he actually imitates the perfected soul's voice by using the first-person "I." He not only *identifies* the voice but also *impersonates* it. So also after treating the psalm, Augustine adds that we hear differently if we hear the psalm spoken "in the person of the Lordly Man" (*in persona dominici hominis*), so long as we "refer whatever is spoken in lowly manner to our weakness, which he carried" (*En. Ps.* 7.20). That is, the psalmist is impersonating Christ himself.

Though related to prosopological analysis, this device of impersonation goes beyond it by hearing a second voice speaking *within* the first voice. What is this peculiar kind of figurative speech? The Greeks called it *prosopopoeia*, literally "face-making." Latin rhetorical handbooks either transliterated the term or translated it as *fictiones personarum*, "imagined persons." *Prosopopoeia* is a rhetorical device whereby an author of a text, or a character in the text, or even the interpreter of a text (as we'll see in Augustine's case) takes up or impersonates the voice of some character, either well known or invented.[14] It stands alongside the host of other rhetorical devices that play with the sound of the human voice: diatribe, a rhetorically staged dialogue that addresses an imaginary proponent in a dispute; personification, which gives the power of speech to an inanimate object; and apostrophe, an imaginary address made to some fictional or abstract figure. Because authors, especially poets, dexterously use all these devices, astute readers must learn to identify not only different *voices* (exegesis of speaking persons), but also different *voice-overs* (exegesis of impersonation). Prosopological exegesis is the work of a text's interpreter, while *prosopopoeia* is the literary device of a text's author.

The best ancient examples of impersonation come from the *progymnasmata* or elementary rhetorical exercises of Greek grammarians like Theon and Hermogenes.[15] Teachers asked students to compose letters that imagined what certain persons might say under given circumstances.

Rhetoricians commended the device, and it was a stock figure of speech declamation. Cicero commended its ability to move the emotions, as did the *Rhetorica ad Herrenium*. The elder Seneca composed many exercises using the device. This figure was so potent that writers counseled that it be used sparingly. So said Quintilian, from whom we have our most detailed theoretical treatment of the device in the ancient world.

> A bolder form of figure, which in Cicero's opinion demands greater effort, is impersonation of characters [*fictiones personarum*] or *prosopopoeia*. This device lends wonderful variety and animation to oratory. By this means we display the inner thoughts of our adversaries as though they were talking with themselves. Or without sacrifice of credibility we may introduce conversations between ourselves and others, or of others among ourselves, and put words of advice, reproach, complaint, praise, or pity into the mouths of appropriate persons. It is also convenient at times to pretend that we have before our eyes the images of things, persons, or utterances . . . (9.2.30–33). We may also introduce some imaginary person without identifying him, as when we say, "Here someone says," or "Someone will say." Or words may be inserted without the introduction of any speaker at all. . . . This involves a mixture of figures, since added to *prosopopoeia* is ellipse, which here consists in omitting any indication of the one speaking.[16]

This device, Quintilian wrote, had the capacity "to bring down the gods and raise up the dead."[17]

Its potential in religious discourse is therefore evident. Recent New Testament scholarship has shown that the apostle Paul uses this device in Romans 7:7–25, where he takes up the voice of a Gentile Christian convert trapped in trying to obey the Law of Moses.[18] Origen referred to *prosopopoeia* in many passages of his *Contra Celsum*, especially as he countered Celsus's own impersonations of skeptical pagans and puzzled Jews looking askance at Christianity.[19] Origen perceived Paul's *prosopopoeia* in Romans 7,[20] and Augustine did too.[21]

Impersonation's consonance of multiple voices within a single character recalls its archaic roots in the theatrical religious drama, where impersonation made the voices of the gods heard upon the earth. A role-playing person "took up" (*suscipio*) or "held up" (*sustineo*) a character mask and assumed that character's voice by speaking through the mask; one spoke "out of" that person, or *ex persona*. (The Latin word *persona* perhaps derived from that image, that is, from *per + sonare*, comes from the one who "makes a sound" (*sonare*) "through" (*per*) the medium.)

It so happens that we know that at this very moment Augustine was thinking about *prosopopoeia* and its conjunctive power, for he used it to spice his work against the Donatist schism that had already split the North African Church for three generations. In a harbinger of Augustine's next two decades of increasing absorption with this conflict, he composed an unusual piece, the *Psalmus contra partem Donati*, or *Psalm against the Faction of Donatus*. This first anti-Donatist work, written about the same time as the first expositions of the biblical psalms, is Augustine's only surviving poetic composition. It addresses the fractious struggle by appealing to the Donatists' suppressed bond of identification with the Catholic Church. The climactic final section of the *Psalmus* enlists the emotional power of impersonation by putting a plaintive appeal for unity into the mouth of Mother Church.[22] Augustine pictures her crying out to the wayward children who have rejected her love and torn her heart:

> Now what if Mother Church herself addressed you calmly, in peace
> And said: "O my children, what complaints have you against your
>   Mother?
> Why have you deserted me? I want to hear it from you now.
> You accuse your brethren, and this lashing out wounds me deeply.
> Many deserted me, but they did so in fear.
> But no one's forcing you to rebel against me so.
> You say you are with me, you see that to be false.
> I'm spoken of as Catholic, and you are of Donatus's sect. . . .
> But what have I done to you, I, your mother, spread across the world?"[23]

Augustine counted on the emotive power of *prosopopoeia*'s personal immediacy.[24] But more importantly for our purposes, this rhetorical practice advanced Augustine's spiritual-theological template for understanding scripture. Augustine also reflected at this time on the Old Testament angels and prophets who spoke God's words in the first person, and the

New Testament apostle who similarly spoke Christ's words (*Against Adimantus* 9.1). Augustine qualified the cause-for-effect metonymy by reference to the personal gift that Christ had given to Paul: please note, Augustine observed, that Paul does not refer to Christ as the one "by whose enlightenment and command I speak; he rather attributes his speech directly to Christ, *by whose gift* he spoke."[25] The "hard" figure of cause-for-effect metonymy emphasizes Christ's transcendence over the human. But by the "gift" that *conjoins* Christ's voice to Paul's, impersonation's "soft" figure of container-for-contained more closely resembles synecdoche, which better expresses the closeness, cooperation, and even communion of the two parties. This trope generates Augustine's different stream of language for discussing the divine Word's relation to time, earth, and humanity. For instance, one psalm exposition from this period uses container-for-contained to help explain scripture's Christological resonance. Psalm 8's inscription, *For the winepresses* (*En. Ps.* 8.2), suggests (among other things) that the divine Word in the church is like a grape. It enters into human words by "commandeering" (*usurpat*) human vocal sounds that encase spiritual understanding as grape skins encase wine. These words enter human ears and penetrate the listening mind, where truth oozes into the understanding, the spiritual "place where 'grapes' are trodden." There it is siphoned into the "vat" of memory, where time and care turn it into the wine of right thinking and virtuous action.

Impersonation appears in Augustine's first psalm expositions in remarkably suggestive ways that, while still experimental, foreshadow the profundities of the later and larger *Expositions of the Psalms*. For instance, after Augustine interprets Psalm 3 from the typical Christological angle (*En. Ps.* 3.1–8), he starts over to interpret the psalm anew "in terms of the person of Christ" (*ad personam Christi*) in another way (3.9). Christ speaks the psalm, yet the words are also those of the church, which praises the Word for "taking it up" (*suscepta*) with the risen Man to "sit at one with him [*una cum illo*] even in heavenly places" (*En. Ps.* 3.9; see Eph. 2:6). That is, Christ's rising also raised up the church "in that Man" (*in illo homine*) because Christ's love guaranteed that "where the head goes the members will follow" (1 Cor. 12:27; Eph. 4:15–16; Rom. 8:35). Christ and church are thus a single entity whom Augustine hears talking in the psalm's speaking *ego;* then he makes Christ's duality-in-unity a mode of scripture interpretation.

Then a third interpretation reads the psalms as the prayer of an individual Christian (3.10). Different voices speak (Christ, church, Christian), though each speaks within what Augustine calls the *totus*, "the whole."[26] The consonance of interpretations stresses the conjunction of voices; indeed, the logic of this exegesis is that the individual Christian prays *within* the church's voice, just as the church prays *within* the voice of Christ. The different voices of the body and the head speak in unison (*simul*) with Christ's voice, but the church and its members speak *through him*. For Augustine the psalms reverberate with several levels of impersonations. On one level the prophet "hosts" all the voices. So in Psalm 3, Christ and the church speak *apud prophetam*, that is, "in the presence of the prophet."[27] But on another level the divine Word takes up and inhabits the prophet's voice, so that the word spoken is truly *God's* word.

Reference to *prosopopoeia* helps Augustine out of some other interpretive jams. We can see Augustine using impersonation to explain an awkward text in the exposition of Psalm 4. Out of overflowing love for his body Christ spoke to God on behalf of his "least ones" (*minimi*) by assuming their identity before God. So as he prayed it was not he, but they, who became "enlarged." He took up not only his people's sins but also *their very persons*. Christ's intercession means that he prayed *for* his people by praying *as* his people. He spoke "for [*pro*] his faithful ones, whose person he took upon himself [*quorum personam sibi imposuit*] also when he said, '*I* was hungry and you did not feed *me*'" (Matt. 25:42).[28]

Convergence of Threads: The Exegesis of Psalm 21

Here we insert Augustine's scintillating new insight about Christ's humanity that he had been learning from Paul's letters: that Christ's humble human will-to-death for us made him "the mediator between God and man." Because Christ became man, a Jew, "born of a woman, born under the law, that he might redeem those under the Law" (Gal. 4:4), Christ's humanity and the Christian reading of the Old Testament are deeply intertwined. Christ "took up" human flesh and a human will-to-death and exhibited this divine condescension exegetically by taking up the voice of the sinner Adam. Augustine now read the work of Christ's intercession back into Christ's human life. Before being raised to God's right hand, he was already interceding for us upon the cross. The exposition of Psalm 21 established the framework for this outlook.[29] The opening paragraph shows Augustine skillfully splicing the Gospel narrative of the Passion accounts and the co-crucifixion insight of the apostle Paul into the words of the psalm title, *To the end, for taking up in the morning, a psalm of David.*

> "To the end," because the Lord Jesus Christ himself speaks, that is, praying for his own resurrection. Now, his resurrection happened on the morning of the first day of the week. He was "taken up" into eternal life, and death will no longer be his master [Rom 6:9]. But these words are spoken in the person of the Crucified One [*ex persona crucifixi*]. The beginning of this psalm has the words that he cried out as he hung upon the cross while also holding fast [*servans*] the person of the "old man" whose mortality he carried [*portavit*]. Now this "old man" was nailed to the cross with him [Rom. 6:6].[30]

This preface set the expository perspective for all the "Psalms of the Crucified" among the early expositions of Psalms 15 through 32. This exegesis rested on a bedrock of spiritual authority because it came from the lips of the dying Savior himself as he prayed from the cross, "My God, my God, why have you forsaken me?" For Augustine the word *me* in this prayer was a figurative act of *prosopopoeia* raised to the power of redemption: Christ took as his own the voice of the sinner Adam. Augustine learned this from Paul's teaching in Romans 5 and 6, where the apostle contrasted Adam and Christ and spoke of the old sinful human self as crucified with Christ. On the cross Jesus's humble human will "took up" the voice of Adam; that very act of embracing human death displayed the exchange of life for death that was the essence of redemption. Augustine discerned its intersection of three texts that so to say triangulated the psalm with the words of the crucified and his apostle: he fused the plaintive cry of Psalm 21:2 with Christ's cry of dereliction in Matthew 27:34 (Mark 15:34), and with Paul's articulation our redemptive union with him in Romans 6:3–9 (especially v. 6). The cross of Christ was now seated in Augustine's rational-spiritual thinking. It is not too much to say that if one might mark a moment of Augustine's emergence from a predominantly religious-philosophical mode to a distinctly Christian mode of spiritual reasoning, this was it. The exposition of Psalm 21 was a watershed in his career as a Christian reader of scripture, and indeed as a Christian. The Word becoming incarnate was an astounding act of saving humility, yet it remained incomplete without the Man's ratifying it upon the cross. The words of the psalm taken from Adam by the Crucified disclosed the very pistons that drove the engine of human redemption, and the exchange of voices between Savior and sinner engineered a magnificent trade of life for death. This was the full emergence of *totus Christus.*

Augustine read the words of the psalmist through the apostle's words as through a Christ-shaped lens. As usual, references to "the end" and "David" still indicated Christ. The Son of David's prayer of anguish on the cross was offered in the human hope of being "taken up" (*susceptio*) in resurrection. The central figure was Adam, whom the dying Jesus held fast (*servo*) to himself; the pronoun *me* enfolded Christ's gracious act of rescue within the guise of the guilty first man. *The crucified Christ spoke in Adam's voice* in order to submerge himself in humanity's sinful *ego*. *Me* referred not merely to general human nature but also to the curse of death stuck fast to it. Christ spoke as one of Adam's mortal issue lost in the maze of the sinful consciousness after rebelling against God, an act so catastrophically numbing that he could not even recall why he had been abandoned. Christ drank Adam's cup of torment to the dregs while confessing to the ignominy of "my" sins.

Christ's crucifixion prayer of Psalm 21 embedded several layers of impersonation.[31] The first was the *prosopopoeia* of the psalmist himself, who prophetically spoke the words of the psalm as the crucified, *ex persona crucifixi* (*En. Ps.* 21.1), which was itself an impersonation in the voice of the first sinner, *ex persona Adam* (21.7). That is, Christ spoke "in the person of the old man whose mortality he carried."[32] As we've seen, Augustine had already pictured Christ the intercessor speaking in the voice of his "least" (4.2), having taken up the voice of his church (3.9). The risen Christ spoke his followers' words at God's right hand in heaven in the aftermath of redemption. But here we find a wider picture: Christ speaks as a mortal man, indeed in the very midst of dying violently upon the cross. Augustine broke fresh ground by picturing Christ in the person of Adam, plunging into the murky world of the sinner and submerging himself in the "I" of one lost in sin (21.3). This human act of "taking up" the sinner on the cross revealed the depth of Christ's humble human love as it ratified and conjoined with humble divine love. It was not only a divine act but also a uniquely human act. At this point love transacted the exchange of redemption. *Prosopopoeia*'s rhetorical transposition of voices provided Augustine with the Christian theological pattern that explained the exchange. While the Word took our flesh and its liability to death, the Man's will-to-death poured out perfect human neighbor-love that fulfilled the law and accomplished redemption. Christ impersonated Adam in order to reveal the structure of redemption that Augustine later called "the marvelous exchange, the divine transaction."[33] Augustine might have called redemption "impersonatory" as long as it was understood that Christ's words and deeds were not mere role play; as divinity truly one with humanity, his figure and reality were truly one and "mediated" the spiritual in the fleshly so as to make the human reality something different. Augustine had another term for it: *sacrament.* Christ's "sacramental" will-to-death gave what it portrayed; and all other events, words, and signs were also sacramental insofar as they partook of it. Because that included all the Old Testament's words and deeds, it too was sacramental, and so legitimated Augustine's figurative reading of scripture.

It is impossible to overstate the importance of Psalm 21 for Augustine.[34] For him it was "the prophecy *par excellence.*"[35] It intersected Israel, Christ, and the Christian, and like lightning in the night illumined the whole Old and New Testament landscape. It underlay the conviction that he eventually expressed as "Christ and the church, the total mystery of all scripture."[36] From then on *totus Christus* assumed a central place in Augustine's biblical work.[37] Constantly recalled in the texts and treatises of the ensuing years, it reinvoked his new fresher and fuller understandings of Christ's redeeming humanity, and of the unity of Old and New Testaments, for the remainder of his days. Augustine had already declared that Christ removed the veil from the Old Testament (not the Old Testament itself; *Adv. Believing* 3.5) and that his self-sacrifice superseded all other sacrifices (*En. Ps.* 2.8). But Christ's redemptive *prosopopoeia* upon the cross in Psalm 21:2 brought Augustine to a new level of understanding, not only

about redemption but also about Old Testament fulfillment. Christ's revelation from the cross included Psalm 21:15, "My heart was made like melt-
ing wax in the middle of my belly." As Augustine put it, the Crucifixion
opened up Christ's enigmatic wisdom in the Old Testament that to this
point had been hard to penetrate. In speaking these words from the cross,
Augustine commented, Christ revealed that the wisdom "which the holy
books spelled out about me was not understood, like something hard and
opaque. But after the fire of my passion set upon it, it became clear like a
pure liquid stored up in the memory of my church." So the cross uncov-
ered the crystalline grace and truth that lay hidden in the murky stories,
characters, rites, and institutions of the Old Testament. Suddenly what
had been obscure to even the most advanced spiritual minds in ancient
Israel became clear to the humblest Christian believer, namely, that God's
truth flowed freely back and forth between the Testaments and yielded itself to figurative reading. Christian preachers and teachers now used figurative reading to nourish new Christians and to train spiritual readers by
continuous spiritual exercises in the era of fulfillment "under grace."

Psalm 21 affected the way Augustine read all the rest of these "Psalms
of the Crucified" and handed him the key that unlocked their mysteries.[38]
Nine of the expositions between Psalms 15 and 32 relate to Christ's death.[39]
Besides the two that spoke about Christ's redemptive suffering from a third-
person point of view (on Psalms 19 and 20), seven others focused directly
on the Crucifixion. Of these seven, three made a link to the Passion narratives of the New Testament (15, 21, 30), while the other four explored
the psalm's paschal implications (16, 17, 27, 29). But most striking fact is
that in these seven expositions, either in whole or in part, *Christ prayed
the psalm in the first person from the cross.*

Unsurprisingly, the *Exposition of Psalm* 17 occasioned Augustine's
first known use of the phrase *totus Christus.*[40] This psalm too was spoken
from the cross; but interestingly, for the first time Augustine heard the voice
alternating between head and body, and at times it was difficult to tell
which is speaking. The title phrase, "to the end," indicated as usual Christ,
"strong-handed in his humanity," but Augustine observed that though the
voice was Christ's the words better fit his body. For verse 2, when the voice
praised the Lord as "my strength . . . my firm support, my refuge, my lib-

erator," the epithet "my strength" pointed to the One "through whom I am strong," that is, to God "my refuge and my liberator," in whom "I sought refuge because you set me free." So Augustine found "Christ and church speaking together here, that is, the whole Christ [*totus Christus*], head and body." But they spoke not merely in unison but on each other's behalf; it was thus an instance of *prosopopoeia* in which Christ spoke on behalf and in the name of the church. Because Christ and church were one body and one voice, Christ could impersonate the church's voice; but the church could also speak in Christ's voice.

DISCOVERING ONESELF EMBODIED IN THE CHRIST OF THE PSALMS

By reading the psalms through the lens of the New Testament, and by drawing out the implications of the Incarnation and the reality of Christ's death, Augustine transformed his framework for understanding scripture. The New Testament had already defined the basic interpretive parameters of psalms interpretation by ascribing certain lament psalms to Christ; then the early church tradition extended that work. Tyconius then spoke of the bipartite body of the Lord in the attempt to distinguish the voices of the Lord and his body in scripture. But Augustine went beyond them all by driving down to the underlying unity of head and body, and to the implied reciprocity between them.

The confluence of Jesus's cry from the cross and Psalm 21:2 was more than a witness to divine grace and love. The bedrock authority of the dying Savior's exegesis of the Psalm 21 disclosed the voice of Christ throughout the whole Psalter and indeed the entire Old Testament. Psalm 21 accordingly revealed not only the mediator's future work but also the preincarnate mediator secretly present in the people, writers, and events of the ancient prophetic people. As he would go on to show, they too were part of the *totus Christus*.[41] New Testament grace appeared in history and language before his advent, when old covenant "sacraments" served as fragmentary but actual means of grace by which the Holy Spirit conveyed knowledge of the mediator's future humility to the people of that time.

Augustine later unfolded the same outlook in greater detail in his exposition of Psalm 45. The metaphor of "the key that unlocks" in *Enarrationes in Psalmos* 45.1 replaced "the fire that melts" of *Enarrationes in Psalmos* 21, but the line of interpretation was the same. Commenting on words in the psalm title, "the hidden things," Augustine wrote that the psalm was "concerned with what is hidden, but as you know, the one crucified on Calvary rent asunder the veil so that the temple's secret places were exposed to view [Matt. 27:51]. Our Lord's cross was like a key for opening what was locked away: so let us be confident that he will be with us now, that these hidden things may be unveiled" (*En. Ps.* 45.1). When Christ transposed all humanity into himself on the cross, he traded humanity's death for divine life. This "marvelous exchange" between spirit and flesh, eternal and temporal, Redeemer and redeemed, introduced heavenly life into earthly life; an exchange of heavenly and earthly nuclei, so to say, brought a new creation into being. That realization set Augustine on the road to seeing how changing historical events could bear God's eternal grace and truth without ceasing to be themselves; temporal things not only anticipated and described the eternal but even manifested and conveyed it. In the words of a psalm that he loved to quote, "Truth has sprung up from the earth" (Ps. 84:12) (e.g., *S.* 185.1–2).

On the one hand the psalmist spoke *as Christ*, while on the other Christ spoke *as Adam* and *as church* and made the figure of *prosopopoeia* his engine of redemption and the template for reading scripture. *Totus Christus* allowed Augustine to take up a position within the text's own precincts. He accordingly read the psalms *as Christ*, that is, as a member of Christ's body who participated in the self-understanding of the head. This way of interpretation embryonically embodied the view that later often pictured Christ at Gethsemane and Golgotha "transfiguring us into himself" (*transfigurans nos in se*); that is, incorporating believers into his person as members of his body, the church.[42] The exchange between Christ and believers—life given for death, justice given for guilt—suggests the chief characteristic of Augustine's Christian hermeneutics, that is, the exchange by which readers project themselves into the scriptures. These early psalms studies, and the later psalms sermons, were training exercises to help readers to practice this self-transposition into the text through Christ's gracious incarnation and death.

Notes

1. "Deum et animam scire cupio. Nihilne plus? Nihil omnino." Cf. Adolph Harnack, *History of Dogma*, vol. 5, trans. Neil Buchanan (1900; repr., New York: Dover, 1961), 110: "In these words Augustine has briefly formulated the aim of his spiritual life."

2. For strictly Christological uses of the phrase, see Augustine, *S.* 92.3, 261.6.7.

3. By the count of Henri Marrou, *Théologie de l'histoire* (Paris: Seuil, 1968), 43, translated by Violet Nevile as *Time and Timeliness* (New York: Sheed and Ward, 1969), 35; noted by Marie-Josèphe Rondeau, *Les commentaires patristiques du Psautier (IIIe–Ve siècles)*, vol. 2, OCA 220 (Rome: Pontificium Institutum Studiorum Orientalium, 1985), 371 n. 1066. Though the CETEDOC Library of Christian Latin Texts count of the phrase *totus Christus* yields less than a quarter of that number, the passages where the idea is discussed or presupposed without being named are many, more than 125 in the *Enarrationes* alone. For major passages that discuss *totus Christus*, see *En. Ps.* 30[2].1.3–5, 32[2].1.2, 37.6, 44.3, 54.3, 61.4, 74.4, 90.2.1, 100.3, 101.1.2, 120.12, 123.1, 130.1, 138.2, and 142.3 and 9. Here and throughout this chapter, *Enarrationes* references list the psalm according to the Septuagint numbering, Augustine's first or second treatment of a psalm appears in brackets (if applicable), then the number of the exposition within the series (if applicable), and then the section number. Thus "30[2].1.3" refers to Psalm 30 (Hebrew 31), second *enarratio*, first homily, third section; "37.6" refers to Psalm 37 (Hebrew 38), section 6.

4. On *totus Christus* as the heart of Augustine's interpretation of the psalms, see Michael Fiedrowicz, *Psalmus Vox Totius Christi: Studien zu Augustins "Enarrationes in Psalmos"* (Freiburg: Herder, 1997), 15. On *totus Christus* as the heart of Augustine's theology generally, see Egon Franz, "*Totus Christus*: Studien über Christus und die Kirche bei Augustin" (Inaugural-Dissertation, University of Bonn, 1956), 95: "Mit dieser Aussage *[totus Christus caput et corpus]* befinden wir uns im Zentrum der Theologie des gereiften Augustin."

5. Augustine, *Ep.* 21.4 (CCSL 31: 49).

6. For a sample of this instruction, see Augustine, *S.* 216; William Harmless, *Augustine and the Catechumenate* (Collegeville, MN: Liturgical Press, 1995), 105.

7. C. H. Dodd, *According to the Scriptures* (London: Nisbet, 1952), 96–103; Barnabas Lindars, *New Testament Apologetic* (London: SCM Press, 1961), 88–110; Donald Juel, *Messianic Exegesis* (Philadelphia: Fortress Press, 1988), 89–117. On Paul, see Richard Hays, *Echoes of Scripture in the Letters of Paul* (New Haven, CT: Yale University Press, 1989), passim, and "Christ Prays the Psalms: Israel's Psalter as the Matrix of Early Christology," in *The Conversion of the Imagination: Paul as Interpreter of Israel's Scripture* (Grand Rapids, MI: Eerdmans, 2005), 101–18.

8. Emile Mersch, *The Whole Christ*, trans. J. R. Kelly (Milwaukee, WI: Bruce, 1938), 227–306; originally published as *Le corps mystique du Christ* (Louvain: Museum Lessianum, 1936).

9. As for instance in *En. Ps.* 37.6.

10. Rondeau, *Commentaires patristiques*, the second volume of which is subtitled *Exégèse prospologique et Théologie*; see especially Hubertus Drobner, *Person-Exegese und Christologie bei Augustinus: Zur Herkunft der Formel una persona* (Leiden: Brill, 1986), and "Grammatical Exegesis and Christology in St. Augustine," *Studia Patristica* 18 (1990): 49–63.

11. Augustine, *En. Ps.* 3.1 (BA 57A: 152).

12. Martine Dulaey observes in her introduction that they read like "school exercises" (BA 57A, 31). Augustine's early psalm expositions stress rather the word as the coefficient, even the inhabitant, of the voice. The Word uses the human voice in order to enter the ears and so into the habits and the memory of its hearers, just as crushed grapes trickle their juice into the wine vat for aging (*En. Ps.* 8.2 [BA 57A: 338]). See above, p. 213.

13. Tyconius, *Liber reg.* 1 (F. C. Burkitt, *The Book of Rules of Tyconius* [Cambridge: Cambridge University Press, 1894], 1.19–2.1): "Dominum eiusne corpus, id est ecclesiam, Scriptura loquatur, sola ratio discernit, dum quid cui conueniat persuadet uel quia tanta est uis ueritatis extorquet" (Whether scripture is speaking about the Lord or about his body, that is, the church, only reason can tell, when what aligns with each one either persuades us or—such is the force of truth—compels us). See Pamela Bright, *The Book of Rules of Tyconius: Its Purpose and Inner Logic*, Christianity and Judaism in Antiquity 2 (Notre Dame, IN: University of Notre Dame Press, 1988), 61–63.

14. Some recent studies have termed this device "speech-in-character." New Testament scholar Stanley K. Stowers discusses the device in "Romans 7.7–25 as a Speech-in-Character (*prosopopoiía*)," in *Paul in His Hellenistic Context*, ed. Troels Engberg-Pedersen (Minneapolis, MN: Augsburg Fortress Press, 1995), 180–202. I draw on his essay in what follows.

15. Ibid., 180–91.

16. Quintilian, *Institutio oratoria* 9.2.37.

17. Quintilian, *Institutio oratoria* 9.2.31. Cicero followed Aristotle's picture of the dead appearing in court to argue the case of understanding a document's intention, which necessarily involved impersonation. Quintilian likewise envisioned its use in a court of law, where a speaker might make someone absent seem present for rhetorical effect.

18. Stowers, "Speech-in-Character," 191–93.

19. Ibid., 188–91; Rondeau, *Commentaires patristiques*, 2: 51–58.

20. Stowers, "Speech-in-Character," 193–97.

21. Augustine, *Simpl.* 1.1.1: "In this passage it seems to me that the apostle has transfigured into himself a man placed under the Law, in whose person he speaks those words" (Quo loco videtur mihi Apostolus transfigurasse in se hominem sub lege positum cuius verbis ex persona sua loquitur [CCSL 44: 8]; cf. *En. Ps.* 102.15). Significantly, Augustine's term for this transposition of voices is *transfiguration*, which clearly shows the rhetorical base of what would become a crucial hermeneutic concept for the later *Expositions of the Psalms*, on which see below.

22. Carl P. E. Springer, "The *Prosopopoeia* of Church as Mother in Augustine's *Psalmus contra Partem Donati*," *Augustinian Studies* 18 (1987): 52–65; Daniel J. Nodes, "The Organization of Augustine's *Psalmus contra Partem Donati*," *Vigiliae Christianae* 63 (2009): 397.

23. *Ps. c. Don.* 270–278, and 287 (BA 28: 188, 190; trans. William Harmless, S.J., *Augustine: In His Own Words* [Washington, DC: Catholic University of America Press, 2010], 245).

24. Like some other devices of this period, extensive use of this rhetorical form was experimental. Yet other briefer passages of impersonation appear not infrequently in Augustine's works. Some instances are well known, as when in *Confessions* he recalls hearing "as it were your voice from on high: 'I am the food of the fully grown; grow and you will feed on me. And you will not change me into you like the food your flesh eats, but you will be changed into me'" (7.10.16; trans. Henry Chadwick [Oxford: Oxford University Press, 1992]). At other times he notes instances in the scriptures, as with Paul's appeal to the Galatians, "My little children, for whom I am again in labor until Christ is formed in you!" (Gal. 4:19). Augustine comments that Paul "spoke this more in the person of Mother Church [*ex persona matris ecclesiae*]" (*Exp. Gal.* 38.1–2 [CSEL 84: 106]). As we are about to see, Augustine drew profound insight from this figure that helped him to explain Christ's redemption.

25. *En. Ps.* 3.6 (BA 57A: 162): "illi tribuit cuius munere loquebar."

26. *En. Ps.* 3.9 (BA 57A: 168). This is not yet quite the "whole Christ" (*totus Christus*) of Augustine's later psalms expositions. Clearly its sense of the unity of head and body is a premise of the later concept; but we do not see here the interactive or transpositive dynamic of the later conception, in which the head and body exchange voices or dialogue together. Here the church speaks using Christ as its mouthpiece.

27. *En. Ps.* 3.9; *pace* Boulding's "in these prophetic words."

28. Augustine had already referred to this parabolic picture of Matt. 25:35–45 in *Gn. c. Man.* 2.25.38, where he wrote of Christians who may be said "not implausibly to bear the person of Christ" (non incongrue sustinet personam Christi; CSEL 91: 162).

29. See Martine Dulaey, "L'interprétation du Psaume 21 (22TM) chez saint Augustin," in *David, Jésus et la reine Esther: Recherches sur le Psaume 21,* ed. Gilles Dorival (Louvain: Peeters, 2002), 315–40.

30. Augustine, *En. Ps.* 21.1 (BA 57B: 132).

31. I leave aside what could be argued to be an act of divine *prosopopoeia,* in which the psalmist is stirred to this act by the preincarnate Word, who, as it were, takes up the human words of the psalmist as his own.

32. Augustine, *En. Ps.* 21.1 (BA 57B: 132): "in personam veteris hominis cuius mortalitatem portavit."

33. Augustine, *En. Ps.* 30[2].1.3 (CCSL 38: 192): "mira commutatio . . . divina commercia . . . mutatio rerum." Christ deigned "to speak in our words, so that we in our turn might speak in his. This is the wonderful exchange, the divine business deal, the transaction effected in this world by the heavenly dealer" (trans. WSA III/15: 322–23).

34. See the comments of Martine Dulaey, "Introduction, Psaume 21: Première explication," BA 57B: 125–31.

35. The phrase is from Dulaey's introduction to *En. Ps.* 21 (BA 57B: 127).

36. Augustine, *En. Ps.* 79.1 (CCSL 39: 1111): "Denique hoc testimonium et Christum et vineam confitetur; hoc est caput et corpus, regem et plebem, patrem et gregem, et totum omnium scripturarum mysterium Christum et ecclesiam" (In short, this testimony acknowledges both Christ and vine, that is, head and body, king and people, shepherd and flock, and the whole mystery of all scripture: Christ and the church).

37. It reappears often in Augustine's sermons, as Hubertus Drobner has shown ("Psalm 21 in Augustine's *Sermones ad populum*: Catecheses on *Christus totus* and Rules of Interpretation," *Augustinian Studies* 37 [2006]: 153–54), but also in his treatises; it is essential to his argument in, for example, *Trin.* 4.3.5–6. *Epistula* 140, written nearly two decades after his time as a presbyter, essentially is an exposition of Psalm 21. See Isabelle Bochet, "Une nouvelle lecture du *Liber ad Honoratum* d'Augustin (= *epist.* 140)," *Revue des Études Augustiniennes* 45 (1999): 335–51.

38. Joanne McWilliam Dewart ("Augustine's Developing Use of the Cross, 387–400," *Augustinian Studies* 15 [1984]: 22) inexplicably dismisses these first psalms expositions with the comment that they present "considerably more than [Augustine] had appropriated intellectually."

39. The treatments of Psalms 22, 23, 24, 25, and 28 feature the church supplicating or acclaiming Christ its head. The speaking voice of Psalm 26 belongs to a new convert within the church, and that of Psalm 31 to a repentant sinner. Psalm 32's exhortation to praise comes from the prophet-psalmist speaking in his own voice.

40. Augustine, *En. Ps.* 17.2 (BA 57B: 16). *En. Ps.* 3.9 came close, referring simply to "the whole" (*totus*). In *div. qu.* 69.10, Augustine made an unusual refer-

ence to *universus Christus,* "the collective Christ," whose many members have been "turned into one" (*unus + verto*).

41. Augustine, *Cat. rud.* 3.5–6.

42. This transfiguration was the foundation of the "marvelous exchange" previously mentioned. When Christ took the form of a slave and clothed us with himself, "he did not disdain to transfigure us into himself [*transfigurare nos in se*]. . . . This is the marvelous exchange" (*En. Ps.* 30[2].1.3 [CCSL 38: 192]). The transfiguration theme appears often in Augustine's preaching, as in *En. Ps.* 32 [2].1.2; *En. Ps.* 142. 9; *S.* 305.4. For a discussion of the theme, see my "Transfiguration: Christology and the Roots of Figurative Exegesis in St. Augustine," *Studia Patristica* 33 (1997): 40–47.

BIBLIOGRAPHICAL NOTE

The standard older survey of the patristic vision of the church as Christ's body is Emile Mersch, *Le corps mystique du Christ* (Louvain: Museum Lessianum, 1936); translated into English by J. R. Kelly as *The Whole Christ* (Milwaukee, WI: Bruce, 1938), it treats Augustine on 384–440. The fullest thematic study remains Egon Franz, "*Totus Christus*: Studien über Christus und die Kirche bei Augustin" (Inaugural-Dissertation, University of Bonn, 1956). Analysis of the idea is typically embedded in larger studies. See especially Michael Fiedrowicz, *Psalmus Vox Totius Christi: Studien zu Augustins "Enarrationes in Psalmos"* (Freiburg: Herder, 1997), 234–378. Fiedrowicz condensed his work for the *Augustinus-Lexikon,* vol. 2, ed. C. P. Mayer (Basel: Schwabe, 1996–2002), see esp. cols. 848–56, and an English précis appears as the "General Introduction" to Maria Boulding's translation *Saint Augustine: Expositions of the Psalms,* 5 vols., WSA III/15 (Hyde Park, NY: New City Press, 2000), see esp. 43–60. Marie-Josèphe Rondeau helpfully includes a perceptive link to Augustine's theme of *transfiguro* in her magisterial *Les commentaires patristiques du Psautier (IIIe–Ve siècles),* vol. 2, *Exégèse prosopologique et théologie,* OCA 220 (Rome: Pontificium Institutum Studium Orientalium, 1985), 365–88.

Among articles dealing with the theme, see Michel Réveillaud, "Le Christ-Homme, tête de l'église: Étude d'ecclésiologie selon les *Enarrationes in Psalmos* d'Augustin," *Recherches Augustiniennes* 5 (1968): 67–94; Pasquale Borgomeo, *L' église de ce temps dans la prédication de saint Augustin* (Paris: Études Augustiniennes, 1972), 191–234; Tarsicius J. van Bavel and B. Bruning, "Die Einheit des *Totus Christus* bei Augustinus," in *Scientia Augustiniana* [Festschrift for A. Zumkeller], ed. C. P. Mayer and W. Eckermann (Würzburg: Augustinus-Verlag, 1975), 43–75; Niel Kelly, "La persona del *totus Christus*: Interpretación christiana de san Augustín," *Augustinus* 36, nos. 140–42 (1991): 147–53; Jozef Niewiadomski, "Gewaltheit und die Konzeption des 'Totus Christus'?" *Augustiniana* 41 (1991): 567–74;

Tarsicius J. van Bavel, "The 'Christus Totus' Idea: A Forgotten Aspect of Augustine's Spirituality," in *Studies in Patristic Christology*, ed. T. Finan and V. Twomey (Dublin: Four Courts Press, 1998), 84–94; Martine Dulaey, "L'interprétation du Psaume 21 (22TM) chez saint Augustin," in *David, Jésus et la reine Esther: Recherches sur le Psaume 21,* ed. Gilles Dorival (Louvain: Peeters, 2002), 315–40; Michael Cameron, "*Totus Christus* and the Psychagogy of Augustine's Sermons," *Augustinian Studies* 36 (2005): 59–70; Michael C. McCarthy, S.J., "An Ecclesiology of Groaning: Augustine, the Psalms, and the Making of Church," *Theological Studies* 66 (2005): 23–48; Hubertus Drobner, "Psalm 21 in Augustine's *Sermones ad populum*: Catecheses on *Christus Totus* and Rules of Interpretation," *Augustinian Studies* 37 (2006): 145–69; Kimberly F. Baker, "Augustine's Doctrine of the *Totus Christus*: Reflecting on the Church as Sacrament of Unity," *Horizons* 37 (2010): 7–24; Andrew Hofer, O.P., "Matthew 25:31–46 as an Hermeneutical Rule in Augustine's *Enarrationes in Psalmos*," *Downside Review* 126 (2010): 285–300.

No monographs exist in English for *totus Christus,* though see S. J. Grabowski, *The Church: An Introduction to the Theology of St. Augustine* (St. Louis, MO: Herder, 1957), 3–70; Guy Leroy, " 'Saul, Saul, pourquoi me persecutes-tu?,' Ac 9,4b, dans le predication de saint Augustin" (PhD diss., Institut d'études théologiques [Brussels], 1986); Goulven Madec, *La patrie et la voie: Le Christ dans la vie et la pensée de saint Augustin* (Paris: Desclée, 1989), 178–85; Bernard McGinn, *The Foundations of Mysticism* (New York: Crossroad, 1991), 248–51; Basil Studer, *The Grace of Christ and the Grace of God in Augustine of Hippo,* trans. M. J. O'Connell (Collegeville, MN: Liturgical Press, 1997), 55–60. The theme is important in Robert Dodaro, *Christ and the Just Society in the Thought of Augustine* (Cambridge: Cambridge University Press, 2004), 97–114; Daniel J. Jones, *Christus Sacerdos in the Preaching of St. Augustine,* Patrologia 14 (Frankfurt: Peter Lang, 2004), 213–38; Jason Byassee, *Praise Seeking Understanding: Reading the Psalms with Augustine* (Grand Rapids, MI: Eerdmans, 2007), 54–96; Michael Cameron, *Christ Meets Me Everywhere: Augustine's Early Figurative Exegesis,* Oxford Studies in Historical Theology (New York: Oxford University Press, 2012), ch. 6. Two recent dissertations explore the theme as important to their topics: Michael C. McCarthy, S.J., "The Revelatory Psalm: A Fundamental Theology of Augustine's *Enarrationes in Psalmos*" (University of Notre Dame, 2003), and Kimberly F. Baker, "Augustine on Action, Contemplation, and Their Meeting Point in Christ" (University of Notre Dame, 2007). On the Christology and ecclesiology of the first Psalms expositions, see also Pierre-Marie Hombert, "La christologie des trente-deux premières *Ennarationes in psalmos* de saint Augustin," in *Augustin, philosophe et prédicateur: Hommage à Goulven Madec,* ed. Isabelle Bochet (Turnhout: Brepols, 2012), 431–63; on *totus Christus,* 456–61.

An Ecclesiology of Groaning

Augustine, the Psalms, and the Making of Church

Michael C. McCarthy, S.J.

In recent issues of *Theological Studies*, the history of exegesis has claimed the attention of biblical scholars, historians, and systematic theologians. Michael Cahill hears a "definite crescendo" sounding from those who study the history of exegesis, and he insists that traditional biblical scholars must now listen to these new dialogue partners.[1] Marie Anne Mayeski adds that systematic theologians will also benefit from joining the conversation. French theologians of the mid-twentieth century, for instance, turned to patristic exegesis as a response to perceived limitations of the historical-critical method. Particularly in their study of typology, they sought to find in the tradition a precedent for treating the Bible, not simply as a deposit of historical record, but as a living, revelatory word in the context of the church.[2] To study the practice of ancient exegesis is to encounter a theological hermeneutics that could complement the more recent efforts of the historical-critical method.

Theologians of the early twenty-first century may continue to retrieve from ancient exegesis an understanding of scripture as the Word of God revealed in the church, but a new set of challenges face us. The church itself may appear far more complex, ambiguous, and problematic than it did in the 1950s. At least in the United States, the actual trials, the sufferings, the scandals of recent history provoke us to ask (with a certain pain and humility) how it is that the church may be considered the context of God's revelation. Here again, though, the actual practice of ancient exegesis—occasional, rhetorical, polemical, constructive—provides us an excellent resource. As a case in point, I shall argue that Augustine's exegesis of the psalms, as demonstrated in his *Enarrationes in Psalmos,* offers us an ecclesiology particularly suitable to a church in crisis. This "ecclesiology of groaning" (as I shall call it) resists formal systematization and idealization precisely because it emerges from the revelatory dynamism of the Word itself, whose mission, for Augustine, crucially includes embodiment in the sullied, vulnerable flesh. Such a dynamism, expressed so poignantly throughout the *Enarrationes in Psalmos,* challenges us to revise our very categories for understanding "exegesis" and "ecclesiology." After a critical evaluation of how these terms may be applied to Augustine's work, then, I shall offer an account of Augustine's theology of the psalms and show how recent social theory may help us find new ways for considering the relationship between biblical commentary and the building up of the church. This "ecclesiology of groaning" provides a new access, not only to Augustine's church, but to our own.

Augustine and Embodied Exegesis

I examine here how the revelatory word operates in the church by highlighting an aspect of patristic exegesis that goes largely unexplored by historical theologians: its social and cultural function. At least since the rise of the historical-critical method, biblical exegesis has remained an overwhelmingly silent affair and has enjoyed a certain independence from an ecclesial setting. "Texts" (as the Bible is so frequently conceived) lie open for scientific examination, inquiry, and comment, but in the scholarly mode such researches are individually pursued and physically mute.[3] For the ancient church, on the other hand, the Bible provided foremost and predominantly a public, oral and auditory encounter. While Augustine himself, for instance, had privileged access to a great library and spent considerable time in private meditation on the written text of scripture, the vast majority of Christians in fourth- and fifth-century North Africa heard the Word of God spoken and explained in the context of liturgical readings and preaching.[4] Augustine comments on the physical demands of hearing the Word toward the end of a long homily on Psalm 147. Contrasting the bodily fatigue of his congregation to the zeal of the crowds thronging the amphitheater, Augustine points to the discipline and stamina of those who patiently study the psalms: "If [those in the theater] had to stand so long, would they still be at their show?"[5]

For Augustine, then, the oral "exegesis" of scripture, unlike the scholarly productions of later history, constituted an event that he would often compare with the spectacles taking place outside his basilica. If practitioners of the historical-critical method may, for their own purposes, appropriately beware of the rhetorical virtuosity of one such as Augustine, the theologian may by no means discount the modality in which scripture and its exegesis is communicated among late ancient Christians. Not only does the ecclesial performance of Augustine and his congregation frame his exegesis, but the practice of that exegesis itself forms the *ecclesia* in a way that is theologically significant. Furthermore, attention to the performative aspects of Augustine's exegesis yields a new way of approaching his ecclesiology. Augustine's actual practice of interpreting the psalms with his community, I argue, "makes" the church: it generates the *ecclesia* at a distinct historical moment. Not only does this complex process call for a revision of what we may mean by ancient "exegesis," therefore, but the practice and performance of that exegesis provide sources for a more dynamic ecclesiology, whose contours are more fully discerned by considering not only what his exegesis *describes* conceptually but also what it *does* concretely.

Augustine's treatment of the psalms provides an especially rich context for examining the practical efficacy of his exegesis. In the *Confessions* Augustine describes his own experience of the psalms as therapeutic (9.4), and indeed throughout his preaching he repeatedly insists that the words of the psalmist are words that members of his congregation may themselves voice in their own condition. A primary strategy of Augustine's exegesis is to show how the psalms apply to his congregation. Unlike passages of other biblical books, the words of the psalms are formally assimilable to the lives of those who hear them: "If the psalm prays, you pray; if it groans, you groan," Augustine asserts. "For all things written here are a mirror to us."[6] Augustine's understanding of the psalms' effect on the soul reflects his acquaintance with ancient philosophical teaching on the affections. The right words (*locutiones*) could heal unwholesome emotions.[7] The

medicinal properties of the psalms' locutions may largely explain the burgeoning interest in the psalms among early ascetics. The rise of monasticism in the fourth century brought a proliferation of psalm commentaries.[8]
Unlike most of these commentaries, however, which seem to be directed at
monastic communities, Augustine's addresses his church as a whole: from
those who have come to the basilica to avoid the temptation of games, cir-
cuses, and fights to the converted astrologer, from the consecrated virgin
to the married mother. In what comes down to us as his *Enarrationes in
Psalmos*, a vast collection of notes and sermons on the psalms given over
the course of almost thirty years (ca. AD 392–422), Augustine speaks directly to a gross and complex populace whom he can hardly idealize.

In extending his commentary beyond the bounds of the ascetical en-
closure, Augustine allows the psalms to speak from that thick and mixed
body. Because he lives at a time of considerable ecclesial tension, of enduring scandal at the lapse of third-century Catholic bishops, of anguished
debates on the nature of the church, and of bitter challenges posed by the
Donatists, his teaching on the *corpus permixtum* has an emotional register
that far exceeds its scope simply as an account of the church. To be a member of such a mixed body is to groan mightily at the obvious iniquities and
imperfections that incorporation entails. To find oneself in such a body is
to share in the laments so powerfully voiced by the psalmist: "My heart
bellows its groans. All my desire is before you, Lord, and my groaning is
not hidden from you" (Psalm 37:9–10). Like the expression of other deep
emotions, however, the groaning of the church resists certain definition: it
possesses a quality that Augustine calls *ineffabilis*. The continued groaning
of the church beggars even Augustine's power to describe fully the range of
problems or theological issues implicit in it. Through his exegesis, however, Augustine actively appropriates for the church the groans that resound throughout the psalter and indicates that, by lamenting with the
psalmist and reflecting deeply and continually on that affect, the church
comes to learn what it is, comes to be what it is. This "ecclesiology of groaning" not only eludes the traditional categories used to describe Augustine's
doctrine of the church but challenges us to find new and far more satisfactory categories, which may arise at least in part from a deeper understanding of the dynamics of his exegesis.

AUGUSTINE AND EMBODIED ECCLESIOLOGY

Like other patristic authors, Augustine offers no formal systematic ecclesiology as such. Throughout the *Enarrationes in Psalmos*, he constantly discusses the church in highly imaginative terms. He draws from the psalms hosts of images so as to meditate on a body that seems almost protean. The *ecclesia* is the moon that waxes and wanes (Psalm 71:7), the earth irrigated and tilled by God (Psalm 36:3), the silvery wings of a dove upon whose back we are borne up (Psalm 67:14), the winepress where the sweetness of fruit may gradually emerge from its bitter skins (Psalm 8:1).[9] However centrally the church figures in Augustine's practice of exegesis, it never becomes an object of particular study as such. Rather, the church itself embodies the complex and exceedingly problematic condition of humanity's return to God, and that body finds rich self-expression in the Psalter. To hunt the works of Augustine in order to construct a conceptually precise *De ecclesia* is to fail in appreciating the peculiar dynamism of ancient thinking about the church, its unsystematic, highly rhetorical, and frequently polemical aspects.[10]

For at least fifty years now, theologians have harvested the corpus of Augustine's biblical commentaries for their ecclesiological content but with a methodology that tends to abstract citations from his actual practice. Few studies have considered the event of his exegesis as itself theologically significant. In 1955, Hans Urs von Balthasar included many passages from Augustine's scriptural commentaries in his anthology of texts on the church.[11] The succeeding decades witnessed two excellent monographs, one on Augustine's understanding of the heavenly church and the other on the "church of this time."[12] Both works relied heavily on Augustine's biblical exegesis, especially that delivered in the course of his preaching. As much as these works brought into relief the complexity of Augustine's thought and the profusion of images he employed to describe the church, they did not consider how his exegesis itself represented the dynamic process in which the church comes to be. Thus a common paradigm, which finds in Augustine two distinct ecclesiologies—the church visible and invisible, the earthly church and the heavenly church—continues to influence our perception and leads to claims that Augustine's sense of church is marked by an

"ultraspiritualism" or Platonic idealization that ignores the concrete ecclesial reality. Speaking of Augustine's treatment of the psalms in the *Enarrationes in Psalmos*, Louis Bouyer remarks that "the 'body' [of Christ] is
so spiritualized that what is corporal about it can no longer be seen."[13]
Yet such a comment betrays the tendency of theologians to isolate discrete statements made in the course of Augustine's preaching from their actual context. We should not ignore that Augustine's discussion of the same
"body" comes from settings where he refers to his sweating before a packed
house, or to the stench generated by his congregation over the course of his
sermon, where he pleads with a great crowd in Carthage to quiet down because his voice is liable to give out or mentions the way they groan when enduring the burdens of incorrigible members of the body.[14] *This* body (i.e.,
the one he addresses, the one that groans through the voice of the psalms)
is hardly marked by an ultraspiritualism.

Augustine does indeed locate this body within an eschatological horizon. The unfinished or unrealized quality of the church always stands at
the center of his reflection. While commenting on the verse that most immediately expresses the theme of the City of God (Psalm 86:4, "Glorious
things are said of you, O City of God"), Augustine reminds his hearers that
as "the wicked city runs its course from beginning to end, so too the good
city is continuously being formed by the conversion of the wicked."[15] The
history within which he places himself and his hearers is the gradual edifi-
cation of Jerusalem; his exegesis is a moment within that history. If we take
Augustine's account seriously, then the object of ecclesiology must always
remain and must always return to that dynamic of conversion, of formation through which Jerusalem is built up.[16]

Not only does this approach to ecclesiology reflect the vitality of Augustine's ancient sense of church throughout his exegesis, but it is one that
fits more recent studies on the proper object and method of ecclesiology.
In his own *Foundations in Ecclesiology*, for instance, Joseph Komonchak
takes Bernard Lonergan's understanding of the church as a "process of self-
constitution," a community that "perfects itself through communication,"
and argues that all reflection on the church must therefore be a "reflection
on this constitutive self-expression and self-realization."[17] Statements about
the church, then, and the multiple images of the church, as well as the actions and historical developments of the church, are significant not only

for their discrete content but also for their quality as themselves constituting the *ecclesia*'s ongoing self-appropriation or "coming-to-consciousness" of itself. Komonchak argues that the study of the church as in the process of self-constitution represents the "foundational" effort of ecclesiology.[18]

Augustine's exegesis of the psalms, as manifested in the *Enarrationes in Psalmos*, constitutes a very significant case in point. Not only does Augustine consistently use images and psalm verses to communicate the experience and nature of the church, but throughout this sprawling work he repeatedly offers a unique and dynamic understanding of the psalms themselves. They are, he asserts again and again, the *uox totius Christi*, the voice of the whole Christ, head and body, the one voice of the Incarnate Word speaking to, with, and within the church. For Augustine, the psalms possess a dialectical character and constitute an ongoing, communicative exchange between God and humanity within the ecclesial body, which prays and meditates upon them. This theologically dynamic conception of the psalms as *uox totius Christi*, therefore, not only serves as a heuristic device grounding Augustine's exegetical enterprise but effectively offers a new key for understanding Augustine's ecclesiology itself. Insofar as ecclesial existence is formed, interpreted, and known in the context of Augustine's psalm exegesis, attention to the theologically complex and dynamic quality of that exegesis represents a significant moment in what Komonchak calls the "foundational effort" of ecclesiology.

The *Enarrationes in Psalmos*, however, not only sets forth the theological model of the *totus Christus*, in which the psalms are interpreted, but also reflects a concrete social context. To the extent that students of Augustine's ecclesiology tend to concentrate on his theological claims in isolation from their situation or the socially productive nature of his exegesis, they indeed risk the kind of theological reductionism or idealization noted above. As Komonchak has insisted, ecclesiology must extend beyond the questions of "hermeneutics of texts" to "hermeneutics of social existence."[19] The *Enarrationes in Psalmos* represents a privileged place where we may engage in both. Here the theological enterprise may gain from the insights of social theorists. Although social theory is avowedly empirical and nontheological, its methods are nonetheless very helpful for understanding more completely the ecclesiology of the *Enarrationes*.[20] While theologians will reorient what they might learn from the human sciences, a consideration of their own dynamism will be crucial. In what follows, therefore, I shall first offer a brief exposition of Augustine's theological hermeneutic of the *uox totius Christi*. Then I shall draw from the work of social theorists to illustrate how Augustine's exegesis may rightly be conceived as a moment of the church's self-appropriation.

The Development of Augustine's Theology of the Psalms

Although most students of the history of exegesis are familiar with Augustine's unique approach to the psalms as the "voice of the whole Christ," many treat it as though it were a univocal concept.[21] In fact, Augustine's understanding of the *uox totius Christi* develops as his Christology develops: increasingly he stresses the revelatory significance of the body. A fuller appreciation of this shifting theology of the psalms, therefore, will have significant impact on the way we understand the relationship between Augustine's exegesis and his ecclesiology.[22] Like other early Christian commentators on the Psalter, Augustine worked out of a tradition that stressed the prophetic function of the Hebrew Bible. The psalms were David's prophecy, and David was himself was a type of the King yet to come. The rule of Hilary of Poitier in the mid-fourth century reflects a basic strategy common to all patristic exegetes: "All prophecy of the psalms must be applied to Christ."[23] Like other authors, Augustine seeks references to Christ through the technique of prosopological exegesis, where the reader of the psalm identifies what person [*prosopon*] is speaking in a given verse or to what character a verse refers.[24] So, for instance, Augustine takes Psalm 2:2 ("Let us burst their chains asunder, and throw their yoke away from us") as referring to those who devised schemes to crucify Christ. Verse 6 of the same psalm, however ("I have been established by God as king over Zion"), is clearly spoken in the person of Christ himself (*ex persona ipsius Domini*).[25]

While Augustine will go on to develop both the Christocentric and the prosopological interpretation of the psalms in a wholly original and rather complex way, he begins the *Enarrationes in Psalmos* in a very traditional manner. In his earliest commentaries on Psalms 1 through 32, thought to be written shortly after his ordination in 391, Augustine seems to accept and apply the principle formulated by his Donatist contemporary Tyconius: that all scripture speaks of Christ and the church, head and body, *de domino et corpore eius*, and that it remains the task of the exegete, therefore, to discern when the reference of verses passes from head to body and vice versa.[26] So he concludes his commentary on Psalm 17 by noting that "whatever things have been said in this psalm that cannot properly fit the Lord himself, that is, the head of the church, must be referred to the church. For the whole Christ speaks here, in which all his members subsist."[27] Likewise, he begins his exegesis on Psalm 24 by stating that the words of this psalm pertain to the Christian people converted to God, and that therefore Christ is speaking, "but in the person of the church [*sed in ecclesiae persona*]."[28]

If Augustine's earlier exegesis, then, manifests the Tyconian concern to distinguish when Christ the head speaks and when Christ the body speaks, increasingly throughout his commentary these voices tend to mix, and his exegesis does not uniformly stress the distinctive voices of the head or body but emphasizes the one voice of the whole Christ. Although Augustine will continue to ask at times who is speaking, and although he will note the change in speakers, the "one voice" of the psalms comes to express, if not actually effect, the union of God and humanity, the one true mediator.[29] By virtue of the Incarnation, Christ did not disdain "to speak in our words so that we in turn may speak in his."[30] Such an exchange of words, rooted in the divine Word's appropriation of human flesh, allows Augustine to emphasize the singularity of the psalms' subject. The "I" who speaks in the psalms is always Christ, the "person" in whom God has definitively joined with all humanity.

Augustine will very frequently refer to the "one voice" speaking throughout the psalms, and all later explanations of the "one voice" of the whole Christ follow the same argument.[31] His second exposition on Psalm 30, for instance, delivered perhaps some twenty years after his first psalm commentaries, reveals a pattern we see again and again.[32] He begins his exposition by considering the inscription *To the end. A psalm for David, an ecstasy*, and explains that *ecstasy* can imply either the activity of heavenly contemplation, where one loses oneself, or fear, where one is beside oneself.[33] After considering the former possibility, Augustine points out that the content of the psalm does indeed suggest fear. Whose fear? Since the psalm is inscribed *To the end . . . for David*, it must be Christ's fear, and yet Augustine also considers the possibility that the psalm refers to our fear. Even though he demurs at the suggestion that Christ was afraid as his passion approached, the self-emptying in which Christ assumed the form of a slave (Phil. 2:7) entails that this fear is, in some sense, his: for "he dresses himself in us" (*nos uestire se*), "assumes us in himself" (*assumere nos in se*), and "transfigures us in himself" (*transfigurare nos in se*).[34] Augustine's language here consistently reflects the change that this act of God's self-giving in Christ effects in humanity: it is a "wonderful exchange" (*mira commutatio*), a "divine transaction" (*diuina . . . commercia*), a "change of reality effected in this world by the heavenly negotiator" (*mutatio rerum celebrata in hoc mundo a negotiatore caelesti*).[35] The human experience of suffering became Christ's because he identified himself so completely with us: "He even said this, that his soul was sorrowful to the point of death, and all of us ourselves said it too with him. Why? Because the whole Christ is head and body. That head is the savior of the body, who has already ascended into heaven; the body, however, is the church, which labors on earth."[36]

Augustine typically relies on several key scriptural passages to justify his conception of the unified voice of head and body, yet always with the intention of explaining that the church's passion is Christ's passion. Most crucially, Christ speaks Psalm 21 from the cross on our behalf. In Acts 9:4 the glorified Christ speaks out of a deep relationship with the laboring Christ on earth: Saul hears the voice from heaven calling out, "Saul, Saul, why are you persecuting me?" Augustine asks how Saul could be inflicting injury on the glorified Christ, and yet the words that Saul hears suggest the complete incorporation of Christ: "He did not say, 'Why are you persecuting my saints' . . . but 'Why are you persecuting me?' The head cries out on behalf of its members, and the head transfigures its members in himself."[37] Augustine draws on Pauline terms to indicate how the incorporation of Christ's head and members sanctions a kind of *communicatio idiomatum*, where one member appropriates the voice of another to express what does not, properly speaking, pertain to it. In Augustine's exegesis, being with Christ ultimately leads to a kind of identity of subject, where Christ speaks not only "in the prophet" but in us, his body. Augustine underscores the unity of the psalms' subject through marital imagery (cf. Matt. 9:5, "They will be two in one flesh; so they are two no longer, but one flesh"). The great mystery, the *magnum sacramentum* (Eph. 5:31–32), of the two in one flesh entails the unity of voice: "If two in one flesh, why not two in one voice? Therefore, let Christ speak, because the church speaks in Christ, and Christ speaks in the church, both body in the head and head in the body."[38]

Augustine's most distinctive and original contribution to the history of psalm exegesis lies precisely in the conception witnessed here: that the psalm (and indeed the entire Psalter) represents in its language, its verbal prayer, the very heart of the Christian mystery—the exchange of God and humanity in the Word-made-flesh, still abiding in the *totus Christus*.[39] To understand the meaning of the psalms, the hearer must already be situated in the ecclesial body. To see oneself in the psalm and be healed by it, one must see one's own passion in the groans and lamentations voiced by the head on the cross. There the labor of Augustine's own exegesis, replete with its own rhetorical dynamics, its own social and cultural function, its performative and practical efficacy, may serve and indeed participate in the transforming grace of Christ in the church. For the "voice is one," so that "you may never exclude the head when you hear the body speaking, nor the body when you hear the head speaking."[40]

UOX TOTIUS CHRISTI:
PERFORMING AND PRACTICING THE PSALMS

The fact that Augustine returns again and again to the *uox totius Christi* does not only reflect its centrality as an exegetical key: the repeated rehearsal of the theme, I argue, is itself theologically significant. Henri-Irénée Marrou mentions that Augustine adverts to the whole Christ over two hundred times in his preaching, and Augustine acknowledges to his congregation how often he repeats himself.[41] At the beginning of his exposition of Psalm 40, for instance, he notes: "I remind you so often, nor does it tire me to repeat what is useful for you to remember."[42] Yet the heuristic framework produces not only Augustine's exegesis but the body reflected in that exegesis. The very process where the body uses and hears its own voice in union with the head contributes to the fashioning of the body as church. Augustine's constant reference to the psalms as the voice of the whole Christ underscores the deeply sacramental quality of the congregation's activity. As the humanity of Christ is a sign of the divine Word making that Word present to the believer, so the church, to the extent that it is united to Christ as his body, makes present the same reality of Christ. For Augustine, then, revelation through the psalms occurs simultaneously with our living the reality they signify: becoming the one Christ by sharing in his voice, being transfigured into himself.[43]

This theological dynamism in Augustine's view of the psalms as *uox totius Christi* impresses upon us his understanding of the church as a "pluriform event" or a "reality in process," not a Platonic idealization.[44] Furthermore, the deeply Christological and ecclesiological foundation of his exegesis may be illuminated by more recent hermeneutical and social theories that stress the productive nature of interpretation. Ricoeur, for instance, stresses the constructive quality of interpretation as an "event" or "making (*poiesis*)" and repeatedly insists that the actual performance of discourse is integral to its meaning.[45] Robert Markus, in his study "Word and Text in Ancient Christianity," avers that Augustine was unique among ancient Christians in insisting on the social construction of meaning.[46] Such a view does not lessen but increases the significance of Augustine's complex emphasis on the ecclesial setting of exegesis. In what follows, then, I shall consider how recent theoretical discussions of performance and practice may enhance our understanding of Augustine's dynamic ecclesiology in the *Enarrationes in Psalmos*.

PERFORMING THE PSALMS:
AUGUSTINE'S EXPOSITION OF PSALM 93

The concept of performance would be particularly appropriate for studying Augustine's exegesis of the psalms, if only because he himself clearly recognized that his preaching was a kind of "performance." Not only do his references to applause and his interaction with the audience reflect the dramatic quality of his scriptural commentary, but, as we have seen, regular remarks that he is preaching in competition with the spectacles and theatrical shows outside imply that they are alternative performances.[47] On one occasion, while commenting on the inscription of Psalm 80 (*For the olive presses*), Augustine says that the presses symbolize the church, where the pure oil oozes invisibly while dregs run outside on the pavement for everyone to see. He compares the dregs to the crowds gathering for the circus shows immediately outside the church that day. By contrast, those who sing and reflect on the psalms are invisibly strained within: "Pay attention to this great spectacle. For God does not fail to provide for us something to look at with great joy. Can the crazy fascination of the circus be compared to this spectacle? Those shows are like to the dregs; this to the oil."[48] The "great spectacle" is the performance that takes place within the church. At the end of the same homily, Augustine tells his audience that, in Christ's name, God has produced constructive entertainments (*diuina spectacula*), which have held them spellbound.[49] Referring to the maritime games (*mare in theatro*) to be celebrated the following day, Augustine urges his congregation to return to the church: "Let us have our port in Christ."[50]

Such explicit references to the theater do not alone justify a consideration of Augustine's exegesis as performance. More recent scholarship on ritual has also identified formal similarities between theater and religious activity. Symbolic acts of interpretation, such as the singing and reflection on the psalms, shape a culture.[51] "Performance" helps generate a community, fashion its identity, and form its self-understanding. Since J. L. Austin's influential distinction between "descriptive" and "performative" statements, scholars have been keenly sensitive to the porousness of the boundary between ritual act and saying.[52] Attention to the way statements may execute some action in their very utterance must clearly affect our understanding of "exegesis," and patristic exegesis in particular. The activity of reciting and reflecting on the psalms tends to "enact" or produce their meaning. Yet taken within a theological horizon, such "enactment" forms part of the sacramental and ecclesial efficacy of the Word.

Augustine's commentary on Psalm 93 offers a fine example of four components that most theorists identify as constituting a religious "performance": (1) an "event" that (2) sets up an interpretative "frame" (3) with a peculiar transforming "efficacy" (4) corresponding to certain "self-reflexive" processes.[53] The psalm itself begs God to arise and give the proud their just deserts (v. 2). The trials that God's virtuous people suffer at the hands of the proud (vv. 4–11) are set in contrast to the blessings that will be given to the virtuous (vv. 12–15). The psalm ends with praise of God, who is a refuge and helper (v. 22) and reaffirms the speaker's confidence that the Lord will bring retribution: "According to their malice will the Lord our God destroy them" (v. 23). Yet through Augustine's exegesis, the church becomes the script with which he works. In his introduction he points out: it seems as only yesterday when we ourselves suffered at the hands of a powerful, unjust family.[54]

The actual context of Augustine's sermon gives it the quality of a very distinct "event." Preaching to an assembly of bishops meeting in Thagaste in AD 414 or 415, Augustine performs before his audience for two hours.[55] He even ends his exposition by anticipating their complaint: "Perhaps the length of this sermon was too laborious for you."[56] Still, he hopes that the role that has caused him to sweat so much will contribute to the salvation of his hearers. Not only does Augustine's preaching to a group of bishops give his exegesis a heightened significance as an ecclesial event, but he avows it is a "command performance": "I have preached as ordered, for the Lord our God has ordered me through my brothers, in whom God dwells."[57] The activity of understanding the psalm is a common work, physically taxing both on the sweating preacher and on the audience, who must be encouraged not to languish: "Pay attention so that, in the name of Christ, we may be strong Christians. There is only a little of the psalm that remains. Let's not flag."[58] The common toil of this commentary, then, forges the text, speaker, and audience in a pursuit of understanding and a trust that, while God seems to allow the wicked to flourish, those who are long-suffering and virtuous shall still find in God their "refuge and hope."

Throughout Augustine's preaching on Psalm 93, he attempts again and again to identify the link between the psalm and the activity in which the audience is currently engaged. The psalm, that is, provides a "frame" in which the church's present sufferings may be interpreted as fulfilling the divine purpose revealed through the very pacing of the psalm. The very progression of the psalm verses is a progression of sympathy between God and the listener. So on verse 3 ("Lord, how long shall the ungodly triumph?"), Augustine notes that God plays the part of one lamenting with you at a moment of painful questioning. Like anyone who wishes to console a friend, God cannot lift a person out of his or her trouble without first grieving in sympathy: "So that he may rejoice with you, first you weep with him; you are sad with him so that you may refresh him. So too both the psalm and the Spirit of God, though knowing all things, seeks with you as if speaking your own words."[59] Through the psalm, God joins Augustine's audience in acting out the part of the righteous sufferer.

Augustine's exegesis, then, creates a moment of self-reflection upon current trials, but the interpretive framework places such tribulation in the context of hope grounded in the Word's own incarnation, death, and resurrection. Augustine explains verse 15 ("Until justice is changed into judgment, all who have justice are right of heart") by noting that a period of suffering must precede final judgment. This time and space prior to judgment is precisely where the church's faith grows, when God waits for members of the church to be converted: "Let the church suffer patiently what the head of the church suffered patiently."[60] In this way, the trials that the psalmist recounts are fashioned into a mysterious discipline of a loving God, who took on himself the vulnerabilities of his body.

While Augustine may be the chief "performer" of the commentary on Psalm 93, the efficacy of the performance lies mostly in the transformation of his audience. He urges his hearers not simply to think about the psalms passively but to live the script reflected in the psalms: "I say this, brothers, so that you may advance from that which you hear. . . . For a good life, led by the commands of God, is like a pen that writes in the heart what it hears. If it is written in wax, it is easily blotted out. Write it rather in your hearts, in your conduct, and it will never be blotted out."[61] The psalm is to effect a remedy both for silent thoughts of despair and for those that break out in words or deeds.

Thus the exposition of Psalm 93 illustrates each of the four concepts that performance theorists commonly apply to a public religious activity. (1) The communal singing of the psalm together with Augustine's lengthy *opus* in the august presence of the North African bishops constitutes an "event" with clear physical and sensory qualities. (2) Through his exegesis, the psalm becomes a "frame" for understanding the painful experience of trial as a necessary condition prior to God's final judgment. (3) As the exegesis advances, members of Augustine's congregation are invited to place their present sufferings more deeply into the context of Christ's life.

Through the psalms, then, the reality of trial becomes the new reality of trial in Christ, whose own sufferings effect our hope, our cure, our transformation. By the end of the psalm we are meant to acclaim God as our refuge and helper and to live out the grace reflected there. (4) Throughout this process of exegesis, members of his congregation are meant to see themselves, via the reflexive properties of the psalm, as living within the mysterious purpose of God, who has become one with us even in the voice of the whole Christ, which they have vocalized.

Practicing the Psalms: Cultivating a Hungry Body

Another approach to understanding the *Enarrationes in Psalmos* as forming the *ecclesia* also derives from the study of ritual, whose practice cultivates a social and cultural environment and creates a *habitus* or set of dispositions that in turn generate further practice.[62] Practice theorists are particularly interested in the way personal agents involved in a religious ritual "embody" schemes that shape the way experience is understood and categorized. The body is a "microcosm of the universe," which enjoys a central place in the "social construction of reality."[63] Knowledge itself is not just propositional or mental but bodily too. Kneeling, for instance, not only communicates subordination to the kneeler but also "produces a subordinated kneeler in and through the act itself."[64] In a similar way, Augustine's practice of exegesis, itself grounded in reference to the body, may be understood as actually "creating" the body of Christ.

Augustine's interpretation of the psalms as *uox totius Christi* turns crucially on the notion that the church, as the body, and Christ, as the head, make up a single organism whose single voice the psalms represent. In Augustine's explanation of the hermeneutical principles, however, Christ's incorporation entails the assumption of immense vulnerability. It is the persecuted body to which the head, in all humility, attaches himself (Acts 9:4), the body that, in the words of the Gospel of Matthew, is hungry, thirsty, estranged, naked, sick, and in prison (Matt. 25:40).[65] As a way of identifying how Augustine finds that vulnerable ecclesial body in the psalms, let us ask what image of "body" is represented in the Psalter or what is the characteristic "voice" of that body as raised in the book of Psalms.

In Augustine's Psalter, the word *corpus* is not often attested. Words for bodily parts, however, are frequently used, as if synecdochically, to refer to the body. Among these words *caro* (flesh), *uenter* (stomach), *ossa* (bones), and *interiora* (inner parts) appear most frequently. In the vast majority of cases, such words denote the deficient, unrealized, vulnerable quality of the body that seeks completion in God alone. In Psalm 15:9, the psalmist proclaims that, having found refuge in God, "even my flesh shall now rest in hope." Psalm 72:26 laments: "My heart and my flesh have failed, but you are the God of my heart." Psalm 37:4 also cries out, "There is no soundness of my flesh in the presence of your anger." Psalm 30:10 asks the Lord for mercy in distress, "for my eye has been disturbed by your wrath, so too my soul and belly," and Psalm 31:3 proclaims: "My bones grew old because of my silence, in consequence of my shouting all day long." In the Psalter, the body is a site of more pain than pleasure. Augustine's exegesis highlights such pain and effectively teaches the church how to be the "body" of Christ.

Nor is that body an abstraction.[66] Rather, in Augustine's exegesis the body manifests natural features of diet and reproduction. Situated in a world whose dangers the psalms so dramatically express, the *ecclesia* as body must constantly find sustenance in its hunger and thirst. Indeed, the "body" of Christ that emerges in the *Enarrationes* is quite strikingly one that seeks to eat and alternately to avoid being eaten. The command to Peter to "slaughter and eat" (Acts 10:13) appears at several points in the *Enarrationes* as a sign of the church's natural growth.[67] Even former persecutors find themselves in the church: "They were eaten by the church. You look for them in themselves, and you don't find them. Look for them in what has eaten them, and they will be found in the church's belly."[68] The image of Christ's body eating the nations, however, frequently stresses the struggle of the body to ingest. For instance, Augustine puts Psalm 30:11 ("My life was impelled by sorrow and my years faded amid sighs") into the mouth of a Christian pastor who, through hard work and preaching, tries to win over and "eat" other people. Such is the nature of the church: "Whenever we win over people for the Lord, somehow the church eats them. What does 'eats' mean? It brings them into its body. For whatever we eat, we bring into our body."[69] For Augustine, however, the particular expression of this psalm verse refers to the discouragement a preacher feels when his work seems ineffectual: "His life is weakened and in want. And a miserable sort of want and hunger it is."[70] So too the hunger of dogs in Psalm 58:15–16 ("Let them be converted in the evening and feel like hungry dogs") refers to the desire of the converted to assimilate others into the body to which they now belong. While they go out to preach, they complain that no one hears and so bark hungrily.[71]

Being the body of Christ and vying to eat the nations, however, also entails the risk of being eaten. Psalm 34:24–26 expresses the fear of one who prays, "Do not let my enemies insult me. Let them not say in their hearts, 'Hooray! Hooray!' to our soul. Let them not say, 'We have swallowed them up.'" Noting again that swallowing means absorbing something into one's body, Augustine warns his congregation that "the world wants to swallow you, but you must swallow the world; draw it into your own body, slaughter and eat it."[72] Indeed, the "teeth of sinners" (*dentes peccatorum*) (Psalm 3:8) represent those authorities who incorporate a person into their own corrupt lives, and the lament that "you have handed us over like sheep for butchering" (Psalm 43:12) refers to those corrupt members of the church who have been "absorbed into the body of the nations . . . devoured by the pagans. The church wails for them as if its own members had been devoured."[73] On the other hand, the exclamation of Psalm 123:3 that if God had not been with us "we would have been eaten alive" leads Augustine to consider the manner in which the church incorporates others into its body—not alive, but having first killed them: "Because no one enters the body of the church without first being killed. What has been dies, so that what has not been may be."[74] Belonging to the body of Christ, that is, involves a conversion of ways: "It is not possible to be eaten by the church unless first killed. Let him renounce the world, then he is killed; let her have faith in God, then she is eaten."[75]

The *Enarrationes in Psalmos* represents a kind of ritual structuring of the ecclesial body. The repeated practice of voicing and reflecting on the psalms produces a "body" characterized by hunger and thirst. Thus Augustine is able to compare his fasting congregation to the parched deer of Psalm 41, for "the church is hungry. Christ's body is hungry."[76] The psalms' references to the flesh express a frightening vulnerability before God and the world, but it is exactly such a body to which Christ the head attaches himself, both in the present moment and throughout all of history. As ritual theorists have noted, the formalized practices of religion constitute a process in which history may be appropriated. Situated in a moment of unfulfilled imperfection and recognizing that the completion of history has yet to be realized, Augustine finds in the psalms references to a long history of trials and persecutions endured by Christ's body, even before the birth of Jesus. Thus on Psalm 128:1 ("From my youth they have often opposed me"), Augustine notes that the psalms speak of opponents who have always caused the church suffering, as if in answer to present Christians who have been wondering whether its languishing is something new.[77] Beginning with Abel, who suffered violence at the hands of his brother Cain, Augustine shows that the church comprises all those who have been persecuted for the sake of righteousness. Not only does such an explanation appropriate this ancient history into the present trials of the church, but it places the whole scope of that history into the experience of the one just man, who suffered in the flesh on the cross.[78]

AN ECCLESIOLOGY OF GROANING

I began by suggesting that, if we are to take the "history of exegesis" seriously, then our very understanding of what "exegesis" is will be reshaped, perhaps challenged, by its actual context. The preconceptions of the historical-critical method are appropriate to its own time and place but differ significantly from the overwhelmingly oral and public nature of ancient biblical proclamation and commentary. Walter Ong's attempt to retrieve this sense of difference between a culture based primarily on spoken language and one dominated by the written word offers insight into the social dynamics operative in ancient exegesis. In the absence of any visual presence of words, spoken words retain their quality as occurrences. As one raised within a culture not far removed from orality, Augustine takes an approach to the psalms that never loses a sense of language as being a "mode of action" and not merely a "countersign of thought."[79] The psalms themselves comprise memorable, neatly patterned, communally fixed and formulaic thought expressions, which add rather than subordinate, aggregate rather than analyze.[80] The verbal "redundancy," parallelism, balance, and polysyndeton characteristic both of the psalms and of Augustine's preaching foster an epistemology where human knowledge is empathetic and participatory and where the value of words lies not foremost in their precise definition but in their "actual habitat," including "gestures, vocal inflections, facial expressions, and the entire human, existential setting in which the real spoken word always occurs."[81] Frames of reference are situational rather than abstract, highly somatic, and very interpersonal.[82] The desire for information, for discovery, is conceived not in terms of securing a *datum* but in terms of forming a personal connection; personality structures are more "communal and externalized"; the act of oral communication unites people in groups.[83] In such a context, the "exegesis" of Augustine the rhetor will have an important socially productive quality.

Augustine's conception of the psalms as *uox totius Christi*, however, offers a framework whose theological dynamism closely corresponds to the social dynamic. The profound Christo-ecclesiological basis of Augustine's exegesis provides scope for seeing the productive qualities of his exegesis as part of the revelatory power of the psalms themselves. New theoretical insights sensitive to the performative and practical force of interpretation may complement, not threaten, theological values and offer new categories for considering what "church" meant to Augustine. The attempt to place a neat neo-Scholastic grid on Augustine in order to delineate his "doctrine of the church" resembles the now suspect attempt to impose a neo-Platonic grid on his reading of scripture. Augustine's mind is far too complex for this attempt at oversimplification, which foreshortens his eschatological horizon, forces premature clarity, denies the troubling depth of the ecclesial scandals in which he spent his career, and reinforces inept idealizations of what the church actually is.

For Augustine, reflection on the church as it is inevitably came with much groaning. At the beginning of his commentary on Psalm 42, he once more asserts the importance of hearing our own "voice" in the psalm: "We should hear the voice [of the church] in all psalms, whether the voice is praising or groaning [*uel psallentem uel gementem*], whether it is rejoicing in hope or sighing in the present condition [*uel laetantem in spe, uel suspirantem in re*]."[84] The most common voice in this psalm, however, is that of inarticulate groaning, which reflects the distress the church feels in present conditions: "All those who make progress and who groan for that heavenly city. . . . Christ's wheat groans amid the weeds and this until the time of harvest shall come, that is, until the end of the world."[85]

Of the four participles Augustine uses throughout the *Enarrationes in Psalmos* to differentiate the various "voices" of the psalms (praising, groaning, rejoicing, sighing), the "groaning" voice is most often heard.[86] The frequent tone of lament in the psalms gives rise to Augustine's recurring reference to the present reality as one in which it is only appropriate to groan. While Augustine himself may rejoice in the hope of things to come, here and now he groans.[87] The inarticulate groans of the church communicate, not a clear idea, but a desire to be at home with God even though we recognize our general distress at our present condition. Hence, on Psalm 30:11 ("My life is imperiled by sorrow, and my years have faded amid sighs"), Augustine notes that our years on earth pass amid groaning, "in groans, not in clear voices" (*in gemitibus, non in claris uocibus*).[88] For God's true servants the groan derives from inner anguish: "He bellows because he remembers the sabbath rest, which flesh and blood do not possess."[89] Even if a servant of God may ostensibly be happy, interiorly the groaning desire reaches the ear of God.[90]

In Augustine's exegesis, a variety of occasions may elicit the groans of the servant who desires the kingdom. Psalm 52, which begins with the complaint, "The impudent one has said in his heart, 'God does not exist,'" is ascribed to one "Maeleth," a name Augustine translates as "for one who labors to give birth or for someone in pain."[91] Augustine explains that such is Christ's body, for whom the psalm is sung, "that unified organism whose head is on high," and who lives in a world "with iniquity increasing mightily" and where the love of many has grown cold (Matt. 24:12).[92] Christ's body suffers and groans among those who deny God through their practical disregard for good. Augustine quotes the line from Matthew ("Whoever perseveres to the end will be saved," Matt. 24:13) to ask:

> Why is persevering a great thing unless one perseveres amid troubles and trials and tribulations and scandals? For no one is commanded to endure good things. But because this psalm is spoken for the sufferer and because it is sung for him, let us see what perseverance is. For the sufferer, the psalm reproves those people among whom he groans, among whom he grieves, and at the end of the psalm, the consolation of the one who grieves and labors in birth is offered and expressed. Who are the people, therefore, among whom we labor and groan, if we are in the body

of Christ. If we live under the head, if we count ourselves among his members, hear who they are.[93]

Psalm 54 also begins with a lament: "Hear my appeal, O God, and do not disdain my prayer; pay heed to me and hear me. I am deeply saddened in my ordeal and very distressed" (Psalm 54:2). Augustine advises that the lament is "for the understanding of David himself" and tells his congregation that "understanding" refers to the church's assessment of the hard situation in which it finds itself and for which it prays deliverance. To seek deliverance, however, is not to seek exclusion from sinners. In his reading of the psalm, Augustine is all too aware of the temptation of the "good and holy" to give in to acts of violent hatred. Indeed, "if we understand, we see that this is a place not of rejoicing but of groaning, not yet a place for exultation but still a place of lamentation."[94] Any illusion that we can live in a place of exultation will lead a Christian to desire separation and to violate his or her fundamental duty of charity in favor of an idealization. Thus, on verses 6–7 ("Fear and trembling came upon me, and darkness covered me. And I said, 'Who will give me wings as though to a dove. Then I will fly away and find rest'"), Augustine notes that a servant of God may not simply fly away from an incorrigible "sinner," no matter how much he or she may wish to do so. "And if the one who cannot be corrected is your own, either through fellowship in the human race or, more importantly, through ecclesial communion, if he is inside, what will you do? Where will you go? Where will you separate yourself, so that you don't have to put up with these things? No: stay present, speak to him, exhort him, be kind to him, challenge him, rouse him."[95] Augustine explains that, like a dove, who is the very symbol of charity, the Christian is affectively attached to those from whom he or she would wish dissociation. Therefore, the dove does not fly away but stays so as to discharge its office of love and accepts those who cause it to groan: "For the dove appears as a sign of love, and in it groans are loved. There is nothing so familiar with groans as a dove; day and night it groans, as if it is placed here where it must groan."[96] The dove does not withdraw from others but lives after the pattern of Christ, who included among his own twelve apostles one who would cause him suffering.[97] To suffer persecution, whether the kind that the ancient martyrs encountered or that which arises on account of the scandalous weakness of others in present times, is a mark of living a devoted life like Christ in the church. For "the church is never free from persecutions."[98]

Indeed, there is even a certain "joy of groaning." Psalm 101, a lament that begins, "Hear my prayer, O Lord: and let my crying come to you," includes the verse "I have eaten ashes as it were bread, and mingled my drink with weeping" (v. 9). For Augustine, this line refers to the Incarnation, in which the Word becomes approachable to us by taking on frailty and mortal flesh and coming to us as one about to die.[99] Since he has united himself to our flesh, then, we can read our words in his. This event of the Word's commingling in a mortal life of tears allows for our ultimate transformation "into the unity of the faith and of the knowledge of the Son of God" (Eph. 4:13). For now, however, while we await the fullness of such transformation, "poverty is our lot here, toil, and groaning."[100] Because in Christ the Word has taken on flesh, Christ's body, the church, may not dissociate itself from human infirmity, "for the sake of his mercy" (*gratias misericordiae ipsius*).

> How does the Word experience toil? How does it groan, the Word through whom all things were made? If he has thought fit to share in our death, will he not give to us his life? He has raised us up in great hope, when we groan in great hope. Groaning includes sadness, but there is a groaning that includes joy too. I think Sarah, who was sterile, groaned joyfully when she gave birth.... Therefore, let us hear Christ poor in us and with us and on account of us.... Therefore one voice, because one flesh. Let us listen and recognize ourselves too in these voices. And if we see that we are outside of him, let us toil to be within him.[101]

———

Augustine's frequent reminder that we groan in the present condition suggests a form of resistance to premature solutions of the multiple problems that he faced as a fifth-century bishop. The eschatological sense, both of scripture and of the church, did not deliver him from real tensions or provide a way for him to escape into an overly spiritualized exegesis or ecclesiology. Rather, it urged patience with pains of disagreement, the effects of scandal, the bonds with those who cause us grief and embarrassment.

His practice of exegesis, finally, was a practice of charity. Both were firmly grounded in his conviction that central to God's revelation was the Word's sharing in the vulnerability of our flesh, the Head's involvement with a body whose complications he did not abandon. Members of a twenty-first-century church, faced with its own complications and seeking in scripture some mooring, would do well to see in Augustine's "ecclesiology of groaning" a salutary warning against the temptation to seek some idealized community of the perfect or to employ strategies for scriptural exegesis that throw off the burdens and ambiguities and disagreements in the body that the Head in fact assumed and transfigured in himself.

NOTES

1. Michael Cahill, "The History of Exegesis and Our Theological Future," *Theological Studies* 61 (2000): 336.

2. Marie Anne Mayeski, "Quaestio Disputata: Catholic Theology and the History of Exegesis," *Theological Studies* 62 (2001): 153.

3. Even Sandra Schneiders's highly regarded treatment of scripture in its full theological and ecclesiological dimensions focuses on the written word. See Sandra M. Schneiders, *The Revelatory Text: Interpreting the New Testament as Sacred Scripture*, 2nd ed. (Collegeville, MN: Liturgical Press, 1999).

4. James J. O'Donnell, "Bible," in *Augustine through the Ages: An Encyclopedia*, ed. Allan D. Fitzgerald (Grand Rapids, MI: Eerdmans,1999), 100.

5. Augustine, *En. Ps.* 147.21 (CCSL 38–40). All psalm numbers and verses here refer to Augustine's *Vetus Latina* version of the Psalter. English translations are mine, though a wonderful new set of translations has been completed as *Saint Augustine: Expositions of the Psalms*, trans. Maria Boulding, 5 vols., WSA III/15 (New York: New City Press, 2000–2004).

6. Augustine, *En. Ps.* 30[4].3.1.

7. Michael Fiedrowicz, "'Ciues sanctae ciuitatis Dei omnes affectiones rectas habent' (Ciu. 14, 9): Terapia delle passioni e preghiera in S. Agostino," *Studia Ephemeridis Augustinianum* 53 (1996): 431–40.

8. Brian E. Daley, S.J., "Is Patristic Exegesis Still Usable? Reflections on Early Christian Interpretation of the Psalms," *Communio* 29 (2002): 204–5. Daley counts at least twenty-one psalm commentaries among Greek and Latin patristic authors.

9. See Augustine, *En. Ps.* 71.10 (church as moon), 36 s.1.4 (as earth), 67.17 (as dove), 8.1 (as winepress). For a catalogue of images, see Amy Germaine Oden, "Dominant Images for the Church in Augustine's *Enarrationes in Psalmos*: A

Study in Augustine's Ecclesiology" (PhD diss., Southern Methodist University, 1990), 265–80.

10. For an example of the attempt to construct a systematic ecclesiology from Augustine, see Stanislaus Grabowski, *The Church: An Introduction to the Theology of St. Augustine* (St. Louis, MO: B. Herder, 1957).

11. Hans Urs von Balthasar, *Augustinus: Das Antlitz der Kirche: Auswahl und Übertragung* (1942; repr., Einsiedeln: Benziger, 1955).

12. Émilien Lamirande, *L'église céleste selon saint Augustin* (Paris: Études Augustiniennes, 1963); Pasquale Borgomeo, *L'église de ce temps dans la prédication de saint Augustin* (Paris: Études Augustiniennes, 1972).

13. Louis Bouyer, *The Church of God: Body of Christ and Temple of the Spirit*, trans. Charles Underhill Quinn (Chicago: Franciscan Herald, 1982), 25.

14. On sweating before a packed house, see Augustine, *En. Ps.* 32[3].2.9: "I see how packed in you are, but you too see how I am sweating!" On the stench, 72.34: "I forgot how long I talked. Now the psalm is over, and I can tell from the stench in here that I have given too long a sermon!" On his voice, 50.1: "I ask for your silence and quiet, so that my voice may be able to keep enough strength after yesterday's labor." For a longer discussion of the groans, 54.8.

15. Augustine, *En. Ps.* 61.7.

16. See Tarsicius J. van Bavel, "What Kind of Church Do You Want? The Breadth of Augustine's Ecclesiology," *Louvain Studies* 7 (1979): 147–71. Van Bavel argues that Augustine conceives the church not as an institution with a fixed and well-defined structure but as a "pluriform event" (147), as a "reality in process [that] has to pass through several phases in order to reach its specific goal" (148).

17. Joseph A. Komonchak, *Foundations in Ecclesiology* (Boston: Boston College, 1995), 49. See Bernard J. F. Lonergan, *Method in Theology* (New York: Herder and Herder, 1972). 363.

18. Komonchak, *Foundations in Ecclesiology*, 53–56.

19. Ibid., 53.

20. In his own analysis of "systematic ecclesiology," Neil Ormerod has noted the resistance among theologians to engage in the methods of human sciences but argues that a full understanding of biblical symbols for church requires the adoption of nontheological categories. See Neil Ormerod, "The Structure of a Systematic Ecclesiology," *Theological Studies* 63 (2002): 11.

21. Michael Fiedrowicz, for example, offers an excellent, comprehensive study of the *uox totius Christi* without tracing developments in Augustine's thinking (*Psalmus Vox Totius Christi: Studien zu Augustins "Enarrationes in Psalmos"* [Freiburg: Herder, 1997]). For a recent critique, see Michael Cameron's review in *Augustinian Studies* 34 (2003): 266–77.

22. Throughout this discussion I am indebted to Michael Cameron, who convincingly argues that shifts in Augustine's Christology in the 390s correspond

to shifts in his understanding of signs and therefore the *Enarrationes in Psalmos.* See his "Augustine's Construction of Figurative Exegesis against the Donatists in the *Enarrationes in Psalmos*" (PhD diss., University of Chicago, 1996), as well as his "Enarrationes in Psalmos," in *Augustine through the Ages: An Encyclopedia,* ed. Allen D. Fitzgerald (Grand Rapids, MI: Eerdmans, 1999), 290–96.

23. Hilary of Poitiers, *Comm. Ps.* 1.2 (CCSL 61.20): "Omnis ad eum prophetia est referenda psalmorum."

24. For a discussion of prosopological exegesis in Augustine, see Hubertus Drobner, *Person-Exegese und Christologie bei Augustinus: Zur Herkunft der Formel Una Persona* (Leiden: Brill, 1986). In patristic commentaries on the psalms more generally, see Marie-Josèphe Rondeau, *Les commentaires patristiques du Psautier (IIIe–Ve siècles),* 2 vols., OCA 219–20 (Rome: Pontificium Institutum Studium Orientalium, 1982–85).

25. Augustine, *En. Ps.* 2.5.

26. See Augustine, *Doctr. chr.* 3.30.42–33.46 (CCSL 32.102–6). The dating of the *En. Ps.* is an extraordinarily complex affair. See Fiedrowicz, *Psalmus Vox Totius Christi,* 430–49, for a table of the variety of scholarly conjectures on chronology.

27. Augustine, *En. Ps.* 17.51: "Quaecumque in hoc psalmo dicta sunt, quae ipsi Domino proprie, id est capiti ecclesiae congruere non possunt, ad ecclesiam referenda sunt. Totus enim Christus hic loquitur, in quo sunt omnia membra eius."

28. Augustine, *En. Ps.* 24.1.

29. See, for instance, traditional concerns in *En. Ps.* 44.4–5. M. Cameron, "Augustine's Construction," 88–116, traces the development of his Christology from one that naturally fit the Tyconian principle (i.e., a "spiritualist paradigm") to one that seriously transformed it (i.e., a fully "incarnational paradigm").

30. Augustine, *En. Ps.* 30[2].1.3: "loqui uerbis nostris, ut et nos loqueremur uerbis ipsius."

31. Augustine, *En. Ps.* 30[2].1.4; 30[3].2.1; 34[2].1; 40.1; 61.4; 68[2].1.; 101 [1].2; 138.21; 142.3.

32. Again, dating is notoriously speculative, but scholarly consensus places this homily after 411. See Fiedrowicz, *Psalmus Vox Totius Christi,* 431.

33. Augustine, *En. Ps.* 30[2].1.2: *Psalmus Dauid ecstasis.*

34. Augustine, *En. Ps.* 30[2].1.3.

35. Augustine, *En. Ps.* 302].1.3.

36. Augustine, *En. Ps.* 30[2].1.3.

37. Augustine, *En. Ps.* 30[2].1.3. Augustine returns to this passage from Acts 9:4 constantly. See, among many examples, *En. Ps.* 26[2].11, 37.6, 39.5, 44.20, 52.1, 54.3, 55.3, 69.3, 86.3, 87.15, 91.11, 100.3, 122.1, 138.2, 142.3, 148.17.

38. Augustine, *En. Ps.* 30[2].1.4. See too similar references to Eph. 5:30–32 in *En. Ps.* 34[2].1, 37.6, 40.1, 54.3, 71.17, 74.4, 90[2].5, 138.2.

39. See Rondeau, *Commentaires patristiques*, 2: 369: "Mais ce qui est fondamentalement nouveau, c'est qu'Augustin érige en principe général, valable pour l'ensemble du Psautier, l'idée que, partout, c'est la voix du Christ qui se fait entendre, parlant tantôt au nom de la tête, tantôt au nom du corps: deux dans une seule voix."

40. Augustine, *En. Ps.* 37.6: "Neque cum corporis uoces audieritis, separetis caput; neque cum capitis uoces audieritis, separetis corpus."

41. Henri-Irénée Marrou, *Time and Timeliness*, trans. Violet Nevile (New York: Sheed and Ward, 1969), 35. See too Borgomeo, *Église de ce temps*, 192–97, on the "frequency of the theme" of the *totus Christus*.

42. Augustine, *En. Ps.* 40.1. See too *En. Ps.* 54.3.

43. Such a dynamic is closely tied to Augustine's concept of biblical authority, which cannot be detached from the authority of the church. Cf. the discussion of Augustine's statement of *Fund.* 5.6 ("Ego uero Euangelio non crederem, nisi me catholicae Ecclesiae commoueret auctoritas") in Pierre-Thomas Camelot, "Autorité de l'écriture, autorité de l'église à propos d'un texte de saint Augustin," in *Mélanges offerts à M-D Chenu*, Bibliothèque thomiste (Paris: Vrin, 1967), 130: "C'est là déjà laisser entrevoir que l'*auctoritas* de l'Eglise n'est pas extérieure ni étrangère à celle de l'Evangile: l'une et l'autre remontent au Christ lui-même." Note also the excellent discussion in Howard J. Loewen, "The Use of Scripture in Augustine's Theology," *Scottish Journal of Theology* 34 (1981): 201–24. In the same way, the inspiration of scripture cannot be conceived apart from the divine activity of forming the church. The biblical "author" is the same as the "author" of the church. The implications of this point of connection for a theology of biblical exegesis are profound.

44. Again, see van Bavel, "What Kind of Church," 147–48.

45. See Paul Ricoeur, *The Rule of Metaphor: Multi-disciplinary Studies of the Creation of Meaning in Language*, trans. Robert Czerny (Toronto: University of Toronto Press, 1977), 39, cited in M. Cameron, "Augustine's Construction," 297. See also Ricoeur, *Interpretation Theory: Discourse and the Surplus of Meaning* (Fort Worth: Texas Christian University Press, 1976), 11: "Linguistic competence actualizes itself in performance."

46. Robert Markus, *Signs and Meanings: World and Text in Ancient Christianity* (Liverpool: Liverpool University Press, 1996), 40–41: "Traditions of interpretation generate communities, and interpretation is a social construction of a meaning related to a text." Given the divine origin of both the community and the "text," however, such generation may be seen as the continued mission of the Word.

47. See Augustine, *En. Ps.* 39.6, 80.2, 80.23, 99.12. Also, on applause, see *En. Ps.* 25[2].8–9; 147.15. Note the comment by Frederik van der Meer, *Augustine the Bishop: The Life and Work of a Father of the Church*, trans. Brian Battershaw and G. R. Lamb (New York: Sheed and Ward, 1961), 427: "Neither in Hippo nor in

Carthage did Augustine have ground for complaining that his hearers were not receptive to their fingertips, and indeed in that day an orator who sought contact with his audience never failed to find it. Augustine certainly did so. Even the transcriptions of the *notarii*, from which much light and shade has naturally disappeared, show us that many sermons were punctuated by loud applause, sometimes, indeed, by complete dialogues between speaker and audience, all of which have been faithfully reproduced."

48. Augustine, *En. Ps.* 80.1: "Intendite ad magnum hoc spectaculum. Non enim desinit Deus edere nobis quod cum magno gaudio spectemus; aut circi insania huic spectaculo comparanda est? Illa ad amurcam pertinet, hoc ad oleum."

49. Augustine, *En. Ps.* 80.23.

50. Augustine, *En. Ps.* 80.23.

51. For a useful overview and bibliography, see Mary Suydam, "An Introduction to Performance Studies," in *Performance and Transformation: New Approaches to Late Medieval Spirituality*, ed. Mary A. Suydam and Joanna E. Ziegler (New York: St. Martin's Press, 1999), 1–26.

52. J. L. Austin, *How to Do Things with Words*, 2nd ed. (Cambridge, MA: Harvard University Press, 1975), originally delivered in 1955 as the William James Lectures. Augustine's own deep anxiety over language in *Confessions* reflects his own self-consciousness of the "performative" quality of speech. The words of classical texts (e.g., the speech of the Vergilian Juno, recounted in *Conf.* 1.17.27) form a notably different person and culture from those of the Bible, particularly when one learns to declaim them *in propria uoce*.

53. Here and throughout the discussion of performance, I am relying on Catherine Bell, *Ritual: Perspectives and Dimensions* (New York: Oxford University Press, 1997), 74–75.

54. Augustine, *En. Ps.* 93.1. What this "domus potentissima" was eludes us but must clearly have been recognized by Augustine's hearers.

55. So Gertrude Gillette, "The Glory of God in Augustine's *Enarrationes in Psalmos*" (PhD diss., Catholic University of America, 1996), 45. *En. Ps.* 93 takes up some thirty pages of the volume in CCSL.

56. Augustine, *En. Ps.* 93.30. "Forte onerosa fuit uobis longitudo sermonis."

57. Augustine, *En. Ps.* 93.30: "iussus feci: nam Dominus Deus noster per eos mihi fratres iussit, in quibus habitat."

58. Augustine, *En. Ps.* 93.24.

59. Augustine, *En. Ps.* 93.9.

60. Augustine, *En. Ps.* 93.8: "Patiatur et ecclesia patienter, quod passum est caput ecclesiae patienter."

61. Augustine, *En. Ps.* 93.30.

62. See Bell, *Ritual: Perspectives and Dimensions*, 77, who cites the following studies of "practice": Marshall Sahlins, *Culture and Practical Reason* (Chi-

cago: University of Chicago Press, 1976); Pierre Bourdieu, *Outline of a Theory of Practice*, trans. Richard Nice (Cambridge: Cambridge University Press, 1977). See also *The Logic of Practice*, trans. Richard Nice (Stanford, CA: Stanford University Press, 1990).

63. Catherine Bell, *Ritual Theory, Ritual Practice* (New York: Oxford University Press, 1992), 94.

64. Bell takes the example of kneeling as not simply communicating a value, say of subordination, so much as "generat[ing] a body identified with subordinating. . . . The molding of the body within a highly structured environment does not simply express inner states. Rather, it primarily acts to restructure bodies in the very doing of the acts themselves" (ibid., 100).

65. Both scriptural verses appear repeatedly in Augustine's explanation of the *uox totius Christi*. See *En. Ps.* 26[2].11; 30[2].1.3; 40.11; 67.25; 69.3; 109.18; and 148.17 for a few examples.

66. Borgomeo underscores that Augustine's concept of the church as body is highly "organic" (*Église de ce temps*, 170). While Scholastic theology held an ecclesiology of the Mystical Body of Christ, such a body is an abstraction: its "diet," as it were, is "strictly vegetarian."

67. Augustine, *En. Ps.* 3.7; 13.4; 30[3].2.5; 34[2].15; 58[1].16; 73.16; 123.5; 149.13.

68. Augustine, *En. Ps.* 98.5.

69. Augustine, *En. Ps.* 30[3].2.5.

70. Augustine, *En. Ps.* 30[3].2.5.

71. Augustine, *En. Ps.* 58[2].9.

72. Augustine, *En. Ps.* 34[2].15.

73. Augustine, *En. Ps.* 43.12. On the teeth of sinners, see *En. Ps.* 3.7.

74. Augustine, *En. Ps.* 123.5.

75. Augustine, *En. Ps.* 123.5.

76. Augustine, *En. Ps.* 44.1, 42.1. See too other passages, esp. Ps. 61:5 ("Cucurri in siti"); Ps. 87:16 ("Inops sum ego, et in laboribus a iuuentute mea"); and Ps. 139:2 ("Exime me, Domine, ab homine maligno"). Borgomeo also insists on the reproductive notion of the body in, e.g., *En. Ps.* 52.1.

77. Augustine, *En. Ps.* 128.2.

78. On the church beginning with Abel, see *En. Ps.* 61.4 (esp. on the blood of Abel); 90 s.2.1, with discussion in Borgomeo, *Église de ce temps*, 30–32. See too Yves Congar, "Ecclesia ab Abel," in *Abhandlungen über Theologie und Kirche: Festschrift für Karl Adam*, ed. Marcel Reding (Düsseldorf: Patmos, 1952), esp. 81–86.

79. Walter J. Ong, *Orality and Literacy: The Technologizing of the Word*, New Accents (New York: Methuen, 1982), 32. Ong relies on the terms of Bronislaw Malinowski, "The Problem of Meaning in Primitive Languages," in *The Meaning of Meaning: A Study of the Influence of Language upon Thought and of the Science*

of Symbolism, ed. I.A. Richards and C. K. Ogden (New York: Harcourt, Brace, 1923), 451, 470–81.

80. Ong, *Orality and Literacy*, 33–38.

81. Ibid., 47.

82. Ong speaks of an oral culture's "verbomotor lifestyle," where individuals are "person-active" rather than "object-attentive" (ibid., 68).

83. Ibid., 69.

84. Augustine, *En. Ps.* 42.1.

85. Augustine, *En. Ps.* 42.2.

86. A word search on the Library of Latin Texts, CLCLT-5 database (Brepols, 2002), reveals the following statistics. Although the generic *cantan** appears sixty-five times throughout the *En. in Ps.*, the voice-specific *psallen** appears fourteen times, *gemen** forty-seven times, *laetan** twenty-seven times, and *suspiran** seventeen times. The preponderance of the voices that "groan" in Augustine's understanding of the psalms is attested throughout the *Enarrationes*. We may also note, however, that even the runner-up of this passage (*laetans*) is only a rejoicing "in hope" rather than for something achieved (*in re*). Borgomeo (*Église de ce temps*, 178) suggests that, for Augustine, groaning is the proper voice of the church of present times.

87. Augustine, *En. Ps.* 31[2].20. "Ita . . . et gaudeo et gemo: gaudeo in spe, gemo adhuc in re."

88. Augustine, *En. Ps.* 30[3].2.5.

89. Augustine, *En. Ps.* 37.13.

90. Augustine, *En. Ps.* 37.14.

91. Augustine, *En. Ps.* 52.1: "Pro parturiente siue dolente."

92. Augustine, *En. Ps.* 52.1.

93. Augustine, *En. Ps.* 52.1.

94. Augustine, *En. Ps.* 54.3.

95. Augustine, *En. Ps.* 54.8.

96. Augustine, *En. Ps.* 54.8: "Columba enim pro signo dilectionis ponitur, et in ea gemitus amatur. Nihil tam amicum gemitibus quam columba; die noctuque gemit, tamquam hic posita ubi gemendum est."

97. Augustine, *En. Ps.* 54.9.

98. Augustine, *En. Ps.* 54.8.

99. Augustine, *En. Ps.* 101[1].2.

100. Augustine, *En. Ps.* 101[1].2.

101. Augustine, *En. Ps.* 101[1].2.

A Psalm "Unto the End"

Eschatology and Anthropology in Maximus the Confessor's *Commentary on Psalm 59*

Paul M. Blowers

Maximus the Confessor has been remembered less as a biblical exegete than as a synthetic theologian of the Greek patristic tradition and a forerunner of the Byzantine scholastics. It is little surprise, then, that his *Commentary on Psalm 59*, one of the shortest of his spiritual or ascetic writings, has received scant attention in the history of scholarship; indeed, even his exegetical magnum opus, the commentary on scriptural ambiguities *Ad Thalassium*, has often been slighted in Maximian studies.[1] Like some of the Confessor's other ascetic works, the *Commentary on Psalm 59* provides little if any internal evidence as to its precise occasion, and in this case there is no named addressee. The thematic content of the work betrays a dating fairly early in Maximus's career, when he was a young monk at Cyzicus, south of Constantinople, and thus probably before his relocation to a monastery in Carthage.[2] Because Psalm 59 (LXX) specifically includes a petition for divine aid in the face of military disaster, Raffaele Cantarella has reasonably conjectured that Maximus wrote the *Commentary* in a time of crisis or impending persecution,[3] presumably around the time when Constantinople was under siege by Avars and Slavs in 626. Polycarp Sherwood, in his reconstruction of the dates of Maximus's works, likewise concurs in dating the *Commentary* very early in his monastic career.[4]

A critical edition of the *Commentary on Psalm 59* by Peter van Deun appeared in 1991 and certainly invites closer consideration of the work's significance in the context of both Maximus's own writing and the larger history of Greek patristic interpretation of the Psalter.[5] In this essay I shall make a few general remarks about both of these trajectories before turning to the content of the *Commentary*, which, I will argue, constitutes an exemplary fusion of Maximus's anagogical method of biblical interpretation, his "realized eschatology," and his Christocentric spiritual anthropology. My translation of the *Commentary* appears at the end of this essay.

Locating the *Commentary on Psalm 59* in Maximus's Corpus and in Greek Patristic Exegesis of the Psalter

Like his larger commentary *Ad Thalassium*, the *Commentary on Psalm 59* presupposes a primarily monastic audience and frames its exegeses in the form of glosses or scholia aimed at elevating the reader beyond the text precisely by probing deep within the text. The *Ad Thalassium* stands technically within the genre of *quaestio-responsio* literature, where the biblical text poses "difficulties" (ἀπορίαι) or "obstacles" (σκάνδαλα) that merit often substantial expositions of spiritual doctrine in order to "resolve" the discrepancies, but the *Commentary on Psalm 59* is a more modest work that strictly follows the discipline of line-by-line elucidation and in this respect is paralleled in Maximus's corpus only by his *Commentary on the Lord's Prayer*.[6] Moreover, Maximus does not dwell on Psalm 59 as a necessarily problematic text, as he does with the biblical passages treated in the *Ad Thalassium*, though he undoubtedly knows Basil of Caesarea's earlier quandary in his homily on this psalm: Why does its inscription open with a celebration of the military successes of David's army (relating to 2 Kings 8:1–14; 10:6–19, LXX; cf. 1 Chron. 18:1–13; 19:6), only to be followed in the body of the psalm by rather gloomy "lamentations and dirges"?[7] Like Basil, Maximus exploits this apparent discrepancy anagogically: David's prefiguration of the "final" victories of Christ is one thing; his prefiguration of our ascetic struggles of mortification and repentance in the prophetic "meantime" is quite another. But the two are inextricably interwoven in the overarching narrative of the soul's spiritual progress.

Whatever the formal differences, the anagogical hermeneutic of the *Commentary on Psalm 59*, unmistakably Origenian in its basic methods and strategies, closely resembles that of the larger work *Ad Thalassium*. I would note just a few examples. Perhaps most obvious is the abundant use of onomastics, where Maximus admits his reliance on earlier authorities.[8] All of the etymologies he uses in the *Commentary* come secondhand; the same is true of the occasional arithmologies he introduces.[9] Perhaps more intriguing in the *Commentary* is Maximus's characteristic rigor about grammatical fine points of the scriptural text.[10] As we will be noting in detail below, the future tense and passive voice used in the inscription to address *those who shall be changed* (τοῖς ἀλλοιωθησομένοις, Ps. 59:1) prove decisive for the overall thrust of the psalm. At verse 6, Maximus makes much of the fact that the prophet, in indicating that God has given his people *a sign to those who fear you to flee from the face of the bow*, uses the specific phrase *flee from the face of the bow* (ἀπὸ προσώπου τόξου) rather than simply *flee from the bow* (ἀπὸ τόξου), since the bow is a figure of devilish passion or sin, which is powerless to the monk apart from its deceptive *facade* (πρόσωπον).[11] At verse 7b, where the prophet beseeches God to *attend to* him, Maximus extrapolates from the prophet's use of an intensive prefix (ἐπι-) in the verb ἐπακούειν. God *hears* (ἀκούει) a penitent suppliant and grants that worthy person forgiveness of sins; but God *attends to* (ἐπακούει) that suppliant when he grants him, in addition, "the direct effects of his spiritual grace."[12] This emphasis on verbs with intensive prefixes as indices of progress in the spiritual life is found in the *Ad Thalassium* as well,[13] and it has a clear precedent in the comments of Origen and Didymus in the celebrated catena on Psalm 118 edited by Marguerite Harl.[14] Maximus stands squarely here in the Alexandrian tradition, leaving no textual stone unturned, since even the minutiae are potentially teeming with insights into the ascetic life. As in Evagrius's *Scholia on Proverbs* and *Commentary on the Psalms*, Maximus views the biblical text as a virtual glossary of the spiritual life that warrants continued probing to tease out its full implications and nuances.

Another feature of the *Commentary on Psalm 59* that parallels the *Ad Thalassium* and is a hallmark of Maximus's hermeneutics is the interest in laying out a whole variety of possible meanings for a single word or phrase in the biblical text. Maximus glories in "pious conjecture" (στοχασμός) and sees no need to scale his different possible interpretations;[15] all may simultaneously have anagogical import, though one meaning may be more obviously compelling than another. The integrity of interpretation is strengthened, not weakened, by study of the text from different angles, in what is an intrinsically heuristic undertaking.[16]

As for Maximus's exegesis of the Psalter in its wider Greek patristic context, the Confessor clearly knows earlier commentaries on Psalm 59. He especially favors the Pseudo-Athanasian *Expositiones in Psalmos* and Basil's *Homily on Psalm 59* and has obviously worked with Gregory of Nyssa's treatise *On the Inscriptions of the Psalms*. Maximus may very well be directly familiar with Eusebius's treatment of Psalm 59 in his massive *Commentary on the Psalms* but doubtless finds it, along with Theodoret's "prophetic" approach in his *Commentary*, to be of limited value. We can only surmise that Maximus knows Origen's *Commentary on the Psalms* and Evagrius's as well. Comparing Maximus's interpretation of the Psalter to that of his predecessors, I have relied heavily on Professor Rondeau's foundational work. Perhaps the most remarkable feature is the thorough lack of methodological novelty in Maximus's *Commentary*. He accepts the standard rendering of David as a sublime prophet and figure of Christ. He presupposes the *prosopological* approach to the psalms and its fruitfulness in conjunction with typology and anagogy. Only once in the *Commentary on Psalm 59* does he use the technical phrase ἐκ προσώπου, seeing David in verse 13 assume the persona of "our common human nature" in petitioning God for help out of affliction;[17] yet the prosopological model, as I will demonstrate further on, is implicit throughout his exposition.

THE INSCRIPTION TO PSALM 59
(εἰς τὸ τέλος, τοῖς ἀλλοιωθησομενοῖς)
AS THE KEY TO ITS INTERPRETATION BY MAXIMUS

Maximus's exegetical forbears were divided on the significance of the titles of the psalms in the Septuagint. Origen, Eusebius, the Cappadocians, Hilary of Poitiers, Jerome, Augustine, and others embraced these permutations of the original Hebrew titles as conveying formative prophetic and spiritual meanings and conditioning the interpretation of the psalms they captioned. Theodore of Mopsuestia, however, found the titles baseless or even misleading, while Diodore of Tarsus specifically warned against enthusiastic prophetic extrapolations from them.[18] Since Maximus has not provided us with a full commentary on the psalms, we have no perspective on his sense of the significance of the inscriptions, or titles, overall. But clearly in his exegesis of the inscription to Psalm 59 he has carefully considered those Greek patristic predecessors who expounded its historical, prophetic, and eschatological import.[19] The psalm is inscribed, as are numerous others in the Septuagint, *unto the end* (εἰς τὸ τέλος), and like three other psalms, *for those who shall be changed* (τοῖς ἀλλοιωθησομενοῖς).[20] Maximus shows no interest in a generic meaning of the inscription but focuses on the keywords τέλος and ἀλλοίωσις as providing the eschatological framework for the spiritual instruction that will follow in his exegesis of Psalm 59.

Earlier Greek patristic exegesis of this inscription provided Maximus a rich diversity of perspectives from which to draw. Eusebius had set the precedent for unfolding the prophetic implications of the inscription's historical referent. David's illustrious victories were to be followed in the future by "a change at a certain time [καιρῷ τινι]" when Israel, like a "flower" or "lily" (using Symmachus's and Aquila's additions to the inscription), would be subjugated by her enemies and would wither in her prime. But for us "now" (καὶ νῦν) there is a further prophetic, even eschatological horizon to this inscription. For the τέλος or change pointed to is that "at the consummation of the ages" (ἐπὶ συντελείᾳ, cf. Heb. 9:26), the future "change" (ἀλλοίωσις) and "transformation" (μεταβολή) inaugurated in the shift from the election of the Jews to the calling of the Gentiles.[21] The author of the Pseudo-Athanasian *Expositions in the Psalms*, whose identity is still contested, takes up Eusebius's interest in the status of Jews and Gentiles, viewing the subject from an eschatological, and now also ecclesiological and ascetic, perspective.[22] Accordingly, David represents in Psalm 59 the πρόσωπον of Christ for *our* spiritual utility (τὸ χρήσιμον) and "instruction" (εἰς διδαχήν), as Christ is the one who "has delivered the change [ἀλλοίωσιν] and renewal [καινότητα] of things at the end of times [ἐπ᾽ ἐσχάτου τῶν καιρῶν)] and who has smitten the foreign—that is, the spiritual [νοητά]—Gentiles." The inscription hails the victory of Christ, as David's seed, over his enemies, and the beginning of the Jewish people's treating Gentiles as kinsmen. Yet the Jews, having become aware of the aid of Christ, are making a "return" (ἐπιστροφή) by petitioning to be worthy of his grace—thus the expressions of lamentation and repentance that follow in Psalm 59:3–6, 11–14.[23]

Basil considers further the moral or ascetic implications of this eschatological title for Psalm 59. Like Eusebius, he sees the ultimate reference of the "end" and "change" as the "fulfillment at the consummation of the ages" (τὸ ἐπὶ συντελείᾳ τῶν αἰώνων ἐκβήσεσθαι, cf. Heb. 9:26; Matt. 28:20). It is a psalm not for those already changed, in the mundane sense of bodily and mental change, but for those (Gentiles), like ourselves, who "*shall* be changed," beginning already with the transition from polytheism to true piety, and is precisely for their genuinely future benefit (ὠφέλεια).[24] Basil's younger brother, Gregory of Nyssa, exploits the ascetic dimension much more dramatically. This inscription, which aims at the τέλος of spiritual victory (νίκη), marks out the frontier between us creatures, who know mutability (τροπή) and change (ἀλλοίωσις), and the immutable God. In keeping with his doctrine of perpetual spiritual progress, or *epektasis*, then, Gregory commends "change" that is a teleologically oriented motion of the soul toward what is superior, modeled in the historical examples of biblical saints and actualized in prayer and the virtuous life.[25]

I mention only one other Greek writer in advance of Maximus. Theodoret, in his exegesis of the inscription for Psalm 59, predictably constrains the eschatological dimension of the text. The text hints enigmatically at a future change (ἀλλοίωσις) and transformation (μεταβολή); there is a mixing of history and prophecy. What is important, however, is simply that "the blessed David, having won the aforementioned victories, foresaw with the eyes of the Spirit the future transgression of the people and the captivity that would accompany it. He foresaw the way of return that would thence come about by divine grace, and he thought it necessary to pre-record both the painful and the pleasant for the benefit of human beings who would be present at those events."[26]

Be that as it may, Maximus, in his turn, pulls out the stops on the eschatological force of the inscription and takes it to all new heights. For

Maximus Psalm 59 is a text par excellence of "realized" eschatology, in which the spiritual David, Christ himself, has assumed within his incarnational economy the tension between the "already" and the "not yet"—that blessed, precarious, mysterious tension which is to be surmounted in the ascetic life. The inscription, however, envisions both the realized and the futuristic dimensions of the τέλος wherein those who are already undergoing change can hope at last to be fully transformed.

> The present psalm is inscribed with the opening words *Unto the end, for those who shall be changed* [εἰς τὸ τέλος, τοῖς ἀλλοιωθησομενοῖς] in view of the transformation and change in deliberative will and in free choice [τὴν γνωμικήν τε καὶ προαιρετικὴν μεταβολὴν καὶ ἀλλοίωσιν], from infidelity to faith, from vice to virtue, and from ignorance to knowledge of God, which have come about for humanity at the end of time [ἐπὶ τέλει τῶν χρόνων] through the advent of Christ. [It is also thus inscribed] in view of the natural change and renewal [φυσικὴ . . . ἀλλοίωσιν τε καὶ ἀνανέωσιν] that will later, in grace, transpire universally at the end of the ages [ἐπὶ τέλει τῶν αἰώνων] through the very same Savior and God, when every human race shall be translated from death and corruption to immortal life and incorruption through the anticipated resurrection. *For an inscription of a title to David*: that is to say, to Christ himself, in view of the destruction of evil, which, in the divine incarnation, itself a kind of "inscription," Christ accomplished in himself as our *Leader and Savior* (Acts 5:31), and which he effects in those who with him live piously in the manner of Christ (cf. 2 Tim. 3:12; Titus 2:12). Yet this phrase also has in view the complete and final disappearance of death and corruption that is yet to happen through Christ.[27]

Especially noteworthy here are the subtle nuances in Maximus's language of the τέλος and transformation. It is clear from other texts of this same period in his career that Maximus was fascinated with the problem, classically posed by Origen in his *Peri Archôn*, of the biblical language of "ages" (αἰῶνες) of time and eternity, and what is relatively and absolutely an "end" of the ages.[28] Exegeting the inscription to Psalm 59, he knows the antecedent tradition of speculation about the τέλος and change. Eusebius and Basil both echoed Hebrews 9:26 in speaking of the *consummation of the ages* (συντέλεια τῶν αἰώνων) inaugurated by Christ's advent but focused more, like Pseudo-Athanasius with his "end of times" (ἔσχατον τῶν καιρῶν), on the *historic* transition from Judaism (or from polytheism, by Basil's account) to the true piety of universal (Gentilic) Christianity. Maximus, sketching from the outset the broader cosmic and transcosmic dimensions of the psalm, instead distinguishes the penultimate "end of *time*" (τέλος τῶν χρόνων), set in motion by the Incarnation itself, and the ultimate "end of the *ages*" (τέλος τῶν αἰώνων), which, though anticipated in the Incarnation, will be completed only with Christ's Second Coming and his annihilation of death and corruption in the final resurrection.[29]

The victorious Christ ("spiritual David") celebrated in the inscription has pioneered a way for us to thrive in the ambiguous circumstances between these two "ends." As Maximus further explains, he is the "Conqueror of time and nature," the two ontological frontiers of historical existence, by having consumed *Syria Soba*, understood as a figure of the disposition of the soul that is "enslaved to time or deceived by this present age."[30] The "change" (ἀλλοίωσις) and "transformation" (μεταβολή) that Christ inaugurates may well include the historic punishment of Israel and calling of the Gentiles, but its more decisive cosmic meaning is the transformation of humanity that would include—and here Maximus adds his own distinctive gloss—a change in "deliberative will" (γνώμη) and "free choice" (προαίρεσις).[31] Within the orbit of Maximus's thought, these concepts, especially that of γνώμη—the individual will that was stunted by the Adamic fall and is destined now to have to "deliberate" in choosing between virtue and vice—signal the ambiguity, yet redeemability, of historical existence after the Fall;[32] and both γνώμη and προαίρεσις must be mortified if they are to be transformed into agents of spiritual progress and participate in the eschatological consummation.

The same holds true for the passions themselves. Like Gregory of Nyssa, Maximus takes *Mesopotamia*, another site of David's victories, as a figure of the soul flooded on all sides by the passions,[33] and the *Valley of Salt* is likewise seen as a figure of the disobedient flesh besieged by dishonorable πάθη. "By communicating with us in the flesh," and by taking on the hostile powers of the devil (*King Adraazar*), Christ has burned this *Mesopotamia*; and he has vanquished the *Valley of Salt* by helping those who are engaged in "invisible battles" with the passions, making possible the purgation of those basic passible faculties, temper (θυμός) and desire (ἐπιθυμία), without which the soul cannot be reordered and stabilized in the advance toward its τέλος, the "good things to come" (cf. Heb. 9:11).[34]

For Maximus, then, the remainder of Psalm 59, some of it penitential, bespeaks both the fait accompli of victory in Christ and the future-oriented vocation of this change (ἀλλοίωσις) and "renewal" (ἀνανέωσις) actualized *now* in the lifelong spiritual mortification "unto the end" where we shall be fully and finally translated to incorruption.

THE FACES/VOICES OF THE TEXT: PROSOPOLOGY AND SPIRITUAL ANTHROPOLOGY IN PSALM 59:3–14

As I noted earlier, Maximus presupposes the prosopological reading of the psalms and has no need to justify its hermeneutical legitimacy. For him the identification of Christ as the "spiritual David" is simply a given. But while (1) the "spiritual David" (= Christ) is sometimes speaking in the text, it is also possible for the πρόσωπον to change to (2) the prophet David speaking on behalf of human nature, or (3) the prophet David speaking on behalf of the individual soul in its ascetic quest. And of course for Maximus, imitating Origen's anagogical method, it is possible for multiple πρόσωπα to be operative at the same time. Most of the time for Maximus the prosopology of the text is simply implicit, framed by the text's overarching Christological and anthropological typologies, such that there is no need to flag the prosopological shifts.[35] Indeed, there are already signals in the shifts of person in the psalm itself: from third person in the inscription, to second-person collective lament (vv. 3–7a), to second-person entreaty with a first-person-singular object (v. 7b), to prophetic first-person quoting of the Lord (vv. 8–10), to first-person singular (v. 11), to second-person entreaty (vv. 12–13), and finally to first-person plural in the concluding resolve of verse 14. For the three prosopic "voices" noted above—Christ, human nature, and the individual soul of the ascetic—the breakdown by verse appears as follows:

VERSE(S)	πρόσωπον
3	2nd person
4	2nd person
5–7a	2nd and 3rd person
7b	2nd and 3rd person
8	1st and 3rd person
9a	3rd person
9b	1st person
10a–b	1st and 3rd person
11	3rd person
12	2nd person
13	2nd person (explicitly ἐκ τοῦ προσώπου τῆς κοινῆς φύσεως)
14	2nd person

Here I can merely remark briefly on how the typologies and proso-pologies work together in service to Maximus's spiritual anthropology. Predictably the expressions of *penitence* in Psalm 59:3–4, 5–7, are ascribed to David as prophet representing the whole of human nature and/or the individual soul in its ascetic struggle, bemoaning the cosmic effects of the Fall and humanity's subjection to judgment, and commending the ascetic imperative of mortification. The prophet's words at verse 4—You *have shaken the earth and disrupted it. Heal its ruptures, for it has been shaken*—indicate a deep sort of repentance. The *earth* here is precisely the human heart (καρδία), and Maximus, in elucidating this *typos*, may well have in mind the classic image from the Pseudo-Macarian homilies of the peni-tent ascetic turning up the "earth of the heart."[36] In Psalm 59, however, it is an image of God's own disciplinary and redemptive disruption of that soil: his shaking up of the connectional sequence of the passions, goading of the fallen conscience, and healing of the ruptures of the heart.[37] Similarly at verse 5, in speaking of God's imposition of *hardships* and the *wine of compunction*, the prophet is evoking the whole scheme of divine disci-pline, both the cosmic pedagogy of God's providence and judgment and, at the microcosmic level of the individual, the means of mortification through "ascetic philosophy" and contemplation.[38]

Assertions of *conquest* in Psalm 59:8–10 are voiced by Christ, the spiritual David, but so too by the righteous soul. Verse 8 signals the shift: *God has spoken in his holy place*, that is, in the person of his incarnate Son, who communicates his divine purpose (σκοπός) not only in the economy of his human incarnation but through his "incarnation" in the λόγοι of his holy commandments.[39] The righteous soul, graced by Christ, thus can claim derivatively to *divide up Sikema (Shechem)* and *parcel out the Valley of Tents*, respectively figures of setting in order the modes of virtue in the context of ascetic practice (κατὰ τὴν πρακτικήν) and of beholding the diverse λόγοι of creation in the context of natural contemplation (κατὰ τὴν φυσικὴν θεωρίαν).[40]

Yet honoring the possible multivalence of the text, Maximus suggests as a more conspicuous interpretation that God himself (in Christ) is claiming to *parcel out the Valley of Tents*, the *tents* being a figure of the churches planted "in every inhabited land."[41] Here the Confessor is clearly beholden to the *ecclesiological* typology proffered by both Pseudo-Athanasius and Basil.[42] Maximus will allow also, however, a *cosmological* interpretation whereby the *parceling* of the *Valley of Tents* is a figure of God comprehending the whole "world of bodies" within his providential knowledge—this because scripture sometimes calls the body a *tent* (cf. Wisd. 9:15; John 2:21; 2 Cor. 5:1–4; 2 Pet. 1:13).[43] Once again, for Maximus, these would not be conflicting readings but kaleidoscopic perspectives on the Bible's richly textured figures.

In verses 9–10, onomastic interpretation largely determines who is making these victorious claims. Subjugated *Galaad* (Gilead) and *Manassês* (Manasseh) are respectively translated "revelation" and "forgetfulness," and thus it is the righteous soul who is effectively speaking here, having acquired revelation of ineffable mysteries and the power to forget the toils of virtue amid the joy of contemplation.[44] *Judah* is the "thanksgiving" uttered by the true king, the incarnate Christ.[45] In verse 10a, *Moab, the washbasin of my hope*, with its peculiar etymology, can be ascribed both to the soul's purification of the body and to the Lord's use, in his incarnation, of the *washbasin* of the flesh to purify us of sin.[46] At last in verse 10b, it is Christ who has stretched out his *shoe* over *Idumea*, translated "bloody clay," a figure of the Incarnation as the Lord's approach into the creation that cannot contain him.[47] But likewise the ascetic soul can claim to have stretched out the *shoe* of its mortified sensual experience over the "bloody clay" of the present worldly age and to have gleaned its true principles (λόγοι).[48] Similarly, it is the incarnate Christ who claims to bring the *foreigners* (i.e., Philistines) into subjection, not only by conquering the invisible forces of evil but by evangelizing all the Gentiles into submission. And with him, then, the righteous soul can claim to have subjugated the *foreigners* in its own ascetic conquest of the demons and its subduing of the passions.[49] Precisely here we have a salient image of Maximus's spiritual anthropology: that of the unruly passions as "Gentiles" who must, within the theater of the soul, be redeemed and transformed as agents of grace in the ultimate τέλος of the spiritual life.[50]

The final petitions of Psalm 59:11–14 represent the prophet speaking either for the righteous soul (v. 11) or for the collective whole of human nature, as Maximus explicitly states in connection with verse 13 (ἐκ προσώπου τῆς κοινῆς φύσεως).[51] The distinctive feature here in these petitions, by Maximus's account, is the request for an assistance in the ascetic life that only God, and more specifically the incarnate Christ, who has himself entered our ascetic conflict, can provide. *Who will lead me into the city of fortification?* (v. 11a). Maximus wholly lifts the *city of fortification* from its historical context (a reference perhaps to the capital city of Edom) and displays it as a multifaceted symbol of the pious soul variously fortified by wisdom, by impregnability, by reason and virtue, by the habitude of true knowledge or pure contemplation.[52] It is a cherished symbol to Maximus, who in the *Ad Thalassium* develops at length the symbol of Jerusalem herself as the ascetically fortified soul.[53] *Idumea* (v. 11b) again comes up, now as a possible symbol of "ascetic philosophy."[54] Such is a spiritual geography through which only the incarnate Logos himself can navigate the faithful, leading the way against the enemy (v. 12) and giving help out of that *affliction* (v. 13) which may be mortality itself or the toil that attends the pursuit of virtue.[55] The end of the *Commentary*, on verse 14, appropriately celebrates the fact that only the God who himself perfectly indwells and contains the virtues and the knowledge of the mysteries of salvation is capable of achieving such a victory.[56] The cherished notion of the divine "incarnation" in the virtues is only briefly hinted at here but is explicit elsewhere in the Confessor's writings.[57]

––––––––

Maximus's *Commentary on Psalm 59*, methodologically, is no dramatic new milestone in Greek patristic exegesis of the Psalter. Maximus has every intention, after all, of building on the work of earlier commentators. Nor does the work in fact represent any significant departure from Maximus's own method of anagogical exegesis. Nor does it set forth themes of spiritual anthropology unparalleled in the Confessor's other ascetic works. Yet precisely in being a commentary specifically on a psalm, with the application of Maximus's anagogical method to it, and with the perspective of the cherished themes of Maximus's spiritual doctrine guiding the exegesis, it is something unique.

Psalm 59, Maximus intimates in his interpretation of its inscription, is an eschatological psalm par excellence that bespeaks the purposive tension between the "realized" end or change that has been inaugurated by the first coming of Christ, and that future τέλος, in the Second Coming and final resurrection, when all humanity will be translated to immortality and incorruption. This is the framework in which the Christian ascetic lives, and moves, and has his or her being. Indeed, we have here Christ himself, the "spiritual David," speaking to us in the victorious efficacy of his incarnation—his incarnational economy being understood in the widest sense as his presence in the flesh, in the contemplated λόγοι of the world, and in the holy commandments, through which the devout soul can participate in Christ's victory. The individual soul, and indeed the whole of penitent human nature, can claim the victorious words of Christ as their own. Thus the "voices" of Psalm 59 bespeak the mysteriously *concurrent* and interwoven experience of the Logos, in his kenotic descent, and of humanity, in spiritual ascent and deification.

Christ's triumphant "incarnation" in the spiritual life of the Christian is nonetheless absolutely commensurate with the Christian's own voluntary growth in grace. Clearly for Maximus any claim the ascetic soul makes to victory here and now is relative. It is a claim that can be made only from the perspective of ongoing repentance, mortification, and progress in virtue, signaled in Psalm 59 by the alternation of expressions of lamentation and conquest. For Maximus the inscription truly does condition the whole of the psalm, since it aims us at what, from our perspective, is perennially a future goal (τέλος) and hope. This, the Fifty-Ninth Psalm, is ultimately *for those who shall be changed,* those destined to be the beneficiaries of the full outworking of the mystery of the Incarnation in the *end of the ages.*

MAXIMUS THE CONFESSOR, *COMMENTARY ON PSALM 59*: A TRANSLATION

Unto the end, for those who shall be changed; for an inscription of a title to David, for instruction, when he set on fire Mesopotamia and Syria Soba, and when Joab returned and struck down twelve thousand in the Valley of Salt (Ps. 59:1–2; cf. 2 Kings 8:1–14; 10:6–19, LXX; 1 Chron. 18:1–13; 19:6).[58]

The present psalm is inscribed with the opening words *Unto the end, for those who shall be changed* in view of the transformation and change in deliberative will and in free choice from infidelity to faith, from vice to virtue, and from ignorance to knowledge of God, which have come about for humanity at the end of time (cf. 1 Cor. 10:11) through the advent of Christ. [It is also thus inscribed] in view of the natural change and renewal that will later, in grace, transpire universally at the end of the ages through the very same Savior and God, when every human race shall be translated from death and corruption to immortal life and incorruption through the anticipated resurrection. *For an inscription of a title to David*: that is to say, to Christ himself, in view of the destruction of evil that, in the divine incarnation, itself a kind of "inscription," Christ accomplished in himself as our *Leader and Savior* (Acts 5:31), and that he effects in those who with him live piously in the manner of Christ (cf. 2 Tim. 3:12; Titus 2:12). Yet this phrase also has in view the complete and final disappearance of death and corruption that is yet to happen through Christ.

[The inscription continues]: *For instruction, when he set on fire Mesopotamia and Syria Soba. . . .* In other words, this psalm, inscribed by the mind of David—that is, by the Christ of God—is for the instruction of us who are being changed and who shall be changed; clearly it aims at the praiseworthy and divine transformation. For Christ alone is the "true King of Israel and the one who sees God,"[59] and who, as the complete Destroyer of evil and ignorance, and as the complete Conqueror of time and nature, through which evil took root among us, *set Mesopotamia on fire* by communicating with us in the flesh; in other words, he set afire the habit of vice that floods us with unnatural carnal passions . . . *and [he set on fire] Syria Soba* . . . , meaning that he also has consumed that disposition [of the soul] which was enslaved to time or deceived by this present age; for *Soba* is translated "seven." So this is clearly an indication of the property of time, since time is hebdomatic.[60] For the devil, who engages in invisible battles, customarily tries to mobilize nature and time together with him in opposing virtue and knowledge, just as *Adraazar* [*Hadadezer*] (cf. 2 Kings 8:3 ff., LXX) engaged the two Syrias against David. For the name *Adraazar*, when translated into Greek, is rendered "dissolving strength" or else "destroying power." The devil, then, is the one who, having by his deceit dissolved the spiritual strength of our human nature through the original transgression of the divine commandment, enslaved humanity to time and nature. For it is utterly impossible to fight against human beings apart from things subject to time and nature.

And when Joab returned and struck down twelve thousand in the Valley of Salt. Everyone who commands for the spiritual "King David"—that is, for our Lord Jesus—*strikes down twelve thousand in the Valley of Salt.* The *Valley of Salt* is the flesh, which through disobedience became like a place of *dishonorable passions* (Rom. 1:26). In it, as in a sort of *valley*, everyone who is pious and devout, through the exercise of reason and contemplation, smites time and nature, or rather the soul's irrational preoccupation with them, in no way cleaving to laws dictated by nature and time, since such a one has reached the summit of virtue and knowledge. For the number twelve signifies time and nature, since [human] nature is pentadic on account of the five senses, while time is hebdomatic, as is quite clear to everyone; and of course combining five with things in seven makes up the number twelve. Perhaps we might say that the number of those destroyed also hints at the triad of the soul's faculties, which viciously through deceit become unnaturally implicated with the tetrad of the [inferior] senses in terms of their inclination, by which inclination every sin is prone to arise.

The spiritual David [Christ] rightly slaughters this number, in the sense that he helps those who endure for the sake of truth, engages intellectually in invisible battles, and wages war spiritually against the powers of evil. For every faculty of the soul, unnaturally incited, is prone to entangle itself with the senses. And thus reason and temper and desire, the general faculties of the soul that are three in number, when multiplied by the four inferior senses,[61] make the number twelve. Four times three and three times four equals this very number, which is destroyed by the one who faithfully allies with the Lord and thoroughly prevails against every invisible and hostile spirit.

At any rate, the present psalm is inscribed with the words *For those who shall be changed* for us; *for teaching* us of the good things to come (cf. Heb. 9:11) by the spiritual David; *for an inscription of a title to David*, in the sense that it proclaims his divine and salvific achievements on our behalf. For, in the view of experts in the interpretation of the names mentioned here, the inscription clearly expresses a proclamation of deeds.

O God, you have repudiated us and destroyed us, you have been angry with us and yet you took pity on us (Ps. 59:3).

God has *repudiated* us whenever, having failed to keep the original commandment, we have appeared unworthy of conversing with him in his presence. He has *destroyed* us whenever he has banished us from the ultimate glory of paradise on account of our wickedness. He *has been angry with* us whenever he has subjected us to the penalty of death as a retribution and punishment for vice. And yet *he took pity* on us when, through his only begotten Son, the divine Logos incarnate, who consented to receive the debt on behalf of all of us, he redeemed us from death (cf. Hos. 13:14) and led us back again into his glory.

You have shaken the earth and disrupted it. Heal its ruptures, for it has been shaken (Ps. 59:4).

He has *shaken and disrupted* our *earth*, that is, our heart, by giving us *the sword of the Spirit* (Eph. 6:17), which intellectually distinguishes *between good and evil* (cf. Heb. 5:14), and *the law of the Spirit* (Rom. 8:2), which *incites* us against the law of the flesh (cf. Rom. 8:6–7), creates within us a praiseworthy battle against the passions, *shakes up* the connectional sequence of the passions within us, and *disrupts* the conscience against preoccupying wicked memories. He has *healed the ruptures* of our heart—

the very ruptures that, having been shaken open and collapsed through disobedience, have endured since the original transgression in paradise—through spiritual regeneration by grace.

You have shown your people hardships, and given us the wine of compunction to drink. You have given a sign to those who fear you to flee from the face of the bow, so that your beloved may be saved (Ps. 59:5–7a).

God has *shown hardships to those who fear him* by means of his commandments, whether by establishing the means of bodily mortification according to ascetical philosophy, or by lovingly disciplining us for our own good (cf. Heb. 12:10) with his manifold providence and judgment—us who, failing to uphold willingly the divine yoke, have come under *the law of commandments* (Eph. 2:15). He *gives us the wine of compunction to drink*, that is to say, he graces us with the knowledge that, in the context of spiritual contemplation, follows upon the purification gained through ascetical philosophy. For all spiritual knowledge penetrates the heart and leads us to comprehend the greatness of God's benefits toward us. He gives *a sign to those who fear him to flee from the face of the bow* by teaching those who fear him *to carry in the body the death of Jesus* (2 Cor. 4:10), whereby sin is brought to a complete standstill. For the power that, through the cross, puts to death *the mind of the flesh* (Rom. 8:6–7) has become the real sign *to flee from the face of the bow*, that is, from the deceptive appearance that manifests itself in created beings. For *the face of the bow*—by which *bow* I mean every devilish passion—is the appearance of bodies, which arouses sense experience, just as the sting of an arrow, in an unseemly way, harms the senses and provokes the soul toward passions. Hence the text says that those who fear the Lord will *flee from the face of the bow*, not "from the bow." For the *bow* of sin, apart from its facade, would not be able to do any harm to those who fear the Lord because of whom *the beloved* of God *are saved*. The *beloved of God* are none other than the thoughts that, in the context of contemplation, preserve divine knowledge. The modes of the virtues, which come about in the context of ascetic practice, *save* these *beloved* thoughts from all error and from all preoccupying memories of sin that perturb the soul.

Save with your right hand, and attend to me. God has spoken in his holy place: "I will rejoice, and divide up Sikema [Shechem] and parcel out the Valley of Tents" (Ps. 59:7b–8).

God *saves with his right hand* by giving his only begotten Son.[62] For the right hand is the Son of the Father (cf. Acts 5:31; Heb. 1:3), who is a ransom given for the salvation of the whole world (cf. Matt. 20:28; Mark 10:45). He *attends to* by granting the righteous, in addition to forgiveness of sins, spiritual gifts—for he "hears" the one who calls upon him, granting first through the suppliant's repentance the forgiveness of sins, but he further *attends to* that suppliant when, in addition to forgiveness of sins, he bestows the direct effects of his spiritual grace. He *speaks in his holy place*—that is, in his incarnate Logos—his divine purpose, *hidden for ages and generations* (Col. 1:26) according to the incarnational economy of his Christ, as if to declare it plainly through his dwelling among us in human form, giving to human life an image of eternal life as its model—an image more sonorous than any voice, being the open demonstration of his good works. Yet he also *speaks* in every *holy place* where his commandments are kept, in the sense of showing the principles of his deeds to be living principles, more sonorous than any audible voice. One who is righteous rejoices when, having been perfected by the grace of the Only-Begotten, he becomes able to *divide up Sikema,* that is, proportionately to subordinate, through wise experience, [certain] human modes of virtue to others in the context of ascetic practice. For *Sikema* is translated "shouldering," which could only mean, then, the habitude that suspends all the passions while producing all the virtues; for they say that the shoulder is a symbol of ascetic practice.[63] Moreover, [one who is righteous] *parcels out the Valley of Tents* by distributing the appropriate principles to each created being in the context of natural contemplation. For the *Valley of Tents* is the cosmos here and now, in which the present, unstable and transient life of all created beings subsists, as in *tents,* according to the variant deliberation and disposition of each being. Or rather, perhaps the *tents* of the present *valley* are the modes of virtue that he who, being able by his *good teaching* (1 Tim. 4:6) to distribute to every creature its proper way to salvation (cf. Acts 16:17), distributes intellectually to those he is instructing, giving appropriate guidance to the habitude of each creature such as will also protect the honorable. Or else the *tents* of the *valley* are the churches of the Gentile faithful (cf. Rom. 16:4) that have staked themselves in every inhabited land through Christ our divine Savior; indeed, this meaning, it seems to me, is more conspicuous than the others. Or yet again, God *parcels out the Valley of Tents* in the sense that he embraces in his knowledge the world of bodies as though it were a *valley of tents*; for in many passages of scripture the body is called a *tent* (cf. Wisd. 9:15; John 2:21; 2 Cor. 5:1–4; 2 Pet. 1:13).

"*Galaad [Gilead] is mine and Manassês [Manasseh] is mine, and Ephraim is the strength of my head*" (Ps. 59:9a).

Galaad, according to one of the translations for this name, means "revelation," while *Manassês* is rendered "forgetfulness." Both revelation and forgetfulness, it seems, accrue to one who is righteous. On the one hand, through contemplation one acquires initiation in ineffable mysteries; on the other hand, one is enabled to forget the toils connected with virtue because of the joy of spiritual contemplation that is obtained from those toils of virtue. *Ephraim* is translated "widening," which is none other than the secure hope, based on faith, of future benefits, a hope that is the *help* of the *head* (Ps. 107:9), or faith, of the righteous. For faith is the *head* of the righteous and of every good work, while the *strength* of the head consists in the secure and unshakable hope of future goods. By this hope, contemplating future things as [already] present, we "widen" ourselves amid afflictions and remain indestructible in the face of tribulations.

"*Judas [Judah] is my king, and Moab the washbasin of my hope*" (Ps. 59:9b–10a; cf. 107:9–10).

Judas is translated "thanksgiving." For thanksgiving for every good thing, through prayer, rules among the saints (cf. Eph. 1:15–16; Col. 1:3–4; Phlm. 5–6). Yet *Judas* can also be understood with reference to the Lord, who is "the true *King* of the spiritual Israel and the one who sees God," and the one who for our sake, when he had become a man, gave thanks to his Father saying, *I thank you, holy Father* . . . (Matt. 11:25; Luke 10:21). *Moab* is translated "bowels of a father," but is understood to mean our body, through which, in the context of ascetic philosophy, as through a bath—which the *washbasin* clearly indicates here—there naturally arises purification from sins. For the *washbasin of hope* is purification, that is to say, the readiness we obtain through a life of purification for the inheritance of good things that, according to our hopes, are being stored up for us (cf. Col. 1:5). And yet *Moab* can also be understood in reference to the incarnation of the Lord. For the *Son of Man* (Matt. 8:20, passim) who was born a man for our sake, and who is able to cleanse and purify us of the taints and defilements of our sins, bears the title of the true *washbasin* of our *hope*.

"I will stretch out my shoe over Idumea [Edom]; the foreigners [Philistines] have been subjected to me" (Ps. 59:10b).

Idumea is translated "bloody clay." But it can also be rendered with reference to the Lord's flesh,[64] through which, as with a *shoe*, the Lord approaches the realm of human affairs, as the creation is otherwise unable to contain its Creator, who is by nature infinite and incomprehensible. *Idumea* can furthermore be understood in reference to the flesh of each one of us, over which we stretch out the foot of the ascetic training and self-control— for so must *shoe* be understood here—that guard the soul from the thistles and thorns (cf. Gen. 3:18; Hos. 10:8; Matt. 7:16; Heb. 6:8) of the devil's wicked powers. For without ascetic training and rigorous self-control the passions of the flesh overthrow the monk who despairs of piety. The *shoe* can furthermore be understood as the soul's sense experience, mortified through reason and contemplation. Through this mortified sense experience the soul, treading on the [individual] senses, passes through the age unscathed, using the medium of sense experience, imagined as a *shoe*, as it gathers up the principles of the age and the differences in form and appearance of visible things for the purposes of the understanding and knowledge of the one and only sovereign reason.

The foreigners have been subjected to me. For when the Lord in his incarnation visited our human dwelling places, he *subjected* to *the strength of his might* (Eph. 6:10) not only the vanquished spirits of wickedness, but all the Gentiles as well, who, being empowered through the summons of the preaching of the gospel, submitted to him. Yet *the foreigners are subjected* also to the one who is righteous when, by stepping on the soil of his flesh with the shoe, as it were, of self-control, which mortifies *the law of sin* (Rom. 7:23, 25; 8:2), that person not only subdues the unclean passions that lurk within him but also conquers the demons who excite them.

Who will lead me into the city of fortification? (Ps. 59:11a).

The *city of fortification*, or the enclosed or *fortified city*, as another translator says,[65] is the wisdom gleaned from many divine and mystical insights by those fortified with the virtues. Or else the *city of fortification* is the condition in which one who is truly pious and devout becomes impregnable and unapproachable to his enemies because of the surrounding defense of holy powers that protect him. Or else the *city of fortification* is the soul that has built itself a wall with reason and life, and become full of all the graces of the virtues. Or still again, the *city of fortification* is the habitude of true and infallible knowledge surrounded by all ethical, natural, and theological insights. Into the *city* of this habitude every pious soul is led by none other than God alone, who draws everyone to himself because of his great and unspeakable goodness.

Or who will guide me as far as Idumea? (Ps. 59:11b).

Idumea, as our earlier account indicated, is the existence of all creatures subject to sense, on which natural contemplation in the Spirit inherently concentrates, whereby *the Creator is proportionately beheld through the beauty and greatness of his creatures* (Wisd. 13:5) by one who is piously gathering up the knowledge of created beings. Or perhaps *Idumea* is virtuous ascetic philosophy for the sake of the flesh, whereby our body becomes a *temple of the Holy Spirit* (1 Cor. 16:19) that is built up with the beauteous material of the commandments. Into this *Idumea* the Lord guides [us], gracing those who love him with the knowledge of visible things, and teaching the mortification of the members of this earthly and mortal flesh.

Or, to put it succinctly, the *city of fortification* is the gnostic contemplation of intelligible realities, while *Idumea* is the knowledge of sensible things. Into these two things only the Wisdom of our God and Father, the only-begotten Son (cf. 1 Cor. 1:21, 24; Eph. 3:10), both *leads and guides* [us]. Hence the prophet goes on to say,

Will not you, O God, who has driven us away? (Ps. 59:12a).

—that is, you, O God, who drove us away in the beginning on account of sin, you who out of your tender mercy (cf. Luke 1:78) had pity on us, *leading (us) into the city of fortification* and *guiding us as far as Idumea* according to our previous exegesis.

And will not you, O God, go forth with our forces? (Ps. 59:12b).

For God will not *go forth* with him who puts his trust in himself, *hoping in his bow* and inscribing his salvation on his own *sword* (Ps. 43:7); rather, God, who goes forth into battle against invisible enemies, goes forth with those who *put down their enemies in* God himself and who *wipe out their foes in his name* (Ps. 43:6).

Give us help out of affliction, [for] salvation coming from human beings is vain (Ps. 59:13).

The prophet, speaking in the person of our common human nature, prayerfully beseeches our God and Savior to *give us help from affliction,* clearly indicating the affliction that has been spread over our human nature because of sin and has pressed it to the very gates of hell (cf. 3 Macc. 5:51; Wisd. 16:13; Matt. 16:18). For *affliction,* in my judgment, is the tyranny and dominion of death and corruption, while *help* is the sure hope of the resurrection granted by grace, for which hope those who see clearly the gloom of death endure without sorrow. Or else *affliction* is toil for the sake of virtue, while *help* is the tranquillity that succeeds this toil by divine grace. In comparison to this tranquillity all salvation coming from human beings is judged to be *vanity* and complete nothingness—for it is right to interpret *vanity* in this way here.

In God we shall wield power, and he shall bring to nought those who afflict us (Ps. 59:14).

They *wield power in God* who do not ascribe to themselves the achievement of the virtues or ascribe to their own wisdom the attainment of the divine mysteries. For God himself alone subsists in these things and wholly contains them, effecting every virtue and granting knowledge, and bringing to nought all wicked demons who oppose themselves to virtue and knowledge and who attempt to afflict those who fear God with vice and ignorance. For he is the Savior of all things because he is also the Creator of all things. *To him be glory and dominion forever and ever, amen* (Rev. 1:6).

Notes

1. A deficit I tried to help remedy in my *Exegesis and Spiritual Pedagogy in Maximus the Confessor: An Investigation of the "Quaestiones ad Thalassium,"* Christianity and Judaism in Antiquity 7 (Notre Dame, IN: University of Notre Dame Press, 1991); also my "The Anagogical Imagination: Maximus the Confessor and the Legacy of Origenian Hermeneutics," in *Origeniana Sexta: Origène et la Bible/Origen and the Bible. Actes du Colloquium Origenianum Sextum, Chantilly, 30 août–3 septembre 1993,* ed. Gilles Dorival and Alain le Boulluec (Leuven: Peeters/Leuven University Press, 1995), 639–54.

2. There are a number of useful surveys of Maximus's career, including his early monastic formation. More recently, see Irénée-Henri Dalmais, "Maxime le Confesseur," in *Dictionnaire de spiritualité ascétique et mystique: Doctrine et his-*

toire, ed. M. Viller et al. (Paris: G. Beauchesne, 1980), 10: 836–37, and "La vie de saint Maxime le Confesseur reconsiderée," *Studia Patristica* 17 (1982): 26–30; Lars Thunberg, *Microcosm and Mediator: The Theological Anthropology of Maximus the Confessor*, 2nd ed. (Chicago: Open Court, 1995), 1–7; Andrew Louth, *Maximus the Confessor* (London: Routledge, 1996), 3–18.

3. See Raffaele Cantarella, *S. Massimo Confessore: La Mistagogia ed altri scritti* (Florence: Ediziones "Testi Cristiani," 1931), 2.

4. Polycarp Sherwood, *An Annotated Date-List of the Works of Maximus the Confessor*, Studia anselmiana 30 (Rome: Herder, 1952), 26, and "Notes on Maximus the Confessor," *American Benedictine Review* 1 (1950): 350–53.

5. *Maximi Confessoris opuscula exegetica duo*, ed. Peter van Deun, CCSG 23 (Turnhout: Brepols, 1991), 3–22. The critical edition of the *Commentary on Psalm 59* appears in this volume with that of Maximus's *Commentary on the Lord's Prayer*.

6. See Blowers, *Exegesis and Spiritual Pedagogy*, 28–73, for an expanded discussion of the plasticity of genre in Maximus's spiritual writings, notably the *Quaestiones ad Thalassium*. Two other works of Maximus in the *quaestio-responsio* genre are his *Quaestiones et dubia* (PG 90: 785–856) and *Quaestiones ad Theopemtum* (PG 90: 1393–1400).

7. See Basil, *Hom. in Ps.* 59 (PG 29: 461B).

8. Maximus, *Expos. in Ps. 59* (CCSG 23: 8.88–89). Van Deun, in his critical edition (CCSG 23), has located the sources of all the onomastic interpretations introduced by Maximus.

9. On the importance of onomastic, or etymological, interpretation to Maximus's anagogy, see Blowers, *Exegesis and Spiritual Pedagogy*, 203–219. Maximus puts in succinctly in *Qu. Thal.* 50 (CCSG 7: 379.32–381.37): "Whoever interprets holy scripture in terms of Christ [κατὰ Χριστόν], in an intellectual way [γνωστικῶς] for the soul, must also diligently study the interpretation of names, which can elucidate the whole meaning of the scriptures, if indeed he cares about the precise intellectual comprehension of the scriptures."

10. This is another legacy of Origenian exegesis heavily used by Maximus. See Blowers, *Exegesis and Spiritual Pedagogy*, 219–28.

11. Maximus, *Expos. in Ps. 59* (CCSG 23: 11.139–47).

12. Maximus, *Expos. in Ps. 59* (CCSG 23: 12.159–65).

13. Maximus, *Qu. Thal.* 59 (CCSG 22: 59.208–67.337); see also Blowers, *Exegesis and Spiritual Pedagogy*, 221–28.

14. See especially Origen's comments on Ps. 118:114, distinguishing between hoping (ἐλπίζειν) and the spiritually superior "hoping in" (ἐπελπίζειν) (SC 189: 374–76 [section 114a]); cf. also Didymus (or else Origen) on the verbs ἐκζήτειν and ἐξερευνᾶν in Ps. 118:2 (SC 189: 194 [3b]); and Didymus (or else Origen) on ἐξερευνᾶν in Ps. 118:29 (SC 189: 398 [129a]). See also Blowers, *Exegesis and Spiritual Pedagogy*, 221 (and n. 176), 223–24 (and nn. 185–87).

15. See, *int. al.*, Maximus, *Qu. Thal.* 55 (CCSG 7: 481.26–483.36).

16. On the importance of unity in diversity in Maximus's exegesis, see Blowers, *Exegesis and Spiritual Pedagogy*, 185–92. The "heuristic" principle in Maximus's theological and hermeneutical method has been analyzed in detail by Vittorio Croce in his *Tradizione e ricerca: Il metodo teologico di san Massimo il Confessore*, Studia patristica mediolanensia 2 (Milan: Vita e Pensiero, 1974).

17. On the Christian roots of this and other prosopological terminology, and the thriving of prosopological exegesis in Origen and his successors, see Marie-Josèphe Rondeau, *Les commentaires patristiques du Psautier (IIIe–Ve siècles)*, 2 vols., OCA 219–20 (Rome: Pontificium Institutum Studiorum Orientalium, 1982–85), 2: 21–34, 40–72. Maximus, *Expos. in Ps. 59* (CCSG 23: 21.322–24).

18. Cf. Theodore, *Exp. in Ps.* (ed. Robert Devreesse, *Le commentaire de Théodore de Mopsueste sur les Psaumes*, Studi e testi 93 [Vatican City: Biblioteca Apostolica Vaticana, 1939]: 334.27–29); Diodore, *Comm. Ps.* 12 (CCSG 6: 70.3–6). I have studied the psalms titled "Unto the End" in a separate essay; see Paul M. Blowers, "Making Ends Meet: Variable Uses of the Psalm Title Unto the End (εἰς τὸ τέλος) in Greek Patristic Commentators on the Psalms," *Studia Patristica* 44 (2010): 163–75.

19. The inscription reads: *Unto the end, for those who shall be changed; for an inscription of a title to David, for instruction, when he set on fire Mesopotamia and Syria Soba, and when Joab returned and struck down twelve thousand in the Valley of Salt.* While, as Basil of Caesarea indicates, there is no scriptural record of the specific episodes alluded to in this inscription (see his *Hom. in Ps.* 59, PG 29: 460C), a general consensus among Greek patristic commentators before Maximus had already connected them with the Davidic military history recounted in 2 Kings 8:1–14; 10:6–19 (LXX); cf. 1 Chron. 18:1–13; 19:6. These passages recount David's campaign against the Philistines (lit. "foreigners," ἀλλόφυλοι) and Moabites, his victory against the Syrian king Adraazar (Heb. Hadadezer) son of Raab of Soba (Heb. Rohob of Zobah), and his slaughter of eighteen thousand Idumeans (Edomites) in the Valley of Salt (all in 2 Kings 8:1–14), as well as Joab's and David's successful campaigns against "Syria Soba" and "Syria from the other side of the [Euphrates] river" (= "Mesopotamia") solicited by Adraazar (2 Kings 10:6–19). Cf. Eusebius, *Comm. in Ps.* 59 (PG 23: 552D–553B); Pseudo-Athanasius, *Expos. in Ps.* 59 (PG 27: 268D); Basil, *Hom. in Ps.* 59 (PG 29: 460C–461C); Theodoret, *Int. in Ps.* 59 (PG 80: 1316C).

20. For other psalms inscribed with *Unto the end*, see, in the LXX, Psalms 4, 5, 6, 8, 9, 10, 11, 12, 13, 17, 18, 19, 20, 21, 29, 30, 35, 38, 39, 40, 41, 43, 44, 45, 46, 48, 50, 51, 52, 53, 54, 55, 56, 57, 58, 60, 61, 63, 64, 65, 66, 67, 68, 69, 74, 75, 76, 79, 80, 83, 84, 108, 138, 139. For other psalms inscribed with *For those who shall be changed*, see Ps. 44 (ὑπὲρ τῶν ἀλλοιωθησομένων); 68 (ὑπὲρ τῶν ἀλλοιωθησομένων); 79 (ὑπὲρ τῶν ἀλλοιωθησομένων).

21. Eusebius, *Comm. in Ps.* 59 (PG 23: 553D–556C).

22. On the problem of identifying him, cf. G. C. Stead, "St. Athanasius on the Psalms," *Vigiliae Christianae* 39 (1985): 65–78; Gilles Dorival, "Athanase ou Pseudo-Athanase," *Rivista di Storia e Letteratura Religiosa* 16 (1980): 80–89; Rondeau, *Commentaires patristiques*, 1: 80–87. On his exegesis itself in the *Expositiones in Psalmos*, see Rondeau, *Commentaires patristiques*, 1: 197–218.

23. Pseudo-Athanasius, *Expos. in Ps.* 59 (PG 27: 268D–269A).

24. Basil, *Hom. in Ps.* 59 (PG 29: 461C–464C).

25. Gregory of Nyssa, *Inscr. Ps.* 2.2 (GNO 5: 72.17–74.1) and specifically on the Ps. 59 inscription, 2.4 (GNO 5: 79.6–82.15). See also the analysis of Ronald Heine, *Gregory of Nyssa's Treatise on the Inscriptions of the Psalms* (Oxford: Oxford University Press, 1995), 16, 46–47.

26. Theodoret, *Int. in Ps.* 59 (PG 80: 1316C–1317A).

27. Maximus, *Expos. in Ps. 59* (CCSG 23: 3.7–4.23).

28. See esp. Maximus, *Qu. Thal.* 22 (CCSG 7: 137 ff.); *Cap. theol.* 2.85 (PG 90: 1164C–D); cf. Origen, *Peri Archôn* 2.3.5 (SC 252: 260–62). See also my study "Realized Eschatology in Maximus the Confessor, *Ad Thalassium* 22," *Studia Patristica* 32 (1997): 258–63.

29. It is possible that Maximus, in speaking of the "end of the ages" (τέλος τῶν αἰώνων), has in mind Paul's reference in 1 Cor. 10:11 to the *end of the ages* (τὰ τέλη τῶν αἰώνων). Paul, however, clearly indicates a realized dimension, as this end has already come upon the faithful (εἰς οὓς . . . κατήντηκε). But as Maximus explains in *Qu. Thal.* 22 (CCSG 7: 137.23–27), these are *ages* not in the ordinary sense but purposed "for the outworking of the mystery of God's embodiment," the economy of the Incarnation in its fullness, in which case the futuristic dimension of this "end of the ages" is crucial. See Blowers, "Realized Eschatology," 260.

30. Maximus, *Expos. in Ps. 59* (CCSG 23: 4.29–5.32; 5.35–37).

31. See Maximus, *Expos. in Ps. 59* (CCSG 23: 3.10–12): the "gnomic" and "prohairetic" transformation has already been inaugurated in Christ. Cf. also Maximus, *Expos. in Ps. 59* (CCSG 23: 13.185–88).

32. On the ambiguity of γνώμη in Maximus, see Thunberg, *Microcosm and Mediator*, 213–18.

33. Cf. Gregory of Nyssa, *Inscr. Ps.* 2.4 (GNO 5: 80.24–81.7); Maximus, *Expos. in Ps. 59* (CCSG 23: 5.33–35).

34. Maximus, *Expos. in Ps. 59* (CCSG 23: 4.24–8.89).

35. On the close interrelation of typology and prosopology, and the possibility for different πρόσωπα to be anagogically operative at the same time in Origen, see Rondeau, *Commentaires patristiques*, 2: 68–72.

36. See Pseudo-Macarius, *Homilia spiritualis* 26.10 (PTS 4: 209.126–28); Pseudo-Macarius, *Logos* 3.3.8–9 (GCS: 33.26 34.19); also Columba Stewart, *"Working the Earth of the Heart": The Messalian Controversy in History, Texts, and*

Language to AD 431, Oxford Theological Monographs (Oxford: Oxford University Press, 1991).

37. Maximus, *Expos. in Ps. 59* (CCSG 23: 9.104–10.115). The interconnections of the various passions, and so too the viciously precise designs of the demons that incite passions, are of considerable importance to Maximus's ascetic theology; see esp. *Qu. Thal.* intro. (CCSG 7: 23.108–35.302).

38. Maximus, *Expos. in Ps. 59* (CCSG 23: 10.120–11.152).

39. Maximus, *Expos. in Ps. 59* (CCSG 23: 12.165–13.175).

40. Maximus, *Expos. in Ps. 59* (CCSG 23: 13.175–84).

41. Maximus, *Expos. in Ps. 59* (CCSG 23: 14.193–97).

42. Pseudo-Athanasius, *Expos. in Ps. 59* (PG 27: 269D): "Divine scripture calls the dwelling-place of all humanity a *valley* (Ps. 59:8). Thus it says, *I will parcel out* for myself *the valley* into *tents*, that is to say, I will bring about the fullest *valley* of churches." Also Basil, *Hom. in Ps.* 59 (PG 29: 465C): "Therefore, after the covenant [= *Sikema/Shechem*] has been divided for all, and the advantage from it has been made common to all those who are having kindness done them by God, then, too, the deep valley of the tabernacles will be measured; that is to say, the whole world, as if by certain lots, will be divided by dioceses in each place" (trans. FC 46: 388).

43. Maximus, *Expos. in Ps. 59* (CCSG 23: 14.197–200).

44. Maximus, *Expos. in Ps. 59* (CCSG 23: 14.203–15.209).

45. Maximus, *Expos. in Ps. 59* (CCSG 23: 15.220–16.226).

46. Maximus, *Expos. in Ps. 59* (CCSG 23: 16.226–37).

47. Maximus, *Expos. in Ps. 59* (CCSG 23: 16.240–17.244). Cf. Basil, *Hom. in Ps.* 59 (PG 29: 468A–B): "The shoe of the Godhead is his God-bearing flesh, through which he approaches human beings."

48. Maximus, *Expos. in Ps. 59* (CCSG 23:17.244–58).

49. Maximus, *Expos. in Ps. 59* (CCSG 23:17.259–18.269).

50. On this theme in Maximus, see my essay "Gentiles of the Soul: Maximus the Confessor on the Substructure and Transformation of the Human Passions," *Journal of Early Christian Studies* 4 (1996): 57–85.

51. Maximus, *Expos. in Ps. 59* (CCSG 23: 21.322–24). See also above, note 16 and related text. In relation to the prophet speaking for the collective whole of human nature, note the shift from petitions for "me" in v. 11 to "us" in vv. 12–14.

52. Maximus, *Expos. in Ps. 59* (CCSG 23: 18.270–19.286; 20.300–301).

53. Cf. Maximus, *Qu. Thal.* 49 (CCSG 7: 351.10–314).

54. Maximus, *Expos. in Ps. 59* (CCSG 23: 19.293–96).

55. Maximus, *Expos. in Ps. 59* (CCSG 23: 19.296–21.335).

56. Maximus, *Expos. in Ps. 59* (CCSG 23: 21.336–22.347).

57. On this theme in Maximus, and its patristic background, see Thunberg, *Microcosm and Mediator*, 323–30.

58. My translation is based on the critical edition of the *Commentary* by Peter van Deun, *Maximi Confessoris opuscula exegetica duo*, CCSG 23: 3–22.

59. On the translation of *Israel* as "the one who sees God," cf. Philo, *Abr.* 57; *Conf.* 56; *Congr.* 51; Origen, *Peri Archôn* 4.3.12; etc. It is a commonplace by Maximus's time.

60. Cf. especially Gregory of Nyssa, *Hom. in Ps. 6* (GNO 5: 188.14–22), on the "hebdomatic" significance of time.

61. The tetrad, or foursome, of "inferior" senses includes those excepting sight: taste, smell, touch, and hearing.

62. The identification of the *right hand* with the Son of God was already well established by earlier patristic exegetes: *int. al.*, Origen, *Fr. Jer.* 2.4 (GCS 6-Origenes Werke 3: 256.1–3); Eusebius, *Comm. in Ps.* 59 (PG 23: 564B); Didymus the Blind, *Comm. in Ps.* 59 (PTS 16: 33.4–5); Cyril of Alexandria, *In Ps.* 59 (PG 69: 1113A); *Glaph. in Gen.* 2 (PG 69: 128A).

63. See Pseudo-Dionysius the Areopagite, *Cel. hier.* 15.3 (PTS: 54.4–5).

64. Cf. Basil, *Hom. in Ps.* 59 (PG 29: 468A–B). See above, note 47.

65. Symmachus from Origen's *Hexapla*; repeated by Eusebius, *Comm. in Ps.* 59 (PG 23: 572B, C, and D).

Septuagint (LXX)/Vulgate, Modern Editions

Psalm 1, Psalm 1

2, 2	30, 31	58, 59	86, 87
3, 3	31, 32	59, 60	87, 88
4, 4	32, 33	60, 61	88, 89
5, 5	33, 34	61, 62	89, 90
6, 6	34, 35	62, 63	90, 91
7, 7	35, 36	63, 64	91, 92
8, 8	36, 37	64, 65	92, 93
9, 9 & 10	37, 38	65, 66	93, 94
10, 11	38, 39	66, 67	94, 95
11, 12	39, 40	67, 68	95, 96
12, 13	40, 41	68, 69	96, 97
13, 14	41, 42	69, 70	97, 98
14, 15	42, 43	70, 71	98, 99
15, 16	43, 44	71, 72	99, 100
16, 17	44, 45	72, 73	100, 101
17, 18	45, 46	73, 74	101, 102
18, 19	46, 47	74, 75	102, 103
19, 20	47, 48	75, 76	103, 104
20, 21	48, 49	76, 77	104, 105
21, 22	49, 50	77, 78	105, 106
22, 23	50, 51	78, 79	106, 107
23, 24	51, 52	79, 80	107, 108
24, 25	52, 53	80, 81	108, 109
25, 26	53, 54	81, 82	109, 110
26, 27	54, 55	82, 83	110, 111
27, 28	55, 56	83, 84	111, 112
28, 29	56, 57	84, 85	112, 113
29, 30	57, 58	85, 86	113, 114 & 115

114, 116:1–9	124, 125	134, 135	144, 145
115, 116:10–19	125, 126	135, 136	145, 146
116, 117	126, 127	136, 137	146, 147:1–11
117, 118	127, 128	137, 138	147, 147:12–20
118, 119	128, 129	138, 139	148, 148
119, 120	129, 130	139, 140	149, 149
120, 121	130, 131	140, 141	150, 150
121, 122	131, 132	141, 142	—, 151
122, 123	132, 133	142, 143	
123, 124	133, 134	143, 144	

Note: Versification between LXX and contemporary English translations frequently does not exactly correspond, since the LXX numbers the psalm inscriptions (or titles).

EARLY CHRISTIAN PSALM COMMENTARIES AND
AVAILABLE ENGLISH TRANSLATIONS

Ambrose of Milan
Explanatio super Psalmos XII. Edited by M. Petschenig, CSEL 64. Edited by Luigi
  Franco Pizzolato, *Sancti Ambrosii Episcopi Mediolanensis Opera 7* (Milan: Bib-
  lioteca Ambrosiana; Rome: Città Nuova, 1980). Translated by Íde Ní Riain,
  Commentary on Twelve Psalms (Dublin: Halcyon Press, 2000).
Expositio de Psalmo cxviii. Edited by M. Petschenig, CSEL 62: 53–510. Edited by
  Luigi Franco Pizzolato, *Sancti Ambrosii Episcopi Mediolanensis Opera 9–10*
  (Milan: Biblioteca Ambrosiana; Rome: Città Nuova, 1987). Translated by Íde
  Ní Riain, *Homilies of Saint Ambrose on Psalm 118 (119)* (Dublin: Halcyon
  Press, 1998).

Ambrosiaster
Quaestiones veteris et novis testamenti 110–12 [on Psalms 1, 23, 50]. Edited by
  Alexander Souter, CSEL 50: 268–98.

Ammonius of Alexandria
Fragmenta in Psalmos. PG 85: 1361–64.

Apollinaris of Laodicea
Fragmenta in Psalmos. In Robert Devreesse, *Les anciens commentateurs grecs des
  Psaumes,* Studi e testi 141 (Vatican City: Biblioteca Apostolica, 1970), 211–23.
  Also in Ekkehard Mühlenberg, *Psalmenkommentare aus der Katenenüber-
  lieferung,* PTS 15: 1–118.

Apollinaris, Pseudo-
Metaphrasis Psalmorum. Edited by A. Ludwich, *Apolinarii metaphrasis psalmorum,* Bibliotheca Teubneriana (Leipzig: Teubner, 1912).

Arnobius, the Younger
Commentarii in Psalmos. Edited by Klaus D. Daur, CSEL 25.

Asterius
Homiliae in Psalmos. Edited by Marcel Richard in *Asterii Sophistae commentariorum in Psalmos quae supersunt: Accedunt aliquot homiliae anonymae* (Oslo: Brogger, 1956).

Athanasius of Alexandria
Epistula ad Marcellinum. PG 27: 12–45. Translated by Pamela Bright in *Early Christian Spirituality,* edited by Charles Kannengiesser (Philadelphia: Fortress Press, 1986), 56–77. Translated by Everett Ferguson, "Athanasius, Epistle to Marcellinus," *Ekklesiastikos Pharos* 60 (1978): 378–403. Translated by Robert C. Gregg in *Athanasius: The Life of Antony and the Letter to Marcellinus,* Classics of Western Spirituality (New York: Paulist Press, 1980), 101–29.

Athanasius, Pseudo-
Argumentum in Psalmos. PG 27: 56–60.
Expositiones in Psalmos. PG 27: 60–545.

Augustine of Hippo
Enarrationes in Psalmos. Edited by D. E. Dekkers and I. Fraipont, CCSL 38–40. Translated by Maria Boulding, *Expositions of the Psalms,* WSA III.15–20.

Basil of Caesarea
Homiliae super Psalmos. PG 29: 209–494. Translated by Agnes Clare Way, *Saint Basil: Exegetic Homilies,* FC 46. Translated by Mark DelCogliano, *St. Basil the Great: On Christian Doctrine and Practice* (Yonkers, NY: St. Vladimir's Seminary Press, 2012), 92–101, 218–26.

Cassiodorus
Expositio Psalmorum. Edited by M. Adriaen, CCSL 97–98. Translated by P. G. Walsh, *Cassiodorus: Explanation of the Psalms,* ACW 51–53.

Cyril of Alexandria
Expositio in Psalmos. PG 69: 717–1274.

Daniel of Salah
Magna expositio super Psalmos; The Great Psalter Commentary of Daniel of Salah. Edited by David G. K. Taylor, 6 vols., CSCO, forthcoming.

Didymus of Alexandria

Commentarii in Psalmos. Edited by L. Doutreleau, A. Gesché, and M. Gronewald, *Didymos der Blinde, psalmenkommentar (Tura-Papyrus)*, 5 vols., Papyrologische Texte und Abhandlungen 4, 6, 7, 8, 12 (Bonn: Habelt, 1968–70). Translated (only Psalm 24) by Albert-Kees Geljon, "Didymus the Blind: Commentary on Psalm 24 (23 LXX): Introduction, Translation and Commentary," *Vigiliae Christianae* 65 (2011): 50–73.

Fragmenta in Psalmos. Edited by Ekkehard Mühlenberg, *Psalmenkommentare aus der Katenenüberlieferung*, PTS 15 (1975): 121–375; 16: 3–365 (1977); PG 39: 1156–1616, 1617–22.

Diodore of Tarsus

Commentarii in Psalmos. Edited by J. M. Olivier, CCSG 6. Translated by Robert C. Hill, *Diodore of Tarsus: Commentary on Psalms 1–51* (Atlanta, GA: Society of Biblical Literature, 2005).

Eusebius of Caesarea

Commentarii in Psalmos. PG 23: 71–1396; 24: 9–78; 30: 81–104.

Evagrius of Pontus

Scholia in Psalmos. May be extracted from printed sources by means of a key in M.-J. Rondeau, "Le commentaire sur les Psaumes d'Évagre le Pontique," *Orientalia Christiana Periodica* 26 (1960): 307–48. Required sources include PG 12: 1054–1686; PG 27: 60–545; and *Origenes in Psalmos*, edited by J. B. Pitra, AS 2: 444–83 and 3: 1–364.

Gennadius of Constantinople

Fragmenta in Psalmos. PG 85: 1665–68.

Gregory of Nyssa

In inscriptiones Psalmorum and *In sextum Psalmum.* Edited by J. McDonough, GNO 5: 24–175. Translated by Ronald E. Heine, *Gregory of Nyssa's Treatise on the Inscriptions of the Psalms* (Oxford: Clarendon Press, 1995).

In sextum Psalmum. Edited by J. McDonough, GNO 5: 187–93. Translated by Brian E. Daley in "Training for 'the Good Ascent': Gregory of Nyssa's Homily on the Sixth Psalm," in *In Dominico Eloquio–In Lordly Eloquence: Essays on Patristic Exegesis in Honor of Robert Louis Wilken*, edited by Paul M. Blowers, Angela R. Christman, and David G. Hunter (Grand Rapids, MI: Eerdmans, 2001), 211–17.

Hesychius of Jerusalem

Fragmenta in Psalmos ex Catena Graecorum Patrum in Psalmos. PG 93: 1179–1340; as Athanasius, *De titulis Psalmorum*, PG 27: 649–1344; and as John Chrysostom, *Commentarius in Psalmos 77–99*, PG 55: 711–84.

Hilary of Poitiers

Tractatus super Psalmos. Edited by A. Zingerle, CSEL 22. Edited by J. Doignon and R. Demeulenaere, CCSL 61, 61A, 61B. Translated (only Psalms 1, 54, 130) by W. Sanday, *Homilies on Psalms*, NPNF, 2nd ser., 9: 236–48. [*Instructio Psalmorum* refers to the preliminary twenty-four paragraphs of the *Tractatus super Psalmos*].

Hippolytus

In Psalmos (fragments). Edited by Hans Achelis, GCS 1.2: 146–47, 153. Translation ANF 5: 170–72.

Jerome

Commentarioli in Psalmos. Edited by G. Morin, CCSL 72: 177–245.
Tractatus LIX in Psalmos. Edited by G. Morin, CCSL 78: 3–352. Translated by M. L. Ewald, *Homilies on the Psalms*, FC 48.
Tractatus in Psalmos series altera. Edited by G. Morin, CCSL 78: 353–447. Translated by M. L. Ewald, *Homilies on the Psalms*, FC 57.

John Chrysostom

Expositiones in Psalmos. PG 55: 39–528. Translated by Robert C. Hill, *St. John Chrysostom Commentary on the Psalms*, 2 vols. (Brookline, MA: Holy Cross Orthodox Press, 1998).

Maximus the Confessor

Expositio in Psalmum 59. CCSG 23: 3–22. Translated by Paul Blowers in this volume.

Origen of Alexandria

Commentarii in Psalmos 1 and 4 = *Philocalia* 2–3, 26. Edited and translated by Marguerite Harl, *Sur les écritures: Philocalie, 1–20*, SC 226. Edited and translated by Éric Junod, *Sur les libre arbitre*, SC 302. Translated by George Lewis, *The Philocalia of Origen* (Edinburgh: T. and T. Clark, 1911), 30–34, 214–24.
Excerpta in Psalmum I. PG 12: 1076–84, 1092–96.

Excerpta in Psalmum VI, XV, XVIII. PG 17: 1076–84, 1092–96.

Homiliae de Psalmis. PG 12: 1319–1410. *Homélies sur les Psaumes 36 á 38*, edited by E. Prinzivalli, SC 411. Translated in M. Heintz, "The Pedagogy of the Soul: Origen's Homilies on the Psalms," PhD diss., (University of Notre Dame, 2008), 88–311.

Libri in Psalmos (Praefatio). PG 12: 1053–1076.

Libri in Psalmos (Fragmenta in diuersos Psalmos in catenis). PG 12: 1085–1320, 1409–1686; PG 17: 105–49.

Prosper of Aquitaine

Expositio Psalmorum. Edited by P. Callens, CCSL 68A.

Theodore of Mopsuestia

Expositionis in Psalmos. Edited by L. De Coninck and M. J. D'Hont, CCSL 88A. Translated by Robert C. Hill, *Theodore of Mopsuestia: Commentary on Psalms 1–81* (Atlanta, GA: Society of Biblical Literature, 2006).

Fragments syriaques du Commentaire des Psaumes: Fragments syriaques du Commentaire des Psaumes (Psaume 118 et Psaumes 138–148). Edited by L. Van Rompay, CSCO 435–36.

Theodoret of Cyrus

Interpretatio in Psalmos. PG 80: 857–1997. Translated by Robert C. Hill, *Theodoret of Cyrus: Commentary on the Psalms,* FC 101–2.

OTHER SOURCES

Achelis, Hans. ed. *Hippolytus Werke.* GCS 1.2. Leipzig: Hinrichs, 1897.

Agnon, Shmuel. *All the Stories of Shmuel Yosef Agnon: Ad Hennah.* Vol. 7. Jerusalem: Shocken, 1978.

Ammonius. *In Porphyrii Isagogen sive V voces.* Edited by A. Busse. Commentaria in Aristotelem Graeca 4.3. Berlin: George Reimer, 1891.

Anatolios, Khaled. *Athanasius: The Coherence of His Thought.* New York: Routledge, 1998.

Andreopoulos, Andreas, Augustine Casiday, and Carol Harrison, eds. *Meditations of the Heart: The Psalms in Early Christian Thought and Practice.* Studia traditionis theologiae 8. Turnhout: Brepols, 2011.

Aspegren, Kerstin. *The Male Woman: A Feminine Ideal in the Early Church.* Edited by René Kieffer. Uppsala: Uppsala Universitet, 1990.

Assmann, Jan. *Moses the Egyptian*. Cambridge, MA: Harvard University Press, 1997.

———. *Politische Theologie zwischen Ägypten und Israel*. Munich: Carl Friedrich von Siemens, 1992.

Atkins, J. W. H. *Literary Criticism in Antiquity*. 2 vols. Cambridge: Cambridge University Press, 1934.

Attridge, Harold W. "Giving Voice to Jesus: Use of the Psalms in the New Testament." In *Psalms in Community: Jewish and Christian Textual, Liturgical, and Artistic Traditions*, edited by Harold W. Attridge and Margot E. Fassler, 101–12. Atlanta, GA: Society of Biblical Literature, 2003.

Attridge, Harold W., and Margot E. Fassler, eds. *Psalms in Community: Jewish and Christian Textual, Liturgical, and Artistic Traditions*. Atlanta, GA: Society of Biblical Literature, 2003.

Austin, J. L. *How to Do Things with Words*. 2nd ed. Cambridge, MA: Harvard University Press, 1975.

Babcock, William S. "The Christ of the Exchange: A Study in the Christology of the *Enarrationes in Psalmos*." PhD diss., Yale University, 1971.

———, trans. *Tyconius: The Book of Rules*. Atlanta, GA: Scholars Press, 1989.

Bader, Günter. *Psalterium affectuum palaestra: Prolegomena zu einer Theologie des Psalters*. Tübingen: Mohr Siebeck, 1996.

Baker, Kimberly F. "Augustine on Action, Contemplation, and Their Meeting Point in Christ." PhD diss., University of Notre Dame, 2007.

———. "Augustine's Doctrine of the *Totus Christus*: Reflecting on the Church as Sacrament of Unity." *Horizons* 37 (2010): 7–24.

Balthasar, Hans Urs von. *Augustinus: Das Antlitz der Kirche: Auswahl und Übertragung*. 1942. Reprint, Einsiedeln: Benziger, 1955.

———. "Die *Hiera* des Evagrius." *Zeitschrift für katholische Theologie* 63 (1939): 86–106, 181–206.

———. "Die Psalmenfrömmigkeit der Märtyrerkirche." In *Die Psalmen als Stimme der Kirche*, edited by A. Heinz. Trier: Paulinus-Verlag, 1982.

Bammel, Caroline. "Origen's Pauline Prefaces and the Chronology of His *Pauline Commentaries*." In *Origeniana Sexta: Origène et la Bible/Origen and the Bible. Acts du Colloquium Origenianum Sextum Chantilly, 30 août–septembre 1993*, edited by Gilles Dorival and Alain le Boulluec, 495–513. Bibliotheca ephemeridum theologicarum Lovaniensium 118. Leuven: Leuven University Press, 1995.

Bandt, Cordula. "Reverberation of Origen's Exegesis of the Psalms in the work of Eusebius and Didymus." In *Origeniana Decima*, edited by Sylwia Kaczmarek and Henryk Pietras, 891–906. Leuven: Peeters, 2011.

Bardy, G. "Commentaires patristiques de la Bible." In *Dictionnaire de la Bible Supplément*, vol. 2, edited by I. Pirot et al., 73–103. Paris: Letouzey et Ané, 1934.

Barker, Andrew, ed. *Greek Musical Writings.* 2 vols., Cambridge Readings in the Literature of Music. Cambridge: Cambridge University Press, 1984.

Basil of Caesarea. *Il Battesimo. Testo, traduzione, introduzione e commento.* Edited by Umberto Neri. Brescia: Paideia, 1976.

Bavel, Tarsicius J. van. "The 'Christus Totus' Idea: A Forgotten Aspect of Augustine's Spirituality." In *Studies in Patristic Christology*, edited by T. Finan and V. Twomey, 84–94. Dublin: Four Courts Press, 1998.

———. "What Kind of Church Do You Want? The Breadth of Augustine's Ecclesiology." *Louvain Studies* 7 (1979): 147–71.

Bavel, Tarsicius J. van, and B. Bruning. "Die Einheit des *Totus Christus* bei Augustinus." In *Scientia Augustiniana* [Festschrift for A. Zumkeller], edited by C. P. Mayer and W. Eckermann, 43–75. Würzburg: Augustinus-Verlag, 1975.

Bekker, Immanuel, ed. *Aristotelis opera.* Vol. 2. Berlin: Reimer, 1831.

Bell, Catherine. *Ritual: Perspectives and Dimensions.* New York: Oxford University Press, 1997.

———. *Ritual Theory, Ritual Practice.* New York: Oxford University Press, 1992.

Berardino, Angelo di, ed. *The Golden Age of Latin Patristic Literature.* Vol. 4 of *Patrology.* Translated by P. Solari. Westminster, MD: Christian Classics, 1986.

Bernardi, Jean. *La prédication des pères cappadociens: Le prédicateur et son auditoire.* Paris: Presses Universitaires de France, 1968.

Bettenson, Henry, trans. *Augustine: Concerning the City of God against the Pagans.* New York: Penguin, 1972.

Blaising, Craig A., and Carmen S. Hardin, ed. *Psalms 1–50.* Ancient Christian Commentary on Scripture. Old Testament 7. Downers Grove, IL: InterVarsity Press, 2008.

Blowers, Paul M. "The Anagogical Imagination: Maximus the Confessor and the Legacy of Origenian Hermeneutics." In *Origeniana Sexta: Origène et la Bible/ Origen and the Bible. Actes du Colloquium Origenianum Sextum, Chantilly, 30 août–3 septembre 1993*, edited by Gilles Dorival and Alain le Boulluec, 639–54. Bibliotheca ephemeridum theologicarum Lovaniensium 118. Leuven: Peeters/Leuven University Press, 1995.

———. *Exegesis and Spiritual Pedagogy in Maximus the Confessor: An Investigation of the "Quaestiones ad Thalassium."* Christianity and Judaism in Antiquity 7. Notre Dame, IN: University of Notre Dame Press, 1991.

———. "Gentiles of the Soul: Maximus the Confessor on the Substructure and Transformation of the Human Passions." *Journal of Early Christian Studies* 4 (1996): 57–85.

————. "Making Ends Meet: Variable Uses of the Psalm Title *Unto the End* (εἰς τὸ τέλος) in Greek Patristic Commentators on the Psalms." *Studia Patristica* 44 (2010): 163–75.

————. "Realized Eschatology in Maximus the Confessor, *Ad Thalassium* 22." *Studia Patristica* 32 (1997): 258–63.

Bochet, Isabelle. "Une nouvelle lecture du *Liber ad Honoratum* d'Augustin (= *epist.* 140)." *Revue des Études Augustiniennes* 45 (1999): 335–51.

Böhm, T. "Athanasius, An Marcellinus: Der Psalter als Mitte des Lebens der Kirche." *Bibel und Liturgie* 77 (2004): 155–60.

Borgomeo, Pasquale. *L'église de ce temps dans la prédication de saint Augustin.* Paris: Études Augustiniennes, 1972.

Børresen, Kari Elisabeth, ed. *Image of God and Gender Models in Judaeo-Christian Tradition.* Oslo: Solum, 1991.

Boulding, Maria, ed. and trans. *Saint Augustine: Expositions of the Psalms,* WSA III/15. Hyde Park, NY: New City Press, 2000.

Bourdieu, Pierre. *The Logic of Practice.* Translated by Richard Nice. Stanford, CA: Stanford University Press, 1990.

————. *Outline of a Theory of Practice.* Translated by Richard Nice. Cambridge: Cambridge University Press, 1977.

Bouyer, Louis. *The Church of God: Body of Christ and Temple of the Spirit.* Translated by Charles Underhill Quinn. Chicago: Franciscan Herald, 1982.

Brakke, David. *Athanasius and Asceticism.* Baltimore: Johns Hopkins University Press, 1998.

————. *Evagrius of Pontus: Talking Back, Antirrhetikos, A Monastic Handbook for Combating Demons.* Collegeville, MN: Cistercian Publications, 2009.

Braude, William G., ed. and trans. *The Midrash on the Psalms.* 2 vols. Yale Judaica Series 13. New Haven, CT: Yale University Press, 1959.

Bright, Pamela. *The Book of Rules of Tyconius: Its Purpose and Inner Logic.* Christianity and Judaism in Antiquity 2. Notre Dame, IN: University of Notre Dame Press, 1988.

————. "Singing the Psalms: Augustine and Athanasius on the Integration of the Self." In *The Whole and Divided Self,* edited by David E. Aune and John McCarthy, 115–29. New York: Crossroad, 1997.

Brown, Peter. *The Body and Society: Men, Women, and Sexual Renunciation in Early Christianity.* 2nd ed. New York: Columbia University Press, 2008.

Brummer, Jakob, ed. *Vitae Vergilianae.* Appendix in *Tiberi Claudi Donati Interpretationes Vergilianae,* edited by H. Georgii. 2 vols. Stuttgart: Teubner, 1969.

Bunge, Gabriel. "Evagrios Pontikos: Der Prolog des *Antirrhetikos.*" *Studia Monastica* 39 (1997): 77–105.

———. *Das Geistgebet, Studien zum Traktat 'De oratione' des Evagrios Pontikos*. Schriftenreihe des Zentrums Patristischer Spiritualität Koinonia-Oriens im Erzbistum Köln 25. Cologne: Luthe, 1987.

———. "'Der Mystische Sinn der Schrift': Anlässlich der Veröffentlichung der Scholien zum Ecclesiasten des Evagrios Pontikos." *Studia Monastica* 36 (1994): 135–46.

———. "Origenismus-Gnostizismus: Zum geistesgeschichtliche Standort des Evagrios Pontikos." *Vigiliae Christianae* 40 (1986): 24–54.

Burn, Andrew E., ed. *Niceta of Remesiana: His Life and Works*. Cambridge: Cambridge University Press, 1905.

Burns, Paul C. "Augustine's Distinctive Use of the Psalms in the Confessions: The Role of Music and Recitation." *Augustinian Studies* 24 (1993) 133–46.

———. *A Model for the Christian Life: Hilary of Poitiers' Commentary on the Psalms*. Washington, DC: Catholic University of America Press, 2012.

Burrus, Virginia. "'Equipped for Victory': Ambrose and the Gendering of Orthodoxy." *Journal of Early Christian Studies* 4 (1996): 461–75.

———. "Reading Agnes: The Rhetoric of Gender in Ambrose and Prudentius." *Journal of Early Christian Studies* 3 (1995): 25–46.

Burton-Christie, Douglas. *The Word in the Desert: Scripture and the Quest for Holiness in Early Christian Monasticism*. Oxford: Oxford University Press, 1993.

Butterworth, G. W., trans. *Origen: On First Principles*. Gloucester, MA: Peter Smith, 1973.

Byassee, Jason. *Praise Seeking Understanding: Reading the Psalms with Augustine*. Grand Rapids, MI: Eerdmans, 2007.

Cahill, Michael. "The History of Exegesis and Our Theological Future." *Theological Studies* 61 (2000): 332–47.

Camelot, Pierre-Thomas. "Autorité de l'écriture, autorité de l'église à propos d'un texte de saint Augustin." In *Mélanges offerts à M.-D. Chenu*, edited by A. Duval. Bibliothèque Thomiste 37. Paris: J. Vrin, 1967.

Cameron, Averil. *Christianity and the Rhetoric of Empire: The Development of Christian Discourse*. Sather Classical Lectures 55. Berkeley: University of California Press, 1991.

———. "Redrawing the Map: Early Christian Territory after Foucault." *Journal of Roman Studies* 76 (1986): 266–71.

———. "Virginity as Metaphor: Women and the Rhetoric of Early Christianity." In *History as Text: The Writing of Ancient History*, edited by Averil Cameron, 181–205. Chapel Hill: University of North Carolina Press, 1989.

Cameron, Michael. "Augustine's Construction of Figurative Exegesis against the Donatists in the *Enarrationes in psalmos*." PhD diss., University of Chicago, 1996.

———. *Christ Meets Me Everywhere: Augustine's Early Figurative Exegesis.* Oxford Studies in Historical Theology. New York: Oxford University Press, 2012.

———. "Enarrationes in Psalmos." In *Augustine through the Ages: An Encyclopedia*, edited by Allen D. Fitzgerald, 290–96. Grand Rapids, MI: Eerdmans, 1999.

———. "Review of Michael Fiedrowicz, *Psalmus Vox Totius Christi: Studien zu Augustins "Enarrationes in Psalmos*." *Augustinian Studies* 34 (2003): 266–77.

———. "*Totus Christus* and the Psychagogy of Augustine's Sermons." *Augustinian Studies* 36 (2005): 59–70.

———. "Transfiguration: Christology and the Roots of Figurative Exegesis in St. Augustine." *Studia Patristica* 33 (1997): 40–47.

Cantarella, Raffaele. *S. Massimo Confessore: La Mistagogia ed altri scritti.* Florence: Ediziones "Testi Cristiani," 1931.

Canty, Aaron. "The Nuptial Imagery of Christ and the Church in Augustine's *Enarrationes in Psalmos*." In *Early Christian Literature and Intertextuality*, vol. 1, edited by Craig A. Evans and H. Daniel Zacharias, 225–35. Library of New Testament Studies 391. New York: T. and T. Clark, 2009.

Casiday, Augustine. "Gabriel Bunge and the Study of Evagrius Ponticus." *St. Vladimir's Theological Quarterly* 48 (2004): 249–97.

———. *Reconstructing the Theology of Evagrius Ponticus: Beyond Heresy.* Cambridge: Cambridge University Press, 2013.

Chadwick, Henry, trans. *Augustine: Confessions.* Oxford: Oxford University Press, 1992.

Childs, Brevard. "Psalm Titles and Midrashic Exegesis." *Journal of Semitic Studies* 16 (1971): 137–50.

Clark, Elizabeth A. *Ascetic Piety and Women's Faith: Essays on Late Antique Christianity.* Lewiston, NY: Edwin Mellen Press, 1986.

———. "Ideology, History, and the Construction of 'Woman' in Late Ancient Christianity," *Journal of Early Christian Studies* 2 (1994): 155–84.

———. "The Lady Vanishes: Dilemmas of a Feminist Historian after the 'Linguistic Turn.'" *Church History* 67 (1998): 1–31.

———. *The Origenist Controversy: The Cultural Construction of an Early Christian Debate.* Princeton, NJ: Princeton University Press, 1992.

Clayton, Paul. *The Christology of Theodoret of Cyrus: Antiochene Christology from the Council of Ephesus (431) to the Council of Chalcedon (451).* Oxford: Oxford University Press, 2007.

Coakley, Sarah. *Powers and Submissions: Spirituality, Philosophy, and Gender.* Oxford: Blackwell, 2002.

Cohen, S. M., and G. B. Matthews, trans. *Ammonius: On Aristotle's Categories.* London: Duckworth, 1991.

Colombás, García. *El monacato primitivo.* 2 vols. Madrid: Biblioteca de Autores Cristianos, 1975.

Congar, Yves. "Ecclesia ab Abel." In *Abhandlungen über Theologie und Kirche: Festschrift für Karl Adam.*, edited by Marcel Reding. Düsseldorf: Patmos, 1952.

Cooper, Alan M. "The Life and Times of King David According to the Book of Psalms." In *The Poet and the Historian: Essays in Literary and Historical Biblical Criticism*, edited by R. E. Friedman, 117–32. Harvard Semitic Studies 26. Chico, CA: Scholars Press, 1983.

Cooper, Kate. "Insinuations of Womanly Influence: An Aspect of the Christianization of the Roman Aristocracy." *Journal of Roman Studies* 82 (1992): 150–64.

———. *The Virgin and the Bride: Idealized Womanhood in Late Antiquity.* Cambridge, MA: Harvard University Press, 1996.

Cowe, S. Peter, "Daniel of Salah as Commentator on the Psalter." *Studia Patristica* 20 (1989): 152–59.

Croce, Vittorio. *Tradizione e ricerca: Il metodo teologico di san Massimo il Confessore.* Studia patristica mediolanensia 2. Milan: Vita e Pensiero, 1974.

Curti, C. "Greek Catenae on the Psalms." In *Patrology: The Eastern Fathers from the Council of Chalcedon (451) to John of Damascus (750)*, edited by Angelo Di Barardino and translated by Adrian Waldford, 618–26. Cambridge: James Clarke, 2006.

Daley, Brian E. "Is Patristic Exegesis Still Usable? Reflections on the Early Christian Interpretation of the Psalms." *Communio* 29 (2002): 185–216.

———. "Theodore of Mopsuestia: Commentary on Psalm 44 (45)." Unpublished paper, 1993.

———. "Training for 'the Good Ascent': Gregory of Nyssa's Homily on the Sixth Psalm." In *In Dominico eloquio—In Lordly Eloquence: Essays on Patristic Exegesis in Honor of Robert Louis Wilken*, edited by Paul M. Blowers, Angela R. Christman, and David G. Hunter, 185–217. Grand Rapids, MI: Eerdmans, 2001.

Dalmais, Irénée-Henri. "Maxime le Confesseur." In *Dictionnaire de spiritualité ascétique et mystique: Doctrine et histoire*, edited by M. Viller et al. 17 vols., 10: 836–47. Paris: G. Beauchesne, 1980.

———. "La vie de saint Maxime le Confesseur reconsiderée." *Studia Patristica* 17 (1982): 26–30.

Dawson, David. *Allegorical Readers and Cultural Revision in Ancient Alexandria.* Berkeley: University of California Press, 1992.

Deun, Peter van, ed. *Maximi Confessoris Opuscula Exegetica Duo.* CCSG 23. Turnhout: Brepols, 1991.

Deusen, Nancy van. *The Place of the Psalms in the Intellectual Culture in the Middle Ages.* Albany: State University of New York Press, 1999.

Devreesse, Robert. *Les anciens commentateurs grecs des Psaumes.* Studi e testi 264. Vatican City: Biblioteca Apostolica Vaticana, 1970.

———. "La chaine sur les psaumes de Daniele Barbaro." *Revue Biblique* 33 (1924): 65–81, 498–521.

———. "Chaines exégétiques grecques." In *Dictionnaire de la Bible,* edited by Louis Pirot, 1084–1233. Suppl. 1. Paris: Letouzey et Ané, 1928.

———. *Le commentaire de Théodore de Mopsueste sur les Psaumes (I–LXXX).* Studi e testi 93. Vatican City: Biblioteca Apostolica Vaticana, 1939.

———. *Essai sur Théodore de Mopsueste.* Studi e testi 141. Vatican City: Biblioteca Apostolica Vaticana, 1948

Dewart, Joanne McWilliam. "Augustine's Developing Use of the Cross, 387–400." *Augustinian Studies* 15 (1984): 15–33.

Dillon, John, and Jackson Hershbell. *On the Pythagorean Way of Life: Texts, Translation, and Notes.* Atlanta, GA: Scholars Press, 1991.

D'Izarny, R. "Mariage et consécration virginale au IVe siècle." *Vie spirituelle,* suppl., 6 (1953): 92–107.

Dodaro, Robert. *Christ and the Just Society in the Thought of Augustine.* Cambridge: Cambridge University Press, 2004.

Dodd, C. H. *According to the Scriptures.* London: Nisbet, 1952.

Dolbeau, François. *Augustin d'Hippone: Vingt-six sermons au people d'Afrique.* Paris: Études Augustiennes, 1996.

Dorival, Gilles. "Athanase ou Pseudo-Athanase?" *Rivista di Storia e Letteratura Religiosa* 16 (1980): 80–89.

———. *Les chaînes exégétiques grecques sur les Psaumes: Contribution à l'étude d'une forme littéraire.* 4 vols. Leuven: Peeters, 1986.

———. "Origène dans les chaînes sur les psaumes: Deux séries inédites de fragments." In *Origeniana: Premier colloque international des études origéniennes (Montserrat, 18–21 septembre 1973),* edited by H. Crouzel, G. Lomiento, and J. Rius-Camps, 199–213. Bari: Istituto di Letteratura Cristiana Antica, 1975.

Driscoll, Jeremy. *The Ad Monachos of Evagrius Ponticus: Its Structure and a Select Commentary.* Studia anselmiana 104. Rome: Pontificio Ateneo S. Anselmo, 1991.

———. "Evagrius and Paphnutius on the Causes for Abandonment by God." *Studia Monastica* 39 (1997): 259–86.

Drobner, Hubertus. "Grammatical Exegesis and Christology in St. Augustine." *Studia Patristica* 18 (1990): 49–63.

———. *Person-Exegese und Christologie bei Augustinus: Zur Herkunft der Formel Una Persona.* Philosophia patrum 8. Leiden: Brill, 1986.

———. "Psalm 21 in Augustine's *Sermones ad populum*: Catecheses on *Christus totus* and Rules of Interpretation." *Augustinian Studies* 37 (2006): 145–69.

Dulaey, Martine. "L'interprétation du Psaume 21 (22TM) chez saint Augustin." In *David, Jésus et la reine Esther: Recherches sur le Psaume 21*, edited by Gilles Dorival, 315–40. Louvain: Peeters, 2002.

———. "Introduction, Psaume 21: Première explication." In *Les Commentaires des Psaumes: Ps 17–25*, edited by Martine Dulaey et al., 125–31. BA 57B. Turnhout: Brepols, 2009.

Duval, Y. -M. "L'originalité du *De virginibus* dans le mouvement ascétique occidental." In *Ambroise de Milan: XVIe centenaire de son élection épiscopale*, edited by Y.-M. Duval, 9–66. Paris: Études Augustiniennes, 1974.

Dyer, Joseph. "The Desert, the City and Psalmody in the Late Fourth Century." In *Western Plainchant in the First Millennium: Studies in the Medieval Liturgy and Its Music*, edited by Sean Galagher et al., 11–43. Aldershot, Hants: Ashgate Press, 2004.

———. "The Psalms in Monastic Prayer." In *The Place of the Psalms in the Intellectual Culture in the Middle Ages*, edited by Nancy van Deusen, 59–90. SUNY Series in Medieval Studies. Albany: State University of New York Press, 1999.

Dysinger, Luke. *Psalmody and Prayer in the Writings of Evagrius Ponticus*. Oxford Theological Monographs. Oxford: Oxford University Press, 2005.

Elm, Susanna. *Virgins of God: The Making of Asceticism in Late Antiquity*. Oxford: Clarendon Press, 1994.

Ernest, James D. "Athanasius of Alexandria: The Scope of Scripture in Polemical and Pastoral Context." *Vigiliae Christianae* 47 (1993): 341–62.

———. *The Bible in Athanasius of Alexandria*. Boston: Brill Academic Publishers, 2004.

Ettlinger, Gerard H., ed., *Eranistes*. Oxford: Clarendon Press, 1975.

———. *Theodoret of Cyrus: Eranistes*. Washington, DC: Catholic University of America Press, 2003.

Ferguson, Everett. "Psalm-Singing at the Eucharist: A Liturgical Controversy in the Fourth Century." *Austin Seminary Bulletin* 98 (1983): 52–77.

Fiedrowicz, Michael. "'Ciues sanctae ciuitatis Dei omnes affectiones rectas habent' (Ciu. 14, 9): Terapia delle passioni e preghiera in S. Agostino." *Studia Ephemeridis Augustinianum* 53 (1996): 431–40.

———. *Psalmus Vox Totius Christi: Studien zu Augustins Enarrationes in Psalmos*. Freiburg: Herder, 1997.

Fischer, Balthasar. "Die Psalmenfrömmigkeit der Märtyrerkirche." In *Die Psalmen als Stimme der Kirche: Gesammelte Studien zur christlichen Psalmenfrömmigkeit*, edited by A. Heinz. Trier: Paulinus, 1982.

Fossas, Ignasi M. "L'Epistola ad Marcellinum di Sant'Atanasio sull'uso cristiano del Salterio: Studio letterario, liturgico e teologico." *Studia Monastica* 39 (1997): 27–74.

Foucault, Michel. *The History of Sexuality.* 3 vols. Translated by Robert Hurley. New York: Random House, 1979–86.

———. "Technologies of the Self." In *Technologies of the Self: A Seminar with Michel Foucault*, edited by Luther H. Martin, Huck Gutman, and Patrick H. Hutton, 16–49. Amherst: University of Massachusetts Press, 1988.

Frank, Georgia. "The Memory Palace of Marcellinus: Athanasius and the Mirror of the Psalms." In *Ascetic Culture: Essays in Honor of Philip Rousseau*, edited by Blake Leyerle and Robin Darling Young, 97–124. Notre Dame, IN: University of Notre Dame Press, 2013.

Frankenberg, Wilhelm, ed. *Euagrius Pontikos.* Abhandlungen der Königlichen Gesellschaft der Wissenschaften zu Göttingen, Philologisch-historische Klasse, Neue Folge, 13.2. Berlin: Weidmannsche Buchhandlung, 1912.

Franz, Egon. *"Totus Christus*: Studien über Christus und die Kirche bei Augustin." Inaugural-Dissertation, University of Bonn, 1956.

Freud, Sigmund. *Five Lectures on Psycho-Analysis.* Edited and translated by James Strachey. New York: W. W. Norton, 1977.

Géhin, Paul. *Évagre le Pontique Scholies a L'Ecclésiaste.* SC 397. Paris: Cerf, 1993.

———. *Évagre le Pontique Scholies aux Proverbes.* SC 340. Paris: Cerf, 1987.

———. "Evagriana d'un Manuscrit Basilien (*Vaticanus Gr. 2028; olim Basilianus* 67)." *Muséon* 109 (1996): 59–85.

Gélineau, Joseph. "Les psaumes à l'époque patristique." *Maison-Dieu* 135 (1978): 99–116.

Gillette, Gertrude. "The Glory of God in Augustine's *Enarrationes in Psalmos*." PhD diss., Catholic University of America, 1996.

Goffinet, Emile. *L'utilisation d'Origène dans le commentaire des Psaumes de Saint Hilaire de Poitiers.* Studia Hellenistica 14. Louvain: Publications Universitaires, 1965.

Gori, Franco, ed. *Verginità e vedovanza.* 2 vols. Opera omnia di sant'Ambrogio 14.2. Rome: Città Nuova Editrice, 1989.

Grabowski, Stanislaus. *The Church: An Introduction to the Theology of St. Augustine.* St. Louis, MO: B. Herder, 1957.

Green, R. P. H., trans. *Saint Augustine: On Christian Teaching.* Oxford: Oxford University Press, 1999.

Greer, Rowan. *Theodore of Mopsuestia, Exegete and Theologian.* Westminster: Faith Press, 1961.

Gregg, Robert C., and Dennis E. Groh. *Early Arianism: A View of Salvation*. Philadelphia: Fortress Press, 1981.

Grillmeier, Aloys. *Christ in Christian Tradition: From the Apostolic Age to Chalcedon (451)*. Rev. ed. Translated by John Bowden. Atlanta: John Knox Press, 1975.

Grünbeck, Elisabeth. *Christologische Schriftargumentation und Bildersprache: Zum Konflikt zwischen Metapherninterpretation und dogmatischen Schriftbeweistraditionen in der patristischen Auslegung des 44. (45.) Psalms*. Leiden: Brill, 1994.

Guillaumont, Antoine, and Claire Guillaumont, eds. *Évagre le Pontique. Traité pratique, ou Le moine*. 2 vols. SC 170–71. Paris: Cerf, 1971.

Guinot, Jean-Noël. *L'exégèse de Théodoret de Cyr*. Paris: Beauchesne, 1995.

———. "L'importance de la dette de Théodoret de Cyr à l'égard de l'exégèse de Théodore de Mopsueste." *Orpheus* 5 (1984): 68–109.

———. "Théodoret à-t-il lu les homélies d'Origène sur l'ancien Testament?" *Vetera Christianorum* 21 (1984): 285–312.

Hadot, Ilsetraut. "Les introductions aux commentaires exégétiques chez les auteurs néoplatoniciens et les auteurs chrétiens." In *Les règles de l'interprétation*, edited by Michel Tardieu, 99–122. Paris: Cerf, 1987.

Hadot, Pierre. *The Inner Citadel: The Meditations of Marcus Aurelius*. Translated by Michael Chase. Cambridge, MA: Harvard University Press, 1998.

———. *Philosophy as a Way of Life: Spiritual Exercises from Socrates to Foucault*, edited by Arnold Davidson. Translated by Michael Chase. Cambridge, MA: Blackwell. 1995.

———. *What Is Ancient Philosophy?* Translated by Michael Chase. Cambridge, MA: Harvard University Press, 2002.

Hamilton, Andrew. "Athanasius and the Simile of the Mirror." *Vigiliae Christianae* 34 (1980): 14–18.

Hamman, Adalbert-G. *La prière*. Vol. 2. *Les trois premiers siècles*. Paris: Desclée, 1963.

Hanson, R. P. C. *Allegory and Event*. Richmond, VA: John Knox Press, 1959.

Harl, Marguerite, ed. and trans. *La Chaîne palestinienne sur le psaume 118 (Origène, Eusèbe, Didyme, Apollinaire, Athanase, Théodoret)*. SC 189–190. Paris: Cerf, 1972.

———. *Sur les écritures: Philocalie, 1–20*. SC 302. Paris: Cerf, 1983.

Harmless, William. *Augustine and the Catechumenate*. Collegeville, MN: Liturgical Press, 1995.

———, trans. *Augustine: In His Own Words*. Washington, DC: Catholic University of America Press, 2010.

Harnack, Adolph. *History of Dogma.* Vol. 5. Translated by Neil Buchanan. 1900. Reprint, New York: Dover, 1961.

Harpham, Geoffrey. *The Ascetic Imperative in Culture and Criticism.* Chicago: University of Chicago Press, 1987.

Harrison, Carol. *The Art of Listening in the Early Church.* Oxford: Oxford University Press, 2013.

———. "Enchanting the Soul: The Music of the Psalms." In *Meditations of the Heart: The Psalms in Early Christian Thought and Practice*, edited by Andreas Andreopoulos, Augustine Casiday, and Carol Harrison, 205–23. Studia traditionis theologiae 8. Turnhout: Brepols, 2011.

Harrison, Verna E. F. "The Feminine Man in Late Antique Ascetic Piety." *Union Seminary Quarterly Review* 48 (1994): 49–71.

———. "Male and Female in Cappadocian Theology," *Journal of Theological Studies*, n.s., 41 (1990): 441–71.

———. "The Maleness of Christ." *St. Vladimir's Theological Quarterly* 42 (1998): 111–51.

Hays, Richard B. "Christ Prays the Psalms: Israel's Psalter as the Matrix of Early Christology." In *The Conversion of the Imagination: Paul as Interpreter of Israel's Scripture,* 101–18. Grand Rapids, MI: Eerdmans, 2005.

———. *Echoes of Scripture in the Letters of Paul.* New Haven, CT: Yale University Press, 1989.

Heine, Ronald E. "The Form of Gregory of Nyssa's Treatise *On the Inscriptions of the Psalms.*" *Studia Patristica* 32 (1997): 130–35.

———. *Gregory of Nyssa's Treatise on the Inscriptions of the Psalms.* Oxford Early Christian Studies. Oxford: Clarendon Press, 1995.

———. "The Introduction to Origen's *Commentary on John* Compared with the Introductions to the Ancient Philosophical Commentaries on Aristotle." In *Origeniana Sexta: Origène et la Bible/Origen and the Bible. Actes du Colloquium Origenianum Sextum Chantilly, 30 août–3 septembre 1993*, edited by Gilles Dorival and Alain Le Boulluec, 3–12. Leuven: Peeters, 1995.

———. *Origen: Scholarship in the Service of the Church.* Christian Theology in Context. Oxford: Oxford University Press, 2010.

Heither, T., ed. and trans. *Origenes commentarii in epistulam ad Romanos.* Fontes Christiani 2/1. Freiburg: Herder, 1990.

Henry, Nathalie. "The Song of Songs and the Liturgy of the *Velatio* in the Fourth Century: From Literary Metaphor to Liturgical Reality." In *Continuity and Change in Christian Worship: Papers Read at the 1997 Summer Meeting and the 1998 Winter Meeting of the Ecclesiastical History Society*, edited by R. N. Swanson, 18–28. Woodbridge: Boydell, 1999.

Heydemann, Gerda. "Biblical Israel and the Christian *Gentes*: Social Metaphors and Concepts of Community in Cassiodorus' *Expositio psalmorum*." In *Strategies of Identification: Early Medieval Perspectives*, edited by Walter Pohl and Gerda Heydemann, 143–208. Cultural Encounters in Late Antiquity and the Middle Ages 13. Turnhout: Brepols, 2013.

Hijmans, B. L. *Askesis: Notes on Epictetus' Educational System*. Wijsgerige teksten en studies 2. Assen: Van Gorcum, 1959.

Hill, Robert C. "His Master's Voice: Theodore of Mopsuestia on the Psalms." *Heythrop Journal* 45 (2004): 40–53.

———. "Psalm 41 (42): A Classic Text for Antiochene Spirituality." *Irish Theological Quarterly* 68 (2003): 25–33.

———. "The Spirituality of Chrysostom's Commentary on the Psalms." *Journal of Early Christian Studies* (1997): 569–79.

———. "Theodoret, Commentator on the Psalms." *Ephemerides Theologicae Lovanienses* 76 (2000): 88–104.

———, trans. *Theodoret of Cyrus: Commentary on the Psalms*. 2 vols. FC 101–2. Washington, DC: Catholic University of America Press, 2000.

———, trans. *Theodore of Mopsuestia: Commentary on the Psalms*. Atlanta, GA: Society of Biblical Literature, 2006.

Hirshman, Marc. *A Rivalry of Genius: Jewish and Christian Biblical Interpretation in Late Antiquity*. Albany: State University of New York Press, 1996.

Hofer, Andrew. "Matthew 25:31–46 as an Hermeneutical Rule in Augustine's *Enarrationes in Psalmos*." *Downside Review* 126 (2010): 285–300.

Holladay, William Lee. *The Psalms through Three Thousand Years: Prayerbook of a Cloud of Witnesses*. Minneapolis, MN: Fortress Press, 1993.

Hollerich, Michael J. "Eusebius' Commentary on the Psalms and Its Place in the Origins of Christian Biblical Scholarship." In *Eusebius of Caesarea: Tradition and Innovations*, edited by Aaron P. Johnson and Jeremy M. Schott, 151–65. Hellenic Studies 60. Washington, DC: Center for Hellenic Studies, 2013.

Hombert, Pierre-Marie. "La christologie des trente-deux premières *Ennarationes in psalmos* de saint Augustin." In *Augustin, philosohie et prédicateur: Hommage à Goulven Madec*, edited by Isabelle Bochet, 431–63. Turnhout: Brepols, 2012.

Horner, George W., ed. *The Statutes of the Apostles, or, Canones ecclesiastici*. London: Williams and Norgate, 1904.

Hunter, David G. "Clerical Celibacy and the Veiling of Virgins: New Boundaries in Late Ancient Christianity." In *The Limits of Ancient Christianity: Essays on Late Antique Thought and Culture in Honor of R.A. Markus*, edited by W. Klingshir and M. Vessey, 139–52. Ann Arbor: University of Michigan Press, 1999.

————. "Helvidius, Jovinian, and the Virginity of Mary in Late Fourth-Century Rome." *Journal of Early Christian Studies* 1 (1993): 47–71.

————. *Marriage, Celibacy and Heresy in Ancient Christianity: The Jovinianist Controversy.* Oxford Early Christian Studies. Oxford: Oxford University Press, 2007.

————. "Resistance to the Virginal Ideal in Late-Fourth-Century Rome: The Case of Jovinian." *Theological Studies* 48 (1987): 45–64.

Irigoin, Jean, et al., eds. *Le Psautier chez les Pères.* Strasbourg: Centre d'Analyse et de Documentation Patristiques, 1994.

Janko, Richard, ed. *Philodemus: On Poems.* Oxford: Oxford University Press, 2000.

Jay, Pierre. "Jérôme à Bethléem: Les Tractatus in Psalmos." In *Jérôme entre l'Occident et l'Orient: Actes du Colloque de Chantilly,* edited by Y.-M. Duval, 367–88. Paris: Études Augustiniennes, 1988.

Jeffrey, Peter. "Monastic Reading and Roman Chant." In *Western Plainchant in the First Millennium Western Plainchant in the First Millennium: Studies in the Medieval Liturgy and Its Music,* edited by Sean Galagher, et al., 45–103. Aldershot, Hants: Ashgate, 2004.

Jenson, Robert. "Hermeneutics and the Life of the Church." In *Reclaiming the Bible for the Church,* edited by C. Braaten and R. Jenson, 89–105. Grand Rapids, MI: Eerdmans, 1995.

Jones, Daniel J. *Christus Sacerdos in the Preaching of St. Augustine.* Patrologia 14. Frankfurt: Peter Lang, 2004.

Jonkers, E. J. ed. *Acta et Symbola Conciliorum quae saeculo quarto habita sunt.* Leiden: Brill, 1954.

Juel, Donald. *Messianic Exegesis.* Philadelphia: Fortress Press, 1988.

Junod, Éric, ed. *Sur le libre arbitre: Philocalie 21–27.* Paris: Cerf, 1976.

Kalvesmaki, Joel. "The *Epistula fidei* of Evagrius of Pontus: An Answer to Constantinople." *Journal of Early Christian Studies* 20 (2012): 113–39.

Kannengiesser, Charles. "Athanasius of Alexandria and the Ascetic Movement of His Time." In *Asceticism,* edited by Vincent L. Wimbush and Richard Valantasis, 479–92. Oxford: Oxford University Press, 1995.

————. *Handbook of Patristic Exegesis.* 2 vols. The Bible in Ancient Christianity 1. Leiden: Brill, 2004.

Kaufman, Yehezqel. *Toledot ha-Emunah ha-Yisraelit* [*The Religion of Israel: From Its Beginnings to the Babylonian Exile*]. 8 vols. Jerusalem: Mosad Bialik, 1960.

Kelly, J. N. D. *Jerome: His Life, Writings, and Controversies.* New York: Harper and Row, 1975.

Kelly, Niel. "La persona del *totus Christus*: Interpretación christiana de san Augustín." *Augustinus* 36 (1991): 147–53.

Kerrigan, Alexander. *St. Cyril of Alexandria: Interpreter of the Old Testament.* Analecta biblica 2. Rome: Pontifical Biblical Institute, 1952.

Kindstrand, J. F., ed. *[Plutarchi]: De Homero.* Edited by J. F. Kindstrand. Leipzig: Teubner, 1990.

King, Karen L. "Which Early Christianity?" In *The Oxford Handbook of Early Christian Studies,* edited by Susan Ashbrook Harvey and David G. Hunter, 66–85. Oxford Handbooks in Religion and Theology. New York: Oxford University Press, 2008.

Kinzig, Wolfram. *In Search of Asterius: Studies on the Authorship of the Homilies on the Psalms.* Göttingen: Vandenhoeck and Ruprecht, 1990.

Kolbet, Paul R. "Rethinking the Rationales for Origen's Use of Allegory." *Studia Patristica* 56 (2013): 41–50.

Komonchak, Joseph A. *Foundations in Ecclesiology.* Boston: Boston College, 1995.

Konstantinovsky, Julia. *Evagrius Ponticus: The Making of a Gnostic.* Farnham: Ashgate, 2009.

Kraemer, Ross S. "Women and Gender." In *The Oxford Handbook of Early Christian Studies,* edited by Susan Ashbrook Harvey and David G. Hunter, 465–92. Oxford Handbooks in Religion and Theology. New York: Oxford University Press, 2008.

Kramer, Bärbel. "Eine Psalmenhomilie aus dem Tura-Fund." *Zeitschrift für Papyrologie und Epigraphik* 16 (1975): 164–213.

Kuffler, Matthew. *The Manly Eunuch: Masculinity, Gender Ambiguity and Christian Ideology in Late Antiquity.* Chicago: University of Chicago Press, 2001.

Kugel, James. "Topics in the History of the Spirituality of the Psalms." In *Jewish Spirituality.* 2 vols, edited by Arthur Green, 1: 113–44. New York: Crossroads, 1986–87.

Lamberton, Robert. *Homer the Theologian.* Berkeley: University of California Press, 1986.

Lambros, S. P. *Catalogue of the Greek Manuscripts on Mount Athos.* 2 vols. Cambridge: Cambridge University Press, 1900.

Lamirande, Émilien. *L'église céleste selon saint Augustin.* Paris: Études Augustiniennes, 1963.

Lampe, G. W. H., and K. J. Woollcombe. *Essays on Typology.* Naperville, IL: Alec R. Allenson, 1956.

Leroy, Guy. "'Saul, Saul, pourquoi me persecutes-tu?,' Ac 9,4b, dans le predication de saint Augustin." PhD diss., Institut d'études théologiques [Brussels], 1986.

Levenson, Jon. *Creation and the Persistence of Evil.* San Francisco: Harper and Row, 1985.

Lewis, George. *The Philocalia of Origen*. Edinburgh: T. and T. Clark, 1911.

Lindars, Barnabas. *New Testament Apologetic*. London: SCM Press, 1961.

Loewen, Howard J. "The Use of Scripture in Augustine's Theology." *Scottish Journal of Theology* 34 (1981): 201–24.

Lonergan, Bernard J. F. *Method in Theology*. New York: Herder and Herder, 1972.

Lossau, Manfred J. *Untersuchungen zur antiken Demosthenesexegese*. Palingenesia 2. Bad Homburg: H. M. Gehlen, 1964.

Louth, Andrew. *Maximus the Confessor*. London: Routledge, 1996.

Lunn-Rockliffe, Sophie. "Bishops on the Chair of Pestilence: Ambrosiaster's Polemical Exegesis of Psalm 1:1." *Journal of Early Christian Studies* 19 (2011): 79–99.

Lutz, Cora E., ed. and trans. *Musonius Rufus: "The Roman Socrates."* Yale Classical Studies 10. New Haven, CT: Yale University Press, 1947.

Madec, Goulven. *La patrie et la voie: Le Christ dans la vie et la pensée de saint Augustin*. Paris: Desclée, 1989.

Magistris, Simon de, ed. *Acta Martyrum ad Ostia Tibernia sub Claudio Gothico*. Rome, 1795.

Malherbe, Abraham J. *Ancient Epistolary Theorists*. Atlanta, GA: Scholars Press, 1988.

Malinowski, Bronislaw. "The Problem of Meaning in Primitive Languages." In *The Meaning of Meaning: A Study of the Influence of Language upon Thought and of the Science of Symbolism*, ed. I. A. Richards and C. K. Ogden, 451–510. New York: Harcourt, Brace, 1923.

Mansfeld, Jaap. *Prolegomena: Questions to Be Settled before the Study of an Author, or a Text*. Philosophia Antiqua 61. Leiden: Brill, 1994.

Markus, Robert A. *The End of Ancient Christianity*. Cambridge: Cambridge University Press, 1990.

———. *Signs and Meanings: World and Text in Ancient Christianity*. Liverpool: Liverpool University Press, 1996.

Marrou, Henri-Irénée. *Histoire de l'éducation dans l'Antiquité*. 6th ed. Paris: Seuil, 1964.

———. *Théologie de l'histoire*. Paris: Seuil, 1968.

———. *Time and Timeliness*. Trans. Violet Nevile. New York: Sheed and Ward, 1969.

Martens, Peter. "Revisiting the Allegory/Typology Distinction: The Case of Origen." *Journal of Early Christian Studies* 16 (2008): 283–317.

Maur, Hansjorg auf der. *Die Psalmenverständnis des Ambrosius von Mailand: Ein Beitrag zum Deutungshintergrund der Psalmenverwendung im Gottesdienst der Alten Kirche*. Leiden: Brill, 1977.

Mayeski, Marie Anne. "Quaestio Disputata: Catholic Theology and the History of Exegesis." *Theological Studies* 62 (2001): 140–53.

McCarthy, Michael C. "An Ecclesiology of Groaning: Augustine, the Psalms, and the Making of Church." *Theological Studies* 66 (2005): 23–48.

———. "*Expectatio Beatitudinis*: The Eschatological Frame of Hilary of Poitiers' *Tractatus super Psalmos*." In *In the Shadow of the Incarnation: Essays on Jesus Christ in the Early Church in Honor of Brian E. Daley, S.J.*, edited by Peter W. Martens, 50–70. Notre Dame, IN: University of Notre Dame Press, 2008.

———. "The Revelatory Psalm: A Fundamental Theology of Augustine's *Enarrationes in Psalmos*." PhD diss., University of Notre Dame, 2003.

McGinn, Bernard. *The Foundations of Mysticism: Origins to the Fifth Century*. New York: Crossroads, 1995.

McGuckin, John A. "Origen's Use of the Psalms in the Treatise *On First Principles*." In *Meditations of the Heart: The Psalms in Early Christian Thought and Practice*, edited by Andreas Andreopoulos, Augustine Casiday, and Carol Harrison, 97–118. Studia traditionis theologiae 8. Turnhout: Brepols, 2011.

———. *St. Cyril of Alexandria: The Christological Controversy*. Leiden: Brill, 1994.

McKinnon, James W. "The Book of Psalms, Monasticism, and the Western Liturgy." In *The Place of the Psalms in the Intellectual Culture in the Middle Ages*, edited by Nancy van Deusen, 43–57. SUNY Series in Medieval Studies. Albany: State University of New York Press, 1999.

———. "Desert Monasticism and the Later Fourth-Century Psalmodic Movement." *Music and Letters* 75 (1994): 505–21.

———. "The Fourth Century Origin of the Gradual." *Early Music History* 7 (1987): 91–106.

———. *Music in Early Christian Literature*. Cambridge: Cambridge University Press, 1983.

McLynn, Neil B. *Ambrose of Milan: Church and Court in the Christian Capital*. The Transformation of the Classical Heritage 22. Berkeley: University of California Press, 1994.

Mercati, G., ed. *Osservazioni a Proemi del Salterio, di Origene, Ippolito, Eusebio, Cirillo Alessandrino e altri*. Studi e testi 142. Vatican City: Biblioteca Apostolica Vaticana, 1948.

Meredith, Anthony. *Gregory of Nyssa*. London: Routledge, 1999.

Mersch, Emile. *The Whole Christ*. Translated by J. R. Kelly. Milwaukee, WI: Bruce, 1938. Originally published as *Le corps mystique du Christ* (Louvain: Museum Lessianum, 1936).

Metz, René. *La consécration des vierges dans l'église romaine*. Paris: Presses Universitaires de France, 1954.

Meyendorff, John. *Byzantine Theology: Historical Trends and Doctrinal Themes.* New York: Fordham University Press, 1974.

———. *Christ in Eastern Christian Thought.* Crestwood, NY: St. Vladimir's Seminary Press, 1987.

Mühlenberg, Ekkehard. *Psalmenkommentare aus der Katenenüberlieferung.* 3 vols. PTS, 15, 16, 19. Berlin: De Gruyter, 1975–78.

Müller, Hildegund. "Theory and Practice of Preaching: Augustine, *De doctrina christiana* and *Enarrationes in psalmos.*" *Studia Patristica* 38 (2001): 233–37.

Munier, Charles, ed. *Concilia Africae, a. 345–a. 525.* CCSL 149. Turnholt: Brepols, 1974.

Nautin, Pierre. *Origène: Sa vie et son œuvre.* Paris: Beauchesne, 1977.

Neuschäfer, Bernhard. *Origenes als Philologe.* Schweizerische Beiträge zur Altertumswissenschaft 18/1–2. Basel: Friedrich Reinhardt, 1987.

Newman, Robert J. "*Cotidie Meditare*: Theory and Practice of the *Meditatio* in Imperial Stoicism." In *Philosophie, Wissenschaften, Technik: Philosophie (Stoizismus)*, edited by Wolfgang Haase, ANRW 2.36.3, 1473–1517. Berlin: De Gruyter, 1989.

Newsom, Carol A. "The Case of the Blinking I: Discourse of the Self at Qumran." *Semeia* 57 (1992): 13–23.

Niewiadomski, Jozef. "Gewaltheit und die Konzeption des 'Totus Christus'?" *Augustiniana* 41 (1991): 567–74.

Nodes, Daniel J. "The Organization of Augustine's *Psalmus contra Partem Donati.*" *Vigiliae Christianae* 63 (2009): 390–408.

Nussbaum, Martha C. *The Therapy of Desire: Theory and Practice in Hellenistic Ethics.* Martin Classical Lectures, n.s. 2. Princeton, NJ: Princeton University Press, 1994.

Oden, Amy Germaine. "Dominant Images for the Church in Augustine's *Enarrationes in Psalmos*: A Study in Augustine's Ecclesiology." PhD diss., Southern Methodist University, 1990.

O'Donnell, James J. "Bible." In *Augustine through the Ages: An Encyclopedia*, edited by Allan D. Fitzgerald, 99–103. Grand Rapids, MI: Eerdmans, 1999.

O'Keefe, John J. "Impassible Suffering? Divine Passion and Fifth-Century Christology." *Theological Studies* 58 (1997): 39–60.

———. "Interpreting the Angel. Cyril of Alexandria and Theodoret of Cyrus: Commentators on the Book of Malachi." PhD diss., Catholic University of America, 1993.

———. "A Letter That Killeth: Toward a Reassessment of Antiochene Exegesis, or Diodore, Theodore, and Theodoret on the Psalms." *Journal of Early Christian Studies* 8 (2000): 83–104.

————. "Rejecting One's Masters: Theodoret of Cyrus, Antiochene Exegesis, and the Patristic Mainstream." In *Syriac and Antiochian Exegesis and Biblical Theology for the 3rd Millennium*, edited by Robert D. Miller. Piscataway, NJ: Gorgias Press, 2008.

O'Keefe, John J., and R. R. Reno. *Sanctified Vision: An Introduction to Early Christian Interpretation of the Bible*. Baltimore: Johns Hopkins University Press, 2005.

Ong, Walter J. *Orality and Literacy: The Technologizing of the Word*. New Accents. New York: Methuen, 1982.

Ormerod, Neil. "The Structure of a Systematic Ecclesiology." *Theological Studies* 63 (2002): 3–30.

Pappas, Harry Spero. "Theodore of Mopsuestia's Commentary on Psalm 44 (LXX): A Study of Exegesis and Christology." *Greek Orthodox Theological Review* 47 (2002): 55–79.

Parvis, Paul. "Theodoret's Commentary on the Epistles of St. Paul: Historical Setting and Exegetical Practice." PhD diss., Oxford University, 1975.

Pásztori-Kupán, István. *Theodoret of Cyrus*. New York: Routledge, 2006.

Peri, Vittorio. *Omelie Origeniane sui Salmi: Contributo all'identificazione del testo latino*. Studi e testi 289. Rome: Biblioteca Apostolica Vaticana, 1980.

Perkins, Judith. *The Suffering Self: Pain and Narrative Representation in the Early Christian Era*. London: Routledge, 1995.

Perrone, Lorenzo. "Rediscovering Origen Today: First Impressions of the New Collection of Homilies on the Psalms in the *Codex monacensis Graecus* 314." *Studia Patristica* 56 (2013): 103–22.

Pitra, J. B., ed. *Origenes in Psalmos*. AS 2. Paris: A. Jouby and Roger, 1884.

Porter, James. "Content and Form in Philodemus: The History of an Evasion." In *Philodemus and Poetry: Poetic Theory and Practice in Lucretius, Philodemus and Horace*, edited by Dirk Obbink, 97–147. New York: Oxford University Press, 1995.

Price, R. M., trans. *Lives of the Monks of Palestine*. Kalamazoo, MI: Cistercian Publications, 1991.

Prinzivalli, E., ed. *Origène: Homélies sur les Psaumes 36 à 38*. SC 411. Paris: Cerf, 1995.

Rabbow, Paul. *Seelenführung: Methodik der Exerzitien in der Antike*. Munich: Kösel-Verlag, 1954.

Ramsey, Boniface. *Ambrose*. The Early Church Fathers. New York: Routledge, 1997.

Refoulé, F. "La christologie d'Évagre et l'Origénisme." *Orientalia Christiana Periodica* 27 (1961): 221–66.

Régnault, Lucien. *La vie quotidienne des pères du désert en Égypte au IVe siècle*. Paris: Hachette, 1990.

Réveillaud, Michel. "Le Christ-Homme, tête de l'église: Étude d'ecclésiologie selon les *Enarrationes in Psalmos* d'Augustin." *Recherches Augustiniennes* 5 (1968): 67–94.

Reydams-Schils, Gretchen. "Roman and Stoic: The Self as a Mediator." *Dionysius* 16 (1998): 35–62.

———. *The Roman Stoics: Self, Responsibility, and Affection.* Chicago: University of Chicago Press, 2005.

Richard, Marcel. "Les premières chaînes sur le Psautier." *Bulletin d'Information de l'Institut de Recherche et d'Histoire des Textes* 5 (1956): 87–98.

Ricoeur, Paul. *Interpretation Theory: Discourse and the Surplus of Meaning.* Fort Worth: Texas Christian University Press, 1976.

———. *The Rule of Metaphor: Multi-disciplinary Studies of the Creation of Meaning in Language.* Translated by Robert Czerny. Toronto: University of Toronto Press, 1977.

Rietz, Walter. *De Origenis Prologis in Psalterium: Quaestiones selectae.* Jena: Pohle, 1914.

Risch, Franz Xaver. "Die Prologe des Origenes zum Psalter." In *Origeniana Decima,* edited by Sylwia Kaczmarek and Henryk Pietras, 475–90. Leuven: Peeters, 2011.

Robitaille, Lucien. "L'église, épouse du Christ, dans l'interprétation patristique du Psaume 44 (45)." *Laval Théologique et Philosophique* 26 (1970): 167–79, 279–306; 27 (1971): 41–65.

Rondeau, Marie-Josèphe. "Le commentaire sur les Psaumes d'Evagre le Pontique." *Orientalia Christiana Periodica* 26 (1960): 307–48.

———. *Les commentaires patristiques du Psautier (IIIe–Ve siècles).* 2 vols. OCA 219–20. Rome: Pontificium Institutum Studiorum Orientalium, 1982–85.

———. "L'élucidation des interlocuteurs des Psaumes et le développement dogmatique (III–V siècles)." In *Liturgie und Dichtung: Ein interdisziplinäres Kompendium,* edited by H. Becker and R. Kaczynski, 509–77. St. Ottilien: EOS, 1983.

———. "L'Épître à Marcellinus sur les Psaumes." *Vigiliae Christianae* 22 (1968): 176–97.

Rose, André. *Les Psaumes: Voix du Christ et de l'église.* Paris: P. Lethielleux, 1981.

Rossi, Maria Assunta. "Ancora sul Commento ai Salmi di Cirillo: A propositio di un recente lavoro sui commentari patristici al Salterio." *Annali di Storia dell'Esegesi* 1 (1984): 45–52.

Rousseau, Philip. *Basil of Caesarea.* Berkeley: University of California Press, 1994.

Russell, Donald A. *Criticism in Antiquity.* Berkeley: University of California Press, 1981.

Russell, Donald A., and Michael Winterbottom, ed. and trans. *Classical Literary Criticism.* World's Classics. Oxford: Oxford University Press, 1989.

Sahlins, Marshall. *Culture and Practical Reason*. Chicago: University of Chicago Press, 1976.

Schlieben, Reinhard. *Christliche Theologie und Philologie in der Spätantike: Die schulwissenschaftlichen Methoden der Psalmenexegese Cassiodors*. Berlin: De Gruyter, 1974.

Schneiders, Sandra M. *The Revelatory Text: Interpreting the New Testament as Sacred Scripture*. Collegeville, MN: Liturgical Press, 1999.

Sheerin, Daniel. "The Role of Prayer in Origen's Homilies." In *Origen of Alexandria: His World and His Legacy*, edited by Charles Kannengiesser and William L. Petersen, 200–214. Christianity and Judaism in Antiquity 1. Notre Dame, IN: University of Notre Dame Press, 1988.

Sherwood, Polycarp. *An Annotated Date-List of the Works of Maximus the Confessor*. Studia anselmiana 30. Rome: Herder, 1952.

———. "Notes on Maximus the Confessor." *American Benedictine Review* 1 (1950): 350–53.

Sieben, Herman-Joseph. "Athanasius über den Psalter: Analyse seines Briefes an Marcellinus." *Theologie und Philosophie* 48 (1973): 157–73.

Slusser, Michael. "The Exegetical Roots of Trinitarian Theology." *Theological Studies* 49 (1988): 461–76.

Smith, John Arthur. *Music in Ancient Judaism and Early Christianity*. Burlington, VT: Ashgate, 2011.

Soloveitchik, H. "Migration, Acculturation, and the New Role of Texts in the Haredi World." In *Accounting for Fundamentalisms*, edited by Martin Marty, 4: 197–235. Chicago: University of Chicago Press, 1994.

Springer, Carl P. E. "The *Prosopopoeia* of Church as Mother in Augustine's *Psalmus contra Partem Donati*." *Augustinian Studies* 18 (1987): 52–65.

Stead, G. C. "St. Athanasius on the Psalms." *Vigiliae Christianae* 39 (1985): 65–78.

Stewart, Columba. *Cassian the Monk*. Oxford: Clarendon Press, 1998.

———. "Evagrius Ponticus on Monastic Pedagogy." In *Abba, the Tradition of Orthodoxy in the West: Festschrift for Bishop Kallistos (Ware) of Diokleia*, edited by John Behr, Andrew Louth, and Dimitri Conomos, 241–71. Crestwood, NY: St. Vladimir's Seminary Press, 2003.

———. "Imageless Prayer and the Theological Vision of Evagrius Ponticus." *Journal of Early Christian Studies* 9 (2001): 173–204.

———. "Prayer." In *The Oxford Handbook of Early Christian Studies*, edited by Susan Ashbrook Harvey and David G. Hunter, 744–63. Oxford Handbooks in Religion and Theology. New York: Oxford University Press, 2008.

———. "The Use of Biblical Texts in Prayer and the Formation of Early Monastic Culture." *American Benedictine Review* 62 (2011): 188–201.

———. *"Working the Earth of the Heart": The Messalian Controversy in History, Texts, and Language to AD 431*. Oxford Theological Monographs. Oxford: Oxford University Press, 1991.

Stowers, Stanley K. "Romans 7.7–25 as a Speech-in-Character (*prosopopoiía*)." In *Paul in His Hellenistic Context*, edited by Troels Engberg-Pederesen, 180–202. Minneapolis, MN: Augsburg Fortress Press, 1995.

Stramara, Daniel F., Jr. "Double Monasticism in the Greek East, Fourth through Eighth Centuries." *Journal of Early Christian Studies* 6 (1998): 269–312.

Studer, Basil. *The Grace of Christ and the Grace of God in Augustine of Hippo*. Translated by M. J. O'Connell. Collegeville, MN: Liturgical Press, 1997.

Sunderland, Anne. "Daniel of Salah: A Sixth Century West Syrian Interpreter of the Psalms." *Byzantinische Forschungen* 24 (1997): 51–61.

Suydam, Mary. "An Introduction to Performance Studies." In *Performance and Transformation: New Approaches to Late Medieval Spirituality*, edited by Mary A. Suydam and Joanna E. Ziegler, 1–26. New York: St. Martin's Press, 1999.

Taft, Robert. "Christian Liturgical Psalmody: Origins, Development, Decomposition, Collapse." In *Psalms in Community: Jewish and Christian Textual, Liturgical, and Artistic Traditions*, edited by Harold W. Attridge and Margot E. Fassler, 7–32. Atlanta, GA: Society of Biblical Literature, 2003.

———. *The Liturgy of the Hours in East and West*. Collegeville, MN: Liturgical Press, 1993.

Tamburrino, Pio. "Osservazioni sulla sezione cristologica dell' *Hom. In Ps. XLIV* di San Basilio." *Revista di Cultura Classica e Medioevale* 8 (1966): 229–39.

Taylor, Charles. *The Sources of the Self: The Making of the Modern Identity*. Cambridge, MA: Harvard University Press, 1989.

Taylor, David G. K. "The Christology of the Syriac Psalm Commentary (AD 541/2) of Daniel of Salah and the 'Phantasiast' Controversy." *Studia Patristica* 35 (2001): 508–15.

———. "The Great Psalm Commentary of Daniel of Salah." *Harp* 11–12 (1998–99): 33–42.

———. "The Manuscript Tradition of Daniel of Salah's Psalm Commentary." In *Symposium Syriacum VII: Uppsala University, Department of Asian and African Languages, 11–14 August 1996*, edited by René Lavenant, 61–69. Orientalia Christiana analecta 256. Roma: Pontificio Istituto Orientale, 1998.

———. "The Psalm Commentary of Daniel of Salah and the Formation of Sixth-Century Syrian Orthodox Identity." *Church History and Religious Culture* 89:1–3 (2009): 65–92.

————. "The Psalm Headings in the West Syrian Tradition." In *The Peshitta: Its Use in Literature and Liturgy. Papers Read at the Third Peshitta Symposium*, edited by Bas ter Haar Romeny, 365–78. Monographs of the Peshitta Institute Leiden 15. Leiden: Boston: Brill, 2006.

Ternant, Paul. "La θεωρία d'Antioche dans le cadre des sens de l'écriture." *Biblica* 34 (1953): 135–58, 354–83, 456–86.

Thilo, G., and H. Hagen, eds. *Servii Grammatici qui feruntur in Vergilii Carmina Commentarii.* Vol. 1. Leipzig: Teubner, 1881.

Thunberg, Lars. *Microcosm and Mediator: The Theological Anthropology of Maximus the Confessor.* 2nd ed. Chicago: Open Court, 1995.

Tilley, Maureen. *The Bible in Christian North Africa: The Donatist World.* Minneapolis, MN: Fortress Press, 1997.

Torjesen, Karen Jo. "Origen's Interpretation of the Psalms." *Studia Patristica* 17 (1982): 944–58.

————. *When Women Were Priests: Women's Leadership in the Early Church and the Scandal of Their Subordination in the Rise of Christianity.* San Francisco: HarperSanFrancisco, 1993.

Trapp, Michael B., ed. *Maximus Tyrius: Dissertationes.* Bibliotheca Scriptorum Graecorum et Romanorum Teubneriana. Stuttgart: B. G. Teubner, 1994.

Trublet, Jacques. "Paumes IV: Le Psautier et le Nouveau Testament." In *Dictionnaire de spiritualité ascétique et mystique: Doctrine et histoire*, 17 vols., edited by M. Viller et al., 12.2: 2552–62. Paris: G. Beauchesne, 1986.

Tugwell, Simon, trans. *Evagrius Ponticus: Praktikos and On Prayer.* Oxford: Oxford University, Faculty of Theology, 1987.

Urbainczyk, Theresa. *Theodoret of Cyrrhus: The Bishop and the Holy Man.* Ann Arbor: University of Michigan Press, 2002.

Usener, Hermann, and Ludwig Rademacher, eds. *Dionysii Halicarnassensis opera.* Leipzig: Teubner, 1904.

Vaccari, Alberto. "La θεωρία nella scuola esegetica di Antiochia." *Biblica* 1 (1920): 3–36.

Van der Meer, Frederik. *Augustine the Bishop: The Life and Work of a Father of the Church.* Translated by Brian Battershaw and G. R. Lamb. London: Sheed and Ward, 1961.

Veilleux, Armand. *La liturgie dans le cénobitisme pachômien au quatrième siècle.* Studia anselmiana 57. Rome: IBC Libreria Herder, 1968.

Veyne, Paul. *A History of Private Life.* Vol. 1. *From Pagan Rome to Byzantium.* Trans. Arthur Goldhammer. Cambridge, MA: Harvard University Press, 1987.

Villani, Barbara. "Zur Psalmenauslegung des Origenes: Einige Beobachtungen am Beispiel von Psalm 2." In *Origeniana Decima*, edited by Sylwia Kaczmarek and Henryk Pietras, 491–506. Leuven: Peeters, 2011.

Ward, Benedicta, trans. *The Sayings of the Desert Fathers: The Alphabetical Collection*. Kalamazoo, MI: Cistercian Publications, 1975.

Weber, R., ed. *Biblia Sacra iusta vulgatam versionem*. Stuttgart: Wiirttembergische Bibelanstalt, 1975.

Wesselschmidt, Quentin F., ed. *Psalms 51–150*. Ancient Christian Commentary on Scripture. Old Testament 8. Downers Grove, IL: InterVarsity Press, 2007.

Wigodsky, Michael. "The Alleged Impossibility of Philosophical Poetry." In *Philodemus and Poetry: Poetic Theory and Practice in Lucretius, Philodemus and Horace*, edited by Dirk Obbink, 58–68. New York: Oxford University Press, 1995.

Wiles, M. F. "Theodore of Mopsuestia as Representative of the Antiochene School." In *The Cambridge History of the Bible*, vol. 1, edited by Peter R. Ackroyd, Christopher Francis Evans, G. W. H. Lampe, and S. L. Greenslad, 489–509. Cambridge: Cambridge University Press, 1970.

Wilken, Robert. *Judaism and the Early Christian Mind*. New Haven, CT: Yale University Press, 1971.

———. "St. Cyril of Alexandria: The Mystery of Christ in the Bible." *Pro Ecclesia* 4 (1999): 454–78.

Williams, Daniel H. *Ambrose of Milan and the End of the Nicene-Arian Conflicts*. Oxford: Clarendon Press, 1995.

Williams, Rowan. "Augustine and the Psalms." *Interpretation* 58 (2004): 17–27.

———. "Christological Exegesis of Psalm 45." In *Meditations of the Heart: The Psalms in Early Christian Thought and Practice*, edited by Andreas Andreopoulos, Augustine Casiday, and Carol Harrison, 17–32. Studia traditionis theologiae 8. Turnhout: Brepols, 2011.

Young, Frances. *Biblical Exegesis and the Formation of Christian Culture*. Cambridge: Cambridge University Press, 1997.

———. "The Rhetorical Schools and Their Influence on Patristic Exegesis." In *The Making of Orthodoxy: Essays in Honour of Henry Chadwick*, edited by Rowan Williams, 182–99. Cambridge: Cambridge University Press, 1989.

Zaharopoulos, D. *Theodore of Mopsuestia on the Bible: A Study of His Old Testament Exegesis*. New York: Paulist Press, 1989.

Zenger, Erich. *A God of Vengeance? Understanding the Psalms of Divine Wrath*. Louisville, KY: Westminster John Knox Press, 1996.

Gary A. Anderson is Hesburgh Professor of Catholic Theology at the University of Notre Dame and president of the Catholic Biblical Association. In addition to many articles, he has authored *Charity: The Place of the Poor in the Biblical Tradition* (Yale University Press, 2013); *Sin: A History* (Yale University Press, 2009); *The Genesis of Perfection: Adam and Eve in Jewish and Christian Imagination* (Westminster John Knox Press, 2001); and *A Time to Mourn, a Time to Dance: The Expression of Grief and Joy in Israelite Religion* (Pennsylvania State University Press, 1991).

Paul M. Blowers is Dean E. Walker Professor of Church History at Emmanuel Christian Seminary. He is a former president of the North American Patristics Society and editor, with Peter W. Martens, of the forthcoming *Oxford Handbook of Early Christian Biblical Interpretation.* In addition to many articles, he has authored *Drama of the Divine Economy: Creator and Creation in Early Christian Theology and Piety* (Oxford University Press, 2012) and *Exegesis and Spiritual Pedagogy in Maximus the Confessor: An Investigation of the Quaestiones ad Thalassium* (University of Notre Dame Press, 1991) and is the editor of *The Bible in Greek Christian Antiquity* (University of Notre Dame Press, 1997).

Michael Cameron is Associate Professor of Historical Theology at the University of Portland and the Latin Patristics editor for the *Encyclopedia of the Bible and Its Reception,* edited by H.-J. Klauck et al. (De Gruyter, 2009–). He is the author of *Christ Meets Me Everywhere: Augustine's Early Figurative Exegesis* (Oxford University Press, 2012); "Augustine and Scripture," in *The Blackwell Companion to Augustine,* edited by Mark Vessey (Blackwell, 2012), 200–214; and "The Christological Substructure of Augustine's Figurative Exegesis," in *Augustine and the Bible,* edited by Pamela Bright (University of Notre Dame Press, 1999), 74–103.

Ronald R. Cox is the Blanche E. Seaver Professor of Religion and author of *By the Same Word: Creation and Salvation in Hellenistic Judaism and Early Christianity* (De Gruyter, 2007); "The New Testament Preaches the Psalms: Problems and Possibilities," in *Performing the Psalms: And the World Imagined in Scripture*, edited by D. Fleer and D. Bland (Chalice Press, 2005), 83–104; and "Traveling the Royal Road: The Soteriology of Philo of Alexandria," in *This World and the World to Come: Soteriology in Early Judaism*, edited by Daniel Gurtner (T. and T. Clark, 2011), 167–80.

Brian E. Daley, S.J., is the Catherine F. Huisking Professor of Theology at the University of Notre Dame. He is a former president of the North American Patristic Society and recipient of the 2012 Ratzinger Prize in Theology. His many publications include *The Hope of the Early Church: A Handbook of Patristic Eschatology*, 2nd ed. (Hendrickson, 2003); *Gregory of Nazianzus* (Routledge, 2006); *On the Dormition of Mary: Early Patristic Homilies* (St. Vladimir's Seminary Press, 1997); and *Light on the Mountain: Greek Patristic and Byzantine Homilies on the Transfiguration of the Lord* (St. Vladimir's Seminary Press, 2013). He is also the translator of Hans Urs von Balthasar's monumental *Cosmic Liturgy: The Universe According to Maximus the Confessor* (Ignatius Press, 2003).

Luke Dysinger, O.S.B., is a monk of St. Andrew's Abbey, Valyermo, and Professor of Church History and Moral Theology at St. John's Seminary, Camarillo, California. He is the author of *Psalmody and Prayer in the Writings of Evagrius Ponticus* (Oxford University Press, 2005) and articles on Christian monasticism and patristic exegesis, including "The Logoi of Providence and Judgment in the Exegetical Writings of Evagrius Ponticus," *Studia Patristica* 37 (2001): 462–71; "Healing Judgment: 'Medical Hermeneutics' in the Writings of Evagrius Ponticus," Studia anselmiana 140, Analecta monastica 8 (2004), 75–104; and "Early Monastic Exegesis: The Basis of Spiritual Direction and Spiritual Exercise," Studia anselmiana 146, Analecta monastica 9 (2009), 423–42.

Nonna Verna Harrison is a former faculty member of St. Paul's School of Theology in Kansas City, an Orthodox nun, and the author of *God's Many-*

Splendored Image: Theological Anthropology for Christian Formation (Baker Academic Publishing, 2010) and *Grace and Human Freedom According to St. Gregory of Nyssa* (E. Mellen Press, 1992); translator of *Festal Orations: St Gregory of Nazianzus* (St. Vladimir's Seminary Press, 2008) and *On The Human Condition: St Basil the Great* (St. Vladimir's Seminary Press, 2005); and author of many articles.

Ronald E. Heine is Professor of Biblical Studies at Northwest Christian University. In addition to having authored a number of articles, he is the editor, with Karen Jo Torjesen, of the forthcoming *Oxford Handbook of Origen*; the author of *Classical Christian Doctrine: Introducing the Essentials of the Ancient Faith* (Baker Academic Publishing, 2013), *Origen: Scholarship in the Service of the Church* (Oxford University Press, 2011), and *Reading the Old Testament with the Ancient Church: Exploring the Formation of Early Christian Thought* (Baker Academic Publishing, 2007); and the translator of many important early Christian works into English.

David G. Hunter holds the Cottrill-Rolfes Chair in Catholic Studies at the University of Kentucky, Lexington. He is a former president of the North American Patristics Society and is the current Editorial Director of the Fathers of the Church translation series. He has authored many articles and a number of translations and is the author of *Marriage, Celibacy, and Heresy in Ancient Christianity: The Jovinianist Controversy* (Oxford University Press, 2007) and the editor, with Susan Ashbrook Harvey, of the *Oxford Handbook of Early Christian Studies* (Oxford University Press, 2008).

Paul R. Kolbet is Lecturer in Early Christianity at Yale Divinity School and Co-Chair of the Augustine and Augustinianisms Group of the American Academy of Religion. He is the author of *Augustine and the Cure of Souls: Revising a Classical Ideal* (University of Notre Dame Press, 2010) and a number of articles, including "Augustine among the Ancient Therapists," in *Augustine and Psychology*, edited by Sandra Dixon, John Doody, and Kim Paffenroth (Lexington Books, 2013), 91–114; "Rethinking the Rationales for Origen's Use of Allegory," *Studia Patristica* 56 (2013): 41–50; "Rethinking the Christological Foundations of Reinhold Niebuhr's Christian

Realism," *Modern Theology* 26 (2010): 437–65; and "Torture and Origen's Hermeneutics of Nonviolence," *Journal of the American Academy of Religion* 76 (2008): 545–72.

Michael C. McCarthy, S.J., is the Executive Director of the Ignatian Center for Jesuit Education and Edmund Campion Professor in Religious Studies and Classics at Santa Clara University. His articles include "Augustine's Mixed Feelings: Vergil's *Aeneid* and the Psalms of David in the *Confessions*," *Harvard Theological Review* 102 (2009): 453–79; "Modalities of Belief in Ancient Christian Controversy," *Journal of Early Christian Studies* 17 (2009): 605–34; "Divine Wrath and Human Anger: Embarrassment Ancient and New," *Theological Studies* 70 (2009): 845–74; and " 'We Are Your Books' (*Sermo* 227): Augustine, the Bible, and the Practice of Authority," *Journal of the American Academy of Religion* 75 (2007): 324–52.

John J. O'Keefe is Professor of Theology at Creighton University. He is the author of, among other publications, "Impassible Suffering? Divine Passion and Fifth-Century Christology," *Theological Studies* 58 (1997): 39–60; (with R. R. Reno) *Sanctified Vision: An Introduction to Patristic Exegesis* (Johns Hopkins University Press, 2005); and editor of Cyril of Alexandria's *Festal Letters*, 2 vols. (Catholic University of America Press, 2009–13).

Scripture citations are indexed to modern editions except where the Septuagint (LXX) is indicated.